Yours affectionately
Theobald Mathew

FATHER MATHEW:

A BIOGRAPHY.

BY

JOHN FRANCIS MAGUIRE, M.P.

AUTHOR OF

'ROME: ITS RULER AND ITS INSTITUTIONS.'

NEW YORK:

D. & J. SADLIER & CO., 31 BARCLAY STREET,

MONTREAL, C. E.:—COR. NOTRE DAME & ST. FRANCIS XAVIER STREETS.

Stereotyped by VINCENT DILL,
No. 24 Beekman St., N. Y.

PREFACE.

IT would be a reproach to the country which he served, no less than to the age which he adorned, were there no record of the life of Theobald Mathew. To allow such a man to pass away, without more notice than a paragraph in a newspaper, an article in a magazine, or a panegyric from the pulpit, would be a stain upon the honour of Ireland. But although I felt this as strongly as anyone could feel it, I did not venture to attempt the task of becoming his biographer until I saw that no other person had intimated an intention of so doing.* Not having found anyone undertaking a duty which more especially belonged to one of his own countrymen to undertake, I resolved on attempting it, notwithstanding that I had to discharge many and varied duties, which involved constant claims upon my time and attention. Setting aside that literary aptitude for the task, in which I but too keenly felt

* The sketch by the late Daniel Owen Madden, though brilliant and spirited, was but a sketch, not a biography; and the interesting and well-written memoir from the accomplished pen of Miss Hill—which formed one of the 'Our Exemplars,' in a little work published in 1861 by Cassell, Petter, & Galpin—did not extend beyond fifty pages. Sketches and brief memoirs of Father Mathew there have been, but no biography.

my deficiency, I had some circumstances in my favour —the principal of which was, my intimate knowledge of the subject of the contemplated memoir. I had known Father Mathew from my childhood; and the feeling which I entertained towards him at that early period of my life, ripened into the strongest and the truest friendship as I grew to manhood. From that time, and up to the year 1849, when he left Ireland for America, I was more or less intimately associated with him, in private as well as in public. He thus became known to me in almost every phase of his career and character—in his weakness as in his strength, in his moments of despondency and gloom as in his hours of happiness and exultation. I beheld him under every circumstance, and in every position—now on the platform, and now in his own home; now in the presence of his equals, and now surrounded by the poorest, the humblest, even the most abject in society. The intimate knowledge of Father Mathew which I was enabled to acquire, was of advantage to my undertaking in many respects; but the more I dwelt upon the memory of his goodness, which was in reality his greatness, the more I despaired of faithfully representing his character in my pages. Of one thing the reader may be sure—that if I have failed in my intended likeness, the failure cannot be attributed to flattery or exaggeration. The qualities of a great heart, throbbing with none but tender, generous, and holy emotions, cannot be exaggerated,—the difficulty is to depict them with anything like a fair approach to their reality. The task—rashly and presumptuously undertaken it may be—is accomplished; and the result of no small labour, but of much greater anxiety, is now placed before the public. And now that it is accomplished, I feel that I have omitted many things which I ought to have done, in order to render the portrait life-like, and in some degree worthy of the original. I also feel that I may have failed in giving an adequate idea of that wondrous movement so providentially originated and so wisely guided by the Apostle of Temperance; but with respect to this portion of my task, there was the danger of imparting an air of dulness to that which I desired to render interesting to the general reader. In one respect, at least, I have been faithful to the life and character of Father Mathew,—in guarding against the voluntary introduction of any topic which would clash with the prevailing tone and temper of one who, devoted Catholic Priest as he was, might be truly said to belong to mankind rather than to party or to sect. If by recording the life I have helped to perpetuate the memory of a great and good man, I have achieved a task of which I may feel some pride; but if the perusal of these pages should inspire others to imitate the virtues of Theobald Mathew, then indeed will his biographer have much reason to rejoice.

CORK: *September* 1863.

CONTENTS.

CHAPTER IV.—*continued.*

CHAPTER V.

CHAPTER VI.

CHAPTER VII.

CHAPTER VIII.

CHAPTER IX.

CHAPTER X.

CHAPTER XI.

CHAPTER XII.

CHAPTER XIII.

CHAPTER XIV.

CHAPTER XV.

CHAPTER XVI.

CHAPTER XVII.

CHAPTER XVIII.

CHAPTER XIX.

CHAPTER XX.

CHAPTER XXI.

CHAPTER XXII.

CHAPTER XXIII.

CHAPTER XXIV.

CHAPTER XXV.

CHAPTER XXVI.

CHAPTER XXVIII.

CHAPTER XXIX.

CHAPTER XXX.

CHAPTER XXXI.

CHAPTER XXXII.

CHAPTER XXXIII.

CHAPTER XXXIV.

CHAPTER XXXV.

CHAPTER XXXVI.

CHAPTER XXXVII.

CHAPTER XXXVIII.

CHAPTER XXXIX.

CHAPTER XL.

CHAPTER XLI.

CHAPTER XLII.

CHAPTER XLIII.

CHAPTER XLIV.

CHAPTER XLV.

CHAPTER XLVI.

FATHER MATHEW:

A BIOGRAPHY.

CHAPTER I.

Born in Thomastown House—His Family—His Infancy—His singular Gentleness and Goodness as a Child—Hiding the Spoons—His influence over his brothers—His Love of Order—The silk Stockings—Taste for Engineering—The Gentlemen with the Tail—Is to be a Priest—His walk from School—Enters and quits Maynooth—Is ordained—His first Sermon—His first Mission in Kilkenny—The Regular Orders—Cause of his leaving Kilkenn.

SOME five miles west of Cashel, the ancient capital of the County of Tipperary, and at the head of a fertile plain, running westward between the Kilmanagh and Galtee range of mountains, locally well known as the 'Golden Vale,' there stands a noble mansion in the midst of a still nobler demesne. Its name is Thomastown. And here, on the 10th of October 1790, Theobald Mathew was born. Thomastown was for many generations the property of a high county family, famous for its wealth and extravagance, and notable in the records of both Houses of the Irish Parliament, but now utterly extinct. The park, two thousand acres in extent, is still in high repute, in a county in which timber is not over abundant, for its long beech avenues, its venerable oaks, and its massive chestnuts, which rival those of Bushy. Pleasure grounds, pieces of ornamental water, and long formal terraces in the old style, lie around Thomastown House—an immense, long-winged castellated pile, not more than two hundred years old. An interesting account of its builder, and of the mode of life he adopted, can be found in Sheridan's 'Life of Swift,' together with a circumstantial narrative of the Dean's visit to Thomastown, and his entertainment there. It is now the property of the Viscount de Chabot, the representative of an illustrious French line, to whom, as the nearest surviving relative, the estate was directly bequeathed by the Lady Elizabeth, or Ellisha (as she is styled in the old peerages) Mathew, daughter of the first and sister of the second and last Earl Llandaff, an eccentric but kind-hearted spinster, of whom further mention must be made hereafter.

With the trunk line of the Mathew family, traced back to Rader, in Glamorgan, by Mervyn Archdale, and other genealogy-compilers after him, this biography has nought to do. Such authentic particulars as can be procured at this time of Father Mathew's immediate family, one of the branch lines, and the only one with any representatives now left, are scanty in the extreme. We know this much for certain—that some time in the second half of the last century, the date of which event cannot be given with accuracy, John Mathew of Thurles married a Miss O'Rahill, a member of a respectable family; that this couple died shortly after their marriage, leaving two daughters* and a son, James Mathew; and that George Mathew of Thomastown, afterwards Baron and first Earl of Llandaff, adopted and educated the orphan boy. In due time James grew to manhood, when he found himself in a very little better position than that of a dependent upon the bounty of his patron; but it is clear that his protector did not neglect the charge he voluntarily assumed,

* Both of the daughters were married—one to Francis Kearney, Esq., whose grandson, the Rev. Dr. Kearney, is Military Chaplain at Ballincollig, and Rector of Carrigrohan, Co. Cork; the other to John Hunt, Esq.—Protestant gentlemen of good position.

for James Mathew remained constantly at Thomastown, and during the long absences of the owner of that grand old place was entrusted with the management of the household and establishment.

While still resident here, he married Anne, daughter of George Whyte, Esq., of Cappa Whyte, she being then in her sixteenth year, and endowed with considerable personal beauty. Even this important step did not sever his connection with Thomastown, for he continued to dwell there for several years afterwards. Children were rapidly born to James and Anne Mathew. The fourth son, named Theobald, was the future founder of the Temperance movement in Ireland. So was it that Thomastown was the place of his birth and infancy.

About the year 1795, James Mathew, finding a young family quickly springing up, and wishing, no doubt, to secure for himself some more permanent footing in the world than his position in Thomastown promised, took a large farm, with a commodious dwelling-house upon it, called Rathcloheen, in the immediate vicinity of Thomastown House; transported thither his wife and children, and so set up for himself. This change he effected without any cessation of kindness and good-will on the part of the now ennobled master of the soil. Lands were let to James Mathew upon easy terms; his flocks and cattle grazed gratuitously upon the rich pastures of the demesne; and things going on well with him, he soon became prosperous and even wealthy, in those halcyon days for farmers of the war time. As years rolled on, no less than twelve children, nine boys and three girls, were born to him. Of these—one having died in her childhood—but one brother and two sisters are now left; and from them, as they were much younger than their priest-brother, but little can be gathered of Theobald Mathew's earlier years.

Theobald was, from his infancy, the favourite child of

his mother. There was something singularly sweet and engaging in the boy, which drew the mother's heart towards him; and his own love for her, which was evidenced in a hundred child-like ways, strengthened the mutual attachment. By his mother's side he preferred passing the hours the others spent in play; and he was consequently somewhat scornfully designated 'the Pet' by his brothers and sisters. At Thomastown House, too, before and after his father's quitting it for Rathcloheen, he was in higher estimation than the rest of the young people. The Earl's daughter, Lady Elizabeth, some fifteen or twenty years the boy's senior, formed an affection for him which never waned during her life.

It does not always happen that the characteristics of the future man are to be traced in the impulses of the child; but in the impulses as well as the habits of the fine sturdy handsome boy, the joy and pride of his fond mother, one may behold, though in modified form, the very same remarkable characteristics of the man who for many years occupied a prominent position in the world, and who owed his singular power over his fellow-man more to the influence of a loving and beneficent nature, than to intellectual superiority or preeminence. In one respect especially the child and the man were identical. From his earliest years, the desire to afford pleasure to others, to be the means of conferring happiness on some one human creature, was his most marked characteristic. Even at this period of his life, this desire had assumed the form of a confirmed habit, which, as years rolled on, became almost as uncontrollable as a passion. Young Theobald, or Toby, as he was familiarly styled, had rather an aversion to the rude sports of his brothers and their young friends and playfellows, although he was gay and cheerful as boys usually are. But while the hardy young fellows were engaged in play, or were absent on some expedition through the woods of Thomastown, Theobald was certain to be found in close attendance on his mother, expressing his love for that fond and indulgent parent in artless prattle, or satisfying his affection by clinging to the skirt of her robe, and looking up into her face, with his sweet innocent glance, beaming from the loveliest eyes of clear limpid blue. Though this strong attachment to his mother, which had a peculiar influence upon his after life, filling him with reverence for good and holy women, was a source of constant ridicule to his brothers, who called him 'the Pet,' addressed him as 'Miss Molly,' and accused him of being always 'tied to his mother's apron-string;' still, from an early age, he acquired an influence over them which they never attempted to dispute or resist, and which he retained and they felt to the last moment of their connection in this world. The boy was in many respects different from other boys. Not only was he most lovable, from his goodness and gentleness, and his invariable habit of seeking to afford pleasure to others; but there was a sweet gravity, even a dignity, in the manner of the child, which was most remarkable at such a period of life. While tied to his mother's apron-string, as his brothers declared him to be, he was not unmindful of their interests, or indifferent to their marked partiality for good things; for he employed the influence which he derived from his mother's love, to coax from her the materials for a little feast, of which he was to be the proud dispenser, and with which it was his delight to surprise them, as they returned home, rosy with health and exercise, and with the appetites of young wolves. To procure a feast—to preside over it—to witness the relish with which the sweet things were, not to say despatched, but devoured—this was a kind of passion with this mere child. Not that he was by any means personally indifferent to such delicacies—what healthy boy ever was?—but that he derived more pleasure from bestowing them on his brothers than in sharing them with them.

When a very little fellow, he was particularly partial to

plum-pudding, for which delicacy, it may be said, he never entirely lost his relish. In after years, he took pleasure in telling how, one Christmas, while the family were still at Thomastown, he quietly secreted, beneath the cushion of a great old-fashioned chair, the silver spoons which had been used with the plum-pudding. Great was the consternation of the servants, and awful the amazement—the utter stupefaction—of the butler, at the sudden and unaccountable disappearance of the plate. The servants were in a lamentable state of alarm, naturally dreading that suspicion should fall upon them ; and as for the family, they did not know what to think of the strange occurrence. At length, Theobald confessed, and not without some degree of pride, that he had put them away in a safe place, so that they might be ready at hand when the next Christmas brought with it its customary pudding. Upon which confession, which relieved many a heart from a load of uneasiness, Lord Llandaff, who was one of the kindest of men, promised his young favourite that, instead of waiting for Christmas, which was then a year distant, there should be a plum-pudding every Sunday—a promise which was received with a vehement shout of delight. This incident occurred while he was yet a very little fellow ; but the recollection of Lord Llandaff's kindness never faded from the retentive and grateful memory of Theobald Mathew.

Though Theobald was the fourth child, with three brothers older than himself, it was singular to observe how he led them, as if by natural right, and how they yielded to him and obeyed him quite as a matter of course. His brothers seemed to feel as if he were different from themselves ; and in more respects than one this difference really existed. He never joined in any cruel sport, or willingly inflicted pain upon a living thing. Coursing, and shooting, and ferretting, in which his young companions indulged, and of their proficiency in which they were boastfully proud, he detested with all his heart. He once witnessed, with horror and compassion, the agony of a poor hunted hare, in her breathless struggles with the fierce dogs; and from that moment he held the sport in abhorrence. The sight of a shattered wing or blood-stained breast of a bird, brought down by his brother's gun, filled the heart of the boy with a sense of pain; for his impulse was to succour and befriend, not to persecute or destroy. Then he was never known to have uttered, not to say an improper word, or word of dubious meaning, but even a light word; and a harsh or unkind expression towards any person was never known to have fallen from his lips. In this respect, as in many others, the child was indeed the father of the man.

In after life, he was remarkable for his love of order, his neatness of dress, and the propriety which, in spite of his voluntary poverty, distinguished the arrangements of his modest dwelling. To find anything out of its right place was, to him, a source of annoyance; it offended against his sense of order and regularity. An incident is told of him, which displays this peculiarity manifesting itself at a very early age. While still at Thomastown, he happened to see, in the breakfast-parlour, a pair of silk stockings on the back of a chair before the fire, where they had been placed, perhaps with a view to their being 'aired' previously to being worn. The indignant disgust of Master Toby may be imagined when it is said that he tore the offending articles from the chair, and flung them into the fire, where they were soon destroyed. As may be supposed, there was a keen search made for the stockings, which were of a valuable kind, and there was much astonishment at their mysterious disappearance. At last, as a desperate resource, Toby was asked if he had seen the missing articles. 'I did,' said the little fellow, 'and I burned them, too.' 'Burned them!—why did you do such a thing, you bold boy?' was the very natural question. 'They had no right to be in the breakfast-parlour;

that was no place for them,' said the boy, sturdily. 'Toby is right,' said Lady Elizabeth Mathew; 'they should not have been put there.' Lady Elizabeth, who was then about twenty-five years of age, thought the loss of her stockings fully compensated by the lesson administered to her attendants from the lips of a child.

Between Rathcloheen and Thomastown, where he was ever sure of being received with affection by Lady Elizabeth, Theobald's early years were happily passed. As each successive year rolled by, he was more an object of love and admiration to young as well as old. This may seem to savour somewhat of exaggeration, when said of a mere child—a boy, with a boy's willfulness; but it will appear more probable when the loving gentle sweet nature of the child is considered—when it is remembered that he was always striving, with kindly ingenuity, to procure some indulgence or gratification for others—for his brothers, who looked up to and obeyed him—for the servants, who adored him—for the poor, who were never tired of invoking blessings on the head of their young benefactor, and who looked upon him as a 'born saint.'

The strange influence which he acquired over his brothers, three of whom were his seniors, was displayed in various ways. Theobald was somewhat of an engineer. The farm-yard and out-offices as well as the dwelling-house of Rathcloheen were indebted for their supply of water to a small stream, which flowed from Thomastown demesne. During the winter it amply sufficed for every purpose, but in the heat of summer the little stream shrank in its bed, and afforded but a scanty supply to the varied wants of the establishment. This partial failure, which was of annual occurrence, excited the interest of Theobald, not alone on account of the practical inconvenience which the loss of the pure element occasioned, but also from the love which he felt for the stream that prattled with such musical voice over its shallow bed, or flashed so brightly in the sunlight; and on a fine summer day there might have been seen a handsome boy, in the midst of a group of fine lads, all bigger than himself, working away with spade or shovel of appropriate dimensions, deepening the channel, improving its levels, or directing its scanty but precious waters into a better course. Many years after these feats of infant engineering, he never could see a rill of spring water running to waste without considering how it might be turned to the best advantage for the use of man; so vivid and lasting, with this impressionable and tenacious nature, were the events and memories of his youthful days.

If Theobald were the 'Pet' of his mother and the 'Miss Molly' of the house, he was not on that account in any way deficient in courage, moral or physical. Quite the contrary, as a rather singular instance will prove. There lived, some half dozen miles from his father's house, a gentleman, to whom alleged acts of cruelty to the peasantry in the time of the Rebellion, then fresh in the memory of all classes, had attached an evil fame. So wicked and inhuman had been the conduct of this gentleman, that the people in the neighbourhood declared he was 'the ould boy himself, all out;' and more than one village gossip, in the blacksmith's forge, or by the kitchen hob, was willing to 'take her Bible' that the object of her horror was gifted with a tail; though the horns, it was admitted, were not ordinarily visible. Theobald heard the story, perhaps, from one of his many pensioned crones, who crossed herself devoutly as she described to her 'darling Master Toby' the supernatural appendage of the gentleman of evil reputation. The strange story, which was firmly believed in by the servants of the house, seized fast hold of the lad's imagination, and he resolved to satisfy himself, by personal inspection, whether Mr. —— were in reality so wonderfully and so unpleasantly endowed. Accordingly, he rose early one morning, and having saddled his pony with his own hands, he galloped or trotted on his journey of more than half a dozen miles, till he reached the gate of the gentleman's demesne ; and there, partly concealed by a projecting portion of the wall, he remained for hours, seated firmly on his pony's back, waiting in the hope of seeing Mr. —— come forth, and thus afford him the opportunity of satisfying his curiosity. He had his trouble for nothing, for no Mr. —— was to be seen that day ; and Toby was at length compelled, by hunger more than by weariness, to turn his pony's head homewards. In a few years after this strange expedition, he met the same gentleman in society, and then convinced himself that, whatever the interior man might have been, the exterior was nowise different from that of ordinary mortals.

The boy seemed to be marked out by nature for something different from other boys. His kindness, gentleness, and unselfishness ; his sweet and cheerful gravity ; his tender compassion for the poor, the lame, the blind, and the sick—including a liberal proportion of impostors among them—who thronged the door-steps and invaded the spacious kitchen of his father's hospitable house ; his wonderful reverence for God's name, which he never lightly pronounced —all marked out Theobald, especially in the estimation of the women of the household, as the future 'Priest of the family.' Mrs. Mathew was a pious Catholic, and, like most good mothers of her creed in Ireland, she hoped to see one of her many sons dedicated to the service of religion. One of the elder boys was 'intended' for the Church ; and a namesake and relative had actually presented him, or his mother for him, with a costly suit of vestments and a valuable chalice ; but, much to his mother's regret, George's 'vocation' proved to be rather a passing impulse, than that irresistible attraction towards the sanctuary which so many young people in Ireland experience at an early age, and which enables them to overcome every obstacle, and resist every temptation to a worldly career. One day, while her now numerous family surrounded the spacious dinner-table, the good lady, looking round with natural pride at her little army of handsome healthy boys, almost involuntarily exclaimed—'Is it not unfortunate! I have nine sons, and not one of them to be a priest!' The boys glanced at George, and blushing George fixed his eyes steadily upon his plate. But the silence was soon broken; for scarcely had the words, which so truly expressed the inmost thoughts of the speaker, been uttered, when Theobald started from his chair, and cried out, with a voice full of emotion, 'Mother, don't be uneasy; I will be a priest.' His mother folded him in her arms, expressing her delight and gratitude in kisses and blessings; and from that moment Theobald Mathew was looked upon as dedicated and belonging to the Church. From that moment, also, his influence over his brothers, which had been singularly great before, was confirmed and increased; which influence, gathering strength as years rolled on, was not always to their personal advantage in after life.

When he had reached his twelfth year, Lady Elizabeth, his constant friend and protectress, announced her intention of educating him at her own cost. She selected for him a school of good repute in Kilkenny, to which he was accordingly sent. Love for his family and kindred was ever with Theobald Mathew one of the strongest and most ardent feelings of his nature. This feeling was nurtured and strengthened in the bosom of a happy home. It was warmed into early vigour in the sunshine of domestic affection, and was never chilled or nipped by coldness or unkindness. While in the school at Kilkenny, he yielded to an uncontrollable desire to see his parents and family, and enjoy in their beloved society the festival of Easter. Without acquainting anyone of his intention, he set out on foot on a journey of between thirty and forty miles; but, sustained by the strong feeling with which he was animated, the affectionate boy got through it bravely, and at the close of a long day arrived, weary and foot-sore, at his father's house, where he was received in the arms of his delighted mother, who only thought of his love for her, and her joy at the unexpected meeting, and hinted no word of rebuke as she strained him to her breast. Many a time, ay a full half century after, did Father Mathew tell of that sweet greeting, which more than repaid the young traveller for the toil and fatigue of that tremendous undertaking.

The late Mr. Richard Sullivan, who for some years represented Kilkenny in Parliament, was a school-fellow of his; and he was often heard to say that there was no more popular boy, nor one more universally beloved by teachers and students, than Theobald Mathew. His mother was frequently gladdened by the tidings of her favourite son's progress in his studies. By no means a brilliant boy, he was attentive and studious, and of good natural parts. The President of the academy, the Rev. Patrick Magrath, was a man of keen discrimination as well as of sound scholarship; and he entertained a high opinion of the capacity of his amiable and attractive pupil, whose attention to his studies and invariably exemplary conduct were the constant theme of his praise.

A writer in the 'Dublin Review,' who wrote of Theobald Mathew in after years, when his name was famous, thus describes him as a boy—the father of the future man; corroborating to the letter the account given of him by the surviving members of his family:—

The writer of this article has been intimately acquainted with the Rev. Theobald Mathew from his earliest boyhood, and he can truly say, that even at that early stage of life he knew nobody so much or so generally beloved as the individual who is now the 'observed of all observers' throughout Ireland. Incapable of anger or resentment, utterly free from selfishness, always anxious to share with others whatever he possessed, jealous of the affections of those to whom he was particularly attached, remarkably gentle in his manners, fond of expressing himself rather in similes than in language; averse from the boisterous amusements to which boys in general are prone, and preferring to them quiet walks by the banks of a river, or by the side of green hedges, in company with two or three select associates. and yet very far from being of a pensive disposition—on the contrary, so cheerful that the slightest ludicrous occurrence turned the smile he generally wore into hearty laughter—he grew up esteemed by everybody who knew him. Even in his boyhood he seemed never to live for himself; and yet by not seeking it he exercised an influence upon those around him, which they never thought of questioning. Such was his character in his early days. And when the writer of these lines, after an interval of thirty years or more, visited Mr. Mathew in the autumn of 1838, he could discern no change in the outlines of that character, except that it was accompanied by a greater degree of physical activity, acquired from almost incessant motion in the performance of sacerdotal or charitable engagements, which seemed to have no end throughout the whole day.

Having gone through the usual course of studies necessary as a preparation for Maynooth, he was sent to that college under the auspices of the Most Reverend Dr. Bray, and matriculated in the Humanity Class, on the 10th of September, 1807.

When the young student entered that famous college, its president was the Very Reverend Dr. Montague, a learned scholar and divine. Theobald Mathew was not destined to finish his scholastic career in the halls of Maynooth. The rules of that institution were then, as now, strict in their character, and rigid in their enforcement. Thus, for instance, it is not allowed that one student shall visit another in his room; as, were it lawful to do so, irregularities and abuses would be likely to follow in consequence; one of which would be the interruption to the studies, which, at a certain period of the year, the student prosecutes in private. But if two or more students assemble in the room of one of them for the purpose of eating, which is defined in the technical phraseology of the college by the term '*commessatio*,' they do so at the risk of expulsion. It may have been that young Mathew did not regard this rule in its serious aspect, or that the temptation of feast-giving was too strong for his powers of resistance; but it is the fact that he violated the rule in a marked manner, by giving a party to a few of his special friends among the students; and the meeting being of a convivial character, the attention of the authorities was attracted to a circumstance extraordinary and unlooked-for in such a place. The master of the feast was at once put under censure; but anticipating expulsion as the result of the formal investigation which was to be held in due course, he quitted the college of his own will, and thus probably avoided what would have been regarded by many, who would never have too closely scrutinised the real cause of offence, as a stigma upon his moral character. The offence, which was quite venial in its nature, was just the one which Theobald Mathew was most likely to commit. It will be seen that it was but a manifestation of that habit of giving, that love for affording pleasure to, or conferring happiness on others, which was one of the most marked characteristics, indeed passions, of his beneficent nature. He left the college in 1808. The time, however, was to come when he, who then hurriedly passed from its walls, was to be received within them with such honours as are but rarely accorded to, and more rarely deserved by man from his fellows—when he was to be hailed with affectionate reverence by venerable priests and learned professors, and with tumultuous acclamations by warm-hearted and enthusiastic students. One might be disposed to think that this unexpected severance of his connection with Maynooth was specially intended by Providence: for, had he gone through the usual course in the classes of that college, he might have become a rural parish priest, even have worn the mitre; and though he was certain of being beloved by his flock, whether of a parish or a diocese, the world at large would, in all human probability, never have heard of the name of Father Mathew.

Stimulated by the edifying example as much as impressed by the poverty of two aged friars, the representatives of the Capuchin Order in Kilkenny, he determined on attaching himself to that lowliest and least influential of the regular orders in Ireland; and, with that object in view, he proceeded to Dublin, where he placed himself under the spiritual care of the Very Reverend Celestine Corcoran of that city. And on Easter Saturday, in the year 1814, he was ordained by the most Reverend Dr. Murray, a prelate whose apostolic virtues commanded the reverence even of his bitterest opponents. That solemn act was the commencement of a friendship which, increasing as years rolled over the heads of the Archbishop and the Priest, terminated only in death. Dr. Murray was through life the faithful friend and powerful supporter of Father Mathew.

On this memorable Easter Saturday was his mother's long-cherished ambition for her beloved son fully gratified. He was now what she had hoped to see him—a priest of the sanctuary, whose voice would be heard in the pulpit, whose consecrated hands would minister at the altar.

It was while on a brief visit to his home, that he was presented with a chalice, one of the most acceptable offerings which can be made to a young priest; and upon its base he had subsequently engraved these words—'*Pray for the souls of James and Anne Mathew, of Thomastown*'—thus associating their honoured names and sacred memories with the celebration of the Holy Sacrifice of the Mass. This was the chalice which he invariably used in private, and to which he was particularly attached.

His first sermon was delivered in the parish chapel of Kilfeacle, in his native county of Tipperary. It was on the occasion of his saying Mass for the priest. He read and explained the Gospel of the day, which proclaims the startling announcement, that it is more difficult for a rich man to enter the Kingdom of Heaven than for a camel to pass through the eye of a needle. His principal auditor of this his first sermon was a village magnate and millionaire, Mr. Scully—considered to be one of the richest men in Tipperary. This rural Crœsus was much struck with the discourse, which was not a little enhanced by the singularly youthful and interesting appearance of the preacher, who rightly explained that it was not the *possession* of riches which was culpable in the sight of God, but the disposition or *use* made of them. Mr. Scully was a very large as well as a very rich man; and meeting the preacher at breakfast, he expressed his personal acknowledgements thus: 'Father Mathew; I feel very much obliged to you for trying to squeeze *me* through the eye of a needle.' The old gentleman was at that time corpulent enough to have blocked up the Camel's Gate of Jerusalem.

Father Mathew's first mission was in Kilkenny, where he joined the small community of Capuchins. The community was small and poor, and their church was not particularly well attended prior to his becoming attached to it. But soon after his arrival a very striking change was effected. The Friary, as it was called, became, ere long, not only popular, but fashionable, thronged by the poor and frequented by the rich. The fame of the young Friar spread rapidly through that Catholic city, and his virtues were the theme of every tongue. His personal appearance was of itself sufficient to excite interest, and his manners quite harmonised with his outward form. In the first bloom and freshness of early manhood, graceful and elegant in his figure and carriage, with a countenance of singular beauty, of expression even more than of feature; winning of speech, polished of address, modest and unobtrusive—the youthful priest was calculated to create the most favourable impression. Those who remember him at that period of his life speak of the extraordinary beauty of his countenance, and the indescribable sweetness of its expression—so good, and pure, and holy —'something angelic'—reflecting faithfully the inward soul. But personal attractions, however they might have commanded attention, or even fascinated for the moment, would soon have failed to influence in his favour, had they not been accompanied by those sterling qualities of mind and heart, as well as that wonderful zeal for the cause of religion, which Father Mathew brought with him to the duties of his sacred calling.

It was in the unobtrusive but onerous and important duties of the confessional that he first distinguished himself. In that confined and comfortless 'box' he was certain to be found almost at any hour, even from the earliest in the morning to the latest at night, during which the chapel was open to the faithful. Here was the principal theatre of his priestly mission; receiving, under the most solemn seal of confidence, the sad story of the sinner, consoling the afflicted, cheering and fortifying the weary spirit, strengthening the feeble against temptation, guiding and directing by his advice and counsel. The poor, as usual, were the first to appreciate his worth; and they, by their lavish praise of the 'new director,' attracted the attention of those of a different class, with whom the youthful priest became an object of the deepest interest, and even veneration. Young as he was in years, and younger still in experience of the world, his advice, even in matters not altogether strictly within the province of a clergyman, was eagerly sought for by many whose hair was streaked with the silver of age. Nor was his advice without its value; for, to an instinctive uprightness, and a stern sense of justice, he united great natural shrewdness and sagacity, with clearness and soundness of judgement.

Even at this early period of his ministry, his efforts as a

preacher were more successful than might have been supposed from the extreme thinness and weakness of his yet undeveloped voice. But there was the one great and much-atoning charm—the evident sincerity of the preacher. Thin and weak, almost shrieking, as his voice was at this time, it reached the heart of the listener, stirring its inmost recesses, and quickening its pulsation with sympathetic fervour. Few men were ever animated with a more ardent love of God and humanity than that which glowed in the breast of Father Mathew, as his whole career testifies; and that sacred love breathed in every word that he spoke from the altar or the pulpit. It is not here necessary to allude to him further as a preacher; for he shortly quitted Kilkenny for Cork, the scene of his future missionary labours, and likewise of his world-wide fame as a great moral reformer.

While in Kilkenny, the benevolence and charity which were the leading features of his character sought every opportunity for their constant exercise. The boy was here repeated in the man. He was never happy unless in doing good. To confer happiness on others seemed to be the instinctive craving of his nature. Had he a pound in his possession, it was only so long as there was no poor person near him with whom he could share it; but had he anything left, after having relieved the wants of the necessitous, it was his greatest delight to surround himself with a few chosen friends, whom he entertained with a warmth and grace of hospitality that specially distinguished him. The boy feast-giver of Thomastown and Rathcloheen was now the modest entertainer of the Capuchin convent in Kilkenny.

His departure from Kilkenny was one of the great events as well as the turning-point of his life. It assisted to place him in that position in which he had the opportunity of best displaying those noble qualities which gathered round him the love and admiration of his fellow-men, and prepared the way for that extraordinary career which rendered the name and character and labours of the humble friar the pride of his country and the property of mankind. It may therefore be not unfitting to explain the cause of his leaving Kilkenny, and taking up his residence in Cork.

At the time when Father Mathew commenced the duties of his ministry, the Catholic Church of Ireland was but slowly emerging from a persecution which had endured, with greater or less severity, and with but occasional snatches of repose, almost from the period of the Reformation. But upon no branch of the Irish Church had that persecution fallen so heavily as upon the Regular Orders. And not only had the Regular Orders to endure the worst malignity of laws conceived in a spirit of hate, and born of fierce and sanguinary times, when passion or selfish policy alone influenced the legislators of those days; but they had also to endure the restraints imposed upon them by more than one bishop of their own Church, in whose diocese the feeble representatives of once proud and illustrious orders sought an asylum, established their poor convent, erected their little chapel, and pursued their mission of unostentatious but active usefulness.

Mr. Fitzpatrick, in his admirable 'Life of Dr. Doyle,' writing of this period, indeed almost of the very year which saw Father Mathew a Capuchin friar in the little convent of Kilkenny, uses these words:—'The Irish friars, at this period, were slighted to such an extent by even the prelates and priests of their own religion, that the Holy See was obliged formally to interfere;' and Mr. Fitzpatrick quotes an official letter from Cardinal Litta to Archbishop Troy, dated the 14th of October 1815, in which the bitter complaints made by the 'Regulars of Ireland' are set forth.

The order to which the young priest attached himself, very much from the humility of his nature, was one of the poorest and most neglected at that time in the country, and certainly offered no worldly attractions to those who joined its few and feeble communities. Of the different subdivisions of the order of Minorites founded by Francis of Assisi, the Capuchins, or cowled, who followed the rigorous precepts laid down by Matthew Barchi, three hundred years after the death of the great saint, were the humblest and most mortified. To this section, represented at that time in Ireland by a few priests in the most important towns, Father Mathew freely and of his own choice attached himself; and with them he cast his lot in the Church. In these kingdoms the Catholic clergy, secular and regular, have but one means of support,—the voluntary contributions of the people. There are, for them, no endowments, no glebes, no rent-charges, no Ecclesiastical Commissioners —the said functionaries being, it may be supposed, superfluous in connection with the Catholic Church. By the people alone are the churches built, the educational and charitable institutions maintained, the Bishops and Parish Priests and Curates, the Monks and Friars of various orders, supported, sheltered, and clothed throughout the entire country. Fifty years since, the priest was necessarily a heavier burden upon the people than he is now. A hundred years ago the Catholic population of Ireland did not exceed a million and a half of souls; and, consequently, when the Church began to revive after her long and dreary night of suffering, and her oppressors at length discovered that no enactment could crush her out of existence, or diminish her vitality, and so gave up actively oppressing, without however repealing the disgraceful laws which continued the power of oppression, the Catholic Bishops endeavoured to keep the number of priests within the closest limits compatible with supplying the spiritual wants of their respective flocks. While acknowledging the value of the Regular Orders, the Irish Bishops, were they so inclined, could scarcely encourage their coming among their already overburdened people, who would have to support them in addition to their ordinary pastors ; and this policy, on the part of the bishops generally, and which in some dioceses assumed the regularity of a system, led to much unhappiness amongst those Regulars who ventured to establish themselves in the different towns. This condition of affairs, so far from deterring, rather induced Father Mathew to join the Capuchins, whose watchword—'*humility*'—was the guiding principle of his life.

As it has been already stated, the young priest had not been long in Kilkenny before his worth was discovered. The Friary, which was not particularly well attended previously, became popular ; his confessional was constantly crowded ; and the people, rich as well as poor, came to him for advice and consolation. But his career in this the first scene of his missionary labours was soon brought to an end. In certain dioceses the Regulars were more restricted than in others. As a rule, they were not endowed with 'functions'—the power of administering Baptism and Extreme Unction, the first and last Sacraments. Their chapels, too, were under particular regulations. For instance, parishioners were not permitted to approach the Paschal Communion within their walls, and friars were restrained from administering it, though at all other seasons except Easter it was permitted. Also, friars could not perform the marriage ceremony without special permission. There were other distinctions between Seculars and Regulars ; but those mentioned were the most remarkable. Many of them hold to this day, and, it must be remarked, without having their justice or necessity questioned.

A circumstance occurred which brought his mission in Kilkenny to a rather abrupt and unexpected termination. The bishop in those days was the Right Rev. Dr. Marum, a highly educated and conscientious man, with however very strong notions of church discipline. On Saturday evening, Father Mathew was, as usual, in his confessional, the doors of which were besieged by a crowd of penitents awaiting their turn for admission. He was closely engaged in his sacred duty, when an ecclesiastic entered the chapel, walked direct to his confessional, and handed him in a document of an urgent nature. Father Mathew opened it, read the first few lines, rose from his seat, and departed humbly from the church, saying to his anxious flock, who felt that something strange was about to happen—'Go to your other clergymen; I have no power to hear your confession any longer.' He had received a command from the bishop to cease hearing confessions, on the alleged ground of his having, contrary to the regulations of the diocese, administered Paschal Communion. A report spread abroad that Father Mathew had been suspended, and the circumstance under which he had received the order from the bishop gave some show of probability to the rumour. It was but a rumour; yet the deprivation so imposed cut him to the soul. He determined to leave Kilkenny without delay, and seek some other diocese; which intention he put into immediate execution. The bishop discovered, when too late, that the complaint on which he so rigorously acted was entirely groundless, and that the young friar had never infringed the regulations of the diocese. Explanations and apologies were offered; but his resolution was not to be changed, and he hastened his departure from the scene of his first mission. Ever after, the bishop deplored his own hastiness in this transaction, and did all in his power to lighten the effects of a blow which he could not recall.

CHAPTER II.

The Little Friary — Father Arthur O'Leary — His Character and Influence — New Coat for St. Patrick — Reply to the Quaker — Father Donovan — Saved from the Guillotine — Attending the Condemned — How the Shirts went — Father Donovan obtains a Colleague, and provides for his Reception — Father Donovan's Ambition — 'Moll in the Wad' — Father Mathew little known at first — Confessional of a Popular Priest — Devotedness of Father Mathew's Friendship.

REMOTE from the din of traffic, and shut out from the public eye, there then, and for many years after, existed in the city of Cork a little chapel of humble pretensions both as to appearance and accommodation. This diminutive place of worship had been erected by a celebrated member of the Capuchin Order, a man whose strong and powerful intellect and scholarly attainments were devoted as well to the defence of his persecuted or endangered faith, as to the promotion of liberal and tolerant opinions, and the maintenance of social order. This was the famous Father Arthur O'Leary. As a priest, he was pious, zealous, charitable ; as a public writer, he was bold, eloquent, of lively fancy, and replete with that humorous vein which is so useful to a cause, and so damaging to an opponent. Fearless and formidable champion to the oppressed, as he proved himself to be during many trying years, while the mass of his countrymen were slowly emerging from an oppression against which it seemed almost useless to contend, it was only natural that Father O'Leary should be loved and honoured by those of his own communion ; while his earnest advocacy of toleration and Christian concord among all men, whatever their faith, and his well-meant efforts to repress lawless and destructive combinations of the peasantry, earned for him the respect of his Protestant and Dissenting brethren. Such, indeed, was his deserved influence with the leading members of the Irish Parliament, that he on more than one occasion saved the Regular Orders from the revival of old penalties, or the imposition of new restrictions. He encountered, and confessedly overthrew, some of the most famous political and polemical writers of the day, and these successful efforts rendered his name celebrated in England as in Ireland; but the production which most added to his fame and enhanced his influence, was one styled 'An Essay on Toleration, or Mr. O'Leary's plea for Liberty of Conscience.' Very much owing to this remarkable work, he was elected a member of a society, partly political and partly social, known as the Monks of St. Patrick, which took its rise under the auspices of Mr Yelverton, afterwards Lord Avonmore, and to which belonged many of the celebrated and leading men of the day. During a debate in the Irish House of Commons, on the Catholic Bill of 1782, testimonies of the most flattering kind were borne to the merits of Father O'Leary. These testimonies were the more remarkable as the assembly in which they were spoken consisted exclusively of Protestant gentlemen. Mr. Grattan described this Franciscan friar as 'poor in everything but genius and philosophy;' and he added—'If I did not know him to be a Christian clergyman, I should suppose him, by his writings, to be a philosopher of the Augustan age.' Mr. St. George would 'for the sake of one celebrated character of their body, be tolerant to the rest.' Sir Lucius O'Brien 'did not approve of the Regulars,' but he spoke with respect of 'the Reverend Doctor Arthur O'Leary.' In five years after, Mr. Curran, during a debate in the same House, thus bore his personal testimony to the character of this remarkable man:—'Mr.

O'Leary is, to my knowledge, a man of the most innocent and amiable simplicity of manners in private life.' A still more interesting evidence of his merit is afforded by his biographer, the late Rev. Thomas England, who states that the late Bishop Murphy of Cork, when a mere youth, was frequently the almoner of Father O'Leary's charities; and that a number of reduced room-keepers and tradesmen were, on every Monday morning, relieved by the good friar. The general average of his weekly charities amounted to 2*l*., and sometimes to 3*l*. His biographer justly remarks—'When it is recollected that the poor Capuchin had no income, except what was derived from the contributions of those who frequented his chapel, the charitable disposition of his heart and mind will be duly appreciated.'

There was a time, however, when the resources of the good priest were not so flourishing, as the following incident will prove. Father O'Leary had many Protestant friends, who admired his ability, and sympathised with his opinions, so full of liberality and Christian charity. One in particular, Mr. Joseph Bennett, a well-known lawyer of the day, was most intimate with the distinguished friar, and frequently visited the little chapel, to enjoy the pleasure of hearing his friend preach. On a certain St. Patrick's Day, Mr. Bennett was in his accustomed place, listening with delight to a noble discourse on the life and labours of the national saint. The preacher and his Protestant admirer dined together the same day. During dinner the latter remarked—'Father O'Leary, that was a splendid sermon of yours on St. Patrick.' 'Didn't I give him a beautiful new coat to-day?' said the preacher in his usual jocular tone. 'Indeed you did,' replied his friend. 'And how much do you think I got for my work?' 'I can't tell—I have no notion; only I know it deserved more than it got.' 'Well, let us see,' said Father O'Leary—'there is the box, on the chair near you. Turn it up, and count its contents.'

The box was turned up, and its contents were counted. '*Eighteenpence-halfpenny!*' exclaimed Mr. Bennett, in deep disgust. 'Well, my dear child,' said the priest, with a smile, 'that's what St. Patrick gave me for his grand new coat.'

Father O'Leary gained more by a reply which he made to a respectable member of the Society of Friends, than by his splendid panegyric of St. Patrick. Going about the city on his annual collection for the support of his chapel, he called into the thriving shop of this worthy Quaker. He made his application, and was answered by a decided refusal. 'Then,' said he, as if speaking to himself, 'I know for whom it will be worse;' and he turned to leave the shop. 'What, friend!' said the Quaker, 'dost thou mean to threaten?' 'Not I, indeed,' replied the friar. 'Then what didst thou mean when thee said thee knew for whom it would be worse?' 'Why, it would be worse *for myself*, to be sure, *if I didn't get the money*,' said O'Leary, with a look of drollery which betrayed the sedate Friend into a hearty laugh. 'Then, if that was all thee meant, here is a guinea for thee,' said the Quaker.

Father O'Leary waged rather a fierce controversy with Dr. Woodward, the Protestant Bishop of Cloyne. Indeed it would be more correct to say he defended himself from a fierce attack from his Right Reverend assailant. It was in reply to an envenomed attack, in which the friars, and O'Leary in particular, were treated with scant courtesy, that a passage, replete with sarcastic humour, thus concludes:—'It is equal to us where a man pays his debts, whether here or in purgatory, provided he pays us ourselves what he owes us; and however clamorous a mitred divine may be about a popish purgatory, *he may perhaps go farther and speed worse*.'

Father O'Leary left Cork for London in the year 1789, when he became connected with St. Patrick's Chapel, Soho Square, in which he officiated till his death, in 1789, in the 73rd year of his age.

In one of his public letters, written in the 'Little Friary,' while yet striking hard blows in the cause of religious freedom, he describes himself as 'a poor friar, buried between salt-houses and stables.' And this was a literal description of his place of residence, the scene alike of his priestly duties and literary labours.

Such was the most famous of the predecessors of Father Mathew, and such the out-of-the-way place in which the young priest recommenced his missionary career. In Cork, as in Kilkenny, the Capuchin Order was represented by two members of the body; and at the time of Father Mathew's arrival, his associate and superior was the Rev. Francis Donovan, of whom some particulars may be given.

At an early period of his life, Father Donovan may have been courteous, refined, and elegant in manner; but at the period when he was joined by his youthful colleague he was not preeminently remarkable for these qualities—which, no doubt, are too often but mere external attractions, and not true indications of the real nature of their possessor. Father Donovan was, in truth, a worthy and pious man, but he was both rough and brusque, and not a little singular in some respects. His life had not been wholly destitute of peril and excitement; for not only had he been the witness of those scenes of horror which have been since then the theme of the philosopher and the property of the historian, but he was made to feel in them a terrible personal interest. Educated in France, at a time when society was heaving with the throes of revolution, he became chaplain to the family of a French nobleman, shortly before the storm burst forth which hurled throne into the dust, and prostrated altar in the mire. The rank of his patron being of itself sufficient to decide his fate before the so-called tribunals of the hour, which were in reality purveyors for the public shambles, he determined to fly from a danger which it would be madness to face, and was fortunate enough to escape to England. The nobleman and his family fled in safety, while the Abbé Donovan was left in Paris, in charge of the hotel and its valuable contents. But as the guillotine was robbed of the Marquis, the Chaplain was made to take his place. It did not require many minutes, or a long deliberation, to find one of his order guilty of treason against the public safety ; and the sentence was a matter of course.

It was a fine, bright sunshiny morning during the Reign of Terror, while yet Marat was a popular idol, and Charlotte Corday was brooding over her thoughts of vengeance away in the quiet province, when a long procession of victims wound its way through the streets of Paris, delighting a populace still unsatiated with blood. On it went, accompanied by a scoffing and yelling rabble, that surged and swayed against the horse-soldiers who guarded the prisoners, and who struggled to reach the scaffold with unbroken line. In one of the rude tumbrils was the Abbé Donovan, who had been actively employed during the preceding night in administering the consolations of religion to his fellow-captives. The goal was at length approached, and the first tumbril was close to the scaffold, on which stood the executioner and his assistants, ready for their dreadful work. Father Donovan, whose appearance was the signal for many a scoff and curse from the savage crowd that were now about to enjoy their daily feast of human slaughter, believed his last moment in this world had arrived; and having whispered a few words of hope and consolation to his companions in misery, he offered up a prayer to God, and prepared to meet his fate with the fortitude of a Christian. But just as he was about to cross the narrow space which appeared to separate him from eternity, an officer, whom Father Donovan ever after described in resplendent colours, rode up to the head of the procession, and raising his voice—'his melodious voice, sir'—above the hoarse murmur of the swaying multitude, cried out—'in the vernacular, sir'—'Are there any Irish among you?' 'There are seven of us!' shrieked Father Donovan, in agonised response. 'Then have no fear,' said the officer, in a voice that sounded to Father Donovan's ears as the voice of an angel; and using his influence with the officials and guards, this man in authority had his seven countrymen put aside, on some pretence or other, and ultimately secured their safety. The guillotine and the friends of 'liberty, equality, and fraternity,' were so fully fed on that day, that both could spare the few prisoners who were rescued from the knife of the one, and the remorseless cruelty of the others. For some time after, as Father Donovan used to tell, he would shake his head rather doubtingly; 'for though,' said he, 'my pate was never any great things of a beauty, I would have felt mighty awkward without it.' In which opinion his friends generally concurred.

This event made a deep impression upon his mind; not so much in consequence of his own extraordinary escape from a fearful death, as from the idea of so many human beings summoned, almost without any preparation, before the Great Tribunal; and he determined that, if he could, he would devote himself thenceforward to the duty of attending on the condemned in their last moments. His wish was gratified; for, some time after his return to Ireland, he was appointed Chaplain to the County Gaol of Cork, but not before he had voluntarily prepared many a poor fellow to meet death with firmness, and in humble confidence in Divine mercy.

Those were times when executions were terribly frequent; as not only were many offences then punished by death which are in these merciful days sufficiently atoned for by a short period of imprisonment, but there were also classes of offences which sprang from the unsettled state of the country, and with which the law dealt relentlessly. Therefore, for a considerable time, Father Donovan had many opportunities of exercising his charity and zeal in bringing the condemned to a true consciousness of their awful position. Rough and ready was the operation of the law in those times. In forty-eight ours after the prisoner stood in the dock, and heard his doom from the lips of his earthly judge, his soul was in the presence of a greater and more merciful tribunal. It is a short time for a man, strong in life, and with every faculty for enjoying existence, to be made to understand that at such a moment he is to die—to become as a clod of earth—cold, senseless—a thing to hide in the ground. A shorter time still in which to prepare for the solemn thought of the world beyond the grave. This fearful rapidity with which execution thus followed upon sentence, rendered necessary the constant attendance of the priest upon the condemned ; and, as a rule, Father Donovan remained up with his penitents for the whole night previous to the fatal morning. It was then the custom to convey the prisoner from the gaol to a place outside the town, where the gallows was erected ; and the bottom of the cart in which he was so conveyed was frequently the platform from which the victim of the law was launched into eternity. Often must the gaol chaplain have thought, as he sat in the cart beside the condemned, perhaps on the coffin which was so soon to receive his lifeless body, of that memorable procession through the streets of Paris, with the long line of tumbrils, in which old and young, the beautiful and the brave, the innocent girl and the strong man, were borne to death, amidst mocking cries, fierce gestures, and flaming eyes. Not that there was any, even the slightest, similarity in the conduct and bearing of the populace in both instances ; for while the one mocked and cursed, the other sympathised and prayed ; still there was enough of resemblance in the one procession to bring the other vividly before the mind.

Father Donovan had many an anecdote to tell of his experience as a gaol chaplain, and of how men bore themselves in the supreme moment of their fate. Though a good-natured man, his temper was not difficult to ruffle ; and on one occasion it was tried rather curiously. A prisoner was sentenced to death on Friday, and was to be executed on the following Monday. Father Donovan was, as usual, most zealous in his attention to the condemned, and employed the best means to bring him to a suitable state of mind. On Sunday, the priest assured his friends that 'that poor fellow up in the gaol was a most edifying penitent, whose thoughts were wholly fixed on heaven.' The hour too soon arrived at which the law was to take its course. The sad procession was slowly winding its way through one of the principal thoroughfares of the city, when the priest, who was absorbed in his pious efforts to complete his good work, was stunned by hearing the condemned man, who sat near him, cry out in a voice expressive of great amazement—'Oh, be the holy powers, that's quare! Yea, Father Donovan, alana, look there!—look at that fine man up there! But what is he doing there at all at all?' The priest indignantly glanced at the cause of this ill-timed excitement, and he saw, over the shop-front of a well-known ironmonger, the, to him, familiar figure of Vulçan, which, cleverly carved in wood and naturally coloured, stood, nude and brawny, leaning in an attitude of repose, the hammer resting on the anvil. The figure was sufficiently life-like to deceive the unhappy culprit, whose dread of death was not powerful enough to repress every emotion of curiosity or surprise.

When engaged in this duty of attending on the condemned in their last moments, it was Father Donovan's invariable custom to wear black silk breeches—this portion of his dress being of cloth on ordinary occasions. So that when the *silk* was seen adorning the well-turned limbs of the chaplain, it was known that the 'law was to take its course;' but when *cloth* was the material worn on a day, generally a Monday, on which an execution was to have taken place, it was equally certain that a reprieve had been received.

To make a 'decent' appearance on the scaffold was a matter of pride, and indeed of consolation, to many a poor fellow; and in the kindness and sympathy of the chaplain the condemned had an unfailing resource, for not only did Father Donovan freely 'lend' his own shirt, to render his penitent 'decent and clean' as he appeared before the public for the last hour of his life, but he as freely 'borrowed' the shirts of his friends for the same purpose. The lending and the borrowing in this case did not, as the reader may suppose, bear their ordinary signification; for neither the chaplain nor his friend ever again saw the article thus lent or borrowed.

From this cause, among others, it was rather hard to keep Father Donovan in shirts, his stock of linen being at times reduced to a very scanty complement, as the following incident will show. . He had been on one occasion invited to join a yachting party by the wealthy owner of a fine boat, in which the good priest had more than once before enjoyed a pleasant sail and an agreeable day. 'Mind you are ready in time, Father Frank; for if we delay, we'll lose the finest part of the day, and have the tide against us besides.' 'Oh, make yourself easy about me; I'm sure to be punctual,' said Father Frank, with an air of confidence that nearly satisfied his friend. 'Very well; but if you are not with us at my house by such an hour, I will call for you at your place.' The morning of the intended excursion arrived, but the friar was not true to his tryst. Time was slipping away, and still no appearance of Father Frank. So the friend proceeded to the well-known cock-loft, in which the unpunctual priest dwelt. To his quick and vehement application to the outer door, a very elderly woman responded, after a cautious Who's there?' by opening it to Mr. ——. 'Is Father Donovan within? I have been waiting for him all the morning.' The old lady made some vague reply, and looked a little confused; but, on being pressed, she admitted that he was still in bed

'In bed! why, what's the matter? is he ill?—he, such an early riser, to be in bed, and a whole party waiting for him! I must see what it means.' So saying, the speaket turned to the door of Father Frank's room, which he found to be locked. He then knocked sharply with his knuckles, crying out, 'Father Donovan! Father Frank! are you within? what's the matter? are you sick?' No answer. More knocking, and renewed appeals to Father Frank. 'Man, I'll kick in the door if I do n't get an answer,' said the impatient gentleman, as the vision of his yacht riding buoyantly at Cove, and straining at her anchor, and his friends waiting ready to start, crossed his mind. This last appeal was effectual, for there was a creaking of the bedstead audible, and then a scramble towards the door, and a turning of the key, and then a shuffle back, and more creaking of the bedstead. In rushed the exasperated owner of the yacht, who could only see a pair of beseeching eyes and a rather red nose above the bed-clothes. 'What does this mean?—are you sick?—do you know the hour?—what's the matter?' The reply was uttered in a plaintive voice—'I had a little disappointment, child.' 'Good heavens! I hope nothing serious? what is it, Father Frank? can I be of any use?' 'No, my dear, none in life; there is only one in the world who can help me now, and that's Molly,' said the occupant of the bed, in dolorous tones. 'Molly! Molly!—what of Molly?—what has she to do with your being in bed?' Well, my child, if you must have the truth, which is always the best, I must tell you that I determined to do honour to your party, and to appear as a gentleman ought; and in a fit of confiding simplicity I entrusted my only shirt to Molly, to do up; and here I am, all this blessed morning, fuming and fretting my life out, and she by the way starching and ironing it! My blessing on you, Molly!—'t is you that would make up linen for the Prince Regent, let alone for a poor Irish friar!' Father Frank's last shirt, save the one in Molly's hands, had graced the person of a penitent of his, who had been hanged the week before, and whose last moments were not a little cheered by the consciousness of the effect produced on his friends and the public in general by the beauty and whiteness of that garment. Molly, the old attendant, at last succeeded in the performance of her task, and the toilet was completed to the satisfaction of Father Frank and his anxious friend; who, it may be added, soon after presented the priest with a good stock of shirts, which, however, went in time the same road as their predecessors.

It was not alone by such small sacrifices that Father Donovan soothed the unhappy men whom he attended to the scaffold. The thought of what would become of their wretched families, when they were no more, would frequently add to the bitterness of their last hours; but the assurance of the priest, that he would take care of them and watch over them, rarely failed in its tranquillising effect. And once that the promise was given, it was sure to be kept, as many of his friends knew to their cost, for Father Frank made them sharers in the good work.

One day, Father Donovan, meeting a respectable lady with whose family he was most intimate, abruptly said: 'Congratulate me!—I have a young priest at last—and a charming young fellow he is, I can assure you.' 'I hope, Father Donovan, you will be kind to him,' remarked the lady. 'Kind to him!—to be sure I will; why not?' The lady evidently suspected that Father Donovan was not always a lamb of gentleness to his young coadjutors; and perhaps she had some reason for so thinking. But whatever he might have been to Father Mathew's predecessors, to him he never gave the smallest cause of complaint. And Father Mathew was the 'charming young fellow' whose arrival he so exultingly announced. Scant, however, was the accommodation for the new comer, and great was the difficulty to provide for his reception. Indeed, it would be hard to find a more miserable hole than what was, in fact and in reality, the Capuchin convent of the city of Cork. It consisted of two small rooms and a kind of closet, formed of what was afterwards the organ-loft of the little chapel; which organ-loft was above the gallery that faced the altar. One of the small rooms was the property of Father Donovan, the other was to become the possession of Father Mathew. To furnish this room for the stranger was a task of no light care to Father Donovan. It had a bedstead, and even a bed, but not a vestige of sheet or blanket. Perhaps, were the truth known, it might be found that sheets and blankets had been made over to some distressed neighbour, who had whispered a sad tale into the ear of that priest of rough exterior but tender heart. To purchase these essential articles was out of the question, in the normal state of Father Donovan's exchequer, and therefore they had to be got by some other means, and were accordingly 'borrowed' of an obliging friend, who would have been delighted to 'lend' a much more valuable equipment for the same purpose.

The difficulty of the bedclothes having been happily got over, there then was the dinner to provide; and how is that to be managed?' thought Father Donovan. Easily enough to him. 'Come with me, child, and I'll show you some of the sights of the city,' said he to the young stranger. Having honestly fulfilled his promise in this respect, he brought him to the door of a respectable-looking house, occupied by a family as remarkable for their worth as for their hospitality. 'Come in here, child; I want to see a friend, to whom I must introduce you.' Briefly introducing his companion to the lady and gentleman of the house, he whispered to him, 'Stay here till I come back, and be sure you wait for me,' and then abruptly quitted the room, leaving the bashful and modest young friar to get on as well as he could with persons to whom he had been previously unknown. He should have waited a long time had he waited for the return of his superior. Poor young priest! that was a day of trial for him. No one possessed more thoroughly the feelings and instincts of a gentleman than he did; and yet, in obedience to the injunction which he had received, he was compelled to remain, though in a state of mental torture, until the usual hour for dinner had been struck by the house clock. The dinner was at length announced, when Father Mathew, whose embarrassment and annoyance were every moment on the increase, rose to depart. 'No, no, Father Mathew,' said the lady of the house, 'you must not go—you are to dine with us—you know we expected you.' 'Expected me, madam!—I assure you I ordered my dinner.' 'That may be, my dear sir; but still you must dine with us. Father Donovan kindly promised us that pleasure, and he was good enough to bring you here himself.' This, then, was the meaning of the whispered injunction, 'Stay here till I come back; be sure you wait for me.' The cordiality and kindness of the good lady and her husband broke down all reserve; and that day was the commencement of a mutual friendship which neither failed nor flagged at this side of the grave.

The two friars became strongly attached to each other; and yet rarely were two men more widely different from each other in many respects. The one, rough and brusque, and not unfrequently passionate and inconsiderate—the other, gentle and courteous, sweet-tempered and thoughtful; the one, occasionally evincing a sublime disdain for the graces and amenities of life—the other, almost formal in the observance of the established rules and customs of society.

But there was this bond which linked the two men together: they each recognised the worth of the other, and they both yearned for some one in whom to centre their affections—one whom to love, and to be loved by. Soon the mutual feeling of regard ripened into the strongest and warmest affection, rendered more sacred, on the one hand, by that paternal feeling which age and a desire to cherish and protect inspired, and, on the other hand, by filial respect, and instinctive reverence for authority, and that natural humility which induced a willing and cheerful obedience.

Father Donovan seemed, as it were, to have got a new lease of life since the arrival of his youthful coadjutor, of whose amiability and goodness he was never wearied of speaking. 'Indeed, Father Donovan,' said a friend to him one day, 'there is really no bearing with you of late, you are so proud since your little Apostle has come to you.' The zeal and holiness of the young priest even then suggested to the mind this most beautiful and sacred form of appellation. In five-and-twenty years after, he was known in every quarter of the globe as the 'Apostle of Temperance.'

If any mortal man could be said to be truly happy, Father Donovan might certainly lay claim to that rare distinction. But there was one cloud that occasionally shadowed his happiness—the want of an organ and a choir. Two difficulties, and rather material ones, stood in the way of the acquisition of the first object. The one was the poverty of the church, the other was the limited space of the building. The church itself exactly measured 43 feet in length, and about the same in breadth ; and from the rails of the altar to the interior of the porch, the space did not exceed 28 or 30 feet. So that, were there money to purchase the organ, there was no place in which to erect it. What might be, and what eventually was, the organ-loft, was then occupied as the dwelling-place of the two priests and an aged attendant. Still, notwithstanding the impossibility of accomplishing his wish, the idea of an organ and choir haunted the brain of Father Donovan, and he determined to accomplish his purpose by some means or other. At length, he believed he had overcome all obstacles, and had realised the darling object of his ambition.

Father Mathew was conscious of a striking change in the manner and bearing of his reverend friend, who suddenly manifested a degree of softness and gentleness not generally common to him, and who walked with a springy and rather boyish step, as if he were revelling in the possession of some joyful secret. 'I have it, my dear boy—I have it, at last—at last, sir!' exclaimed Father Donovan one day to his friend, in a tone of exultation. 'Have what, my dear Father Donovan?' gently enquired Father Mathew. 'Why, the organ, my dear boy! I have such a treat for you for next Sunday. Yes, sir; the organ. I knew I'd have it at last.' 'An organ! my dear Father Donovan; how are we to get it, and where are we to put it?' was the natural question. 'It's all right. I got it, sir—a most beautiful instrument; and as for room, it won't occupy any space. You will be sure to be delighted, and so will our poor people. I tell you what it is, the *Adeste* is heavenly. Wait till you hear it.' Father Donovan then explained how he had procured a barrel-organ, which played a number of sacred airs, such as the *Adeste fidelis* and the *Sicilian Mariners' Hymn*; and that these could be fittingly introduced during Mass, and also at Vespers. The musician would be under his control, and he (Father Donovan) would be responsible for the admirable effect of this delightful innovation. The Sunday, fraught with anticipated triumph to Father Donovan, arrived. The organ and its operator were in the little chapel, and Father Donovan was having a vigilant eye to both. Nothing could be a more decided success than the *Adeste*, as many besides Father Donovan thought it 'heavenly;' nor was its effect lessened by the plaintive sweetness of the *Hymn*. Tears of rapture stood in the eyes of Father Donovan. It was a moment of unalloyed triumph, such as mortals experience but rarely in this life. The Last Gospel was just being read by Father Mathew, who was the celebrant, when the operator commenced a third air; but—horror of horrors!—instead of one of those gentle and spirit-breathing strains that lift the soul to heaven in a flood of holy melody, out rattled the two-well-known air of '*Moll in the wad!*' It would be impossible to describe the bewilderment of the congregation, or the rage and confusion of poor Father Donovan, at this 'awful scandal,' which nearly threw him into a fever, from shame and humiliation. His friends were, thenceforward, rather cautious in their allusions to mechanical music, and indeed organs of all kinds; and as for the remotest reference to '*Moll in the wad*,' that would have been a rashness as fatal to peace, as it would have been cruel and ungenerous to the sorely-afflicted friar.

For a time, little was known of the young priest, who was rarely to be met with beyond the precincts of his chapel, and who with difficulty could be drawn from the retirement of the miserable apartment which was appropriated to his use. Miserable indeed it was in every respect; for not only was it bare of furniture, and mean and poor in its accommodation, but the vitiated air from the congregation, whose clothes were frequently saturated with rain, ascended to this as well as to the adjoining chamber, producing its natural effect even upon his youthful frame and robust constitution. If one desired to see Father Mathew, the most likely place in which to find him was the confessional. As in Kilkenny, the number of his penitents rapidly increased, and with them, of course, increased the labour which he had to undergo in consequence of his growing popularity.

To those who know little or nothing of this branch of the duty of a Catholic clergyman, it would be almost impossible to describe with accuracy its wearying and engrossing nature. Constant attendance in a crowded court is fatiguing to the lawyer, whether he be actually engaged in business or otherwise; but can its irksomeness, which is relieved by mental excitement, or by the interest felt in the conduct of a case, be compared to the dull, monotonous, terrible drudgery of the priest, who is popular with the poor, and whose confessional is therefore much frequented? Some idea of the labour undergone by Father Mathew in this department of his priestly duty may be understood, when it is mentioned that, on certain days in the week, he was in his confessional as early as five o'clock in the morning. In this box, his portion of which was about the width of an ordinary arm-chair, he generally sat till eight o'clock, if he had to say mass; or till nine, if he had not: but as soon as breakfast was over, he was to be found in the same place, with an anxious crowd at either side, each person awaiting his or her turn to kneel at one of the two compartments. Were it Saturday, or the vigil of a festival, the duty, which commenced at five in the morning, did not terminate till ten, and frequently eleven o'clock, at night. Towards evening the number always increased, as it was then only the working people could conveniently attend. In this confined box, surrounded by those whose poverty was painfully evidenced in the wretched condition of their clothing, the unpleasantness aggravated by the wetness of the weather or the heaviness of the atmosphere, Father Mathew was pent up, oftentimes for fifteen hours, as well during the stifling heat of summer as in the numbing cold of winter; but though this constant attendance was a fearful tax upon his strength, and no small strain upon his constitution, he never wearied of his work but persevered in it with the most extraordinary energy and the most marvellous punctuality.

Let the reader imagine the young priest, in this little chapel, seated in that circumscribed box, surrounded by a crowd, poor, badly clad, with garments reeking with moisture; and then think of the various trades and occupations in which the penitents had been engaged up to the moment they had entered the sacred building. There was the dealer in salt fish, the workman in the chandlery, those engaged in killing meat for market or curing it for exportation, the makers of puddings and sausages, and, omitting many others, the lamplighters of the city !—the odour from whose clothes, however tolerable in the open air, must have been overpowering in a confined and ill-ventilated place. For eighteen or twenty years after Father Mathew had made Cork his future home, oil lamps were alone used in its streets ; and this mode of illumination required a considerable staff of lamplighters. So soon as Father Mathew's fame spread abroad, the lamplighters turned to his confessional ; and these poor fellows, whose clothes literally reeked with fish oil in every stage of decomposition, though most excellent and edifying Christians, were about the least savoury of human beings. At first, these highly flavoured penitents were almost two much for the jaded stomach of the young priest to endure ; but he never, in any way, manifested the slightest repugnance to their close neighbourhood, and ere long it became to him a matter of indifference.

It was in the confessional that he laid the foundation of his future fame. His reputation as a spiritual director spread from parish to parish of the city, gradually it reached to its remotest confines, and so travelled far beyond ; until, subsequently, it was said, with as much of truth as of pleasantry—that if a carman from Kerry brought a firkin of butter into the Cork market, he would not return home until he had gone to confession to Father Mathew. It may here be mentioned that, in order to hear the confessions of people from the country, many of whom then spoke no other language than Irish, Father Mathew set himself diligently to learn the native tongue ; and that after a time he became sufficiently conversant with it for the purposes of his ministry.

An incident occurred to him on one occasion which left a deep impression on his mind. It was on a Sunday morning, when he had been engaged in the church from six o'clock until after ten, in hearing confessions, celebrating Mass, and again hearing confessions. He had been in his confessional the night before till eleven o'clock; so that, when on this morning he was about to leave the church in order to get his breakfast, it might well be supposed that he was both hungry and weary. But as he was about to leave, four sailors rolled in, and requested him to hear their confessions. 'Why did you not come at a more reasonable hour?' asked Father Mathew, in a tone of momentary irritation; 'I can't hear you now, come in the morning.' The sailors turned to go, when a devout poor woman, who had witnessed the interview, gently approached him, and touching his arm, said, in a voice of respectful entreaty, 'They may not come again, sir.' This implied remonstrance made an instantaneous impression on his mind; and running after the sailors, who had left in the meantime, he brought them back to the confessional, and remained with them until he had administered the sacraments to each. He then entertained them at breakfast, and dismissed them in a happy state of mind. He afterwards thanked the poor woman, 'through whom,' he said, 'the Holy Ghost had spoken to him.'

In some years subsequent to the period of which we now treat, a Catholic lady said to an elderly servant in her house—'Well, Kitty, how do you like Father Mathew as a director?' Wisha, purty well, ma'm.' 'What do you mean by "purty well?"' enquired the mistress. 'Well, indeed, ma'm, he's a beautiful director, not a doubt about it; but—' here Kitty paused. 'What do you mean by your "but?"' persevered the mistress, whose interest was excited by the manner of her servant. 'Then, ma'm, the way of it is this—the worse you are in the beginning, the more he'd like you, and the better he'd use you; but if you didn't improve very soon, there is no usage too bad for you.' The mistress was strongly in favour of Kitty not changing her new director.

Day by day, did the young friar win his way to the hearts of the poor, and to the respect and confidence of the rich. The people could not think of him without love, or speak of him without enthusiasm. He was so gentle and compassionate to them, so respectful to poverty, in which, as he frequently said, he ever saw the image of the Redeemer; he was so earnest in his desire to rescue the erring from vice, and to raise the fallen to a new life ; he was so full of fervour and zeal, and yet without harshness or austerity—that he took captive the affections of all who came within the reach of his influence. This is not the testimony of one; it is that of hundreds.

As the circle of his acquaintance became extended, so likewise was multiplied the number of his friends ; and, with Father Mathew, once his friend, his friend for ever—for that must have been a quarrelsome and perverse person indeed, whose conduct severed the sacred tie with one who literally revelled in the delights of friendship. He thus began to be more generally known ; and as he became more known, so did his influence extend among the class whose aid and assistance were frequently of use to him in the promotion of those good works to which he soon turned his attention.

An instance may here be given of the strength and devotedness of his friendship. It was in the summer of the year 1817, when he had been about three years in Cork, that that city was visited with an outbreak of fever of a peculiarly malignant character—in fact, the worst form of typhus ; a disease which has long made its home in Ireland, and which, in the period of pressure arising from scarcity of food, is sure to manifest its dreaded presence. Father Mathew was then very intimate with a family of great worth, well known and universally respected on account of their religious and charitable disposition. The eldest son, who was then springing into manhood, was struck down by the sickness, which was making fearful ravages amidst the poor, and rapidly picking out its victims from among the wealthier class, to which the family in question belonged. Their residence was some distance, perhaps a mile and a half, from Father Mathew's little crib in Blackamoor Lane, where, like his predecessor, Father O'Leary, he was 'buried amid salt-houses and stables.' But, as early as five o'clock in the morning, the watchman, were he in the way, might have seen a slight active figure climbing the wall which surrounded the pleasure ground attached to the residence, and rapidly making its way to the rear of the building. This was Father Mathew, whose anxiety for the safety of his young friend was so intense, that he sought the earliest intelligence of how he had passed the night, but whose consideration for the people of the lodge would not suffer him to disturb them at that hour to open the gate for him, and admit him in the usual way. The invalid, who was the object of so much solicitude, recovered from the attack, and lives to this day to tell, with grateful emotion, of a friendship so earnest and so sincere.

CHAPTER III.

Father Mathew establishes Literary and Industrial Schools — Attracts the Young to him — Founds valuable Societies — Economy of Time — Punctuality in keeping Appointments — Early Rising — Same Kindness to all — His lavish Charities — Instances of his Kindness — The imaginary Temptation — The Dean's Bees — He loses his youngest Brother — Instance of his Humility — His Preaching — His Passion Sermon — Charity Sermons — Establishes a Cemetery — The Cholera of 1832 — His Services in the Hospital — Saved!

BECOMING, after a time, thoroughly acquainted with the teeming population around him, their wants, their necessities, their virtues as well as their vices, he witnessed with pain the operation of two parent evils—ignorance and idleness; and he determined, so far as he could, to provide the usual remedies to counteract their baneful influence—namely, education and employment. There were some few schools in the city for the humblest class of the community; but at the time when Father Mathew drew round him active co-operators in his benevolent work, education was much more restricted than it is at present, when it is placed fairly within the reach of all who desire to avail themselves of its advantages. As to industrial training, it was not much thought of in those days. The efforts which Father Mathew then made, in establishing a school in which industrial was combined with literary training, and in forming associations at once educational and charitable, were the fruitful germs of undertakings of far greater magnitude, which were afterwards developed into widely-extended and permanent usefulness. He opened a school for female children, and procured for it the attendance of a number of ladies who, at his earnest solicitation, devoted themselves with zeal to its superintendence. In this admirable school, which was established in a large store adjoining the Friary, hundreds of children were instructed in the ordinary rudiments of literary knowledge, and were also taught plain and other work, which was made for them a source of profit and support. They also received from those good ladies, whom they had so much reason to respect, lessons of piety and virtue, which strengthened while they formed their moral character, and prepared them to resist some of the worst temptations common to their condition of life. This school progressed and prospered, and was ere long felt to be a blessing to the neighbourhood. Father Mathew cherished it as the apple of his eye. In the year 1824 there were 500 pupils, grown girls as well as children, in this school. The upper loft, or apartment, was occupied by 200 girls, who were constantly employed in various kinds of work during the hours in which they were not engaged in learning the ordinary lessons taught in such schools. The lower loft of the store contained 300 children, a large proportion of them of tender years. There was also an evening or night school for boys, many of them orphan or deserted children, but all of the very humblest and poorest class.

To attract the young towards him by every honest art of persuasion and inducement, and to acquire and maintain over them a salutary yet gentle control, was with him an instinct as well as a policy. And few men were more calculated than he was to win the confidence of the young, and to inspire them with a deep interest in what they were taught, and a sentiment of personal devotion to their teacher. Father Mathew naturally preferred adopting the suggestion of the *blandi doctores* of Horace to the stern maxim of Solomon. The *crustula* were, in his esteem, a more effectual agent than the rod. Sweet smiles, and gentle words, and tender caresses, and timely presents, and occasional feasts, and pleasant trips into the country—these were some of the means which he employed with a number of interesting boys and youths of the middle class, whom he attracted to his church, and formed into societies, whose objects were at once religious, educational, and charitable. They attended at the altar, and, by their decorum of conduct and gravity of demeanour, and the neatness and even picturesqueness of the costume which he had provided for them, added considerably to the pomp and impressiveness of the religious ceremonial for which the 'Little Friary,' as it was commonly called, became remarkable under Father Mathew's auspices. The young men taught catechism, and instructed poor children to read and write; and they improved their own minds through the aid of a well-stocked library, which their patron established for their use and enjoyment. They also visited the sick, and relieved their physical wants, as well as read for them and prayed with them. Here, in the Josephian Society of forty-four years since—for it was established by its founder in the year 1819—was the precursor of more than one association which in this day proves to be of so much advantage to its members, and which bridges over, as with a bridge of gold, the chasm that divides the different classes of society—especially those who possess almost everything, and those who want almost everything.

Father Mathew was most remarkable for his faculty of economising time. A favourite proverb of his was—'*Take time by the forelock, for he is bald behind;* and few ever so uniformly and persistently practised the wise lesson which it teaches as he did. He made time by husbanding and economising it. Rising early, generally about five o'clock, and, if necessary even earlier, he got through much business while other men were still in bed. Though, like all who are constantly engaged in some engrossing pursuit, he felt the day rapidly pass, he nevertheless found it to suffice for the discharge of his varied duties. He seemed to have the right moment for everything, and this too when his duties became more onerous and pressing, and the claims upon his attention were multiplied in consequence alike of his great popularity, and the every day widening circle of his acquaintance. In his appointments he was punctual to the minute, always at the appointed place at the appointed moment. 'In fact,' to use the words of a brother clergyman who knew and loved him from the first year of his ministry in Cork, 'he was never once absent from where his duty called him, whether by a public necessity or a private claim, or where his presence could console the afflicted, or give hope to the despairing.' It might be added that he was as punctual as punctilious in his visits of friendship, and even of ceremony; though it must be admitted that he contrived to combine a little business with occasions of the kind. For instance, when visiting at the house of a friend, he was sure to ask after the 'young gentlemen' of the family; and when the young gentlemen appeared, perhaps in obedience to a special summons, and that he had fondled and caressed them, as usual, he contrived to whisper into their blushing ear, 'My dear, you are forgetting me altogether; I have not seen you of late,'—a hint which was unfailingly understood, and which was generally successful. So that these visits of friendship enabled the watchful shepherd to keep his young flock from straying into devious paths. But whatever the duty, public or private, he was certain to perform it with exemplary regularity; and thus, by early rising, and the assistance of a programme, carefully prepared in the morning, Father Mathew got through an amount of work which three or four really active and energetic men, not possessing his method, would have found it hard to have equalled. Being one day asked by a friend how he contrived to rise so early as he did, he answered, while pointing to an adjoining cooperage, then in full operation, 'If I were a cooper, and bound to Mr. ——, I should be up as early, so as to be at my work at the appointed time, and thus become pleasing to Mr. ——, my master. But I have a higher calling, and I serve a better Master ; and am I to be less desirous of pleasing that Master than I should be to satisfy Mr. ——?'

It will be seen how this habit of early rising, and the method with which he provided for each hour of the day, served him in those wonderful exertions which he subsequently displayed in his mission as leader of the temperance movement.

Father Mathew was a gentleman by birth and association, and his tendencies might have naturally led him to seek the society of persons of the higher rather than of the humbler class ; but there never was a man who was more thoroughly free from the vice of toadying to the great—whether the greatness were derived from power, position, wealth, or the accident of birth. He was respectful to those who held a high position, and deferential to authority, whether ecclesiastical or civil ; but though full of humility and modesty, still there was a kind of unconscious dignity, and even nobleness, in the man, which kept him free from the slightest taint of meanness or cringing. When occasions drew together the representatives of various classes in the social scale, there was not a shade of difference in his manner to one more than to another—the same genial courtesy, the same consideration, the same kindly interest and cordial politeness. Father Mathew's manner was polished, but it was not artificial. There was this difference between it and the mere conventional politeness, which complies with the outward forms and observances of society, but which has no heart in it ; Father Mathew was kind and courteous from thorough goodness of disposition, which is the true foundation of that quality which we understand as 'gentlemanly.' A true gentleman is always considerate to the feelings of others ; and this delicacy of sentiment is as often found under the homespun of the peasant as under the broadcloth of the courtier. In this sense Father Mathew was preeminently a gentleman. To the poor he was respectful and tender, indeed almost reverential. 'They,' he used to say, 'will be as high in heaven as the highest in the land.'

The circumstances of the Friary were now different from what they had been before Father Mathew's arrival. The church, though miserably small, displayed an air of neatness and elegance, and the condition of the clergymen attached to it was much improved. Father Mathew received a considerable number of offerings and 'intentions;'* but as his pecuniary resources were increased, so were his charities multiplied. If he gave but little before, it was because he had only little to give, and he now gave abundantly because he had much to give. His daily duties brought him into contact with miseries and wretchedness in every imaginable form, and he never saw distress, in whatever shape, without attempting to relieve it. Here, in the midst of a poor and populous district, was a fitting theatre for the benevolent labours of such a man as Theobald Mathew. To give, and give with open hand, was with him, independently of its being a duty binding upon a minister of religion, a positive pleasure, an intense gratification—a kind of voluptuous enjoyment. Not only did he give charity himself, but he encouraged others to give it. 'Give, give, give!—have no fear of giving. What you have, you got from God; and be assured you will never be the worse of what you give in His name.' This was his answer to a person who talked of caution and prudence in the exercise of this great Christian virtue. He certainly had no fear of giving, giving with open hand and unstinted measure. Besides his regular pensioners, who were the very poor, he had a large number of room-

* Money given to a priest for masses to be offered up for some special purpose and intention.

keepers whom he constantly relieved. Then there were orphans, who clung round his very heart ; and widows, whose claim on his compassion was irresistible. Where he possibly could, he provided for the one, and relieved the other. There was a class, however, to whom he was peculiarly tender and respectful—those who, to use an expressive phrase, had seen better days. Nothing could surpass his delicate consideration for their sensitive feelings. If he could not himself relieve persons of this class without hurting their susceptibility, he did so in secret, and without his name being known or his hand seen. Instances might be mentioned of families in distress, or under a cloud, and who had at one time been prosperous, and had carried a high head in their day, being visited by some one who, in the dusk of evening or the darkness of night, enquired of them at the door, handed in a letter, and then vanished. The letter contained money—money sadly needed—but the donor was unknown ; and it was only in years after that those who had been thus made the bearers of his bounty, revealed the fact that Father Mathew was the unknown benefactor whose delicate charity assisted those families in their hour of need, perhaps rescued them from despair. The clerk of his chapel was frequently the medium through whom this timely bounty reached its intended object ; and speaking on one occasion of his lavish charities, the clerk adopted this rather expressive mode of describing his superior's faculty or love of giving :—Look, sir ! here is my notion on the subject,—if the streets of Cork were paved with gold, and if Father Mathew had entire control over them, and could do what he liked with them, there would not be a paving-stone in all Cork by the end of the year.'

Surely the boy was, in this instance, the father of the man. The child who clung to his mother's side, and fondly importuned her for her little feasts for his brothers, and indulgences for the servants, and alms for the poor, was here reflected in the priest, whose whole thought was how he could do good—how feed the hungry, and cover the naked, and raise the fallen—how minister to the sorrowful and the afflicted.

A case in point will exhibit the delicacy of his respect for those who had seen better days, and his quick sympathy with their feelings at what they considered the worst degradation of poverty. It was that of two young and attractive girls who, though delicately nurtured and carefully educated, unfortunately had no claim by birth upon their father's property. So long as they lived with their father, they knew nothing of sorrow or humiliation, and the world was to them without a cloud. But the father resolved to marry; and as there was no possibility of their being received by his future wife, he was compelled, through his selfishness, to make them over to the protection of relatives, who, having apprenticed the poor girls to the dressmaking business, gave themselves little further trouble about them. One of the girls bore the change bravely; but the other, who was delicate in constitution, and sensitive of disposition, gradually pined away, and, ere many months had passed, died. The father and his wife had left the country, and the surviving girl was as utterly desolate as she was destitute. What to do she knew not. To defray expenses of a funeral she had no means whatever; and her mistress, being either unwilling or unable to provide better, was about to have the remains of the dead girl carried to the grave in a rude shell, or parish coffin. Bold and brave as she was, the surviving sister could not endure this crowning indignity; for, in her mind, this was poverty in its most odious and revolting aspect. A thought struck her—she would appeal to one who had always been kind to her and her sister. Quitting the mean apartment, in which lay the body of the poor young creature, and the rude shell that had been brought for its reception, she rushed through the streets, and, wild and almost breathless, reached the Friary, where she found Father Mathew. Flinging herself on her knees before him, she could only sob out, 'Oh, Father Mathew! oh, Father Mathew!' 'My dear child, what is the matter? tell me, what has happened?' 'Oh, Father Mathew, they are going to bury my poor sister in a parish coffin!' This was repeated hysterically by the unhappy girl, whose strength and courage were now completely broken down. 'No, my dear child; they shall not do so. Rise up, my poor child, and have no fear. I will have her buried properly,' was Father Mathew's instantaneous reply. And he fully redeemed his word; for he went that moment to a respectable undertaker, and gave the necessary directions; and as early as five o'clock the next morning, there was a hearse and pair of horses at the door, and a chaise for the officiating priest, who, it need scarcely be said, was Father Mathew. In an hour after, he was found in his confessional; as he would not allow even a luxury of the kind—the luxury of doing good—to interfere with his ordinary, but, with him, imperative duties. It is pleasing to know that this considerate generos ity produced the most salutary effect upon the mind of the young girl, who soon regained her former strength and courage, and persevered at her employment till she learned to maintain herself independently.

Another case will afford the reader a further insight into the character of Father Mathew, and will also serve to show on what solid foundations rested the daily increasing fame of this good and holy man. A miserably poor woman, long and helplessly bedridden, had for her sole support on earth an only daughter, a girl of angelic sweetness, who lived but to minister to her afflicted mother. By incessant toil at her needle, this delicate girl just earned as much as enabled her to supply her mother with necessaries, and an occasional comfort; but for herself, her thin and scanty dress and transparent fingers told with terrible eloquence of her bitter struggles and heroic self-denial. To feed her bedridden mother, she starved herself. If the holiest and most exalted love could have borne her up in her hard struggle, she might have fought the good fight successfully; but the poor child sank under the fearful pressure, and died—as such die—in peace. The wretched mother was stunned by a blow for which she had not been prepared. She was blind, and could not see the fatal hectic upon her darling's cheek, though she might have noticed the faltering footstep and the failing voice. Nor, such was the loving deception practised upon her by her daughter, could she have imagined that, while she had enough to satisfy her wants, her poor child was at that very time dying of hunger. In her despair, this bereaved blind creature lifted her voice, and in her momentary madness blasphemed God—Who took from her, as she foolishly thought, her only support. She raved and cursed in the frenzy of her grief. Father Mathew heard the sad story, which at once excited his compassion. The scene of this misery was a wretched garret in one of the worst lanes of the city. Thither he went without delay, but not before he had provided himself with necessaries and comforts suited to the condition of the invalid. He found her still inconsolable, and raving in her despair; but soon his gentle voice, fraught with tenderness and compassion, made this helpless creature feel that God had not abandoned her, even in this world. With his own hands he fed her; nor did he leave her bedside until he had brought her to a right state of mind, and placed her in care of a person whom he had provided to attend and take charge of her. Next day, he constructed an altar in that dismal garret, and afforded her the unwonted consolation of being present at the celebration of the Holy Sacrifice. The poor creature, who was naturally religious and resigned to the will of Providence, perfectly recovered her right mind. She did not, however, long survive her daughter; but so long as she lived, she was supported and watched over by Father Mathew. Her death was full of peace and gentleness, and, in her last audible prayer to the Throne of Mercy, the name of her child was coupled with blessings upon her benefactor. Father Mathew concluded his good work by following her body to the grave, where it was laid by the side of that young creature whose short life had been that of a martyr and a saint.

Father Donovan died about the year 1820, to the deep sorrow of his attached friend, who during their intimate connection had looked upon him as a father, and loved him with the tenderness of a son. The effect which this loss produced on the mind of Father Mathew was very painful : for a time his nervous system was completely prostrated. It was during this distressing period of physical and mental prostration that he imagined himself to be tried by the following temptation. Resisting the kindly importunities of his friends, who sought to distract his grief by the influences of agreeable society, he shut himself up in his unwholesome chamber, and there brooded in secret over his gloomy thoughts. As he sat one evening by himself before the fire, whose flickering light filled the room with fantastic shadows, a voice seemed to whisper in his ear—'Father Mathew, that Cognac in the cupboard is delicious. You have not tasted it. Why do n't you try it ?' Yielding to the delusion, Father Mathew replied, audibly—'Tea is much better.' 'But you did n't taste the Cognac—it is delicious—only try it,' whispered the imaginary voice. 'No ; tea is much better,' replied Father Mathew, now starting up in alarm. He seized his hat, and almost ran the short distance which separated the Friary from the residence of Dean Collins, the Parish Priest of St. Finn Barr's. He told the cause of his abrupt visit to his venerable friend, who was then in his seventieth year. 'It was a suggestion of the Evil One, my child, and you did well to resist it,' was the answer of the Dean. The next day, the Cognac, which had been given as a present to Father Mathew, was sent by him to a friend. The voice was never audible again, simply because the nerves had recovered their wonted strength.

In those days there was not that cordial feeling which now happily exists between the different orders of the clergy ; and the earnest support of a powerful friend, like the Dean and Vicar-General of the diocese, and pastor of the parish in which his chapel stood, was of no small service to Father Mathew, the Capuchin. But that friendship was fairly won by sterling merit and by good works. It would be difficult to conceive a grander or more imposing High Priest than Dean Collins, as he stood upon the altar, engaged in some solemn office of his ministry. Tall and commanding in stature, the snowy whiteness of his hair imparted a venerable majesty to his aspect. His face was beautiful in feature, but more beautiful in expression. His eye was large, dark, and soul-searching, but its light was usually softened by the tenderness of his disposition ; and it was only when he had to deal with the base or the mean, or when he thundered at some scandalous abuse, that it flashed like lightning. Dean Collins had all the graceful dignity and bearing of a gentleman of the old school, and, in society, his fascination of manner was most remarkable. An able and learned man, he was still as simple as a child. Of powerful intellect and great wisdom, he was modest and unpretending. Originally well educated, and a scholar of considerable attainments, he was not satisfied with knowing only what he had learned in his youth ; but during his long career as a missionary priest, he steadily kept pace with the progress of the age ; and to his latest moments he was thoroughly conversant with the literature, the philosophy, the discoveries of the time, as well as a keen observer of the political changes by which nations were influenced either for good or ill. He did not love learning in a selfish spirit ; he equally loved to disseminate it. The memory of the days when it was surrounded with danger to those who sought to drink from its spring, was ever present to his mind ; and he spared no effort to procure its waters pure and unpolluted for the children of his flock. His almost dying words will best represent his zeal in the cause of education, and his vivid recollection of the evil days that had gone.

It was a few days before he died ; and he lay stretched on a sofa, the sunlight and the soft breeze of summer entering through the open casement. One of his curates, the Rev. Wm. O'Connor, was with him in the room. Suddenly, the Dean said, in a low but impressive voice—'Do n't you hear the bees, Father William?' 'No, sir ; I do not,' answered his curate, who went over to the window, to look into the garden into which it opened. 'Do n't you hear the boys in the school, laying up honey for the winter of life?' Do n't you hear the bees now, Father William?' 'Yes sir, indeed I do ; I hear *your* bees.' They were his bees, for it was he who had built the hive for them, and called them together to possess it. 'Well I remember,' continued the dying priest, 'when I was learning my classics, I had to watch on the ditch side to protect the life of my teacher. The older boys used to take that necessary duty in turn ; and many a time has my eye wandered over the surrounding country from the pages of my *Virgil*, to see if there was a spy or an informer in sight. But now see how it is! The finger of God is there. Here are 600 boys below, gathering in the honey ; and there are 600 girls above, with the good nuns—and we are not afraid of anyone. We need not watch now. No wonder I should say—*Magnificat anima mea Dominum!*—My soul doth magnify the Lord.'

This good man gave his unreserved friendship to Father Mathew, simply because he believed in him, and honoured his worth. 'Oh, Dr. Collins,' said a lady to the Dean, 'I have been just listening to a sermon from Father Mathew, and I have been greatly edified.' 'My dear,' answered the venerable priest, '*his life is a sermon.*'

The death of Father Donovan threw additional labour upon Father Mathew, who, with the assistance of occasional help, undertook and discharged all the duties himself. In this laborious work he soon found distraction for his sorrow. But he was ere long to suffer the keenest affliction of his whole life. This was the death of his youngest brother.

Though the fourth son of his parents, Father Mathew became, on their death, and as it were of right, the recognised head of the family. His eldest brothers regarded him as their natural guide and superior, and his younger brothers looked up to him as to a father; and, certainly, no father could be more solicitous for the welfare and happiness of his children, than was Theobald Mathew for the welfare and happiness of his brothers. Robert was the youngest of all the children, and Father Mathew took upon himself the care of his education. He brought him to Cork, where he lived with him, not in the cockloft of the Friary, for he had been literally driven from that miserable hole by a succession of fevers—but in a small house in the neighbourhood, of which he became the tenant. Robert was the great joy of his life. A gay, lively, cheerful boy, innocent as an angel, and more beautiful than angels are generally represented—he filled the house with pleasant laughter, and revived, by his sports and gambols, the recollections of his brother's youth. Every day was a holiday to the priest so long as he had Robert to welcome him as he returned home, wearied after many hours of duty in the church, or in attendance by the bedside of the sick. The little fellow used to lie in wait behind the door when he heard the familiar footstep, and then, springing out from his place of well-known concealment, jump on the neck of his brother, with whom the pleasant prank never tired, or lost its charm, because it delighted the merry and affectionate boy. Father Mathew kept Robert at a day-school of high character in the city ; but he never otherwise left him from his care. The truth is, he would have spoiled the boy, had he not been of the most amiable disposition ; but such was his fondness for his young charge, that he gratified his every wish. Robert grew to be a high-spirited lad, strongly imbued with a love of adventure, which was not a little stimulated by the stories and descriptions indulged in by his brother Charles, who was then, and had been for some time previously, engaged in the African trade. Nothing would content Robert but to go with Charles, and share with him the dangers and the excitements of trade in a strange country and with a strange people. Father Mathew was much pained at the idea of losing the boy, who was at once his pet and companion, his plaything and solace ; but Robert's vocation was for the sea, and he was not to be driven from his fixed idea. It was at length decided that he should make the next voyage with Charles ; and too soon came the hour when he was torn from the arms of his brother Theobald, and consigned, with cautions and blessings, with tears and prayers, to his future guardian. Those who remember Robert at this time, as he was emerging from boyhood, speak of him with the utmost admiration —for the grace and elegance of his appearance, the extreme beauty of his countenance, and his frank and engaging manners. The vessel sailed for her distant destination ; and many a fervent prayer, murmured at the altar, or uttered by the bedside at night, followed her path across the ocean. The time came when the good ship was expected on her voyage home ; and as the days grew into weeks, so did the anxiety of the priest increase. Often, as he returned from some duty, he fancied that he should be met with the old surprise, and that the same loving arms would again cling round his neck. But it was the will of God that it should be otherwise. Theobald Mathew was never more to hear his brother's voice, or feel his circling arms, save in some happy dream, from which he was to awake in sorrow. The thoughtless boy, profiting by the temporary absence of his brother Charles, and bidding defiance to his strict injunctions, proceeded on an excursion to shoot pelicans, and, exposing himself to the fierce heat of the sun, in his eagerness to come on his game, received a sun-stroke, from which he died in a few hours. Charles returned only in time to see that there was no hope for the unhappy youth, whose rashness was not only fatal to his own bright young life, but fatal to the happiness of one at home, who loved him with more than the love of a father. The blow was a fearful one to that fond heart. It literally crushed it for a time. The mother that bore him could not have felt a keener pang of anguish than did poor Father Mathew for the loss of that engaging youth. Indeed, the feeling of the elder for the younger brother had in it much of womanly tenderness. Besides, Father Mathew had been bequeathed the boy by his mother ; and he ever felt, in addition to that natural affection which such intimate relationship inspires, that he was paying back, through his love for Robert, an instalment of the large debt of affection which he owed to the memory of that revered parent. For some time he was quite inconsolable, plunged in an agony of grief ; but religion came at length to his aid, and in the contemplation of the sorrows and sufferings of his Divine Master, he learned the duty of resignation, and obtained sufficient strength to assume at least an outward composure of manner. It was a hard struggle, however, with one of his affectionate disposition ; and his eyes would fill with tears and his features quiver with emotion, not only at the slightest allusion to the happy past, but at any circumstance which recalled it too vividly to his mind. It was pitiable, said an intimate friend, to witness the vehemence of his emotion, and the struggles which he made to subdue his feelings. It was a poor consolation to him, but one of which he eagerly availed himself, to order the erection of a monument over the distant grave which held the remains of his lost brother; and in a few years after, in the cemetery which he founded in Cork, he raised another monument to his memory, bearing this inscription:—

SACRED TO THE MEMORY OF
ROBERT MATHEW,
WHO DIED IN THE BIGHT OF BENIN, MAY 27TH, 1824,
AGED 16 YEARS.

Yet think not, dear youth, tho' far, far away
From thy own native Isle thou art sleeping,
That no heart for thy slumber is aching to-day,
That no eye for thy mem'ry is weeping.*

For more than thirty years, as the 27th of May came round, this tomb was decked with the fairest flowers, emblematic of the bright young life which had been extinguished on that fatal day.

The healing influence of time, and the teaching of that religion which he not only preached, but made the guide of his daily life, restored Father Mathew to apparent cheerfulness; but those by whom he was known most intimately, state that he did not for many years entirely recover, if he ever did, from the effects of that shock; which effects were

* These lines were taken from a little poem, written by one who combined much sweetness and grace of expression, with a bard's full share of misfortune and disappointed hope. The song of *Gougane Barra* affords, however, a far more favourable specimen of his powers. Calanan loved and honoured Father Mathew, and he offered him the tribute of his sympathy in the rather feeble verses from which the above lines were taken.

The first part of the poem referred to, which is descriptive of romantic scenery familiar to many a modern tourist, is as follows:—

'There is a green island in lone Gougane Barra,
Where Allua of songs rushes forth as an arrow;
In deep-valleyed Desmond—a thousand wild fountains
Came down to that lake from their home in the mountains.'

manifested in frequent fits of despondency—the more gloomy and profound when they followed some scene of gay conviviality of which he had been the life and centre.

Theobald Mathew was a man of strong feelings and quick emotions. He was as keenly alive to sorrow as to joy, to wrong and insult as to benefit and kindness. But while he felt the sting, he did not resent the injury. He suffered all the more acutely that he did not retaliate. The impulse was there, for he was only human, with a man's strength and a man's weakness ; but he resolutely beat down his rebellious nature, and rather sought to disarm his antagonist of the moment by a kind word, which 'turneth away wrath,' than to triumph in an angry conflict. He had a grand proverb which taught him the value of time, but he had a still better maxim which taught him the value of temper : '*A pint of oil is better than a hogshead of vinegar.*' Keenly sensitive and naturally excitable, he still was able to control the impulse which would prompt him to resent or retaliate. To use his own words, he 'struggled hard with the bitterness of the moment ;' and the struggle invariably ended in victory over self. That 'pint of oil' was a grand peace-maker.

Father Mathew had great humility of disposition, natural, as well as the growth of reflection. An incident will happily exemplify this humility, as well as the Christian charity of the man. A lady, in mistaken friendship, and believing that she was doing well in 'putting people on their guard,' resolved to perform this kind office for her favourite friend. Being at a dinner party, where many guests were assembled, and where the conversation happened to turn on Father Mathew and his good works, she heard him spoken rather hardly of by a clergyman, who, perhaps, might have spoken without much consideration, or in a spirit of momentary opposition to the general feeling, which was strongly in favour of the subject of conversation. The lady was deeply mortified at the remarks made, and could not rest, poor soul, until she had poured her complaint into the ear of her unconsciously outraged friend. Father Mathew heard her patiently, without betraying the slightest emotion of resentment, and then meekly replied—'My dear madam, I am very sorry indeed that my acts have not the approbation of this clergyman, for he is a truly good man, and one whose good opinion I value highly ; and I only hope that I may merit it in future better than I have hitherto done.' The lady was stunned by the reply, and could not at the moment say whether she was more annoyed with the assailed or with the assailant. Some time after, the same clergyman contracted a bad fever, while attending the sick ; and the first priest found at his bedside, and the one most constant in his attentions to the dying man, up to the last hour of his life, was the Rev. Theobald Mathew.

He was now about twelve years in Cork, and was most popular with persons of every class and creed. In those times religious differences were more strongly marked than in these happier days ; and the state of the Catholic question, which was to be settled in a few years after by the Act of Emancipation, was such as to keep alive much anger and bitterness in the public mind. But even then, and while such elements of strife were in constant action, Father Mathew was respected by his Protestant and Dissenting brethren, who, notwithstanding his being a devoted Catholic Priest, could not fail to recognise in him the true type of the Christian minister. His manner and appearance were greatly in his favour. Kind, cordial, and courteous, he was deferential without the slightest tinge of sycophancy ; and his appearance was pleasing and prepossessing in the highest degree. Handsome in person, with a countenance full of sweetness and expression, his natural gifts were heightened by the extreme neatness and simple elegance of his dress. While he looked the gentleman every inch, he was still unmistakably the priest. A brother clergyman, speaking of Father

Mathew in those days, says, 'He was the most irreproachable man I ever knew, and the pink of a gentleman. No one ever lived more within his ministry than he did. He was then what he was to the last—a mild, kind, gentle, unassuming man—always the same.' 'There was,' says another clergyman, 'a quiet gravity in his manner, with an air of genuine sanctity—something of the altar and the sanctuary always about him.' No one was more thoroughly devoid of affectation, and no one was more truly what he appeared to be—religious without austerity, good without parade, charitable without ostentation; devoted to his church, and in every thought a priest, but free from the slightest taint of sectarian rancour or intolerance. And this with him was not the result of calculation, or even of reasoning; it was instinctive, and sprang from his very nature.

CHAPTER IV.

Father Mathew as a Preacher — Earnestness his chief Attraction — Cotemporary Sketch of his Pulpit Oratory — His Sermons free from sectarian Bitterness — His Charity Sermons — His Pictures of the sublime Charity of the Poor — Intensity of his Emotion — The Man and the Preacher one — Establishes a Cemetery — The Cholera of 1832 — His untiring Exertions — The Hospital — Saved! — Give! give! give!

FROM the year 1820, his reputation as a preacher had been steadily advancing ; and at the time of which we now speak—six years after that date—he was admitted to be one of the most popular preachers of the day. This was at a period when the Cork pulpit was adorned by men whose powers were of the very highest order. Father Mathew was not a man of shining abilities, nor was he a profound or severely-trained scholar. Neither had he fashioned his style upon the best models, or improved his taste by a thorough acquaintance with those authors whose works are the classics of English literature. He was not then certainly an accomplished pulpit orator, if at any period of his life he could lay claim to that distinction ; and in the earlier years of his ministry he was frequently guilty of errors of taste, and violations of those rules laid down by rhetoricians of ancient and modern schools. And his voice, which at first was shrill, weak, and puny to the last degree, still lacked that strength and volume which practice and confidence imparted to it in later years. But those who for the most part thronged to hear him, and crowded his little church with that object, were not either inclined to be critical, or very capable of criti cism. They came, in an humble spirit, to hear the Gospel expounded—to be told of the mercy and goodness of God—of the beauty and holiness of charity—by one whose life was the living example of the precepts he taught. What was it to them, if a simile were false, or a metaphor out of place, or an image occasionally tawdry, or a sentence wanting in polish, or a chain of reasoning loose and inconclusive?—they crushed into that little temple to listen to the word of God preached by a man of God; and in that expectation they were never disappointed. Once within that church, they yielded themselves implicitly and unhesitatingly to his spiritual and moral guidance, and they went with him whither he led them. Ay, and even those few who ordinarily could sit coldly in judgement upon the excellencies or the defects, the style or manner of a preacher, and who, perhaps, came just to see something of the young priest of whom the 'common people' and the 'old women' talked so much—even they, cool critics and lofty judges, as they held themselves to be, found themselves suddenly surprised by strange dimness of vision and a chocking sensation in the throat, at the unpretending pathos of the preacher. What was the charm that held spell-bound the close-packed hundreds beneath the pulpit, that riveted the attention of the crowded galleries, and moved the inmost hearts even of those who had come to criticise? The earnestness of the preacher. Not the earnestness of the actor, who simulates, with cunning declamation and by impassioned gesture, the ardour of nature. No; it was the earnestness of truth, of sincerity, of belief. Father Mathew practised what he preached, and believed what he so persuasively and urgently enforced. Then, the emotion, which his voice made manifest to the ear, and which his agitated features made visible to the eye, was real, genuine, springing from the heart, thrilling his nerves, warming his blood, quickening his pulse—felt in every fibre of his frame. There was established between the preacher and the audience the most complete and perfect identity of feeling, the result of the sympathy which they mutually felt.

From one of a remarkable series of papers, entitled 'Sketches of the Cork Catholic Pulpit,' published about the year 1826, and which were written by a clergyman, whose fame as a pulpit orator is equalled by his reputation as a profound scholar,* a passage or two may be aptly quoted, so as to afford the reader a clearer impression of the Father Mathew of that day. The writer, after paying an eloquent tribute to the character of the preacher, to whom, he says, the reverence of all classes of the community was spontaneously and unreservedly tendered, thus describes the effect produced by his preaching on the mind of one who rather came to judge than to sympathise :—

> We have ourselves more than once gone to hear this preacher, with the express intent of duly and fairly estimating his powers as a speaker, and have summoned to our aid as much of our critical bitterness as we conceived sufficient to preserve our judgement uninfluenced by the previous charm of his character. We were not listening to his affectionate, earnest, and pathetic exhortation more than ten minutes, when our criticism—our bitterness—our self-importance, left us; all within us of unkind and harsh was softened down—our heart beat only to kindlier emotions—we sympathised with our fellow-christians around us. We defy the sternness and severity of criticism to stand unmoved, though it may remain unawakened, while Mr. Mathew is preaching; and this surely is no mean criterion of the excellence of his character, and the efficiency of his ministry in the pulpit.

His personal appearance is thus minutely sketched :-

> He has the advantage (though he appears to make little use of the advantage) of possessing a finely formed middle sized person, of exquisite symmetry ; the head, of admirable contour, and from which a finished model of the antique could be cast; the countenance intelligent, animated, and benevolent; its complexion rather sallow, inclining to paleness; eyes of dark lustre, beaming with internal peace, and rich in concentrated sensibility, rather than speaking or kindling

* The Very Rev. M. B. O'Shea, Archdeacon and Pastor of St. Patrick's, Cork.

with a superabundant fire ; the line of his mouth, harmonising so completely with his nose and chin, is of peculiar grace ; the brow, open, pale, broad and polished, bears upon it the impress not merely of dignified thought, but of nobility itself.

The concluding passage is at once a description and a testimony :

His principal talent lies in the disposal of the persuasive topics. He is fond of appealing—and in truth he does it with success—to the warm devotional feelings that have their fixed and natural seat in the Catholic bosom ; to the devotional recollections and associations that alternately soothe and alarm the Catholic mind. To all these he appeals ; matters so full of thrilling interest, and of inherent eloquence, that they burst on the soul with an all-subduing, instantaneous and electric force, purifying and ennobling the commonest phraseology that happens to be selected as their vehicle. Thus has this excellent young man gone on, notwithstanding many imperfections, which may yet be removed by ordinary study and attention, preaching earnestly and successfully, and enforcing truth and illustrating the beauty of the doctrine of his religion, by the noblest, the fairest, the most convincing comment—the undeviating rectitude, the unspotted purity, the extensive and indefatigable beneficence of his life. *O, si sic omnes!*

His Passion sermon, which he preached generally twice on Good Friday, was a marvellous success. The subject is of itself sufficient to inspire the human heart with the profoundest emotions of sympathy and compassion, and to fill the soul of the Christian with reverential awe. But as the preacher led his breathless audience, step by step, through each stage of that tremendous tragedy, that sublime agony, they were themselves the horror-stricken spectators of those memorable scenes. They glowed and shuddered, they sighed and wept, until, in the supreme moment, when the Great Atonement is consummated, they were so overwhelmed with sorrow, that sobs and cries testified to the depth of their emotion, and the triumph of the preacher. But is 'triumph' the right word, where there was neither art nor artifice—no deliberate attempt to work upon the feelings of susceptible piety? The preacher was as much moved as were those whom he moved. He was present in spirit with the beloved ones at the foot of the Cross, his features, as his soul, convulsed with the liveliest grief and horror; and those who saw that working countenance and that heaving breast, and heard those thrilling accents, could not but feel the keenest sympathy with his almost terrible emotion.

There was another charm in Father Mathew's preaching—it was utterly divested of religious, or, more correctly speaking, sectarian bitterness. He was not a controversialist. Controversy, which too often stands for conflict, was not suited to his natural temperament; neither, perhaps, was his mind sufficiently trained by theological study to enable him to wield with effect against an opponent, and with safety to himself, those sharp-pointed weapons which, while slaying one's antagonist in argument, too frequently penetrate beyond the robe, and wound the sacred side of Religion. He was not a deeply-read theologian, and with Canon Law he was but imperfectly acquainted; indeed, so little so, that he occasionally committed himself by mistakes which, though of small importance in the esteem of laymen, assumed a grave aspect in the consideration of the severely-trained student of Maynooth or the Sorbonne. Few men, however, were better Biblical scholars than was Father Mathew. With the Sacred Scriptures he was intimately and profoundly conversant. There was not a line from Genesis to Revelation with which he was not familiar. Imbued with the purer spirit of the New Testament, his imagination was yet captivated by the grandeur and the beauty of the Old. In its sublimity, as in its sweetness, the Bible was thoroughly mastered by this Brother of the Capuchin Order. Thus he had at will, and ready for every occasion, as for any emergency, quotations from gospel and parable, from hymn and canticle, from prophecy and proverb; and if he could not wrestle in tough argument, or flash logic in keen strife of intellect, he could disarm with an apt quotation, or safely intrench himself behind a maxim which might not be disputed. His sermons were eminently scriptural, breathing certainly more of the meek spirit of Him who taught so lovingly on the Mount, than of those fierce kings and mighty captains of Judea, whose words sound like trumpet blasts, and whose deeds ring again with the clang of battle.

Of his charity sermons I may here make mention, although his reputation for these more ambitious efforts of pulpit oratory was of somewhat slow growth ; and it was not until about the date of his adhesion to the temperance cause that he was eagerly sought after by those interested in the management of such charities as were either wholly or partly sustained through appeals of that nature. Here again, his earnestness, his character, his life, rendered his preaching not to say impressive, but irresistible. He pleaded with all the fervour of his soul for those whom, of all others, he loved the most—the poor, the afflicted, the suffering, those sunk in sorrow or lost in shame. The charity which glowed in his own breast he imparted, even if momentarily, to those whom he addressed. In these sermons there was not the least attempt at display—no elaborately prepared and carefully studied preface, in which the orator, in measured sentences of graceful cadence, might exhibit the range of his scholarship, and his acquaintance with the learning of the historian or the speculations of the philosopher. Father Mathew was too earnest, too direct and practical, for display of any kind. He gave out his text, and plunged right into the midst of his subject—telling his audience what were the commands and injunctions of God as revealed in the Old Law and taught in the New—what were the duties of the rich to their brethren the poor. He painted the poor lovingly and truthfully, in their sufferings and in their patience, in their profound misery and in their exalted charity ; and while he touched the heart by pathetic descriptions, and stirred it by impassioned appeals, he shamed the niggard alms-giving of the wealthy by narrating instances of the sublime generosity of the poor to the poor. A beautiful instance of this boundless charity, so frequently evinced by the humblest in the community, formed a striking feature in one of his most successful sermons, preached first in Cork, with great advantage to the cause for which he appealed, and afterwards preached in Dublin with a success almost unprecedented. It will afford the reader an idea of the happy manner in which he imparted a human interest to his religious exhortation :—

If I were to pause to enumerate but the hundredth part of the many generous deeds of mercy performed by the poorest of the poor, of which I myself have been witness, I would occupy the whole of the time which this discourse should last. Permit me, however, to state one simple case of facts :—A poor woman found in the streets a male infant, which she brought to me, and asked imploringly what she was to do with it? Influenced, unhappily, by cold caution, I advised her to give it to the churchwardens. It was then evening. On the ensuing morning, early, I found this poor woman at my door ; she was a poor water-carrier ; she cried bitterly, and said—'I have not slept one wink all night for parting with that child which God had put in my way, and if you will give me leave, I will take him back again.' I was filled with confusion at the pious tenderness of this poor creature, and I went with her to the parish nurse for the infant, which she brought to her home with joy, exclaiming in the very words of the prophet—'Poor child, though thy mother has forgotten thee, I will not forget thee.' Eight years have elapsed since she brought to her humble home that exposed infant, and she is now blind from the constant exposure to wet and cold ; and ten times a-day may be seen that poor water-carrier passing with her weary load, led by this little foundling boy. Oh! merciful Jesus, I would gladly sacrifice the wealth and power of this wide world to secure to myself the glorious welcome that awaits this poor blind water-carrier on the great accounting day ! Oh ! what, compared to charity like this, the ermined robe, the ivory sceptre, the golden throne, the jewelled diadem !

Father Mathew was not content with reaping his present harvest ; he sowed in the richest soil of the human heart seeds of compassion and tenderness, which afterwards brought forth good fruit, in many a holy work and charitable undertaking. For the orphan especially he appealed with resistless pathos. At times, his words produced an electrical effect, and haunted the memory with unfading freshness. To this day, the writer remembers, as vividly as if they were spoken but yesterday, though they were heard by him more than twenty years since, these words, delivered with all the force of the sincerest conviction: 'I never meet in the street a ragged child, asking me for charity in the name of God, that I do not think I see the infant Jesus, with outstretched hands, and hear the petition for human mercy emanating from the lips of the Divinity.'

Answering those who allege they would wish to do good, but that they are afraid of imposition, he thus answered: 'Wretched excuse! It is safer to be imposed upon by nineteen, than to allow one deserving object to depart unrelieved. Many, says the Sacred Text, imagining they received weary hungry travellers, entertained angels.'

His pictures of the hospital, the garret, the sick and the dying poor, the expiring father of the destitute family, were as full of pathos as his pictures of the heartless rich man, breathing his last in the midst of gorgeous luxury, which his eye then loathed, were striking and terrible to the imagination. The preacher prayed and implored, and his wailing tones called forth the responsive tear; but he likewise thundered against the selfish, the hard-hearted, the cruel, the grinder of the faces of the poor and the betrayer of innocence, in the language of immortal wrath, and denounced their guilt with the awful anathemas of the Sacred Word.

Occasionally, his emotion completely overpowered him; as an instance will show. It was while he was preaching the annual charity sermon for the Magdalen Asylum. He drew a captivating picture of one whom he had personally known— a pure and sinless girl, happy in her unconscious innocence, gay as the lark in the morning sky, the spring of the fawn in her step, the light of gladness in her eye, and prayers of thankfulness to God on her virgin lip. Then bringing the dark figure of the seducer into this Eden of innocence, he depicted him marking out his prey, lying stealthily in wait for her, haunting her footsteps, flattering her artless vanity, encompassing her with snare and pitfall, never relinquishing his hellish pursuit, till, by foul and devilish perfidy, he had accomplished his fatal purpose, by the ruin of his victim. The preacher described the struggles, the prayers, the weaknesses, the helplessness of the poor young creature, thus lost to honour and to virtue. And then he told how, after he had missed her from her accustomed place before the altar, he met her one wild night in the public street, and how, covered with shame, she sought to elude his grasp. She was not yet hardened in her hateful life; but her beauty was gone, her light extinguished in a night of horror; and as he pictured the defilement of that poor human heart, once the tabernacle of the living God; he burst into a passionate flood of tears, overpowered by the emotion which his own words excited. There was not a dry eye in the congregation; but the charity gained largely by this irrepressible outburst of feeling.

No man was more thoroughly represented by his own words than Father Mathew; and a single passage from one of his charity sermons offers, as it were, a key to his whole life. 'Mercy! heavenly mercy! Had the Deity never spoken—had He never revealed, by prophet or apostle, that mercy was His will—its innate excellence, the high honour it confers upon us, *the delicious, the ineffable pleasure we enjoy in its exercise*, would be sufficient to point out to us the necessity of this indispensable duty.'

An idea of the good sense of the man and the simplicity of his style, may be gathered from a reply which he made to a brother clergyman of eminent ability, and most remarkable for his gifts as a preacher, who observed to Father Mathew how difficult it was at times to select a subject, and to know what would please a cultivated congregation. 'My dear sir,' said Father Mathew, 'preach for the poor, and your preaching will always serve for the rich.'

Amongst the many useful and indeed necessary works with which, in a religious and social point of view, his name is indissolubly linked, was the establishment of a new cemetery —that which has been for more than thirty years known as the 'Botanic Graveyard,' or 'Father Mathew's Cemetery.' It derived its former name from the fact, that the ground purchased by Father Mathew, and leased to him in January 1830, had been for several years known as the Botanic Gardens, attached to the Royal Cork Institution. These grounds had long been remarkable for their beauty, the admirable manner in which they were laid out, and the variety and rarity of the trees, shrubs, and other botanical treasures with which they were adorned. Even at this day it is no uncommon thing to hear it said that such a person had been buried in the 'Botanic Gardens.' Father Mathew was impelled to take this important step by two considerations,—the desire to relieve the poorer classes from the heavy and oppressive burial-fees then exacted in the established graveyards of the city, and the necessity of putting an end to a condition of dependence which Catholic pride felt to be alike galling and degrading. This state of things sprang out of the religious condition of the country, and the lingering pressure of the still unrepealed Penal Laws. He had a keen remembrance of a circumstance which excited intense feeling at the time, and which may be mentioned, as it tends to illustrate the grievance for which a practical remedy was now sought to be obtained. It occurred shortly after the passing of the Burial Act in 1825, when Dean Magee—determining to enforce the authority acquired by the new law, which, while professing to be a measure of relief, in reality perpetuated exceptional and unjust legislation — gave orders that no clergyman should be allowed to pray in the churchyard of St. Finn Barr's without permission from him. The first message to that effect was delivered by a subordinate on the occasion of the burial of a respectable Catholic in that graveyard. The deceased gentleman had been much esteemed for his charitable disposition, and his many good works ; and a large concourse of persons, of all classes, testified by their presence the respect in which they held his memory. The venerable Dean Collins, whose name has been previously mentioned, as one of Father Mathew's best friends, attended the funeral, accompanied by several clergymen, of whom Father Mathew was one ; and as the Dean was in the act of reciting the solemn service for the dead, he was most indecently interrupted, to the grievous indignation of the excited multitude. He was imperiously commanded, by the express directions of Dr. Magee, to desist from the performance of the Catholic service over the remains of a Catholic parishioner. Dr. Collins raised his tall figure to its fullest height, and, turning to the bearer of the unchristian mandate, which had been rudely and even insolently conveyed, said, in a voice which was heard by all present : 'Go, sir ! tell your superior that I will not comply with his indecent and untimely command. No law, civil or ecclesiastical, that I know of, prohibits any man, clergyman or other, from offering up a few prayers for the dead, within the precincts of a churchyard or on the high road, when there is no introduction, or, if he please, obtrusion, of the peculiar ceremonial of the Catholic Church. Go, sir, and tell your master he will not find me, or my brother priests, obedient to his command. Go and tell Dean Magee that I will pray to God when, where, and in what manner I please, without asking permission of Dean Magee.' A deep murmur of sympathy rose from the very heart of that insulted assembly ; and were it not for the nature of the occasion, and the chastened feeling which it naturally induced, a wild cheer would have rung through that graveyard, scaring the rooks in the old trees that cast their solemn shadows upon the quiet graves beneath, and perhaps startling those who were on the watch, to witness how the Dean's rash conduct had been borne by the 'bondsmen' of that day. It is sufficient to say that the spirited and becoming resistance of Dean Collins put an end to scandals of the kind; for we do not find in the records of Cork that any similar attempt was made by the dignitary who became, in some years after the incident referred to, Archbishop of Dublin. The occurrence, nevertheless, made a deep and lasting impression upon the local community, and in no small degree influenced Father Mathew in the important undertaking which was so soon to be crowned with the most complete success.

It required very little, either in arrangement or outlay, to adapt the beautiful grounds to the purpose for which they were now destined. The cypress and the willow, the cedar and the palm-tree, were there in blended beauty; and fragrant shrubs and bright evergreens delighted the eye at every step. Soon, the modest mound, with its simple cross, marking the last resting-place of the lowly dead, dotted the space liberally reserved for free burials; and soon, too, the headstone, elaborately carved, and the tomb and monument, simple and elegant, or costly and ambitious, afforded their evidence of the want that had been experienced, and of the grateful readiness with which this most useful and benevolent undertaking had been availed of by the wealthier classes of the Catholic community. On January the 25th, the lease was perfected; and in the following month there was erected, in the central avenue, a great stone cross, which is overshadowed by a veritable cedar of Lebanon, and beneath which, according to his living intention and dying injunction, now rests all that is mortal of the good man by whom the cemetery was founded and the cross was erected.

In seven or eight years after the conversion of these grounds into a cemetery, there was a motion made, in the

Irish Court of Chancery, to restrain Father Mathew from using portions of the adjoining ground for the same purpose. The circumstance is only of this value, that it affords an opportunity of quoting the testimony of the opposing counsel, as to the disposition made by Father Mathew of the revenue derived from burials. Mr. Sergeant Warren, who appeared for the plaintiff, used these words :—'It is quite true, my lord, that the defendant here has been actuated, in the course he has taken, by the purest and most benevolent motives—these I give him the fullest credit for. I doubt not that he has bestowed (as stated in his answer and in his proofs) the profits arising from the cemetery in works of charity, and that, so far from deriving any personal benefit, he is rather a loser, by the payment of part of the rents of the lands out of his own resources.' It is not always that such testimony is borne to a defendant by the counsel of the plaintiff.

Very soon, indeed, was the necessity for this additional receptacle for the dead terribly manifested. In 1832, the cholera, the dread of which had been haunting the minds of those who daily noted its eccentric but fatal track, burst out in Cork with fearful malignity. It had for its fitting birth-place and cradle one of the filthiest dens in one of the most crowded and worst-ventilated districts of the city. There it appeared in its most awful aspect, appalling the community by the rapidity of its stroke, the brief struggle of its victim, and the wild dread of contagion which its very name evoked. The people were filled with dismay, as each hour brought with it new tidings of its spreading from house to house, from lane to lane, from street to street, from district to district. The calamity, severe and terrible as it was, had this much of good in it—it called forth the courage, the devotedness, and the generosity of the principal inhabitants, whom it united together, even as one man, irrespective of all political or religious distinctions whatever. Many instances of the greatest heroism and of the most extraordinary munificence could here be mentioned ; but allusions to individuals might seem invidious and unfair ; and, besides, those who distinguished themselves most by their fearless exertions and by their unstinted generosity, are now numbered with the dead, and are, we humbly trust, enjoying, in a happier world than that which they adorned by their virtues, the reward promised to those who walk in the way of the Lord.

This was just the occasion to call into their fullest activity the qualities of a man like Father Mathew. At this time we can only faintly remember the confidence which he inspired, and the blessings which followed his footsteps, as he rapidly passed through the streets on some mission of charity; but we have been favoured with a communication from one who bears a grateful memory the generous aid which he, the pastor of the parish in which the plague first broke out, received from his brother priest. The writer is the Catholic Archdeacon of Cork, the Venerable M. B. O'Shea, now pastor of St. Patrick's, then pastor of SS. Peter and Paul :—

I have at this moment (Feb. 11th, 1863) the most vivid and grateful recollection of the generous and heroic zeal displayed by my revered and beloved friend, Father Mathew, when, with the unselfish devotedness of a martyr and an apostle, he threw himself into the midst of the peril, when the terrible *reality* of Asiatic cholera smote my parish first of any locality in Ireland, in April 1832. When the first stunning effect of the blow had subsided, as it speedily did, a noble spectacle was exhibited by the union of all ranks, professions, and creeds, while resolutely and fearlessly confronting the calamity, and aiming at its mitigation by all the resources which humanity, religion, and science are sure to bring into play, in the presence of a fearful crisis. Amongst those who at that awful period took a conspicuous part, not only in unwearied attendance by the bed-side of the plague-stricken sufferers, but also in suggesting and practically carrying out sanitary and remedial measures for the relief of the sick in private houses and in the public hospitals, Father Mathew was ever foremost, and always indefatigable. What most deeply affected me *then*, and which the memory even now, at the distance of more than thirty years, fills me with the mingled emotions of gratitude and of reverential regard, was the visit he paid me in the very early stage of this dire calamity, when my hard-worked curates and myself were overwhelmed with incessant calls by day and night, before there was time for the erection of a temporary hospital, and before the pestilence had spread over other and distant districts of the city and suburbs—the centre and focus of the disease being a block of narrow ill-ventilated streets and lanes in the immediate neighbourhood of my residence, where the cholera raged with peculiar virulence. Two or three days after the first terrific outburst of the pest, and as soon as the awful tidings reached Father Mathew's ears, he hastened to my house, and, with open heart and arms, embraced me ; and, while offering his consolation and sympathy, tendered me his valuable services and the offices of his sacred ministry, for the comfort and spirtual aid of my poor afflicted parishioners, at every hour by night or day that I should refer to him. This offer, unexpected and unsolicited on my part, was, of course, promptly and gratefully accepted ; and nothing could equal the noble untiring efficiency of the support he then gave me until the benefit and blessing of his ministrations to the sick were required away from my central district, in the southern quarter of the city, which, in less than a fortnight after, was doomed to undergo its own share in the prevailing scourge.

Quitting the district in which he had laboured so zealously as a volunteer, Father Mathew devoted himself, almost exclusively for a time, to the more legitimate sphere of his duties, his own parish. Here the plague raged in all its horrors, and at every hour of the day the brave priest might be seen going from house to house, performing the duties of his ministry amidst sights and sounds that appalled the stoutest heart, and shook the strongest nerves. But this was not all he did in that trying time.

One of the largest hospitals in the city was established at a little distance from his dwelling in Cove Street, and was attended by a full staff of clergymen, who spared no labour in that trying moment. In order to ensure the presence of a clergyman at every hour of the day and night, it was arranged that the duty should be taken in turn ; and Father Mathew requested, 'as a favour,' that he should be apportioned the hours from midnight to six in the morning—the very hours which even the most zealous might be excused from selecting. But Father Mathew knew how little reliance could be placed on mere mercenaries, gathered together for the occasion, and performing duties of a depressing and even revolting nature. In whatever part of the city he might have been during the day,—in the garret or the hovel in the remotest suburbs, or by the bed-side of a friend who had been suddenly struck down,—he was unfailingly punctual in his attendance in the hospital during the long and weary hours of night. Gentle and mild as he was, still there was not a nurse or an assistant in the hospital that did not stand in awe of the vigilance of Father Mathew, or who would willingly have incurred his rebuke. If the nurses watched the patients, Father Mathew watched both nurses and patients; and while he was present, there was no such thing heard of as a nurse or attendant nodding at her post, or relaxing in her attention to the sick. An incident, to which he oftentimes referred in after life, and which was soon known through the city, exhibited the value and necessity of his vigilance and supervision.

He had administered the last rites of religion to a young man, in whom he had a special interest, and having received a summons to another part of the hospital, he hurriedly quitted the ward, from which he was absent but for a short time. On his return, he approached the bed in which he had left the young man alive; but the bed was now unoccupied. 'Nurse, nurse! what has become of the young man who lay in this bed?' asked Father Mathew. 'Dead, sir,' was the laconic answer. 'Dead!—it cannot be—where is he?' 'The corpse is taken to the dead-house, sir.' 'I can't believe he is dead—I must go myself and see,' said Father Mathew; and he at once proceeded to the ghastly chamber to which the dead were borne, previous to being taken out for interment. It presented an awful spectacle indeed. At one end was a pile of miserable coffins, the merest shells, made of thin boards, and knocked together with a few nails. Some of these wretched receptacles were on the floor, either with their lids fastened down, or open and awaiting their future occupants. On tables, and also on the floor, lay a number of bodies, in each of which a heart throbbed and a soul dwelt a few hours before. Some lay, blue and distorted, in the sheet in which they had been snatched from the bed on which they died ; more were wrapped, like mummies, in similar sheets, which had been covered with pitch or tar, liberally laid on to prevent contagion. Amidst that scene of death in its most appalling aspect, there was a horrid bustle of life ; coffins being nailed down with noisy clatter—sheets being rapidly covered over with a black and seething substance—bodies being moved from place to place, and tumbled into their last receptacle with the haste and indifference which a terrible familiarity with death engenders in the minds of a certain class—orders hoarsely given—figures moving or reeling to and fro ; for it was necessary that those who performed the horrid and revolting duties of that chamber should be well plied with whisky : it was the custom of the time and the necessity of the moment. Into this scene of horrors, partly lighted by a few coarse flickering candles, Father Mathew hurriedly entered. Even the strongest might have recoiled at the spectacle which met his sight ; but he only thought of the object of his mission. There lay the body, and near it were two men preparing the tarred sheet in which they were to wrap it. 'Stop, stop !' said Father Mathew, 'surely the young man can't be dead !' 'Dead, your reverence ! God forbid you or me would be as dead as that poor fellow—The Lord have mercy on his sowl !' said one of the men. 'No, no, I can't believe it—I was speaking to him a moment before I left the ward—let me try.' 'Wisha, try, if you plaze, your reverence ; but he's as dead as a door-nail; and shure it does n't take long to carry a man off in those times—God be between us and harm!' There was a momentary suspension of the loathsome work as Fathew Mathew knelt down beside the body, and pressed his hand lightly over the region of the heart. A group, such as few, save perhaps those who loved to paint the terrible and the hideous, would desire to see near them, clustered round the devoted priest; and not a sound was heard for a time in that chamber of death. There was a suspense of a moment—it seemed an age—when Father Mathew cried out exultingly—'Thank God! he is alive!—I feel his heart beat—thank God, thank God!' It was quite true—life was not extinct; and restoratives having been applied, the young man was removed to another part of the hospital—and in a few days after he was able to pour forth his gratitude to him who, through God's mercy, had rescued him from inevitable death; for had but another minute elapsed, he was lost to this world for ever. As may be supposed, this incident had a salutary effect in the hospital, though it was little wanted to render as untiring as ever the sleepless vigilance of Father Mathew.

The physicians who were associated with him in that fearful time spoke ever after with enthusiasm of his zeal, his utter disregard of self, and his munificent generosity; for, from his own resources, he constantly sent the most costly wines and spirits to the hospitals, as stimulants to be used by the patients, and also for the staff, who, as he then believed, required their use after the discharge of their arduous and exhausting duties.

The reputation of Father Mathew was much enhanced by his marvellous labours at this period—which labours never ceased until the temporary hospitals were closed, and confidence was fully restored to the public mind. Nor indeed were his labours over even then, though they assumed another form; for there were widows to assist, and orphans to educate and provide for; and to this holy duty he applied his utmost energy, and devoted every shilling he could spare from the other objects of his seemingly exhaustless bounty. 'Give ! give ! give !'—so he preached, and so he practised ; and when he gave his last shilling, he gave it in the name of God, confident that God would send him more to give.

CHAPTER V.

A Holiday-getter and a Feast-giver—Gentle Rebuke—Taught in a good School—His kindness to young Priests—Grand party in the Cock-loft—The 'Bore' from the Country—His Success as a Peace-maker—The flounced 'Habit.'

THE nature of Father Mathew was eminently *paternal.* The innocence and gaiety of childhood had for him an unfailing charm. He was interested in the plays and sports of youth ; and the more they yelled and shrieked in the delirium of childish enjoyment, the greater was his delight, especially if, as was often the case, he had been the promotei and patron of the day's amusements. To promote their enjoyment and add to their happiness was with him to live over again his own youth at Rathcloheen. No one better knew the genuine tastes and likings of little people than Father Mathew. He knew that apples and oranges, and nuts, cakes, and sweet things, including toffy and 'bull's-eyes,' were to them the *summum bonum* of earthly felicity ; and that these, with an out-of-door holiday, when they could run, and shout, and tumble, and play all manner of wild pranks, were, in their esteem, to be preferred to the finest clothes in the world. And accordingly he made a reputation for himself with the young people of the city, as a holiday-getter as well as a feast-giver. Indeed, his visit to any school, whatever the effect it had upon the solemn master or the sedate mistress, sent a thrill of joyous expectation through the scholars of all degrees ; for not rarely was the glad announcement made, in words that surpassed the most ravishing music.—'Young gentlemen, Father Mathew has asked for a holiday for you, and I cannot refuse him anything he asks for.' 'Young ladies, ditto, ditto.' But if he obtained the holiday, he also provided a feast; and often times the fine old place occupied by his brother Charles, at Lehenagh, a couple of miles outside the city, was the scene of the twofold enjoyment. Entertaining a profound reverence for youthful powers of digestion, he looked on placidly while sturdy boys crammed themselves with quantities of pastry, the fourth part of which would have consigned a full-grown man to the care of his doctor. Considerate to children in general, to orphans he was peculiarly tender; and invariable presents of large bags of apples and nuts, sent on the eve of All Saints—an occasion devoted by youth to perpetual crunching and testing of teeth, as by those somewhat older to the mysteries of melted lead, &c.—to the orphans in the Asylums, and to the children in the House of Industry, exhibited the interest which he felt in these unfortunate little ones. These he frequently had taken to the green fields, and to the pleasant meadows along the river's side, but under the care of watchful guardians. Such excursions were always preceded by a good breakfast, and were usually wound up by a more solid entertainment, both being at his expense. His feeling towards children may be further illustrated by the following incident.

During certain days of Holy Week, it is the custom, in Catholic countries, to remove the Blessed Sacrament from the tabernacle on the high altar to a side altar, which, with pious care, is elaborately prepared for its reception. This altar is decorated with the richest velvets, the choicest silks, or the most sumptuous brocades—with lace, and flowers, and jewellery—whatever, in fact, is costly and precious in the eyes of the world. Hundreds of waxen lights flood the altar with their radiance, and enhance the effect of the drapery and the decoration. The effect is still further heightened by the sombre gloom of the rest of the church, and the blank desolation of the high altar, upon which not only is there no light burning, but which is entirely shrouded in purple, emblematical of the mourning of the Church, and the Passion which it commemorates. The small or side altar is the object of devout attraction, and typifies the tomb which received the sacred body of the Redeemer. On these days it is customary for the faithful to 'make their rounds'—that is, to go from church to church, and to offer up in each certain prayers appropriate to the solemnity of the occasion, and to do so with a suitable intention. Nothing can exceed the devout and decorous bearing of those who perform this religious exercise; even the children, as a rule, are reverential in their manner, and repeat their prayers with edifying gravity. But a few are sure to be thoughtless and noisy, and, perhaps with the best intention in the world, are rather distracting by their behaviour. The little Friary, or Father Mathew's Chapel, as it was indifferently called, was at all times, at least since his connection with it, remarkable for the splendour and beauty of this altar, and for the extreme richness and elegance of its decoration. The most costly and beautiful articles were lavished upon it in profusion by the good ladies who thus evinced their piety, and their respect for the priest whose virtues they revered. The temper of these excellent ladies was not at all times proof against the incursions of troops of little ones, whose clattering footsteps resounded in the hushed chapel, and whose artless admiration, uttered too often in a tone of voice more suited to the open air, than to a place of solemn worship, was rather trying, more especially to those interested in the maintenance of decorum. The annoyance occasioned by these incursions excited the anger of a lady, one of the voluntary teachers in the adjoining school, and whose position gave her peculiar authority. She was in the act of driving before her a noisy bevy of very young children, when Father Mathew came up, and, drawing away her attention from the little intruders, said, 'My dear madam, why are you driving these children out of the chapel?' 'Oh, Father Mathew,' answered the lady, 'they were making such a noise, that they were disturbing the congregation; and really, I must say, Father Mathew, I wonder how *you* can tolerate them, going in and out, as they do.' 'My dear madam, you must remember the words of our Divine Redeemer, who said, *Suffer these little ones to come unto me, and forbid them not, for of such is the kingdom of Heaven.* If they come from curiosity now, they will come to pray another time; and you cannot tell what impression is made upon the mind of the very youngest child that enters the House of God.' The lady never again, whatever her temptation to do so, interfered with the movements of these questionable worshippers.

The sports and gambols of youth were pleasing to the good man's heart, but the spectacle of their piety raised him, as it were, to the seventh heaven. He could scarcely restrain his emotion as he administered to them the First Communion, or witnessed their performance of some work of charity. By teaching and by example, he encouraged his young friends to do good to their fellow-creatures; and when he saw that his teaching was not in vain, that the seed which he had planted in their heart was bearing abundant fruit, his happiness was very great.

Passing through one of the principal streets of Cork, he saw two of his special *protégés*, two young lads of respectable position, standing in a door-way, and deeply engaged over something contained in a little book. 'Good morrow, boys!' said Father Mathew, as he shook hands with his young friends, and gave to each of them his usual caress, which was a soft pull of the ear. 'What are you doing here, my dears?' After some little show of reluctance, they told him that they were collecting for a case of urgent charity, which at the time excited the liveliest compassion. A poor young mother, with a number of helpless children, had been left utterly destitute by the sudden death of the head of the family, who had held a respectable rank in his native city. And the young lads, taught in a good school, had, of their own accord, taken up the case, and were going from door to door, seeking for contributions. 'Why did n't you tell *me* of this?—why not call on me?—why pass me by, my dear?' said Father Mathew to the elder lad, who had the care of the little book in which the subscriptions were entered. 'Why, Father Mathew, we were really ashamed to apply to you; we knew you had more calls on you than any one else, and you are always giving charity.' 'But, my dear, you were wrong in not coming to me. It would have pained me if I had not the pleasure of aiding you in your good work. Put my name down for 5*l*. I have not the money now, but call on me in two days for it at my house.' When the lads came at the appointed time, they were radiant with triumph. 'Oh! Father Mathew, you have done us such good! The moment *your* name was seen, every one had confidence in the case; and see! we have got over 200*l*.! We are so much obliged to you.' 'No, my dear boys, it is I who ought to be so much obliged to you, for doing such a work of charity for this poor family. God will bless you for it, now and hereafter. It is by such acts that we do honour to God's holy name. Thank you, boys—thank you.' And with another fond pull of the ear, and the promised 5*l*., the delighted lads were dismissed.

Those of a different faith felt almost the same respect for Father Mathew, and the same confidence in his purity of life and integrity of motive, as did the members of his own communion. A rather remarkable proof of the esteem in which he was held by Protestants may be mentioned. The conductors of one of the very first classical schools of the city, well known to more than one generation as 'Hamblin's School,' made a special application to Father Mathew, requesting him to teach catechism and give religious instruction to the Catholic boys on a certain day in the week; and on every Thursday, for several years, the catechism was taught and the instruction given by him in the school. The school-boys, Protestant as well as Catholic, liked Father Mathew, who, it must be said, found an easy road to their hearts by procuring for them an occasional holiday, and inviting the whole school out to Lehenagh, where, as one of the pupils of that day now states, they were 'gloriously treated.' The surviving member of the then existing partnership in the conduct of that celebrated seminary, speaks of Father Mathew in the warmest terms of respect and affection. 'He was,' says Dr. Porter, 'one of the kindest, one of the best, and one of the most benevolent men I ever knew—a man of true liberality of mind, and a thorough gentleman.

To young priests, as well as to young men intended for the ministry, Father Mathew was invariably kind; and many a grey-headed pastor, by the zealous assistance which he afforded to the Apostle of Temperance, paid back the debt of gratitude which he had incurred in his youth—perhaps in the hour of sickness, or at a time when the offices of friendship were most needed. Young priests just left college, and yet without a mission, are not usually in the most affluent circumstances; and at such a time an act of kindness is peculiarly acceptable. Father Mathew, when an opportunity of the kind was afforded him, would say, as if he were asking a favour rather than conferring a benefit, 'You must oblige me and come and say eight o'clock Mass for me for the next fortnight. Do so, my dear sir, if you possibly can.' Of course, the young priest was only too glad to accept the invitation; and it was thus, among other kindly devices, that Father Mathew was enabled to render a substantial service without hurting the pride or lowering the self-respect of him whom he served. If a young priest were sick, formality was then out of the question. He entered the sick room as a father would that of a son; and if anything were wanted, which was often the case, he ordered it to be sent in at his expense, and insisted upon its being as freely used as it was freely given. He provided a careful nurse, where it was necessary to do so, and supplied every requisite, either during the stages of the disease, or during the tedious convalescence; and were change of air and a milder climate considered essential to recovery, a bank-note, slipped into the hand of the patient, with a gentle pressure and an imperative whisper—'You *must*, my dear. You will seriously pain me if you refuse'—placed the means of health at the disposal of the invalid. Hundreds of instances of his kindness to his brethren in the ministry might be recorded of him; but it will be sufficient to say, that never was his sympathy or his assistance sought for in vain, and that it was more frequently proffered than solicited.

He was also fond of assisting young persons who had an evident vocation for a religious life, to prosecute their studies, and realise their pious intention. If he felt convinced that the vocation was real, and that they were likely to serve religion, and reflect credit on the Church, he encouraged and fostered their piety; and were they in circumstances which rendered material aid necessary, he contrived to send them to Rome, or to some college at home, to accomplish the object of their desires. He considerably strengthened his own order in Ireland by his selection of subjects, and by his liberality in enabling them to complete their course of study.

That remarkable trait in his character—his hospitality—merits special notice. Hospitality is not always a proof of generosity or kindness of disposition, for there are many who freely entertain from ostentation, or a wish to eclipse their neighbours; but Father Mathew's hospitality was born of his nature—it sprang from his heart—it manifested itself in his youth—it grew and increased with his years.

He had not been long in Cork, when his brother Charles, returning from one of his voyages, came to pay the priest a visit. Proceeding to the Friary, he ascended the stairs that led to the gallery, or loft, which was occupied by the two friars, Father Donovan and Father Mathew. As he approached the top of the stairs, he was surprised to hear bursts of laughter, and other unmistakable indications of jollity and pleasure; and on entering the low-ceiled room belonging to his brother, he was quite taken aback at the spectacle which met his astonished gaze. There was a company of about twenty surrounding a well-served table, plentifully supplied with glasses and decanters, hot water, lemons, sugar, wine and whisky, the usual and orthodox 'et ceteras;' and Father Mathew at the head of the table, 'looking,' said Charles, 'as happy as a king—quite in his element—delighted at seeing so many people enjoying themselves.' Songs and toasts, wit and humour, fun and jollity, were the order of the evening; but at a reasonable hour—earlier, perhaps, than most of the guests thought necessary—the party broke up, and the brothers were left alone to talk over the past, and speculate as to the future. The guests of that evening were, some of them, his brother clergymen—others, the friends with whom he had become acquainted since his arrival in Cork, and who, loving him then, loved him to the last.

When a grand entertainment of this kind was given by either of the friars, it was necessary to convert the other chamber into a kitchen; and Father Donovan came out in great force on such occasions, for he had quite a genius for cooking.

'Poor Theobald Mathew,' says a brother-priest, fondly looking back to the earliest years of his mission, 'was never so happy as when he had a dozen of us around him. He was as good a host as ever lived—full of innocent gaiety, and as easily amused as a child.' Fond of company as he was, especially when he himself was lord of the feast, he was never, even once, guilty of excess, or indeed of the slightest approach to it. As an intimate friend of his happily remarked—'He was always cautious, but convivial—fond of seeing people enjoy themselves, but never once bordering on being the worse of wine.' Singularly abstemious himself, he did not in any way run counter to the custom of the day, much less so when he assumed the duties of a host; in which capacity he neither spared his wine, nor refrained from pressing his guests to 'help themselves.' In those days, the idea of any man wilfully abstaining from the use of the 'gifts of God,' was never dreamed of; or if a case were mentioned where a person did not drink wine, or had an aversion to whisky-punch, it was at once set down to eccentricity, or to some constitutional tendency—perhaps, to insanity—which might be developed by the use of stimulants. Father Mathew then took the world as he found it, never imagining that a day was to come when he was to lead a crusade against its most deeply-rooted customs, and to assail strong drink with all the enthusiasm and ardour of a Soldier of the Cross. He may have been constitutionally, or from taste, averse to the free use of wine; but his prevailing motive was the danger of giving scandal, and the necessity which compelled him, *a priest*, to be more circumspect than other men. A glass or two of wine, or a 'tumbler of punch,' carefully and dexterously 'watered,' was the extent of his indulgence. And, as an invariable rule, long before the hand of the clock pointed to ten, he slipped away from whatever company he happened to be with, and was on his way to his apartment in the Friary, or to his modest, though afterwards historic, house in Cove Street.

Father Mathew was a most agreeable companion; for, what is a thing very rare to be met with, he combined the two opposite qualities of being a first-rate listener and a first-rate *raconteur*. His powers as a listener were rather severely but successfully tested on one occasion, when he obtained unmerited credit for the display of other qualites which had no possible opportunity for their exercise. Among the guests whom he entertained that day was a thorough-paced bore from a neighbouring town, who not only talked of himself, his affairs, his opinions, his views of things in particular and things in general, his wisdom, his sagacity, his extraordinary depth of penetration, &c., but took good care that no one else should as much as edge in a word. A mill, with a fine head of water, and the machinery in full motion, could scarcely vie with this sublime bore, who, though he contrived to do his duty manfully at dinner, and with the 'materials' afterwards, never stopped the flow of his discourse for a single minute. He literally held Father Mathew by the ear for the whole of that evening. But his host was in one of his grandest listening moods. He looked full at his loquacious guest, with eyes beaming with benevolence, nodding from time to time 'like a mandarin,' occasionally ejaculating 'Ah!' in a tone of surprise or sympathy, and, on very rare occasions, affording breathing time to the speaker by such expressions as 'Dear me, sir!' 'How very strange!' 'It is quite wonderful, my dear sir!' This was the extent of Father Mathew's share in that evening's conversation. And yet, when the unwearied bore bade good night to his host, and got out into the street, he clutched the arm of the disgusted friend, who had introduced him and brought him to dine, saying, 'My dear fellow, I had no idea that Mr. Mathew was so agreeable a man. I assure you, I have been most pleasingly disappointed in him. So full of anecdote! So charming a companion! Such sound common sense! Really I do n't know when I spent so delightful an evening.'

Now a bore of this kind was a positive relief to Father Mathew, who rejoiced when he could have some one with him who relieved him of the trouble of talking. But few could enter more usefully and profitably into conversation than he could, when he pleased, or who narrated striking events or described circumstances of personal occurrence with better effect.

Though leading a life of extraordinary activity, and absorbed in the duties of his ministry, he still found time for reading other than strictly professional works. He was generally acquainted with the literature of the day, and could criticise with acuteness the merits of a popular work, pointing out, with unfailing accuracy, its good or evil tendency, its fallacies or its truths. To books of travel he was much inclined ; but where the traveller penetrated some new country, explored virgin forests, or described the habits, customs, modes of life, and superstitions of a wild race, Father Mathew was captivated by his pages. For natural history he had the greatest partiality, as it enabled him better to understand the benignity of Providence, its care for all created things, and the wonderful adaptation of the animal creation to the sphere in which it was destined to exist. Whatever, in the wonders or the beauties of creation, spoke of the glory, the greatness, or the beneficence of the Supreme Being, filled the heart of Father Mathew with thankfulness and praise. He was likewise deeply interested in biographical works, especially when their subject was the life of a man eminent for his public virtue, the devotion of his talents or energies to the good of his country, the elevation of his race, or the redemption from bondage of some down-trodden branch of the great human family. 'Plutarch's Lives,' which contain so many instances of heroic virtue and lofty deeds, had a peculiar charm for a nature such as his, which, while compassionate towards human weakness, soared above everything low, or mean, or little When he did not read himself, he contrived to have one of his young friends to read for him ; and after a good dinner, and a pleasant chat, which placed the most timid at his ease, the request was made : 'Perhaps, my dear, you would be good enough to read some pages of an interesting book for me ?'—which request, it need scarcely be added, was irresistible as a royal command. Thus there were two persons benefited by the reading, the listener and the reader.

Father Mathew had extraordinary success as a peace-maker. To restore peace in distracted families was the very thing which he most delighted to do, as well from the natural prompting of his disposition as from a sense of religious obligation. His visits under such circumstances were those of an angel. It was impossible to resist the tenderness of his pleading or the earnestness of his importunity ; and many a husband and wife had reason to bless his timely interference ; and so also had many a parent, to whom the wayward child was restored, in duty and affection, by his persuasive counsels. Generally, he was sent for in cases of the kind ; but were he not sent for in a case which had come to his knowledge, he would contrive to make a visit at the right moment ; and not even the haughtiest or most self-willed could quarrel with Father Mathew, or feel humiliated by his good offices. 'I declare, sir,' said a gentleman to his friend, one day in the public street, as Father Mathew left them, 'I believe that man has some extraordinary power about him. I had not the best feeling towards him, on account of something that annoyed me ; but, sir, I do assure you, the moment he grasped me by the hand, there was an end to my anger. I can't say what it is ; but if we lived in another age, I should be inclined to say there was magic in it.' 'Would that we had more of such magic and such magicians in these days,' was the answer of his friend.

To be a peace-maker was one thing, but to be a match-maker was quite another. To overtures of every kind which had match-making for their object, he lent a deaf ear. He had no objection to see his young friends happy—quite the contrary ; but with the young people themselves, their parents, and their friends, Father Mathew left such matters. Nor were tempting offers wanting, offers which might well shake the firmness of most men. It is a positive fact that one gentleman offered him so much as a thousand pounds, if he brought about a marriage with a lady on whom the gentleman had fixed his—intentions. The offer was declined with good temper.

Father Mathew was made the repository of many a tale of sorrow or of shame, the slightest betrayal of which would have brought misery or dishonour to many a home; but he was also made the recipient of absurd confidences, and his advice was gravely asked respecting matters which, to say the least, were not altogether within his province. An instance of the latter kind may be mentioned. Father Mathew often told it himself, and never without a laugh at its oddity. A very old and poor woman called on him one day, and desired particularly to speak with him in private. Her countenance denoted much mental pertubation, and a sigh or two gave warning of the afflicting nature of the coming disclosure. 'Well, my dear,' said Father Mathew, 'you seem disturbed; what is the matter?' 'Oh, then, your reverence, it's my "habit" that's troubling me, and I came to ask your reverence what would you advise me to do with it?' 'Your "habit," my dear?' 'Yes, indeed, your reverence, the "habit"—it wo n't let me rest easy with thinking what I'm to do with it.' 'Why, my good woman, what is the matter with your "habit," and what can I possibly do for you?' 'Well, your reverence, here's the way it is,—I have the "habit" for a long time, for, you know, one must always be prepared, and shure we do n't know the moment when our hour may come; and, your reverence, I tried it on the other night, and'—(here a sob choked her utterance)—'and—and—your reverence—it's too short!' This sad announcement was followed by another burst of emotion. 'But, my dear, what?' —'Oh, your reverence, I hadn't a wink of sleep for the whole night with thinking of it—and the disgrace of it!' The matter was becoming serious, and poor Father Mathew was quite bewildered. What could he do for her, unless give her money to purchase a new 'habit?' But no; it was not money, but advice, she required—not a new 'habit,' but to know what to do with the 'habit' to which she had been accustomed, and which she associated with the happy ending of her life. A bright idea struck him, which, with as much gravity as he could summon to his aid, he imparted to his anxious applicant, who seemed to hang in suspense on his very look. 'Well, my dear, that being the case, I recommend you to put *flounces* to it.' It was a beautiful idea, and it brought peace and consolation with it. The old lady grasped at it with avidity, and gratefully thanked his reverence for his suggestion, and declared she would go home that moment, and carry it into immediate execution. She left her adviser with a benediction, and an assurance that she was now happy in her mind. The reader will best judge of the nature of the suggested addition, when it is stated that the habit referred to was a kind of shroud, in which devout people, belonging to certain lay orders, or religious societies, were laid out or 'waked' in when dead.

Doing good everywhere, consulted by rich and applied to by poor, promoting every useful or charitable object, possessing the respect and confidence of all creeds and classes in his adopted city,—such was Father Mathew, when called upon to assume a new position, and to undertake duties which, while disturbing the entire course of his priestly life, drew him from the even tenor of his missionary career, to new scenes, new acquaintances, a new field of action, new labours, and new anxieties.

CHAPTER VI.

The House of Industry and its Inmates—The Pioneers of the Cause—William Martin's Appeal—Grave Deliberation—Father Mathew crosses the Rubicon.

FATHER MATHEW had been for some years one of the governors of the House of Industry—The Cork Workhouse of those days—in which the poor waifs and strays of society, the wretched and the broken-down, the victims of their own folly, or of the calamities, accidents, and vicissitudes of life, found a miserable home. To a man of his nature, such an assemblage of destitute and helpless human beings was a cause of the truest sympathy, as of constant enquiry and consideration. He possessed the key to open harder hearts and unlock closer breasts than theirs: and many a tale of folly and of sin was whispered in his ear, in accents of self-reproach, by the miserable inmates of that house. The dilapidated drunkard excited his compassion, but the orphan child of the drunkard made his heart bleed with sorrow. While he saw, in that last of asylums, many a victim of the changing fashions of the day, of manufacturing industry turned into a new channel, of sickness or decrepitude, he likewise saw in its dismal wards the dupes of their own besotted folly, the slaves of a passion that seemed to be as uncontrollable as it was fatal in its consequences. Here, in this wretched abode, was the worldly ruin which, from the pulpit and in the confessional, he had so often depicted as *one* of the results of this destructive vice ; and in the hospitals, in the jail, in the lunatic asylum, as in the haunts of infamy, he witnessed other phases of the same terrible infatuation. On the Board of Governors, with Father Mathew, was one who, himself a convert to the doctrine of total abstinence, never failed to direct his attention to a case more remarkable in its distressing features than another, with the observation—'Strong drink is the cause of this.' And having excited the compassionate sympathy of his hearer, he would add, 'Oh, Theobald Mathew! if thou would only give thy aid, much good could be done in this city.'

Long before Father Mathew had the slightest idea of taking any part in the temperance movement, William Martin had made up his mind that Theobald Mathew was, of all others, the man best suited to render it successful. For some eight or ten years previous to the now recognised commencement of the movement in Ireland, attempts of various kinds had been made in Cork to diminish, if possible, the evils of intemperance, and bring the working classes of that city to believe in the virtue of sobriety. Among those who were the early and the most prominent labourers in the then unpromising field, were the Rev. Nicholas Dunscombe, Richard Dowden, and William Martin. The first was a Protestant clergyman; the second was a distinguished member of the local Unitarian body, remarkable for his broad philanthropy, and his advanced opinions on all questions of social progress and reform; and the third was the honest and earnest Quaker who afterwards gloried in the title of 'Grandfather of the Temperance Cause.' These men, and a few others of inferior note, worked resolutely and bravely, but with comparatively little success. They had not the ear, and therefore found it impossible to reach the heart, of the local community. They were, in the first place, of a different religious persuasion to that of the great bulk of the population, and, in the second place, they preached a doctrine which excited the wonder of some, but the ridicule of more. A few believed, and became converts, and the tiny rivulet swelled in the course of time to larger dimensions; but it never flowed with the strength and volume of a stream. Mr. Dunscombe was earnest, and spoke with all the force of sincerity, but, comparatively, in vain—with no result adequate to his zeal and his persistent advocacy. Richard Dowden employed every art of the practised orator to enforce his views, or to obtain even a single convert. He now tried what fun, and humour, and comical description could do, and, if that failed, he had recourse to eloquent denunciation and passionate appeal; still the numbers in his society might have been easily counted. William Martin gave his testimony, and essayed his powers of persuasion; but laughter and derision were for years the only apparent result of his well-meant efforts. Now and then, others, including some excellent members of the Society of Friends, spoke in persuasive accents, and made affectionate appeals to audiences more or less incredulous and unsympathising, which were generally drawn together more from curiosity, or perhaps a hope of witnessing 'some fun,' than from any other motive. Tea-parties were occasionally held, and these celebrations attracted many young people, who came rather in search of amusement than with the desire of being instructed or improved. What the pioneers of the movement could do, they did; but notwithstanding the earnestness, the sincerity, and the single-mindedness of its advocates, the doctrine was unpalatable, or it was ridiculed as absurd, or condemned as fanatical, and its practice was regarded, almost generally, as a kind of eccentricity very nearly bordering on madness. 'Now, moderation—if these people only stopped there—is all well in its way, and is commendable rather than otherwise, for we ought to be moderate in the use of the gifts of God; but total abstinence!—why *that* is the dream of a madman, and a downright flying in the face of Providence.' This is how those who condescended to 'argue' the question delivered themselves of their indignant feelings. There was, besides, a kind of lurking suspicion that there was some concealed object, something lurking in the back-ground, in this desire on the part of Protestants 'to entangle Catholics in their societies.' This suspicion, utterly without foundation, was still not devoid of a certain influence in closing the ears of the working classes against well-meant advice and disinterested advocacy. So that, while a few laboured zealously and perseveringly to preach the cause, they advanced but slowly and painfully, as it were inch by inch, and made little headway against the tide of popular indifference or popular mistrust. In vain a reformed veteran, whom excess had brought to the verge of the grave, to decrepitude and misery, appealed to his then vigorous upright form, and his comfortable dress and decent position, to convince his hearers of the benefit which *he* had received from a total avoidance of the cause of his former ruin and disgrace. With as little profit did a respectable mechanic refer to his years of folly and tribulation, and contrast them with his present security and independence. The advocates were listened to, and applauded, but rarely was their example imitated. The right man was wanted for the cause, and he was soon to come.

'Oh, Theobald Mathew, if *thou* would but take the cause in hand!' was the constant appeal of William Martin to the benevolence of the most popular and influential priest of the day. These appeals were not addressed to a dull ear or an insensible heart. '*Thou* could do such good to these poor creatures,' were words which haunted the memory and stirred the conscience of Father Mathew. For some time he made no sign which could indicate that he was seriously considering the proposal to undertake the leadership of the movement. But never was a grave proposal more anxiously considered in all its bearings. Seriously and solemnly did Theobald Mathew commune with himself in the solitude of his chamber, and fervently and humbly did he pray to God to vouchsafe him light and guidance.

Father Mathew was now in his 47th year, and possessed an extensive and profound experience of his fellow men. In every phase of life and grade of society, and under every circumstance common to a large community, that experience had been gained. In the mansions of the rich, in the garrets of the poor, amongst those endowed with the wealth of the world, and those to whom a week's sickness brought with it the horrors of actual want, he had witnessed the working of a vicious and, unhappily, a too-pervading habit. He had seen the happiness of the brightest home wrecked by the weakness of a father, by the folly of a husband, or by the deeper and more terrible misery caused by the infatuation of the mother and the wife—ruin and dishonour brought upon young men who had entered upon life with buoyant hopes, and the most brilliant prospects of success. He had beheld the prosperous merchant, the successful trader, the energetic manufacturer, sink gradually into bankruptcy and decay. With even greater sorrow, he had seen the light of genius, extinguished in hopeless gloom, and splendid talents flung recklessly away, as if they were not the special gifts of God to a chosen few. To use his own expressive words, he had seen the stars of heaven fall, and the cedars of Lebanon laid low. In the prison, the mad-house, the hospital, the workhouse, he recognised the victims of this absorbing passion. Poverty and disease, debasement and crime, he in a great measure attributed to its baneful influence. He admired and was proud of the intelligence of the artisans of his city, but he deplored their recklessness and their improvidence. He knew many, many families, that ought to be independent, and even in the enjoyment of comforts, plunged in a state of chronic misery, and frequently indebted for a single meal to the accommodation of the pawn-office—children in rags and squalor, with coarse words upon their young lips—wives despairing and broken-hearted —husbands debauched or brutal.

All this, and more, had pressed upon his mind, filling him with sorrow and dismay, not imagining how a remedy was to be had for an evil of such magnitude, so deeply-rooted and so widely-spread. Was there not Religion?—why could it not prove of avail in this instance? Surely, it had accom plished greater miracles—why not this? But the difficulty—and no man knew it better than Father Mathew—was how to bring the influence of religion to bear upon the habitual and confirmed drunkard. The drunkard was not the one to attend to the ministrations of his clergyman; he frequently failed to comply with one of the most obvious duties of the Christian—namely, to go to his place of worship on the Sunday. If he occasionally made resolutions of amendment, he neglected to fortify those resolutions with the graces of religion. His fatal habit was a bar between him and the religious influence. He fought against it, derided it, or kept it at a distance; and if he yielded to it at last, it was, perhaps on his bed of damp straw, to which drink had brought him, or on a pallet in the hospital, to which an accident or injury received in some savage conflict had consigned him. Then indeed he *promised* amendment for the future; but Father Mathew knew, alas! too well, how, once out of danger, such promises, extorted by fear, were broken in health—broken as easily as strong men break bands of straw—or, like the impress of the foot on the sand, were washed away by the next wave.

What *could* he do?—Father Mathew asked himself in the solitude of his midnight musing—what could he do for the people he so truly loved? how could he benefit the poor, in whose sorrows, sufferings, and poverty he recognised the image of his Redeemer? Was there really a remedy in this pledge of total abstinence, this total avoidance of the cause of the evils he deplored? Would it, could it be ever adopted—that is, generally, or to any extent? Were not the habits, customs, feelings, and associations of the Irish people opposed to this total renunciation of a long-accustomed indulgence? Were all the social enjoyments to be given up? Was *moderation*, that which he had practised during his entire life, and which he had so often seen enhance the delights of friendly intercourse—was this to be condemned as an evil? Was wine to be banished from the table, and anathematised as an unmitigated mischief? Did not hundreds of his own personal friends, his most esteemed and honoured friends, men of blameless lives,—good and religious and charitable,—did not they use it and enjoy it, and in moderation too? Was he to tell them that *they* were doing wrong?

Then, there were vast interests which would be imperilled by the change from a habit which was so universal. Enormous capital was invested in breweries and distilleries. Thousands of families were living in independence by this trade, discharging all the duties of citizenship, educating and providing for their own children, and not neglecting the children of the poor; contributing to the charities, supporting every useful institution, and freely responding to every appeal on behalf of religion. Were there not fully five hundred retailers of drink in his own city, almost every one of whom he knew, and from many of whom he had obtained liberal assistance in his good works? and were their families to be thrown on the world, and by his hand, too?

Then again, would the attempt succeed, as he was told it would if *he* would only aid it? Was not the opposing power too great to be overcome? The personal interests of those engaged in the trade—the habits and customs of society—the weakness of man's nature,—were not these fatal obstacles to the success of so desperate an attempt? Was it prudent, was it wise, was it honest, to undertake so tremendous a task, when, in all human probability, the result would be none other than failure? Besides, there were the friends whom he would pain, the friendships which it might sever, the injury which it would inflict. Nay, his own flesh and blood—the brothers of his youth—their young children, whom he loved with such yearning fondness—the husband of his sister,—these would be among the victims of his mission, were that mission to be successful! Was he also to abandon the darling object of his life, that noblest ambition of the Minister of Religion, the completion of a temple to the worship of the Deity?

Such were the thoughts that passed through the perplexed mind of the good priest, as he remembered the frequent appeal, 'Oh! Theobald Mathew, if *thou* would only give thy aid to the cause, what good thou wouldst do for these poor creatures!' and passed in review the dangers and obstacles which he would have to encounter, could he bring himself to take so formidable a step. Vanity had no seductions in a moment and in an issue like this. The responsibility was too awful, the risk too terrible, the consequences of success too grave, the shame of failure too bitter. In prayer, on his knees before his God, he sought for guidance from on high; and if, after long and anxious deliberation, and frequent mental struggles, he became at last convinced that the cause was one in which, for the sake of his people, he ought boldly and unreservedly embark, and if he decided on placing himself at the head of the movement, may we not believe that he received the guidance which he so reverently sought?

He did not decide until after long and anxious deliberation; but once having decided, he acted promptly, as a man whose mind was thoroughly made up. Like Cæsar, he had crossed the Rubicon.

CHAPTER VII.

He consults William Martin—'Here goes, in the name of God!'—The Horse-Bazaar—The Movement Progresses—Billy Martin—William's Oratory—William's gentler Breathings—The Reconcilement.

THAT was a joyful day to honest William Martin, on which, early in April 1838, he received a message from Father Mathew, requesting his presence that evening at the house in Cove Street. William, as he afterwards assured his friends, 'had a presentiment of what was about to happen,' and for that day he carried his sixty-eight years as jauntily as if they had been only thirty. At the appointed moment he was at the door, which was open for his reception; and there, at the threshold, stood his friend Theobald Mathew ready to receive him, his handsome countenance radiant with kindness and good nature. 'Welcome, Mr. Martin; welcome, my dear friend. It is very kind of you to come to me at so short a notice, and so punctually too.' 'I was right glad to come to thee, Theobald Mathew, for I expected that thou had good news for me.' 'Well, Mr. Martin, I have sent for you to assist me in forming a temperance society in this neighbourhood.' 'I knew it!' said William; 'something seemed to tell me that thou would'st do it at last.' 'My dear sir, it was not a matter to be undertaken lightly, and I feel that there are many difficulties in the way.' 'There are difficulties in everything we do,' remarked William; 'but thou knowest we must conquer them.' 'Very true, my dear friend, we must try and do so. You remember that, a considerable time ago, you spoke to me on the subject at the House of Industry.' 'I remember it well, and that I often spoke to thee about it, and told thee that thou were the only man that could help us.' 'At that time,' continued Father Mathew, 'I could not see my way clearly to take up the question; but I have thought much of it since then, and I think I do see my way now. I have been asked by several good men to take up the cause, and I feel I can no longer refuse. How are we to begin, Mr. Martin?' 'Easily enough,' said honest William. 'Appoint a place to hold the meeting, fix a day and hour,—and that's the way to begin.' 'Will Tuesday next, at seven o'clock, in my schoolroom, answer?' asked Father Mathew. 'It's the very thing,' said William, who added,—'This will be joyful news for our friends. Oh! Theobald Mathew, thou hast made me a happy man this night.' An affectionate pressure of the hand was the response.

This, indeed, was great news for the friends of temperance—for those who had struggled so long, and in vain, to arrest even the decent attention of the community, and who had seen such little result from their many years of earnest and disinterested labours. They rejoiced unfeignedly, and wisely considered that the cause was thenceforth destined to advance; though no one could have then imagined that it would ever have assumed the importance which it obtained in scarcely more than a year from that date. People do not anticipate miraculous revolutions; and what was to happen was of this class.

When it became generally known through the city that Father Mathew had taken this important step, some applauded him, and said that it was in keeping with his other good works; but a much larger number ridiculed the notion of his joining the 'fanatics.' Those who were inclined to take a lenient view of his folly, said he had lost his usual good sense, or attributed his conduct partly to a momentary impulse, and partly to his natural unwillingness to say 'no' to any application. 'And then, those temperance fellows have been so pestering and bothering the poor man, that he could not resist their importunities.' To say the truth, many of his friends were deeply disgusted at what they regarded as an unaccountable freak, or, at the best, an instance of pitiable weakness.

The meeting was not a very large one, whatever its future influence upon the country and upon its people. Of course, the veterans were there to witness the triumph of their courage and fidelity. Several of the personal followers of Father Mathew were there also. But of those in whose behalf he had consented to place himself in a position from which his natural modesty shrank, there was a small attendance. It mattered little, however, what the attendance was, whether small or great; it was the work to be then undertaken which was of importance. The place of meeting was auspicious and appropriate. It was the schoolroom in which, for nearly twenty years, since when it had been established by the good priest who now placed himself at the head of another movement for the good of the people, many hundreds, nay thousands, of the children of the poor had been taught, trained, and fed within its walls, and prepared, by knowledge and by industry, for the better discharge of their duties in life.

Father Mathew took the chair, and opened the proceedings in a short address. He briefly described the object for which he had called his friends together, and referred to the frequent applications that had been made to him by gentlemen who differed from him in religion, but who were known and respected for their worth and benevolence.

These gentlemen (he continued) are good enough to say that I could be useful in promoting the great virtue of temperance, and arresting the spread of drunkenness. I am quite alive to the evils which this vice brings with it, especially to the humbler classes, who are naturally most exposed to its temptation, and liable to yield to its seductive influences. I have always endeavoured, as a minister of religion, to discourage drunkenness, not with the success I desired, it is true; but I yielded to no one in my wish to see our working classes sober and self-respecting. I could not refuse to listen to the many appeals made to me. Your respected friend Mr. Martin has often asked me to do what I am about to do this night—and Mr. Olden, whom you well know, has told me that 'the mission was from God, and that I should not reject it.' My dear friends, I much fear that your kind partiality has made you overlook my many defects, and attribute to me merits which I am very far from possessing; but if, through any humble instrumentality of mine, I can do good to my fellow creatures, and give glory to God, I feel I am bound, as a minister of the Gospel, to throw all personal considerations aside, and try and give a helping hand to gentlemen who have afforded me so excellent an example. Indeed, if only one poor soul could be rescued from destruction by what we are now attempting, it would be giving glory to God, and well worth all the trouble we could take. No person in health has any need of intoxicating drinks. My dear friends, you don't require them, nor do I require them—neither do I take them. Many of you here have proved that they can be done without, for you are strong in health, and in the possession of all your faculties. After much reflection on the subject, I have come to the conviction that there is no necessity for them for any one in good health; and I advise you all to follow my example. I will be the first to sign my name in the book which is on the table, and I hope we shall soon have it full.

Father Mathew then approached the table, and, taking the pen, said, in a voice heard by all, and remembered by many to this day—'Here goes, *in the name of God!*' and signed as follows,—'Revd. Theobald Mathew, C. C., Cove Street, No. 1.'

It is not possible to describe the exultation of William Martin, and the deep satisfaction felt by others; it is sufficient to say that sixty names were enrolled that night, including the names of some who, now much advanced in life, are still faithful to the promise of that memorable evening—the 10th of April 1838.

From that moment Father Mathew became public property. His time was thenceforward no longer his own, and his house was soon to lose its accustomed privacy. Day by day, there grew upon him an amount of labour, labour of body and of mind, such as perhaps no other man ever went through, and which, could he at all have anticipated it when he wrote that signature in the book, might have appalled even his self-sacrificing spirit. Now indeed his twenty-five years of devotion to the service of his fellow-citizens proved of infinite value to him. His reputation, for every virtue which could adorn a man or a priest, had long been established in the hearts of the mass of the population, with whom his name had become a household word, the type of goodness, and charity, and compassionateness. No man had ever more successfully prepared the way for his own work, or so securely laid the foundations—broad, deep, wide, and solid—of his own future fame, as he had done during those five and twenty years. In his confessional, in his pulpit, in the squalid garret, in the haunts of fever, by the bedside of the sinner, in the wards of the cholera hospital, in his munificent charities, in his unostentatious benevolence, in his acts of untold kindness and generosity—*in his whole life*—lay the secret of his marvellous success—of the miraculous progress of the movement of which he had now become the leader. He may have been, and indeed was, derided by many, though only for a short time; but no one was foolish or wicked enough to question either the sincerity of his conviction, or the purity of his motives. Theobald Mathew's character was beyond the reach of calumny. In the reverence of the people for that character was based the foundation of the temperance cause in Cork—in Ireland—in Scotland and England—in America. No other man could have done the work; he did it, because he was the right man to do it.

At the next meeting, to which the public were invited through placards, the signatures were very much increased; for once it was generally known that Father Mathew had 'a society of his own,' the interest of the working classes was attracted towards it. Soon the crowds became so great, that fears were entertained of the security of the loft of the old store, in which the meetings were held on two nights in the week, and also on Sunday, after 'last Mass.' Curiosity, no doubt, attracted numbers to these meetings. They desired to ascertain for themselves what Father Mathew *really* said, and if it were possible that he recommended people to give up drink of every kind, and that he adopted the motto of 'Billy Martin'—not to 'touch, taste, or handle,' what William unflatteringly designated as 'poison' and 'brewer's wash.' To their great amazement, they found that their faithful and beloved friend, the friend of the poor and the needy, whose every effort had been devoted to the service of the people, did advise them, in simple and affectionate language, to avoid a certain cause of danger, and to prefer solid comforts, to a false and fleeting gratification. He told them some of the facts of his experience, which facts now assumed a more startling significance to his own mind; and, depicting in forcible but unexaggerated language the misery and ruin, the sorrow and disgrace, which drink brought upon society, especially on those who lived by the sweat of their brow and the labour of their hands, he exhorted them to think of their own interests, their children's welfare, their happiness in this world and in the next, and, with the courage of a truly Christian people, to free themselves from the bondage of a degrading habit. Coming from any one, such advice was good; but urged by Father Mathew, it was irresistible. Thus more was done by him in a few weeks for temperance in Cork than had been accomplished in twice that number of years before.

It became therefore indispensable that a suitable place should be found, which would be capable of accommodating the thousands who flocked to the preaching of the new doctrine. Fortunately, it was found in the Horse Bazaar, a great covered space, in which, for years after, more than 4,000 persons were frequently assembled. It was quite convenient to, and within a few yards of, Father Mathew's house in Cove Street, and was placed unreservedly at his disposal by one of his sincerest friends and most devoted followers, Mrs. O'Connor. It was in this vast and dimly-lighted building that temperance was rocked and nursed, and that the sturdy infant grew strong and robust and bold, until eventually it attracted public attention to what it was doing. At first, Father Mathew did not speak at any length, and preferred that the speaking should fall to the share of others ; and the walls of the Bazaar rang night after night with fervid and impassioned oratory such as, whatever some may think to the contrary, a theme of the kind is calculated to elicit and inspire. Nor was there any lack of really clever speakers now surrounding Father Mathew. He had nearly all the old practised advocates, who had the usual arguments at their fingers' ends ; but he had likewise men of ability and enthusiasm, who flung into their advocacy all the ardour of their youth, and who, with the versatility and vivacity common to their country, enlivened their addresses by humorous descriptions and witty and amusing sallies. The speaking had the charm of variety and contrast. Following after the homely good sense and oftentimes unconsciously comical oratory of 'Billy Martin,' as people would persist in calling him, there flashed a brilliant speech from Frank Walsh, a barrister of local celebrity, one of the best popular orators of the day, and a man beloved for the genial kindness of his disposition. Frank Walsh was an invaluable aid to Father Mathew, and was one of the first to make attractive the meetings of the Bazaar. He could elicit the tear by his pathos, and delight his audience by his playful fancy and happy mimicry. Then some honest artisan, conquering his bashfulness, narrated his experience, sometimes with homely simplicity, but as often with genuine humour. Then there was the Secretary, James M'Kenna, who had known the two sides of the question from personal experience, and whose speeches frequently partook of the character of rhapsodies, rather startling to the ear of the critic, but to which the evident sincerity of the speaker imparted the genuine ring. There were others; but it is not necessary that their names should be mentioned. Suffice it to say, that scarcely in any community could any cause have been better supplied with advocates, or a leader sustained by more zealous and devoted lieutenants.

The movement rolled on majestically. The hundreds rapidly swelled into thousands, and the thousands were, before the year was at an end, to become hundreds of thousands. Thus, in three months from the day that Father Mathew signed the book 'in the name of God,' the number on the roll was 25,000; in five months, it was 131,000; and in less than nine months—from April to December of the year 1838—it was 156,000. So the temperance reformation went on, swelling like the tide, till it rushed with the force of a torrent, and eventually assumed, so to speak, the dimensions of an ocean. No wonder that 'Billy Martin' should occasionally, in the exuberance of his delight, depart from the decorous placidity of the Friend. As this worthy man had much to do with inducing Father Mathew to join the movement, or rather to create and lead it, the present may be a fitting time to give the reader an idea of what 'the Grandfather of the cause' was like.

At the first time of his adopting temperance notions, which were decidedly repugnant to his social and convivial habits, he was far advanced in life; and when he signed his name on the 10th of April 1838, he was within two years of the patriarchal age of seventy. But he was as strong as an elephant, and as active as a horse—the two animals he invariably introduced into what may be termed his sensation speeches. Broad, sturdy, and vigorous, he had gone into the cause with all the earnestness, honesty, and obstinacy of his nature. Honest and upright in his dealings, he was just the man to 'stand no nonsense,' and to despise half measures from the bottom of his soul. William was a philanthropist, and abhorred slavery and oppression of every kind. He was a negro emancipationist, and an enemy to capital punishment;

but to no cause did he devote a tithe of the ardour and energy that he did to temperance. He had given up whisky-punch and wine and porter himself; and why should n't every-one do the same? He made the sacrifice,—if it were a sacrifice,—and he should like to know why every other person in the world should not do likewise?

For years, William had been accustomed to decorate his shop-window with flaring placards and startling pictures, which silently though forcibly advocated his darling cause. Whatever came from the temperance printing-press which most strikingly illustrated the folly, the ruin, or the disgrace of drunkenness, or depicted in the most glowing colours the advantages which followed in the path of sobriety, found a place in this picture-gallery of his. No caricature of the 'miserable drunkard' was too broad for his taste; it was impossible that the colours could be laid on too thick or too dark for William's satisfaction. Besides, as he said, the public were to be frightened if they could not be argued out of the folly and wickedness of their drinking habits; and the ladies too, he added, should be shown 'what came of their drinking their couple of glasses of their nice port and their beautiful sherry.' There were pictures to suit every understanding. Those who could not be won by examples of domestic felicity, in which a lady in pink, with a very small child sitting on the carpet at her feet, and a gentleman in a blue coat and yellow trowsers, reading by a lamp, pleasingly figured, were appealed to through their grosser sense—the concupiscence of the eye—by the representation of a prodigious plum-pudding, bristling with huge almonds, or of a mammoth round of beef; while those who were insensible to persuasion, and should be dealt with sternly, were aroused to a sense of their danger by an internal scene, in which a gentleman was represented in the act of administering a second and evidently a superfluous blow to his wife, with a poker of gigantic demensions; or a street scene, in which the 'groggery' and the brewery and distillery were represented as being under the direct superintendence, and indeed active management, of Satan and a host of hoofed and horned satellites. The mass of the community at that time regarded total abstinence as the wildest of wild dreams, and the most foolish of absurdities; and, in their eyes, he who preached it was either a fool, a knave, a dupe, or an impostor. But William did not care a button as to what people said or thought of him; he resolved that if they would not listen to the truth, they should *see* it. Therefore everything novel and astounding found an honoured place in his shop-window; and when a crowd gathered and gaped, great was his rejoicing thereat.

He delighted in all the catch-words of temperance oratory, and repeated with undiminished relish certain couplets and scraps which enriched the harangues of the ordinary temperance platforms—such as

> Drink of the fountain bubbling free;
> 'T was good for Samson, and 't is good for thee.

Though a Friend, and a lover of peace, William was a fierce zealot in temperance. Indeed I am thoroughly convinced that he would have cheerfully gone to the stake—of course, after first sturdily fighting against it—in defence of his principles; and it is much to be feared that he would not have dealt over mercifully with the 'groggeries,' which were the objects of his special detestation—had he them in his power. He preached total abstinence on many occasions with an energy and vehemence startling to unaccustomed ears. His speech was at times rather a war-whoop than an appeal to the reasoning faculties. In this respect he was a remarkable contrast to those members of the Society of Friends who had joined at an early period. Bland and gentle in manner, and persuasive in advocacy, they, when compared with William, were as the softest whispering of the gentlest zephyr to the swell and roar of the storm. Nor was William Martin always in the stormy mood : he could be humorous and playful, and relished fun amazingly, as well as indulged in it, to the vast delight of his audience—especially after the company had enjoyed a more than usually satisfactory tea.

The writer well remembers the amazement depicted on the countenances of two American Friends, whom Father Mathew had brought with him to a 'soirée,' while listening to a speech from William. He was in majestic force this night, and seemed evidently determined to afford his transatlantic brethren a lively idea of how things were done in Ireland. He revelled in comical pictures and droll incidents, and he wound up with his favourite queries, which clinched the argument, and left his imaginary opponent trampled beneath his sturdy feet. Imagine this broad-shouldered vigorous old man of seventy roaring out the following questions and answers, his voice swelling in volume and his vehemence culminating to a force quite prodigious at the final and crushing assertion—'What does the Race-horse drink ?—Water ! What does the Elephant drink ?—Water ! ! What does the Lion drink ?—Water ! ! ! It is good for Man, Beast, and Bird ! ! ! !' As hes houted out the last word, which he usually pronounced as if it were spelt with a 'u' instead of an 'i,' he was carried away by his energy, and literally roared and stamped—the American friends looking on in indescribable amazement, perhaps either dreading apoplexy for the impassioned orator, or the sudden giving way of the floor, which, no doubt, William sorely tried. Father Mathew thoroughly relished his friend William's exhibitions of 'earnestness and sincerity,' as he rather mildly designated these grand outbursts. The following, which was accurately reported at the time—it was spoken in 1843—will afford a favourable specimen of William Martin's gentler breathings :—

'Well, my friends, how things are changed !—thanks to your good President. I remember the time when I was the scoff and scorn of all Cork.' Here an old lady, from the root and vegetable market, with a deep lace frill to her snowy cap, which was ornamented with a broad ribbon of the most brilliant hue, remarked, in a consolatory tone—'Do n't mind what they did, Mr. Martin, darling—'t is you had the sense, and they had n't. God bless you! you knew what was good for poor craytures, and 't is finely you are this blessed night, sure enough.' When the good humoured laughter which this sally provoked had subsided, the speaker continued his address—''Tis a great change for the better. But I knew how it would be. When that meeting was held on the 10th of April, 1838, and your respected President undertook the task, I felt as if a load was taken off my shoulders, and put upon Theobald Mathew's.' Mr. Martin, finding his audience to be in the most amiable mood, thus pleasantly relaxed :—

I will just tell you an anecdote, to show you how foolish a poor fellow may become when he has a little drop in. There was a man named John Turner, who thought that he should go to the public-house, and take a pint of porter ; he had 2*s*. 6*d*. in his pocket, besides the price of two pints. Well, John Turner went in, and called for one pint, and then he called for another, and at last poor John Turner fell asleep. Now there were some 'purty boys' in the tap-room at the time, and they got a cork and burned it over the candle, and smeared poor John's face, until he became like a black. Well, one said that he ought to cut off one of John's whiskers; and when that one was off, they did n't think it was fair but to cut off the other, until John Turner was clipped as bare as a fighting cock. 'Let us look at his pockets,' said they; and they looked in, and saw 2*s*. 6*d*., and they took it out. After that they got a looking-glass, and put it opposite to him, and then they shook him to waken him. John opened his eyes, and rubbed them, and took a peep in the glass. 'O dear! is this me?' said John—'no it can't: it must be some other man. I was a fair man, and I had whiskers on me— and this fellow is black, and has n't a hair on his face. Oh dear! oh dear!' said poor John, 'who am I at all? Well, if it is me,' said John, 'I 'll soon find out, for I had 2*s*. 6*d*. in my pocket: and if I have n't it, I can't be John Turner.' He put his hand in his pocket, and there was no 2s. 6d. to be found—so he said that he could n't be John Turner. He then thought that if anyone should know him, it should be his wife; so he rolled and staggered to the door, and he rapped, and he says—'Is it here one John Turner lives?' 'It is,' says his wife, who opened the door. 'Am I John Turner?—look at me, and tell me am I John Turner?' 'You are not John,' says the wife. 'John had a nice fair face, and had fine whiskers—and you have none; and John, my John, used to walk steadily, and hold himself up like a man—but you are staggering about like a drunken fool, and you are nearly doubled up.' 'Oh dear! oh dear! then who am I?' said John Turner. 'No matter who you are,' said the wife—'you are in want of a lodging, and you must be taken in.' So she let him in; and I suppose when he awoke in the morning he found out that he was poor John Turner himself. It is said there is 'nourishment' in strong drinks, but I say it is in the *eating* that the nourishment is to be found. When I eat, I find, as the lady said who took the port wine, that it is doing me good down to my very toes. Here I am in my seventy-second year, and I am strong and healthy without their 'nourishment.' Oh, take the pure bubbling stream—

Drink from the bubbling fountain free,
'T was Sampson's drink, 't is good for thee.

William sat down on this occasion, as he did on most others, amid a storm of applause. The same old lady with the grand cap rushed over to him, and seizing his hand, exclaimed, 'God bless you,' Mr. Martin—'t is you 're the splendid man of your age. Faith 't is n't every young fellow that's like you—strong an' hearty you are this day, my old buck! God spare you to us for another twenty year, at any rate.' William was affected, but somewhat embarrassed, by the old lady's enthusiasm, which was fully shared in by her female friends in his neighbourhood.

A little incident in which William Martin was concerned, will afford an interesting idea of the character of the man whom he sincerely admired. William could, when he so liked, and that was not rarely, be as obstinate as a mule. Father Mathew was quick, hot, and, at times, obstinate also. In fact, he had so long, not to say influenced, but even ruled, others, that he was—at intervals, and rarely, to be sure—

impatient of contradiction. William was rough and resolute; his friend warm and somewhat self-willed. Some question arose respecting which the two friends had a difference of opinion, and neither would yield to the other; and so they fell out—William leaving the house in high dudgeon. Scarcely had the broad back of the sturdy Quaker been lost sight of at the corner of the street, when poor Father Mathew's anger vanished like smoke, and gave place to the keenest compunction. He was most unhappy at the notion of his having wounded the feelings of his good old friend, and would have followed him and implored his forgiveness, if he believed it would have been of any use. William was grieved in his own way, and became several degrees more gruff in consequence. A kind friend interposed, and explanations and assurances of mutual regard and esteem followed. Father Mathew quickly availed himself of the opportunity afforded to him, and proceeding to the place of business of honest William, flung himself upon his neck, and, kissing him on the cheek, humbly implored his pardon. That was another proud day for William Martin, between whom and Father Mathew no cloud, small even as a man's hand, ever again interposed.

CHAPTER VIII.

The Pilgrimage to Cork—'Father Mathew's Parlour'—The House in Cove Street—His man John—The Great Powers of the Kitchen and the Pantry—The happy working of the Cause.

THE 200,000 on the roll of the society in the month of January, 1839, were not exclusively from the city and county of Cork. It is true, the city and county contributed a large portion of the entire; but the number was partly made up by those who poured in from the adjoining counties of Kerry, Waterford, Limerick, Clare, and Tipperary—and even from remote Galway. The tidings of the great moral reformation worked in Cork quickly spread, through the agency of the public press, throughout the island, and to all parts of the United Kingdom. The speeches of Father Mathew and his assistants were copied from one paper into another, and with them accounts of the success of his mission, the benefits which it conferred on the community as well as on the individual, and the evils which it remedied or prevented. Attention was thus arrested and interest excited, and it was only natural that those who read or heard accounts of what was doing in Cork, should come to the conclusion that what was good for Cork was good for other places, and that what had done one person good would do another person good; and so, as Father Mathew did not come to them, they resolved on coming to him. Thus it was that the public conveyances brought numbers into Cork every day, and that multitudes of pilgrims might be seen on the roads leading into the city, with their little bundles in their hands, and generally lame and foot-sore after their long journey. To Cove Street the pilgrimage was directed. To see Father Mathew—to take the pledge from him—to be touched by him and blessed by him,—this was sufficient reward for the longest and most painful journey. But never did Father Mathew send the poor pilgrim from his door without having first fed and comforted him, and, where necessary, provided for his safe and easy return. A seat on a public car, or something in the pocket, enabled the poor traveller from a distance—often of 50 miles, sometimes of 100 miles—to return happy and joyful to his home. Thus, through the accounts given by the early pilgrims, of the good man who had heard their story, who had sympathised with them, who had blessed them and prayed for them, who had treated them as a father and a benefactor, was the fame of Father Mathew spread abroad, even more effectually than through the columns of the public press. The expense entailed on Father Mathew by what may be described as this pilgrimage to Cork, the Mecca of temperance, was considerable; and before he ever sold a single medal, he was involved in debt to the amount of 1,500*l.*, notwithstanding the numerous offerings which he continued to receive as a priest. His resources were not increased, but his expenditure, even thus early in the movement, was so to a very great extent.

The lower apartment, or parlour, which was on a level with the street, was converted into a reception room for those who came to take the pledge: and here was the book in which the names were enrolled, and here the pledge was administered. It was in this celebrated apartment that scenes such as the following might be daily witnessed. At all hours of the day and evening—even to ten or eleven o'clock at night—'batches' of ten, twenty, or even thirty, might be seen waiting to be enrolled. Some were sober and penitent; others smelling strongly of their recent potations, and ashamed to commit themselves by uttering a word; more boisterous and rude, their poor wives and mothers endeavouring to soothe and keep them under control. One of this class—a big, brawny fellow, with rough voice, blood-shot eyes, and tattered clothes—would roar out:—'I won't take the pledge—I 'll be——if I do. Is it me! What oc-oc-occasion have I for it! I won't demane myself by taking it. I always stood a trate, and I 'll stand it again. Me take it! Let me go, woman! I tell you, lave me go!' 'Oh, Patsy, darlin', don't expose yourself. You know I 'm for your good. And what would his reverence say to you if he heard you? Do, alana, be quiet, an' wait for the holy priest.' 'Well, hould off of me, any way. Can 't I take care of myself? Can 't I do what I like? Who 'll dare say I can 't?' 'Oh Patsy, Patsy, darlin'!' 'Is, indeed! Patsy, darlin'! Let me go, woman!'—and, bursting away from the trembling hands of the poor creature, who struggled to hold the drunken fool; Patsy would make a wild dash to the door, amidst muttered expressions of sympathy, such as—'God help you, honest woman! 't is you 're to be pitied with that quare man.' 'Yes,' another would remark, 'an' a fine man he is, and a decent man, too, if he 'd only be sober.' But just as Patsy was about effecting his escape, and swearing that 'he would never be the one of his name to demane himself by taking their dirty pledge,' he was certain to be arrested by Father Mathew himself, who at a glance knew the nature of the case. Catching Patsy with a grasp stronger than that from which he had escaped, Father Mathew would say, in a cheerful voice to Patsy, as if that gentleman had come of his own free will to implore the pledge at his hands—'Welcome! welcome! my dear. Delighted to see you. Glad you are come to me. You are doing a good day's work for yourself and your family. You will have God's blessing on your head. Poverty is no crime, my dear child; it is sin alone that lowers us in the eyes of God.

Kneel down, my dear (a strong pressure on Patsy's shoulder, under which Patsy reluctantly sinks on his knees), and repeat the words of the pledge after me ; and then I will mark you with the sign of the Cross, and pray God to keep you from temptation.' What could poor Patsy do, but yield, as that magnetic hand rested affectionately on his tangled locks? And so Patsy's name was added to the long muster-roll of the pledged.

We doubt if there was a tap-room in Cork in which a more decided odour of whisky and porter—or, as the phrase went, 'strong drink'—was apparent, than in 'Father Mathew's parlour'—especially on the evenings of Saturday and Monday, but more especially on the latter. The odour did not however ascend higher, for a door, covered with faded green baize, shut off the upper from the lower part of the house; into which, if the reader has no objection, we shall take a peep.

If Father Mathew lived in a cloister, he could not have lived more modestly and quietly than he did. His principal room—his *only* room, save that in which he slept—was at once breakfast and dining-room, study and reception-room. It certainly did not exceed sixteen feet from wall to wall. Not a morsel of carpet concealed the well-washed boards; while the furniture consisted of the barest necessaries—a centre table, a sideboard, a side-table, some chairs, and a writing-desk. On the side-table was a large-sized bust of Lord Morpeth, the popular Secretary of Ireland, and friend of Father Mathew. Two enormous volumes of the Sacred Scriptures, one containing the Old and the other the New Testament, flanked the bust; and a glass filled with flowers, when flowers were in season, completed the adornment of this show-table. On the wall opposite the fire-place hung a good oil painting—a portrait of Cardinal Micara, the head of the Capuchins, who had constantly exhibited the deepest interest in the career of the illustrious Irish friar. Opposite the windows, a good engraving of a celebrated picture of the Holy Family was suspended. But, framed with richness and glazed with reverent care, was a marvellous production in worsted, intended to represent, and fondly believed by the donor and artist as well as by its grateful recipient to represent, the religious profession of St. Clare. The desk was fearfully bespattered with ink, and otherwise exhibited signs of being an article of furniture more useful than ornamental. But everything, save the said desk, was neat and in perfect order. If it were poverty, it was willingly and honestly assumed; but the neatness and order bespoke the presence and influence of a gentleman. In this modest apartment the Apostle of Temperance was visited by many of the great and distinguished of the earth, and here he exercised a hospitality which made those who partook of it experience that most agreeable of all feelings in the mind of a guest—namely, the consciousness of being welcome, and *at home*.

There was one, however, in that house who, in it, was a much greater man than its master. That was the servant John. Now, as much of Father Mathew's internal comfort and peace of mind depended upon John, and the mood in which he happened to be in, it is necessary to say something of that august potentate of the pantry.

John was a dried-up, wizened-faced, dapper old bachelor, who entertained the most exalted opinion of his own wisdom and knowledge of the world, and the profoundest contempt for nearly every human creature, save Father Mathew and his own marvellously-old mother. John was sour of visage and still more sour of speech. The gleam of his small eyes, and the downward curl of his thin lips, were pretty good indications of his general state of mind, which was apt to be ruffled at the slightest provocation. He was eminently aristocratic, and hated to be bored by the poor. For his part, he did n't know what the priest wanted with them, or they with him; but he could unhesitatingly say that he detested their knocks at the door, their constant enquiries, their vulgar manners, and the sight and smell of their clothes. John had served in a noble family—hence he was an infallible authority on all matters of taste, style, and fashion. He had been in London—therefore he was equally an authority on foreign travel and the world in general. There was one article which he specially prized, and which, indeed, divided with Father Mathew and his venerable mother that small amount of affection which he condescended to bestow upon anyone or anything save himself. This was a silver watch of formidable dimensions, which was encased in *three* leather wrappers, no doubt as a precaution against chill or rheumatism. If one desired to conciliate the favour of the magnate, one perhaps might achieve that grand result by respectfully requesting to know 'what the exact hour was.' John would graciously proceed to satisfy a curiosity so natural, and would draw forth the well-protected time-piece, and gravely divest it of its three wrappers ; then, having glanced with a kind of scientific air at the dial, which was of prodigious surface, he would loftily announce the time, to the minute and to the second ; having done which, he would caress the back with a tender hand, and at once restore the valuable article to its wrappers and his fob.

This sweet-tempered bachelor did not at all admire little boys. He did n't know what good they were, or why they were brought into the world, unless to stuff themselves unpleasantly with pastry, to spoil tablecloths, and to worry deserving and inoffensive servants. It was a source of anguish to him to be compelled to allow the priest's two nephews—boys keen after sweets, and of daring appetite—to have the run of his pantry. But, 'John, give the boys that pie,' was too direct a command to be resisted ; and John would retire with a grumble, while Father Mathew would stand looking on, his hands deep in his pockets, and a smile on his face, while the boys ploughed deep into the contents of a pie-dish, and made paste and fruit vanish before their combined attack. No doubt John must at times have wished that some unlooked-for ingredient had been mixed with the sweets, to punish the lads for the liberties which, on too frequent occasions, they took with him, and especially with his age.

The priest was in the habit of inviting young people to breakfast, always to John's disgust. On one occasion, a young fellow, nervous and awkward, spilled his tea, and upset his egg—the shame of which double catastrophe was terribly enhanced by the display of John's sublime disdain, and the ostentatious solemnity with which the mischief was temporarily repaired. The poor lad felt himself in a social Coventry,—banished from polite society for ever.

John was a good servant, so long as he did not attempt to play the part of master. He was neat of hand, clean in person and in habit, and an admirable cook. In the artistic laying of the cloth for dinner, and the scientific arrangement of the table, there was not, as he often declared, his superior in the universe; and really few could excel him in his soup and coffee. John brought in the soup-tureen with a solemnity of deportment which would have done honour to a master-of-ceremonies; and as it was distributed to the guests, he awaited with grim dignity the accustomed praise. Should an unhappy guest look dissatisfied, or even indifferent to the merits of the elixir, he was lost—marked down from that day in John's darkest tablets. But if he praised it in this fashion —'Really, this soup is so delightful, that I must trouble you again, Father Mathew'—he won the artist's heart—took it by storm. There was, however, one commendation for which he always looked, and which he invariably obtained—that of his master, who would have drunk the soup were ditch-water its principal ingredient, rather than have pained his old follower. The usual formula of approval was thus pronounced —'Very nice, indeed. Why, John, you are getting better every day.' These words were like sunlight to John's moral landscape. His sour features brightened with delight, and for the moment the natural vinegar and lemon-juice were banished from his thin lips.

John loved his master, in his own way, and after his own fashion ; but he had a mission to fulfil, and that was to tyrannise over that master, and to retain Biddy, the woman servant, in a state of abject subjection. He succeeded in the former object rather too well ; but in the latter he had not equal success, for Biddy was a woman of spirit, and stood on her rights, defending them with the valour of a heroine against the encroachments of the enemy. Little knew the admiring world outside the difficulty which the Apostle of Temperance had to maintain even an armed neutrality between the Great Powers of the Kitchen and the Pantry in Cove Street, or the many and unavailing efforts he had made to effect a solid and lasting peace on terms honourable to both. When peace did reign between the Powers, Father Mathew rejoiced in spirit.

We shall renew our acquaintance with our friend John.

There was no flagging in the good work, as the gradually widening circle of the 'batches' in the Horse Bazaar, and the increasing numbers pouring into the parlour in Cove Street, sufficiently attested. The interest of the local community was excited in the movement, and the pride of the citizens of Cork was gratified by the fact of their city being the birth-place and cradle of a great moral reformation. But a deeper feeling was aroused, as the practical results of sobriety were being daily manifested, not only in the greater quietness and good order of the streets, but in the material and moral improvement of those who adopted this once much-ridiculed pledge of total abstinence. The numbers in the prisoners' dock in the Police Court were steadily diminishing, week after week ; masters and employers expressed their satisfaction at the improved conduct of their servants and work-people ; the attendance of children in schools became more steady and continuous as their parents became sober and self-respecting ; and the appearance of the people generally was marked by an air of comfort which they had not previously exhibited. If the trade of the publican was lessened, which undoubtedly it was, those who dealt in necessaries and humble luxuries were correspondingly benefited. Temperance-rooms began to spring into existence ; and in these members gathered together, and drew other members towards them, as well by the example which they afforded, as by the inducements they held out. Working men could sit at the bright fire of the reading-room without risk of temptation, hearing the news, discussing the topics of the hour, or glorying in the progress of the cause from which they were taught to expect great honour and lasting advantage to their country. These reading-rooms ere long assumed a very important feature in the movement, and became one of its most effective means of practical organisation.

During all this time Father Mathew was as much the priest as ever. The same early hours, the same attendance in the confessional, the same attention to his clerical duties, the same activity and punctuality in whatever he had to perform. The Father Mathew of 1838 and 1839 was in all respects, save one, the same as the Father Mathew of any year since his arrival in Cork ; and that one exception was in the greater labour which he was compelled, from his new position, to undertake, but which he cheerfully, and indeed delightedly, went through. Doubt and uncertainty as to the step which he had taken, and the course which he was now fairly entering upon, vanished altogether from his mind at the spectacle of the rags and misery, the squalor and wretchedness, the sorrow and crime and ruin, which the experience of each succeeding day proved to be the consequence of the prevailing habit of a people naturally possessed of the highest moral and social qualities. Whatever may have been his former apprehensions as to the difficulty he would have to encounter, and the risk of failure in his undertaking, he had entirely forgotten that he ever entertained such a sentiment. In fact, Father Mathew had caught the contagion of the movement, and was now as confident and fearless as the least responsible member of his already vast society. From a timid yet willing convert, he had warmed into an enthusiast; and that too, ere many months had passed since he used the memorable words—'Here goes, in the name of God!' There was not a man in Ireland whose heart and soul were more thoroughly enlisted in the cause. He saw in it the social redemption of the individual, the national elevation of the country; and he gave himself up to it without reserve, in the spirit of a Christian and a patriot. And he had his reward in the happy faces and decent appearance of the people, as he met them in the streets, saw them in their homes, or observed them in the body of the church, or at the rails of the altar.

It was thus, in four years from the commencement of his work, that, at a 'festival' in the town of Nenagh, he happily referred to the motives which had induced him to undertake the task:—

This great temperance movement which we witness, was not lightly thought of by me; it was not the result of sudden excitement; it was not the impulse of a moment, that induced me to undertake the share I have had in it. I pondered long upon it; I examined it carefully; I had long reflected on the degradation to which my country was reduced—a country, I will say, second to none in the universe for every element that constitutes a nation's greatness, with a people whose generous nature is the world's admiration. I mourned in secret over the miseries of this country; I endeavoured to find out the cause of those miseries, and, if that were possible, to apply a remedy. I saw that those miseries were chiefly owing to the crimes of the people, and that those crimes again had their origin in the use that was made of intoxicating drinks. I discovered that if the cause were removed, the effects would cease; and with my hope in the God of universal benevolence and charity, reposing my hopes in the

Omnipotent, I began this mission in Cork, with the cordial assistance afforded me by persons widely differing in creed, and particularly by members of the Society of Friends in that city. Four years have passed away since the grain of mustard-seed was sown ; many perils were encountered ; many objections had to be met ; misrepresentation had to be combated ; opposition had to be faced. I went on, notwithstanding all. The grain of mustard seed grew by degrees into that mighty and majestic tree that has overshadowed the land, and under whose peaceful and protecting branches we are met this evening.

Invitations now began to pour in upon Father Mathew from many parts of the country, more particularly from the adjoining counties, soliciting his presence, that he might administer the pledge, and organise local societies. For some time he did not yield to these entreaties, however supplicatory and pressing ; but his compassion for the pilgrims from a distance, who so often knelt before him hungry, fainting, and foot-sore, at length prevailed over his reluctance ; and from that moment might be said to have commenced a new phase in the movement, whose progress thenceforward was prodigious, and whose success was almost miraculous.

CHAPTER IX.

He visits Limerick — Extraordinary Excitement caused by his Visit — Its Result — Visits Waterford — Speech of Bishop Foran — Whimsical Occurrence — First Sale of Cards and Medals — In Borrisokane — Goes to Dublin — Denies he can effect Cures — Simplicity and Efficacy of the Pledge.

THE city of Limerick was the first scene of his missionary labours. He had been invited to visit that city by his venerable friend, the Right Rev. Dr. Ryan, a man simple and homely in manner, but of solid good sense, and true Christian piety. Father Mathew the more readily yielded to the invitation, as his doing so afforded him the opportunity of visiting his sister, Mrs. Dunbar, to whom he was tenderly attached, and to whom he had always stood more in the relation of a parent than a brother. The announcement of his intended visit—of the coming of the 'Apostle of Temperance'—produced the most extraordinary effect, as it was borne from village to village, from town to town, from county to county, along the banks of the noble Shannon, and far away into the wilds of distant Connemara. Father Mathew, of whom mothers told their children, and the old, by the fireside, spoke with reverence, was coming to Limerick! The first week in December 1839 was a memorable time in that fine city. Even on the day before he was expected to arrive, the principal roads were black with groups of people from all parts of the county, from the adjoining counties, and from the province of Connaught. During the next day, the streets of Limerick were choked with dense masses—with a multitude which it was impossible to count, and whose numbers were guessed at, as being something fabulous. It was an invasion, a taking of the town by storm. The necessaries of life rose to famine prices—for who could have anticipated such a mighty rush?—and where were food and drink to be found for those myriad mouths? What the authorities, the Bishop and his clergy, and the good citizens could do, to relieve the necessities and minister to the wants of the strangers, they generously did. The public rooms were thrown open for their shelter at night; for were the town ten times its size, it could scarcely have afforded ordinary sleeping accommodation for those who now stood in need of it. Father Mathew's reception was an ovation such as few men ever received; indeed still fewer had ever excited in a people the same blended feelings of love, and reverence, and enthusiasm. Though with a serious and solemn purpose in their minds, the people rushed towards him as if possessed by a frenzy. They struggled and fought their way through living masses, through every obstacle, until they found themselves in his presence, at his feet, listening to his voice, receiving his blessing, repeating after him the words which emancipated them, as they felt, from sin, sorrow, and temptation.

With considerate kindness, the authorities had taken such precautions as would have sufficed on an ordinary occasion; but the following extract, from a biographical notice, written in a few months after, by the late Rev. James Birmingham, P. P. of Borrisokane, will show with what result on this extraordinary occasion:—

So great was the rush of the temperance postulants, that the iron railing opposite the house of Mr. Dunbar, the rev. gentleman's brother-in-law, in which he had stopped, were carried away, and a number of persons were precipitated into the Shannon. Fortunately they were all safely picked up, and no further accident occurred. I have been told by those who were spectators of the scene, that some of the horses, with their riders, of the Scots Greys, who attended to keep order, were occasionally lifted from the ground, and carried away for a short distance by the rushing multitude; and so densely were the people crowded, that several, in their eagerness to approach Mr. Mathew, ran along to their destination quietly and securely on the heads and shoulders of the vast assemblage.

After four days of incessant labour—preaching and exhorting so long as the least remnant of voice was left him—Father Mathew concluded one of the most successful of all his temperance missions, and one that imparted an amazing impetus to the progress of the cause, which, in those four days, had obtained 150,000 additional disciples and propagandists. Thenceforward there was no going back, no halt or hesitation—the word was 'Onwards!'

Though Limerick may claim the honour of the first missionary visit of the Apostle of Temperance, Waterford claims, through the Right Rev. Dr. Foran, the good Bishop of that day, the distinction of being the first city which invited him. That invitation was given in the following letter, which is the more important as it describes, in a few words, the earlier phases of the wondrous popular movement:—

Waterford: November 4, 1839.

VERY REV. DEAR SIR,—Anxious to cooperate with you in your zealous and, under God, successful undertaking of bringing the people of this country to habits of temperance and sobriety, I, and the clergy of this city, are doing what we can to induce our flocks here to enroll themselves in your society. A great number of habitual drunkards have willingly come forward and expressed their ardent desire to become members of your Temperance Society, but many of them, from their extreme poverty, are unable to defray the expense of a journey to Cork. If you could make it your convenience to come here, any time between this and Advent, and begin the good work in this city, you would, I have no doubt, do incalculable good. While you are here, my house shall be yours. May I request, at your convenience, a few lines in answer?

I remain, very reverend dear sir,
With esteem, yours faithfully,
✠ N. FORAN.

The success which attended the first visit may be best

described in the words of the amiable prelate, whose apostolic character was depicted in the sweetness of his countenance, and the mildness and gentleness of his manner. On a subsequent occasion, when the *élite* of Waterford were assembled in the Town Hall to do honour to Father Mathew, Dr. Foran, when responding to the mention of his own name, said:—

Your Chairman told you that I was the first Catholic Bishop who invited Father Mathew to his diocese. It is true I was. The cause of temperance commenced in Waterford before Father Mathew visited our city. When he was administering the pledge in Cork, and when the fame of his great mission had gone abroad, hundreds of the people of Waterford journeyed to Cork, and on foot, at an inclement season of the year, in order to become enrolled under his banner. Some good and humane gentlemen, on seeing this, came forward and offered to raise a sufficient sum to send the people on cars. 'No,' said I, 'but we can write to Father Mathew to come to us for a day or two.' I did write accordingly, and Father Mathew acceded to our wishes. He came to Waterford in December, 1839, and spent three or four days here. I thought at the time that three or four thousand persons might be induced to join his standard within that period; but what was my extreme astonishment, as well as gratification, when in three days not less than 80,000 received the pledge at his hands!

In the course of his address, the speaker thus explained why he, as a bishop and a patriot, lent his aid to the temperance movement:—

My dear friends, why should I not encourage this movement, and sanction and support it by every means in my power? If I did not do so, I would not be an Irishman; if I did not do so, I would not be a Christian; and if I did not do so, I would not be a Bishop. I would not be an Irishman if I did not countenance and support the great cause by every influence I possess—and I am an Irishman; and being an Irishman, I love my country, as every Irishman does. Loving my country, I wish for its peace, happiness, and prosperity; and I am convinced that until the people of Ireland become an entirely temperate, sober, and moral people, they never can enjoy prosperity or happiness. I would not be a Christian or a Priest if I did not encourage and sanction the movement, for no one can assert that either the temporal or eternal interests of mankind can be obtained without the practice of sobriety. Much as I value temperance, if it did no other good but merely render the people of Ireland sober, I would not think much of it. But you all know that drunkenness was the curse of the country, and the chief cause of its degradation. You know that faction fights resulted from it, and that many victims have been offered up to its dreadful power. It is a many-headed monster; it is not the parent of one crime alone, but it drags a thousand others in its train. The habitual drunkard is a swearer, a blasphemer; he is a bad man, a bad father, a bad husband, a bad son, a bad member of society; and therefore a person addicted to this vice will be liable to fall into a thousand others. Look at the mighty reformation already effected in the people of this country!—they have become a sober and a thinking people; they have improved in every relation of life, as fathers, husbands, brothers, sons, and members of society—they are more than ever devoted to the practice of true religion, and more obedient to the commandments of their God. These are the advantages of temperance, and if they did not come in its train, I should not value it. But they do follow from its practice, and therefore it is my bounden duty as an Irishman, a Christian, and a Bishop, to support the temperance movement by every influence within my limited jurisdiction.

The good Bishop who thus spoke is, if we are to believe in the promises made to the just, now enjoying in heaven the reward of his virtues in this life.

It was in Waterford, on an occasion subsequent to Father Mathew's first visit, that the following whimsical occurrence took place. The hall of the Court House was too confined in its space to accommodate the vast numbers that pressed on continually to take the pledge, and the weather being then peculiarly severe, the meetings were necessarily held in the Catholic Cathedral, a very fine and spacious building. In one of the enormous batches, of which there were several during the day, was a poor fellow who was decidedly 'the worse of liquor'—in fact, unmistakably tipsy. He nevertheless managed to repeat the words of the pledge with due gravity and decorum; but no sooner had Father Mathew approached him to mark his forehead with the sign of the Cross, as was his custom, than the new member of the Temperance Society clutched his leader by the skirts of his coat with such a grasp as a drunken man can take, and, in a voice much broken by hiccups, cried out—'Father Ma–ma–chee, darlin', you m–m–ust k–k–iss me!' 'My dear, do let me go. God bless you, my dear child; be a good boy for the future. There—do let me go,' said Father Mathew. 'No, Father Ma–chee, darlin', I won't l–l–ave go my hoult till I get wan k–k–iss!' 'Oh, my dear, do let me go!' 'No; wan is all I ax, an' I m–m–ust have it. Do n't r–r–efuse a poor fellow-craychure wan kiss—only wan!' persisted the tender soul. Several gentlemen, including the clergymen in attendance, approached, and tried to pacify Jim, and induce him to quit his hold of Father Mathew's coat; but all to no purpose. Jim was determined to have his 'wan k–k–iss.' 'Jim, avick, ar' n't you ashamed of yourself—the holy priest!—an' in the chapel, too!' remonstrated an old woman near him. 'Jim, you bosthoon you! quit yer hould of his reverence this moment!' insisted a sturdy friend at the other side. 'No, not till I get wan k–k–iss; no, af I died for it, I won't lave go.' Father Mathew, seeing that unpleasant consequences were likely to ensue if Jim's rather inconvenient request were not at once complied with, resolved to make him happy, and accordingly kissed Jim on both cheeks, saying, 'Now, James, my dear, go home and remain quiet, and be a sensible boy for the future.' The 'boy,' we may remark, was not much short of forty years of age. Jim relinquished his grasp of the skirt of the coat, and retired, proud of his achievement.

It was of very common occurrence to see a tipsy or even drunken man take the pledge. With many, this drunkenness was the result of premeditation. They were resolved to have a parting 'dhrop of the crayture;' and, with tears in his eyes, and even heart-rending sobs, more than one poor fellow tossed off his last pint of porter, or swallowed, 'at a mouthful,' his last glass of whisky. Father Mathew was often asked why he administered the pledge to persons 'in a beastly state ;' but his answer was, 'I will never refuse the pledge to anyone, and I find that people who come to me drunk remain faithful to the pledge.' A Protestant magistrate, from Macroom, in the county of Cork, communicated to the writer a remarkable instance in support of this statement. He says :—

An accidental occurrence gave me the honour of an acquaintance with the great and good Father Mathew. I was waited upon by several of the townspeople to request my company at a temperance meeting, at which Father Mathew was to preside. The evening passed most happily. Several persons had the pledge administered to them ; and among the number, a shoemaker was hauled in, quite unable to speak or walk, from sheer drunkenness. I at once objected to his getting the pledge, but Father Mathew resolved on giving it, and was right. *That man kept it.*

Father Mathew returned to Cork for the Christmas, and returned as a conqueror. The quarter of a million of pledged teetotallers which that memorable journey added to the ranks of the society, produced an effect throughout the whole country such as could not have been anticipated. Local societies were called into existence, reading-rooms were established, and bands were formed. The organisation soon became complete ; and, ere long, there was scarcely a parish in any part of Ireland that had not its society, its room, its banner, and its band.

And with the growth of the society, and the perfection of its organisation, increased the expenditure entailed upon its leader. To meet the enormous expense which his temperance mission involved, Father Mathew adopted the plan of issuing cards and medals, which were sold at a profit, but which were not purchased by the twentieth of those who took the pledge, and whose names were inscribed on the register. We shall have subsequently to deal with this matter of cards and medals, as much misconception was created by the alleged enormous gains made by their sale ; not, to be sure, in the first flush of the miraculous progress of the cause, but at a later period. We must at present refer somewhat further to the manner in which the movement progressed.

Having discharged his ordinary priestly duties during the important festival of Christmas with the same zeal as previously distinguished him, dispensed charity with a still more unsparing hand, administered the pledge during all hours of the day and evening, visited the temperance rooms, given audiences, taken counsel with his lieutenants, assisted materially to extend and strengthen the organisation in Cork, and having moreover visited with unfailing punctuality his host of friends in the city, he again set out on his mission.

The most remarkable meetings held during the next three months were those held in Parsonstown, King's County, and in Dublin. An eye-witness, the Rev. Mr. Birmingham, thus describes the scene in Parsonstown :—

> On entering the area, on which stands the Roman Catholic Chapel, a scene presented itself highly calculated to stir up, even in hearts not very susceptible of such impressions, feelings of intense interest and of awe. In front of the chapel was stationed a large body of police, presenting a very fine and well-disciplined force ; outside these were the rifles on bended knee, with bayonets fixed and pointed, forming a barrier to oppose the rushing multitudes ; whilst within and without this barrier, to keep the passages clear, the cavalry, 'in all the pomp and circumstance of glorious war,' with flags waving to the wind—moved up and down in slow and measured pace. Beyond, and as far along the streets as the eye could reach, were the congregated masses swaying to and fro with every new impulse, and by their united voices producing a deep, indistinct sound like the murmur of the ruffled waters of the sea. Within the vicarial residence, and in strong contrast to the stirring scene without, sat the mild, unassuming, but extraordinary man, round whom had collected this display of martial pomp and numerical force. He seemed perfectly unconscious of the excitement he had produced, and spoke and acted as if he regarded himself as the least remarkable man of the age. Here I had been introduced by a friend to the Apostle of Temperance.

It is not necessary to trace Father Mathew's progress through the country on that occasion ; it is sufficient to say that it was marked by the same wonderful enthusiasm on the part of the people as was displayed at Limerick and Waterford. The good priest of Borrisokane, who has been already quoted, thus describes the results of a casual visit which was paid to his own parish :—

Mr. Mathew arrived late at night, and unexpectedly. Only a few had been aware of his arrival; and in the morning, when I waited on him, the postulants were but thinly scattered up and down the street. I asked Mr. Mathew to do me the honour of spending the day with me. He expressed his regret that time did not permit him, and stated that he should be off the moment he had received into the society the few who presented themselves. Fame, however, was busy in trumpeting the rev. gentleman's visit to our neighbourhood; and I became indebted to the number and enthusiasm of those who poured in to be enrolled, for the honour of receiving at my humble board the distinguished guest, whose company, it had appeared, I should for that day be obliged to forego. Each moment Mr. Mathew was on the point of moving away; but each moment brought numbers from the surrounding parishes, who having heard that the rev. gentleman had been in Borrisokane, threw aside their various implements of industry, and hurried in to enlist themselves under the standard of temperance, and receive the good man's benediction. Fatigued and breathless, men, women, and children, rushed forward indiscriminately to take the pledge. Mr. Mathew could not bring himself to disappoint such eagerness, or damp such ardour. He was consequently obliged to remain; and standing on a stone seat under a venerable ash tree — now more venerable than ever — he received in this small town, without any previous notice having been given, 7,000 or 8,000 souls.

Next in importance, as to its effect upon the country, and, indeed, upon the United Kingdom, to his visit to Limerick in December 1839, was that which he paid to Dublin on the 28th of March, 1840. It was bringing the movement into the capital and heart of his country. He was ardently welcomed by the Most Rev. Dr. Murray, the prelate by whom he had been ordained thirty-six years before, and the friend who had been faithful to him through life. Father Mathew was now famous; and his sermon, preached for one of the orphan institutions of Dublin, was a striking success. Long practice had imparted to his voice the strength and volume which it lacked during many years of his ministry; but the simplicity, persuasiveness, pathos, and earnestness which at all times distinguished his preaching, had lost nothing of their charm. The collection amounted to between 300*l*. and 400*l*.

The great area of the Custom House, or Beresford Place, was selected for the open-air meetings; and, day after day, from an early hour, the indefatigable Apostle was at work in his mission. One or two extracts from his addresses on this occasion are of special interest. In the following he publicly disclaims, not for the first or even the hundredth time, having any power whatever to effect cures; and he justly denies that he ever in any way encouraged the people to think that he could effect them:—

My dear friends, I wish to allude to a certain subject, to which I adverted on the first day I attended here—it is with regard to the great number of infirm and sick persons that are coming here to take the pledge. I mentioned before what brought them here. They attend to join the society in consequence of the exaggerated accounts they received from those who had been drunkards, and who, to encourage others to become teetotallers, showed the benefit they enjoyed from being temperate in their habits. They state that their health, which had been impaired by the use of intoxicating liquors, became renewed, and that their constitutions, which were broken down, were repaired by the practice of temperance. The first person I heard speak on the subject was Mr. Smith, the great teetotaller, who stated that persons who for years could not work, when they became teetotallers, were able to resume their avocations. This induces people who are suffering from various diseases to come to me, under the impression that I could cure them; but it is not in my power to afford them relief; that is all in the hands of God. I received an anonymous letter on the subject, finding fault with my conduct; but I do n't mind those attacks, it is my wish to please and satisfy all. St. Paul said he would himself be an anathema for the sake of his brethren. Some persons say, why not put them away;—but I would not envy the feelings of the man that could treat these poor people so unkindly. Persons who are free from superstition have brought me to those sick persons, to gratify them; and when I went to them I did not refuse them my blessing. I went through no ceremony of any kind, but simply invoked a blessing on them, and it is no harm to do that to anything, animate or inanimate, or to any creature, rational or irrational. Whatever the consequences may be, though I do not wish to see them coming here, I will not refuse them my blessing, or, rather, refuse to ask God to bless them. If, for one moment, I relieve them from pain of mind, or despondency of heart, I care not what is said about it, for it should not give scandal. Several of those persons have been turned out of hospitals incurable; and it is natural that when man cannot afford them aid, they apply to heaven for it. Persons of strong religious belief have importuned me to give them a blessing and let them go away. I cannot, as I said before, bless them, but I can say, 'God bless you.' I use neither candle nor holy water, nor go through any ceremony, but merely give them a blessing. I have seen Protestants invoking a blessing.

The efficacy and simplicity of the pledge are most happily described in the following passage, which is quite characteristic of the use to which he applied his familiarity with the Scriptures:—

I do not know how it is possible, but I can assure you there is very little difficulty in adhering to the pledge. I have been told by numbers in all parts of the kingdom that they had not the slightest trouble in adhering to the pledge, or the least wish to break their promise. The pledge appears to be, in fact, as fast binding as the strongest oath, though nothing could be more simple than it is in detail. Simplicity, however, never takes away from the efficacy of any proceeding. It reminds me of the case of Naaman the Syrian, who, when he went to the prophet to be cured of leprosy, was told to go and wash himself in the Jordan. He at first refused, on account of the simplicity of the cure, and said that he had rivers enough in Syria to bathe in if he thought bathing could do him any good; but his servant at length said to him, 'Father, if the prophet had bid thee do some great thing, surely thou shouldst have done it: how much rather what he now said to thee: wash, and thou shalt be clean.' Naaman then went and did as he was desired, and he was at once cured, and his skin became as the skin of an infant.

During his stay in Dublin, he was treated with the greatest distinction by persons of all classes and creeds, who vied with each other in evincing their respect for 'the moral regenerator of Ireland,' as he was now frequently termed. Several young men of the higher class, including a number of the students of Trinity College, took the pledge at his hands. But the most remarkable feature in his first visit to Dublin was thus, in two years after, described by himself when addressing a meeting in Glasgow :—

When in Dublin, administering the pledge in Beresford Place, I happened to allude to the necessity and importance of the ladies doing their duty in this respect, when I was told that if they could obtain a convenient place, a number of them would take the pledge. Well, a meeting was called in the Royal Exchange, and 500 ladies enrolled themselves teetotallers

CHAPTER X.

Admirable Conduct of the Irish Publicans—Curious Letter of a Publican—Respect of the Brewers and Distillers for Father Mathew—George Roe of Dublin—Father Mathew visits the College of Maynooth—Extraordinary Scene—The Duke of Leinster—Visits Carlow—Incidents of his Visit—Testimonies in the House of Lords.

THAT there should have been some opposition to the temperance cause, was not only what was natural to expect, but what Father Mathew had fully anticipated from the first. Strange to say, and much to their credit, the opposition, such as it was, did not arise from the publicans of the country. That they were seriously injured by the spread of temperance was certain, and that they would be injured still more was inevitable; but still their conduct throughout the entire continuance of the agitation, for a period of some eight years, was in the highest degree creditable to their good feeling. The following letter from a publican is amusing for more reasons than one, and will indicate the effect produced, even thus early, by the movement upon the retail business of the trade. It need scarcely be said that 'the respectable farmers' sons' referred to had improvised an ingenious excuse for not paying their lawful debts:—

Newbawn, New Ross: May 16, 1840.

REV. SIR,—I beg leave to inform you that about a year ago I commenced public business, in a house which cost me upwards of 100*l*. I gave credit to respectable farmers' sons to a considerable amount, but, in consequence of they having taken the Temperance pledge, they say that you would not allow them to pay for any kind of intoxicating liquor. I therefore humbly request that you will write a few lines to my parish priest, the Rev. Mr. Ryan, on the subject, as it will be the means of keeping myself and family from begging. *I do hereby pledge myself to resign this business the moment Mr. Ryan shall have received your letter, and that I will take the Temperance pledge myself, as my son has done.*

Awaiting with anxiety your favourable reply, I have the honour to be,

Rev. sir,

Your most obedient servant, &c.

MICHL. CANNON.

At a period subsequent to the date of this letter, Father Mathew thus alluded to the fact that numbers of the retailers throughout Ireland had joined his society, while he happily replied to those who interestedly cried out against it and its principles :—

There is no public good effected without some individual injury being occasioned ; the introduction of steam-engines, for example, put, necessarily, many hands out of employment ; the railroad conveyances have seriously affected stage-coach proprietors, and those who had hack-coaches and cars to let out for hire ; but the public is confessedly benefited by such improvements. In the making and vending of spirits and other deleterious drinks, many have previously made a livelihood, and some a fortune, whilst not a few of them have been sufferers to a considerable extent. *I am, however, happy to say that numbers of them have nobly come forward and joined our society.* To be sure, in every change, be they ever so pregnant with blessings for the community, some interested persons will be always found to stand up and oppose their progress ; and so it is with us. Some concerned in the manufacturing and retailing of deleterious drinks cry out incessantly against our society. They forcibly remind me of the conduct of the people of Ephesus to St. Paul, when he came among them to preach the Gospel, and diffuse the blessings of Christianity. Many of them were silversmiths, whose principal emolument arose from the making of statues of the goddess Diana (the idol then worshipped at Ephesus), and their constant cry then was, 'Great is Diana of the Ephesians!' Thus it is always with many in this country engaged in the spirit trade, who are heard to cry out incessantly, 'Great is Whisky! Potent is Ale! Great is Whisky! Potent is Ale!' But I say to you, 'Greater, far greater still, is Temperance—greater, far greater still, is Teetotalism.'

Many testimonies of the respect paid to Father Mathew by those who had large capital embarked in the manufacture of whisky and porter, and whose interests had been seriously injured by the spread of temperance, could be adduced; but that manifested towards him by one of the most eminent distillers, and one of the most honourable and high-minded men in Ireland—George Roe, of Dublin—made a deep impression upon the temperance leader, and is honourable to both. Father Mathew made a short visit to Dublin, with the object of collecting for his new church, which he had very much neglected, and in fact had been compelled to sacrifice to the cause to which he had now devoted all his energies. Among others on whom he called was George Roe, to whom, as he afterwards said, he 'appealed in fear and trembling.' The answer was characteristic of the princely-minded gentleman. 'No man,' said George Roe, 'has done me more injury than you have, Father Mathew; but I forget all in the great good you have done my country.' And he presented his proud and delighted applicant with a handsome donation.

And among the distillers and brewers of his own city he possessed many friends, to whom he was never afraid to present himself in the cause of charity. The Beamishes, the Crawfords, the Wises, the Murphys, the Hewitts, the Lanes, the Dalys, and others, never failed to evince their respect for Father Mathew; and when the citizens of Cork met, in 1857, to commemorate his memory by a public statue, Colonel Beamish, the head of the great establishment of Beamish and Crawford, was one of the most eloquent eulogists of his fame and character.

Father Mathew had now—indeed, even before the year 1840—become every inch a leader. Each day his ardour seemed to be, if possible, on the increase. Next to the duties of his ministry, the promotion and spread of temperance was the great object of his life. To widen, deepen, and strengthen the foundations of the great fabric which he had reared up ; to extend its influence among the higher classes ; to enlist men of talent and zeal in its advocacy ; to induce employers to set an example to their work-people ; to prevail on masters and mistresses to do the same to their servants ; to attract the young and innocent into the ranks ; to interest the feelings of his brother-priests in the progress of a cause which, as he said, next to that of religion, ought to be the one dearest to their hearts—in fine, to go on until the inhabitants of the country were gathered into one great temperance fold, was his fixed resolve. Assist the cause, and you complimented him. Do so even by an admission of its usefulness, and you pleased him ; do so by your own personal example, and there was no sacrifice which he would not willingly make for your advantage. But look coldly on it, and you pained him ; sneer at it, and you wounded him ; attack it, and you roused his indignation. As a leader, he valiantly stood in the van, and challenged the enemy to strike at his shield. Assail the society, and you assailed him ; attack its members, and it was he who felt the blow. The 'cause' had become part of his very being ; and this was one of the reasons of his marvellous success. Nor was he averse to meet his opponents, or to encounter their opposition by the trenchant logic of common sense, in such vigorous language as this :—

What filled our gaols and bridewells ? The effects of intoxication. What crowded the very lunatic asylums? Drunkenness and its effects. What fed the very gibbets ? Drunkenness. I never will give up until we are freed, with the blessing and the assistance of God, from all these deplorable evils ; and if I encounter during the progress of my career the sneers of some, and the contumelies of others, I must expect it. Some there are, and it is strange, look with an evil eye upon me. But cannot I say in the words of St. Paul, 'Am I your enemy, because I tell the truth ?' Let them show me anyone brought to misery or ruin by total abstinence. Show me anyone brought to gaol or bridewell by total abstinence. Show me anyone sent to the lunatic asylum from total abstinence. Oh, no! not a single one.

After having enrolled hundreds of thousands in various parts of the island—50,000 in one place, 100,000 in another—and become the moral leader of 2,000,000 of his countrymen, Father Mathew, in the June of 1840, wisely turned to the fountain source of the religious teaching of the Catholics of Ireland, all of whom he hoped to embrace in his society,—namely, to the College of Maynooth, to which he had been invited by the President. Within its walls were being trained the future priesthood of Ireland ; and if he could but enlist their young and warm hearts in his cause—the cause of the country they loved—it would be of greater permanent advantage than if another million, carried away by the impulse of the moment, were added to his ranks. His reception was an ovation, his success great beyond his most sanguine expectation. Of those outside the college walls no less than 35,000 were computed to have taken the pledge ; and as to what took place within its walls, the following, from a glowing description written by one of the students who was among the 'postulants,' and who was inflamed by the generous excitement of the hour, will afford the reader a vivid idea of the effect produced by this memorable visit, and of the extraordinary enthusiasm which the presence and preaching of Father Mather excited in the minds of hundreds of educated young men, whose days were divided between severe study and the practices of piety. If such were the effect produced by the Apostle in the halls of an ecclesiastical college, what must not it have been in the market-place, or on the hill side, with working people and peasants for his auditors? The student, who writes in all the impassioned ardour of his first feelings, thus depicts the scene :—

I had the good fortune to be present in the great hall of the college when the professors and students knelt down with edifying humility under the inspiring eloquence of an humble priest. The scene was majestically grand; it threw back the mind upon itself; it drew forth in full light all that is high and all that is amiable in the Irish heart; and to a day-dreamer, like myself, recalled in tender recollection the memory of other times, and looked for a while like their revival. On an elevated bench, which extends along one side of the quadrangular room, stood the Apostle of Temperance, 'reasoning of justice and temperance and the judgement to come.' The able and amiable Dr. Hughes, Bishop of New York, was present on every occasion, and showed by his feelings how deeply he loves the land of his birth. Mr. Mathew was supported on either side by the maters and professors of the college. The room was piled to the utmost extremity by the students and several distinguished strangers were occasionally present. A small vacant space under the bench was the hallowed spot consecrated to the virtue of temperance. The words of wisdom which he uttered were followed by deep emotion—they won the heart and subdued the judgement. No pen can describe, and none but an eye-witness can conceive, the stirring effect produced on a thoughtful spectator by the appeals of Theobald Mathew—the conflicting emotions of joy and astonishment in his audience, and the thunders of involuntary applause that greeted each new accession of converts as they moved deliberately forward in successive files, and with eager emulation, to the arena of virtue and heroic self-denial.

For the more convenient management of so great an institution the discipline of the college wisely separates the senior and junior parts of the community. The good man, after his first successful essay in the senior college, requested to be led to the junior house. He briefly stated the object of his mission. They listened in silent wonder; their innocence was startled by the turpitude of the unfelt gratification, and their humility was alarmed by the exalted act of virtue they were invited to imitate. No postulant appeared, and the holy man retired with perfect composure, but not without hope. Their own reflections created a speedy revolution of sentiment, and they requested him to return. He hurried with eager zeal to see them again, and the little Benjamins, as he endearingly called them, repaid his paternal solicitude by fully emulating, at each successive visit he paid them, the generous enthusiasm of their seniors.

The writer's feelings are further described by his own act, and the hopes to which the success of the day gave rise in the mind of an ardent youth :—

Yielding cheerfully myself to the many generous examples I had seen in the town and in the college, I did what an Irishman should do under such circumstances. I must be like them, said I; I will do as they have done; after ages will bless this day; and, folding my arms in deep deliberation, I knelt amongst the crowd, I registered in heaven my solemn promise of total and perpetual abstinence, and got the benediction of Father Mathew.

The fruits of this visit to Maynooth were 35,000 of the people, 8 professors of the college, and 250 students.

During his visit to Maynooth he was the guest of the Duke of Leinster, at Carton. This amiable nobleman—'Ireland's only Duke,' as he was termed by O'Connell—received Father Mathew with the greatest distinction. Indeed, it might be said with justice that his attention to him was extraordinary; for the housekeeper of Carton said she never received an order as to the arrangements or preparations which she should make for the reception of the most distinguished nobleman, even for the Lord-Lieutenant; but when Father Mathew was expected, the duke requested that she would take 'particular care' in her arrangements for his reception. If he were a crowned monarch instead of a lowly friar, he could not have been treated with greater respect and distinction by his noble host.

In the month of October of the same year, he visited Carlow, near which town there is a lay and ecclesiastical college, in which the illustrious Dr. Doyle had been a professor many years before. The meetings were held in the cathedral; and such was the enthusiasm excited by the addresses of the Apostle of Temperance, and the ardour of the thousands who rushed forward with impetuosity to adopt the pledge, that the students of the college speedily caught the contagion, and made known their desire to imitate the general example. Father Mathew was delighted at the intelligence, it being that, of all others, which he most longed to hear. He appointed to meet the students in the evening, and having dined at a late hour in the college, with a large party assembled to do him honour, he proceeded to the refectory of the ecclesiastical students when their supper was over. Several of the lay students were admitted on the occasion, as they had expressed a wish to take the pledge at the same time. He won the hearts of the students by his affectionate manner, as he went from table to table, and enquired of them of their parents and friends, many of whom he had personally known, and spoke to them of their town, or their parish, or of something in which they were interested. He then addressed them on the object of his visit.

My dear young friends (said he) I am inexpressibly delighted at hearing that many among you are disposed to take the pledge. I am well aware no one present requires words of advice or encouragement from me, as a necessity does not exist for your becoming pledged tc the principles or practice of total abstinence. But your example will have a powerful influence on many others, who will be induced to emulate your virtuous and noble resolution, either through motives of religion and moral purification, or from necessity and a distrust in their own weakness in withstanding those strong temptations to indulge in excess, which were so frequently, and are still, presented in Ireland. The humbler classes in this country naturally look to their clergy for good example as for direction, and hence it affords me the greatest possible delight to find the young aspirants to the priesthood, and also the young gentlemen of the lay college, prepared to make sacrifices which cannot fail to give great edification to the people.

Father Mathew then administered the pledge to a considerable number, and requested that if any others desired to do the same on the morrow, they would do so on the steps of the high altar in the cathedral, 'in presence of the assembled thousands of their countrymen;' and he added, 'The Almighty would bestow His choicest graces and blessings on them, in return for their generous and sublime resolve.'

Those of the ecclesiastical students who had not taken the pledge on this occasion, held serious communion with themselves during the night, and asked for direction from on high. The result of their earnest deliberation was, that a largo additional number resolved on affording an example in their own persons. A respectable clergyman, who was then one of the students of the college, has furnished the author with an interesting sketch of Father Mathew's mission to Carlow, from which is taken the account of what happened on the following days:—

On the day following, the students who had resolved on taking the pledge ranged themselves on the steps of the platform before the high altar, whilst a vast multitude assembled in the nave and transepts of the cathedral. With a feeling of proud gratulation, Father Mathew pointed to the band of students who were prepared to set an example to the people, and after an animated address to the congregation, the candidates knelt down and repeated the words of the Total Abstinence pledge after the great representative of the temperance movement. Immediately afterwards, the good Father, full of emotion and bending over each student in succession, embraced him warmly, and kissed him on the cheek, whilst he repeated words of the following import on passing before the line of kneeling ecclesiastics: 'God bless you, my dear sir! God bless you! God bless you, my dear young gentlemen!' Before leaving Carlow, he requested a list of the names of all those students to be left with his secretary, and no long interval elapsed until each one received from him the gift of a silver medal, as a *souvenir* of the occasion, and as a token of the Very Rev. Father's grateful appreciation of this accession to the ranks of his teetotallers.

Whilst successive congregations filled the cathedral at intervals during each day, the late Most Rev. Dr. Healy, Bishop of the dioceses of Kildare and Leighlin, was in almost constant attendance, as a spectator, whilst he seemed truly anxious in every way to promote the success of the good Father's mission. Although the pious missionary frequently disclaimed all pretentions to the possession of supernatural or miraculous powers, yet such was the faith and fervour of the peasantry, that many afflicted with various diseases felt desirous of receiving the pledge at his hands, and of obtaining his benediction, in confident expectation that they would experience instant relief and a permanent cure. In very many instances, by a sort of preternatural effort, cripples were seen casting away their staves and crutches, as no longer needful, whilst they walked erect, or nearly so, to the great astonishment of all present, Protestants as well as Catholics. In those instances, pious ejaculations resounded through the cathedral, both from the afflicted patients themselves and from the crowds that flocked around them, within and without the sacred building. For any restoration of this kind, Father Mathew invariably requested the people to give all praise and glory to God, under whom he was an unworthy instrument, permitted to exercise the duties of a holy ministry, and to effect only what he believed to be a great social reformation.

All day on Tuesday the crowds pouring into the cathedral were in no manner diminished, and the sun went down without the slightest interruption to the immense mental and physical exertions of Father Mathew.

At an early hour on Wednesday he was similarly employed; but his engagements elsewhere obliged him to leave by the midday coach, which awaited his arrival on the Dublin road. The good Father sent his luggage forward, and remained himself in the cathedral to the last possible moment, when he told the people he must absolutely leave, but he promised that he would take the first available opportunity to return again and resume the labours of his abundant harvest in Carlow. The coach had been already delayed beyond its time, and Father Mathew, with a hurried grasp of the hand to a few of the numerous friends about him, and a courteous adieu waved to others, ran through the College Park by the nearest route to his destination. Groups of men had contrived to scale the college walls, and these threw themselves on their knees before him, asking to take the pledge before he should leave. In breathless haste, it was administered in a number of instances, and whilst he was in rapid motion across the park. Others, again, had passed round the road to the coach, where a great multitude of men, women, and children were collected. It was utterly impossible to comply with their urgent requests to be enrolled, as the coach-driver was obliged to ply his whip with vigour, to make good his time between the intermediate stages to his ultimate destination.

On Friday, July 10, 1840, the Marquis of Westmeath asked a question in the House of Lords, which elicited valuable testimony in favour of the temperance movement. He called attention to what he termed a 'proclamation,' which had been issued by the Lord Lieutenant of Ireland (Lord Ebrington), in which this passage occurred: 'To the benefit which the temperance pledge has conferred upon Ireland, in the improved habits of the people, and the diminution of outrage, His Excellency bears a willing and grateful testimony.' He desired to learn whether this proclamation was authentic or not.

The Marquis of Normanby could give no official answer on the subject; but he would say, from all the information which he had received with respect to the movement then going on in Ireland, he was convinced that a most beneficial change had been effected amongst the people by the pledge.

The Earl of Devon said that, so far as he had an opportunity of judging, a great and substantial good had been done. I believe, continued the noble earl, that it has been effected by perfectly legitimate means and legitimate exertions, and that it is as little connected with fanaticism, with party, or with appeals to religious feelings of a peculiar character, as could be imagined. I have myself heard Father Mathew address the people; and his manner is such as any noble lord who hears me might adopt in addressing a public body in support of such an object. It is, I conceive, *pessimi exempli* to speak in reproachful terms of that which has been productive of very great good.

The Earl of Wicklow thought that the temperance societies were calculated to effect much good; and the individual who had devoted himself to the furtherance of the temperance movement deserved the greatest praise for what he was doing.

CHAPTER XI.

Other Valuable Testimonies—The Marquis of Lansdowne—The Duke of Devonshire—The Traveller Kohl—Mrs. S. C. Hall—Father Mathew's Despondency—Dean Coll's Consolation—Stopping the Royal Mail.

DURING the year 1840, Father Mathew received the most flattering and consolatory expressions of approval from some of the foremost men of the day; for, in spite of the triumphant nature of his progress, and the love and admiration of the people, he was occasionally depressed by some sneer, taunt, or false accusation, wantonly or maliciously levelled at the society, its principles, its practice, or its usefulness. Such testimonies, then, as the following, from the Marquis of Lansdowne, which awaited him in Cork, on his return from an arduous campaign, were like sunlight to his soul. If he were easily depressed—we do not by any means say daunted—he was easily cheered and encouraged. He had plenty of courage, both moral and physical, and no lack of self-will—even a strong tinge of obstinacy; but he possessed the sensitive heart of a woman, and a susceptibility that at times became almost morbid in its intensity. He took great pride in the letter which we now quote. This letter was personally handed by the noble writer to Mr. Donnelly, who acted as one of the secretaries in charge of the temperance register and other books. Donnelly was on this day enjoying unusual idleness, it being generally known that Father Mathew was absent, and was not to return for some days. There was no one in the little parlour save the book-keeper, when a quiet-looking, neatly-dressed, elderly gentleman entered the apartment, and, taking a seat near the window, fell into pleasant conversation with its idle occupant. He asked him a variety of questions, as to the progress of the cause, the number on the roll, and the effects already produced; and made special enquiries as to the labours and charities, as well as the daily life, of Father Mathew; all of which questions were frankly and unreservedly answered. The quiet-looking and kindly-spoken gentleman appeared much pleased at the information afforded him, and, on rising to take his leave, he handed his card to Donnelly, requesting him to present it to Father Mathew. Donnelly looked at the card, and was 'struck of a heap,' as he said, at having treated a great nobleman as if he were 'nobody at all;' and he stammered out an apology for his apparent want of respect. 'Not at all, my good sir,' said the marquis; 'you owe me no apology whatever; you have nothing to blame yourself for; you answered all my questions freely and satisfactorily; and perhaps had you been told who I was, I might not have learned as much as I am happy to know.' The marquis then left the house; but he had not gone ten steps from the door, when he turned back, and, drawing a letter, which he had ready in the breast-pocket of his coat, he handed it to Donnelly, saying: 'Give that to Father Mathew, with the Marquis of Lansdowne's kindest wishes.' This was the letter:—

Cork: Sept. 15, 1840.

REV. SIR.—I am near the conclusion of a journey through a considerable portion of the south of Ireland, in the course of which I have myself had, everywhere, repeated occasion to observe a most remarkable change for the better in the appearance of the population, and to be assured by others on whom I could rely of an equally manifest improvement in their character and conduct, produced by the extraordinary success of your unremitting endeavour to introduce amongst them confirmed habits of temperance and self-control.

I had hoped to have had an opportunity, at this place, of expressing to you personally the deep sense I entertain, both as an Irish proprietor and a public servant, of the value of your exertions, obviously conducive, as they must prove under all circumstances, to the maintenance of peace and order, and to a greater developement than could by any other means be attained, of every social virtue.

Your temporary absence from home has alone prevented my doing so, and I trust I may be permitted to take the only method in my power of recording these sentiments in a mode that may not be disagreeable to you, by inclosing a draft for 100*l.*, and requesting the favour of you to apply it to the use of any one of the institutions for the benefit of your poorer countrymen in which you take an interest, and which, in your judgement, stands most in need of pecu niary assistance.

I am, rev. sir, with sincere respect,

Your obedient servant,

LANSDOWNE.

Rev. T. Mathew.

The writer of the above kindly letter is now no more, having died in the early part of this year, at the venerable age of 82 years.

Among the other distinguished personages who sought the acquaintance of Father Mathew about this time, was the late Duke of Devonshire, a nobleman of princely character, and one of the best and kindest of the landlords of Ireland, in which country he possessed vast estates. The duke, who was then stopping at the Imperial Hotel, in Cork, wrote a courteous letter to Father Mathew, requesting that he would honour him by a visit. Father Mathew at once availed himself of the invitation, and waited on his Grace, who received him with every mark of respect. The interview was equally agreeable to both, and was the commencement of a friendship which was sincere and earnest to the last. The duke, who was every inch a gentleman—a gentleman whose courtesy and kindness sprang from goodness of heart—was charmed with Father Mathew. He admired him particularly for his disinterestedness in embarking in an undertaking which he knew must entail injury upon his own family, whose interests he sacrificed to the public good. Having seen and spoken with the temperance leader, the duke no longer wondered at the influence which he exercised, or the success which he had achieved. He said he found him to be a man of such divine countenance, and of a manner so marvellously winning, that he could now easily understand how the people were moved, as by an impulse, to fall down before him. The impression produced upon the duke by this interview was communicated to the writer by a gentleman intimately connected with his Grace, and who was present on the occasion.

The descriptions given of Father Mathew at this period of his life were sometimes both felicitous and accurate. Perhaps that written by the Russian traveller Kohl is among the best. It is in these words :—

> He is decidedly a man of a distinguished appearance, and I was not long in comprehending the influence which it was in his power to exercise over the people. The multitude require a handsome and imposing person in the individual who is to lead them, and Father Mathew is unquestionably handsome. He is not tall, he is about the same height and figure as Napoleon, and is, throughout, well built and well proportioned. He has nothing of the meagre, haggard Franciscan monk about him; but, on the contrary, without being exactly corpulent. his figure is well rounded, and in excellent condition. His countenance is fresh and beaming with health. His movements and address are simple and unaffected, and altogether he has something about him that wins for him the goodwill of those he addresses. His features are regular, and full of noble expression, of mildness and indomitable firmness. His eyes are large, and he is apt to keep his glance fixed for a long time on the same object. His forehead is straight, high, and commanding, and his nose—a part of the face which in some expresses such intense vulgarity, and in others so much nobleness and delicacy—is particularly handsome, though somewhat too aquiline. His mouth is small and well proportioned, and his chin round, projecting, firm, and large, like Napoleon's.

Mrs. S. C. Hall, who enjoyed his intimate friendship, presents him in his moral as well as his physical aspect :—

> The expression of his countenance is peculiarly mild and gracious. His manner is persuasive to a degree, simple and easy and humble,

without a shadow of affectation, and his voice is low and musical, such as moves men. A man more naturally fitted to obtain influence over a people easily led, and proverbially swayed by the affections, we have never encountered. No man has borne his honours more meekly, encountered opposition with greater gentleness or forbearance, or disarmed hostility by weapons better suited to a Christian.

Occasionally the despondency, which was somewhat constitutional with Father Mathew, was displayed in a manner sufficiently marked to excite the attention of his audience. His address in Limerick, in the October of 1841, partook largely of the gloom that for the moment seemed to pervade his mind. It may have been the necessary consequence of the tremendous labour of mind and body to which he was at the time exposed, it being then in the very whirl and rush of the movement, to which each day imparted additional strength and velocity; or it may have arisen from the slightest remarks of some anonymous opponent, or the venomous sneers of some malicious caviller. The passage quoted will indicate the irritation under which it was spoken :—

But though, in becoming a teetotaller, the individual taking the pledge becomes a new man—though he has ideas of self-respect, and decorum, and propriety which he had not experienced before, and though he is no longer the reckless and improvident character he had been, yet I must say there are persons who expect too much from teetotallers, and who think that they should all be perfect. Their faults are magnified, whilst their virtues are shaded; the lapses they make are invested with attributes that do not belong to them, whilst the good they do is never taken into consideration. It is thought by those who are thus severe upon the teetotallers, that human nature does not belong to humble life—but I say that the cabin beneath whose lowly roof it is supposed no human sentiment is cherished, covers as much of the workings of the heart, as yonder proud mansion that graces and adorns the banks of your majestic Shannon. I have been blamed for many matters connected with the temperance society, for which I think no blame should be attributed to me, or to those who are blamed with me. I cannot express the sentiment of sovereign contempt which I entertain for those who thus betray the feelings that agitate them. Some of them raise the cry; and the least vice they themselves have is their utter want of every virtue. Some others say that I should prevent females to attend *soirées*, while their own daughters and wives, perhaps, mingle in the crowded ball-room, and whirl in the maze of the profane waltz. Some say that I should prevent persons to sit in their temperance rooms and enjoy each other's society in that respect; whilst they themselves, the victims of drunkenness, may be seen reeling through the streets to their homes, after spending their nights in the tap-room or tavern. They will not see the frailties of teetotallers as they see the frailties of other men.

He then talked of friends who had left his side and faltered in the race, and spoke in a tone of such despondency as excited the sympathy of his listeners, and, among the others, of Dean Coll, the Parish Priest of Newcastle, a man of great learning, and who possessed more of the readiness and manner of the popular orator than many of his contemporaries. The Dean was a staunch supporter of the cause, and a firm friend and ally of its leader; and thus, in a spontaneous outburst, which at the moment produced an electrical effect—the whole audience being charged with the right sympathy—he offered that consolation to his friend of which he stood then so much in need:—

Mr. Mathew told of friends leaving him. No friend, my dearest friend (said the venerable Dean), shall leave you. Fear not—no friend shall depart from you. There is no man who is not the subject of critical and vile and slanderous malignity when he rises to dignity; but I do not hesitate to denounce it folly in any man who doubts that you are the commanded messenger of God. Enemies, you say, pursue you. Fear them not, wherever they be. It is the mark of God's servant to meet with the cross, and to be obliged to bear it. But, dearest friend and brother in the sanctuary, to go on in the glorious mission for which you are destined, be not troubled at the persecution of enemies; in every peril God shall be your shield, and your country shall be your protector. (Here the whole company stood up and responded to the sentiment by an outburst of enthusiasm seldom witnessed.) No! you need have no fear. You are sustained by the sanction and cooperation of those whose opinion you should prize. The venerated Bishop of the diocese would be present this evening, were he able to be so. The Catholic prelates throughout the land were the active cooperators in the movement. No; fear not! You have the support of all whose support is worthy of appreciation —pursue your way, as you have begun it, and as you have gone on, until a drunkard shall not be seen to reel through the land we love.

The reader may imagine the effect produced by this passage upon a meeting composed exclusively of those who respected Father Mathew as a leader, venerated him as a priest, and loved him as a man. Father Mathew never forgot that evening.

A circumstance that occurred in the town of Athy, will give an idea of the eagerness with which the people availed themselves of every opportunity to take the pledge. At this time, the Great Southern and Western Railway of Ireland was scarcely hatched in the brain of its projector, and the 'mail' was the quickest mode of conveyance between the cities and chief towns of the country. The mail coach between Dublin and Cork, when coming from Dublin, stopped at Athy sufficiently long to admit of the passengers breakfasting in the hotel of that town. On the day in question, the coach stopped as usual; but one of the inside passengers having been recognised by the group then invariably awaiting the arrival and the departure of the 'mail,' a shout of joy was raised, which resounded through the quiet little town; and in a minute the cry 'Father Mathew is at the hotel!' was heard almost by every human being of the entire population. Soon a dense crowd of some thousands assembled; and by the time the coach ought to have started, that vehicle was wedged round so completely, that to think of moving it one inch from the hotel door until Father Mathew had administered the pledge to those who now clamoured for it at his hands, was quite out of the question. Father Mathew had no desire to delay the coach, which was, in fact, stopping the principal correspondence of the south of Ireland; but what could he do, but endeavour to diminish the numbers by giving them the pledge, and thus get rid of the obstruction? And he at once commenced to do so with more than ordinary expedition. But as fast as he got rid of one large batch, another much larger took its place—and all this time the crowd becoming more dense, in consequence of frequent accessions from the surrounding country ; so that it positively was not until after a delay of *five hours*, during which Father Mathew worked as he never worked before in his life, that the Royal Mail was well out of the town of Athy. The incident made considerable noise at the time, and some of the papers were very indignant with the 'friar,' and his audacity in stopping Her Majesty's Mail, and interrupting the correspondence of the country ; and one journal went so far, in its wrath, as to suggest that he should not be suffered to travel by a similar conveyance again. The then agent in Cork* sent the article—it was from an English paper—to Mr. Purcell, the proprietor of the coaches and contractor for carrying the mails ; and the reply which that gentleman made was, to enclose to his agent a letter for Father Mathew, in which he assured the audacious stopper of Her Majesty's Mail, that he would confer a favour on him, Peter Purcell, 'by making free use of all his coaches to further the holy cause of temperance.' This liberal offer, of which Father Mathew gratefully availed himself, was of considerable advantage to the latter, as the coaches of Mr. Purcell traversed the principal highways of the kingdom.

The same privilege was granted by Mr. Bianconi, the well-known owner of the public cars of the country.

In the public Press of Ireland Father Mathew had a powerful and consistent supporter. No matter what its politics, it advocated the spread of temperance, and spoke with respect of the motives and services of its distinguished advocate. Irish journalists generally adopted this policy and tone from an earnest desire to promote so good and useful a cause,

* Mr. Anthony Murray.

and out of sincere respect for the character of the man ; but it occasionally did happen that the opportunity of bestowing praise on Father Mathew was availed of to strike a blow at another great Irishman, who rivalled the temperance leader in his hold on the affections of the mass of his countrymen, and whose impassioned appeals in favour of legislative independence produced a still greater impression upon their minds, than the milder and less exciting addresses of the moral reformer. Thus it was that not only did Father Mathew receive a large share of praise and encouragement on his own account, but he was indirectly indebted to Daniel O'Connell for no small amount in addition. With the conductors of most of the Irish journals he was on terms of friendship. Those who opposed his religious faith, or who were in constant antagonism to the active popular political movement of the day, experienced genuine pleasure in meeting so good a man on neutral ground ; and once that they had formed any acquaintance with him, the charm of his manner soon ripened the acquaintance into friendship. As for the popular journalists, who were mostly of the same faith as himself, they united their sympathy and their personal affection with their support. Not a few of the leading journalists of Ireland had joined the society; and there was not a newspaper in the kingdom in which a considerable proportion of the staff—Editors, Reporters, Clerks, Compositors, Messengers, Printers' Devils, and all—had not taken the pledge, and did not, at one time or other, possess the temperance medal.

Father Mathew was intimately acquainted with the young gentlemen who attended his meetings in the capacity of reporters, and he was ready on every occasion to show them attention and kindness. The Cork newspapers were then, as they are now, spiritedly conducted, and commanded efficient reporting staffs, every member of which was known to the 'Apostle' as his 'dear young friend.' Among others in whom he was sincerely interested was L.——, who was a first-rate hand at his profession, and whose attachment to Father Mathew was observable in the care he bestowed on his speeches. On one occasion L—— went down to Fermoy, to report a 'great demonstration,' and he put up at the same hotel with Father Mathew. Poor L—— was not remarkable for his strength of mind or tenacity of purpose, and, yielding either to the weakness of his nature, or the solicitations of his more sceptical friends, he, to use the popular phrase of the day, 'broke the pledge:' he, however, insisted he had only 'surrendered it.' At any rate, he was not then a 'teetotaller,' though he did not think it necessary to apprise his friend Father Mathew of that fact. L—— was at his little table, on the platform, working diligently with the pencil at times, and taking his leisure at others, as some well-membered passage was repeated by the speaker. Father Mathew was urging on his hearers the fact that no one had suffered in health or pocket from having taken his advice; and happening to glance at L——'s handsome face, he found, as he believed, a happy illustration of the health which the 'steadfast teetotaller' was sure to obtain and retain; and placing his hand fondly on the head of the horrified L——, he thus continued, to his victim's ineffable confusion—'Look, my dear friends!—here is a fine specimen of a faithful teetotaller (L—— blushing deeply)—he never tastes anything stronger than water or tea (L——'s confusion increasing). There is the hue of health on his countenance—not the flush of strong drink (L—— red as a peony, and his pencil paralysed). He, my dear friends, will never, please God! barter his moral independence for a fleeting gratification. He will not be like Esau, who sold his birthright for a mess of pottage (L—— wishing devoutly that the ground might open and swallow him, or that, at the very least, some fearful accident might happen to the platform). No, my dear people, my young friend here is a faithful follower of the cause, and will never turn his back on the pure and spotless banner.' Fortunately, here the personal allusion ceased, and the fondling hand was taken from the head of the victim ; for had the torture continued a minute longer, as L—— afterwards assured his friends, something dreadful would have happened him. It was, however, not all over with him yet. Father Mathew and L—— breakfasted the next morning at the same table During breakfast, L—— desired the waiter to bring him his bill. 'Oh, no, my dear,' said Father Mathew, 'you are my guest here—you must not pay anything.' 'Thank you, sir, not at all—I assure you I must pay my own bill. Waiter, bring it to me at once.' 'Waiter, do no such thing. Everything must be included in mine. I could not think of allowing it.' L—— made a last desperate effort—'I assure you Father Mathew, Mr. —— (the proprietor of the journal he represented) would be very indignant with me if I allowed you to pay my bill. Waiter, bring it to me.' 'Do what I insist upon, waiter,' said Father Mathew, with a manner that was not to be disputed. L—— looked at the waiter, and the waiter looked at L——, and L——'s glance of despair was only matched by the waiter's look of comical perplexity. Before the document respecting which this struggle took place was produced, L——was seated on 'Bian,' * his back turned to the hotel. During the previous evening and night, poor L—— had sought consolation in rather deep potations ; and in the bill which was thrust into the pocket of the Apostle of Temperance there was a fearful list of 'materials' for whisky punch, and 'goes' of brandy and water ! For a month after, L—— fled from the face of Father Mathew ; but when they afterwards met, the latter did not, by the slightest sign, exhibit his knowledge of the fact that poor weak L——had sold his birthright for a mess of pottage.

It was somewhat about the same time that two members of the Cork press were sent to an important meeting of the same character. Having performed their duty, they imme-

* A popular abbreviation for Bianconi's car.

diately drove to a distant village, at which the night mail was to stop, and in which they had taken their seats; and they dined, and then wrote out their report. At the appointed time the mail arrived, and they occupied their places. There was but one other inside passenger, and he was muffled up in a corner, and was quite silent, and was supposed by the friends to be indulging in a comfortable nap. The friends, as soon as they were well settled, commenced a lively chat. At length, one asked the other this question—'Jack, what do you think Father Mathew is doing now?' 'What is he doing?—why, taking a good stiff tumbler of punch, such as you and I, Dick, will take, please the Fates, at the next stage.' 'Punch! nonsense, man. Surely you are jesting. You do n't think Father Mathew is such a hypocrite.' 'Faith I do n't care what he is, my boy; but I am sure the jolly old buffer is taking a stiff tumbler at this moment—and I wish I had the same.' When the coach arrived at the next stage, the gentlemen of the press got out, and, entering the inn, called for the promised beverage. They had got through about half of their smoking tumblers, when the guard entered, saying, 'Come, gentlemen, time is up; please make haste.' 'Hallo, guard!' said Jack, the more convivial of the two, 'take something.' 'I thank you kindly, sir, no—I'm temperate.' 'You, coachman—won't you have a drop this cold night?' 'No, sir, thank you all the same. I hav' n't tasted anything for years, and, please God, I never will. But I 'm as much obliged to you, sir, as if I took what 's in the house,' said the man of the whip.' 'Tell me, guard, who is that you have in the coach with us? Do 'nt you know him, sir? He 's one the country ought to be proud of. It 's Father Mathew!' It is not necessary to represent with accuracy the exclamations uttered by the doubter of the consistency of the temperance leader; it is enough to say that he precipitately abandoned the remainder of his punch, and, scrambling up to a seat behind the coachman, thus accomplished the rest of his jour ney. The other, on entering the coach, received a warm shake of the hand; but not a word was said by Father Mathew of the conversation which he no doubt fully heard, For he asked where was Mr.——; to which the reply was made, that 'the inside of the coach did not agree with him, and that he preferred the fresh air.' The sceptic must certainly have been peculiar in his tastes, for the night was frightfully raw.

To one of these two gentlemen of the press a circumstance occurred, shortly after, in London, which was near having been attended with unpleasant consequences, and which strongly impressed him with the value of temperance, and the danger that might arise from too intimate an association with those who drank in excess. Both of the actors in the scene are since dead, but both were personally and intimately known to me for several years. Mr. ——, who held the position of assistant-editor of one of the Cork journals, determined to retire from the drudgery of the press, and establish himself in London in some other profession or business. The companion of his journey to the metropolis was Richard ——, who had for many years occupied the position of chief of the reporting staff on the same paper, and had just received an engagement as a Gallery Reporter on a leading morning journal. Richard at once commenced his duties, for which he was eminently capable; but Mr. —— determined to indulge himself a little before he seriously set about his new profession. Drink was his besetting weakness. Differing, however, from most Irishmen, he did not drink out of good fellowship, or from a love of company: his indulgence was solitary and selfish. 'Richard,' said Mr. —— one day to his friend, who lodged with him in the same house, 'I wish you would take charge of some money for me.' 'Why should I take charge of it?—can't you put it in the bank?' replied Richard. 'I don't like putting it in the bank, and you will oblige me if you keep it for me; it's only for a few days.' 'Be it so,' said Richard. The amount was between 200*l.* and 300*l.*, and consisted of bank bills, notes, gold, and silver. Honest Richard had as little notion of money matters as he had of the philosophy of Confucius; but, acting upon what seemed to him like a presentiment, he drew up a docket, in which he represented the different sums that made up the whole amount entrusted to his care. He then deposited the precious charge in a box in his bedroom, and thought no more about the matter. Scarcely had Mr. —— placed his money in safety, than he made elaborate preparations for a prolonged and systematic debauch. Wines, brandies, spirits of all kinds, were profusely ordered and sent in. For a fortnight, or longer, the solitary drinker continued his carouse. At the end of that time he was seen one morning to descend the stairs, dressed with more than ordinary neatness—for he was quite a dandy in dress—and to leave the house, with steady step, but with face of deadly paleness. Richard, after his previous night's work in the Gallery, resolved to refresh himself by a ramble in the parks. On his return, he was surprised to find the entire household assembled in the common sitting-room, and two strange men with them. No sooner had the unsuspecting reporter entered the apartment, than one of the strange men deliberately placed his back against the door, as if to bar all egress; while the other, addressing Richard, asked him if he were Mr. ——. 'That's my name,' said Richard. 'Then, sir, I am sorry to tell you I am here from Bow Street, on a serious charge against you,' said the officer. 'What,' said the Irishman, 'have the girls been saying anything against me?' Much more serious than that, sir; Mr. —— has charged you with embezzlement!' 'Good God!' exclaimed Richard, now thoroughly alarmed, and turning to Mr. ——, who sat at the table, his face pale as that of the dead, 'could *you* have done so?' 'It grieved me much to do so,' replied Mr. ——, with the solemn air of a Brutus about condemning his son to death; 'but it was my duty, Richard, and I could not avoid it.' 'Did Mr.

—— entrust you with his money?' enquired the officer. 'He did certainly,' was the reply; 'but come with me, gentlemen, and I will show you where it is.' Most fortunately, the money was correct to the shilling. 'In the name of God, what induced you to make such a charge against me?' asked the poor young fellow of the wretched drunkard, when all had again returned to the sitting-room. 'My dear Dick,' sobbed Mr. ——, bursting into a flood of tears; 'I would trust you with a thousand pounds!' The officers retired in unutterable disgust; and, ere an hour had passed, Richard had established himself in other lodgings, and had 'registered a vow in heaven' as to three things—to adhere to the pledge for twelve months—never again to take the charge of any man's money—and to keep as far away as possible from one liable to an attack of *delirium tremens.* The vow was religiously observed.

As may be supposed, there was much similarity in many of Father Mathew's speeches, for he delivered hundreds of such in the year. By local allusions, and illustrations borrowed from some circumstance or event of the day, he imparted as much novelty to each speech as the nature of the subject well admitted of; still, to an accustomed ear, especially that of a reporter, the general similarity was obvious. A very young and talented member of the Cork press, and who is now making for himself a reputation in the very highest class of periodical literature, was specially instructed to attend a certain meeting, and to be sure and give Father Mathew 'a full and careful report.' The meeting was held on Sunday—a beautiful bright day in summer, which invited to pleasure and enjoyment—but it was not honoured by the attendance of the representative of the palladium of our liberties. He was far away, outside the harbour, amidst the young and the gay, revelling in the enjoyment of his self-given holiday. Nevertheless, the next issue of the paper contained a long, elaborate, and careful report of Father Mathew's speech of the day before, which, besides arguing the question with more than usual force, contained some admirable descriptions and powerful appeals, and was enriched by several local allusions and personal references of a complimentary character. Thus, for instance, the people of the parish and their 'beloved pastor' came in for more than their share of affectionate eulogy; even the band was praised for 'its delightful performance,' and 'the fidelity of the members of the reading-room' was held up to all societies as a shining example. The speech told wonderfully. 'Really,' said a knowing one, 'that's the best speech Father Mathew ever delivered.' And Father Mathew thought the same; for when he next met the reporter, he shook him by both hands, saying, 'My dear J——, that was a most beautiful report. I do'nt think I was ever better or more faithfully reported in my life.' The modest reporter blushed, and answered, 'I was afraid, sir, you might not have been pleased with it.' 'Pleased, my dear! why it was literal. Only it was rather better done than I spoke it.' The mind of the reporter was much relieved by this assurance; for the report had been prepared the day *before* the meeting was held, and was borrowed from Father Mathew's former speeches, which were contained in the newspaper file. It was ingeniously supplied with such novelties, in the way of courtesy and compliment and illustration, as the reporter knew would have to be introduced on the occasion. It was not until many years after that the proprietor of the paper heard of this ingenious instance of 'literal' reporting.

CHAPTER XII.

His Reception in the North — Expenses of his Mission — His Unceasing Generosity — The Temperance Bands — The Appeal and Response — The 'Poor Dhrummer' — A Village Tea-party — 'Beautiful Music' — Who paid for the Music.

FATHER MATHEW'S success in the Province of Ulster was far greater than he or his friends could have anticipated ; as, from various reasons, into which it is not within the scope of this work to enter, the spirit of sectarian strife was more active and acrimonious in that portion of Ireland than in the provinces of the West and South. There was one reason for the existence of this feeling in the North, which did not apply to the other provinces—the population were, at least in some counties, about equally divided between the different religious denominations. Thus, while, as a rule, the Western and Southern counties were Catholic, the Northern counties had a nearly equally balanced number of followers belonging to the two great denominations, of Protestant and Catholic, including Presbyterians under the head Protestant.* It must be admitted that no other Catholic priest could have succeeded in conciliating the goodwill, and indeed in arousing the enthusiasm, of the sturdy Presbyterian and the strong Orange Protestant of Ulster. Had Father Mathew been a controversialist, who had wrestled in theological conflict, like his distinguished predecessor Father O'Leary, not only would the heart but the very highways of Ulster have been closed against him. But, as before stated,

* By the census of 1861, the three Churches were thus represented in Ulster : Catholics, 963,687 ; Protestants, 390,130 ; Presbyterians, 511,371.

polemical controversy was repugnant to his nature; and strife of any kind, especially in the name of religion, he would neither take part in, nor do anything to promote. His character had gone before him, and his presence accomplished the rest. As he said himself at a meeting in Newry, in 1841, to which he had been invited by the Right Rev. Dr. Blake, Catholic Bishop of Dromore—'that Bishop after St. Paul's own heart,' as Father Mathew described him—the progress of temperance in the North had been one continued triumph. 'I had, it is true,' he added, the aid of the press of Ulster, of all parties; and I rejoice that some of the most talented conductors of that press are here to-night.' On the same occasion he thus described the manner of his reception in the North:—

We had no military, no police, no constables; but, in lieu of them, we had several excellent young gentlemen from Belfast, Lisburn, and other places, who kept order. I must here speak particularly of young Mr. Hancock, of Lurgan, whose efforts in the preservation of the peace, and in aid of the cause, were most laudable. I had the happiness of being the guest of his amiable mother, whilst in Lurgan; and I had the honour, also, of being the guest of the noble proprietor, Lord Lurgan. Col. Blacker there met me, and read to me a beautiful poetical tribute to the success of teetotalism, during the reading of which every eye in that gilded saloon beamed with pleasure. In coming originally to the North, I had great difficulties to contend with. I was told I would be assassinated in Ulster; but I had confidence in my cause, as I came in the name of the Lord, proclaiming aloud, 'Glory to God in the highest, and peace on earth, to men goodwill.' I knew the people of Ulster were too virtuous to refuse me their aid in this total abstinence movement, on any sectarian grounds. I had also too much reliance on the honour of Irishman to suppose the people of this province would arise in their might, and crush one humble individual, who was merely trying to promote public morality. In the words of the poet, slightly altered, I may say, in conclusion—

Blessed for ever the day I relied
On Ulster's honour and Ulster's pride.

On a subsequent occasion he referred to his further experience of the kindness and good feeling almost universally manifested towards him by persons of the most opposite opinions on all matters of importance, and showed how, by his tact and good nature, he converted into a compliment that which some few ill-conditioned or ill-mannered persons intended as an insult to the Popish Priest:—

When I was about visiting Cootehill, there was a great number of placards posted about the place cautioning me not to go there, as it was supposed the Protestants would not receive me kindly; and the Catholic Bishop wrote to me not to visit the place; yet I went there, and the first person who met me, and who gave me the most cordial welcome, was the Rev. Dr. Douglas, rector of Cootehill, together with all the respectable Protestants of the town. I discovered afterwards that the person who got the placards printed and posted up was no other than a Catholic publican of the town. I met some of my warmest friends from Armagh to Caledon, amongst whom were Messrs. Ellis, Moore. and many others, who, for the sake of good example and edification, took the pledge, in order to induce others to do the same; and I can tell them that from the time I went into Ulster till my last visit to Drogheda, I have received the greatest kindness at the hands of all persons and parties. At Clones there were two orange flags raised there when I visited it, and, instead of an insult, I thought this a very great compliment, never having seen one or being honoured with one before, and when I saw them I called for three cheers for the orange flag, and the Catholics and Protestants became the greatest friends from that day forward, and during three days while I remained there, the different parties were the best friends imaginable. I could have apprehended nothing save goodwill and kindly feeling from one end of Ulster to the other, and this was amply demonstrated by my visits to Lurgan, Lisburn, Belfast, Downpatrick, Derry, and other places; and the 'Prentice Boys' of Derry showed me the greatest kindness, but it was not to me alone, but to the glorious cause. Thousands of them came out to Moira from Belfast and other places, and actually detained me three days longer than I intended to have stopped; and was not this truly delightful?

Invitations now continually poured in upon him from all parts of Ireland—from bishops and parish-priests—from presidents of temperance societies—from noblemen and gentlemen, who desired to obtain for their poor neighbours and their own dependents the advantage of his presence. Generally speaking, when he was invited to a town by a clergyman, it was with two objects in view—that he might administer the pledge to the people, and preach in aid of funds for the erection or completion of a church, a convent, or a school. And thus, wherever he went with this double object, he was sure to be himself one of the most liberal, indeed *the* most liberal contributor to the charity on behalf of which he appealed. It was no uncommon thing for him to hand 10*l.*, or even 20*l.*, to his friend, the clergyman who had invited him to his parish, and who, in so doing, had conferred on him the greatest of all favours—namely, afforded him the opportunity of prosecuting his mission. The local temperance society was always certain to benefit by his visit. If they were in difficulty from debt, he released them from their embarrassment, and set them on their legs again; for he wisely regarded the reading-room, with its hundred or couple of hundred members, as a rallying-point and a stronghold for the cause.

Mr. Purcell and Mr. Bianconi had, no doubt, acted in a kind and thoughtful manner towards Father Mathew, when they made him free of their coaches and cars; still the cost of an inside seat in a mail coach did not represent the fiftieth part of the expense of an ordinary journey made by Father Mathew during the ardour of the campaign. From the moment he quitted Cove Street, in the City of Cork, until he returned to it again, after having traversed half a dozen counties, his hands were continually in his pockets—'giving—giving—giving.' At every place the coach stopped, a crowd soon surrounded him; and among the crowd—including the lame, and the blind, and the sick, the very old, and the very young—money was scattered profusely. It literally rained silver upon those occasions. This unreflecting and even reckless liberality may not have been wise or prudent; but it was utterly impossible that Father Mathew could have reflected, or could have calculated, when his compassion was excited, or his charity appealed to. His eye and his ear were direct avenues to his heart: and when these conveyed sights of misery and voices of distress, the heart responded to the appeal, and the hand instinctively followed the impulse of the heart. Thus he gave with open heart and open hand, and could no more refrain from giving than he could refrain from feeling sympathy or expressing compassion.

A few lines from a letter written to him, about this time, by a clergyman who was compelled to proceed to Rome to prosecute a cause in which he was personally interested, will further exhibit the generous nature of this good man. The writer says :—

> I accept with gratitude the sum of 60*l.* which you offered me, and will punctually repay it. Less would do, but I may have to stay two or three months, and I cannot return without making church and altar purchases, particularly if I succeed.

A respectable widow, of straitened means, called on him one day, to consult him about her son, a promising lad whom she wished to place in a certain collegiate institution: and thinking that Father Mathew might have sufficient influence with its conductors to obtain admittance for her son on reduced terms, she applied to him to that effect. 'I am sorry, my dear madam,' said Father Mathew, 'that I cannot do what you desire. I am sure the terms cannot be reduced, as they are already barely sufficient to meet the expenses of the establishment.' 'Dear, dear! what am I to do?—I am sorry, sir, to have troubled you; but, really, as you know, my means are so small, that it would be impossible for me to exist on what would remain after paying the pension,' said the poor lady, in the most affecting tones. 'Well, my dear madam, I tell you what you can do—bring me the sum you say you can afford to give, and I will pay it for you; and we will arrange it in that way, and your boy must have his chance of working his way, and being an honour and credit to his good mother.' 'God will bless you, sir, for you have many a widow's blessing, and mine among them,' replied the now happy woman. The money was regularly handed to Father Mathew, for transmission to the college, and the young lad received an education through which he advanced in life; and it was not till many years after, that the widow discovered that the full sum had been paid for her son, and that Father Mathew had regularly made good the balance out of his own pocket.

Hundreds of such instances as the following might be given, as an evidence of 'how all the money went.' It is the concluding passage from a letter written, rather early in the movement, by the Rev. Mr. Molony, of Rosscarbery, in the county of Cork, and addressed to a Cork newspaper:—

> I beg to add that he has literally forced on me a most splendid donation for the completion of the chapel, and that he has left with me, gratuitously, cards and medals for the vast number of poor people who had enrolled themselves.

It will be necessary to refer to the alleged receipts for cards and medals in a subsequent place. We now desire to say something of what were at once the pride and glory of the local societies, and a source of constant anxiety and expense to Father Mathew. These were the Temperance Bands.

Father Mathew had not the slightest knowledge of or taste for music. He could scarcely distinguish one air from another; and as for 'turning a tune,' he could as soon have turned the universe. In conversation, or in addressing an assembly, his voice was pleasing and melodious; but when, at High Mass or Vespers, he was compelled to sing—if the word can properly apply in his case—his voice was a croak, and his performance was mournful and dismal beyond description. The simplest Gregorian chant was too much for Father Mathew. In fine, he had '*no ear*' for music. Still he loved to be thrilled and stunned by the alternate shriek and roar of the genuine Temperance Band. He delighted in the shrill fife and the shriller piccolo, and in the rattle of the small drum and the thunder of the big—simply because these harmonious sounds emanated from a band; and where there was a band, there also was a reading-room; and where there was a reading-room, there was a stronghold of temperance, a source of strength and encouragement to the weak and the vacillating, as well as a tribunal of public opinion formidable to the backslider. He also liked the bands because they amused the people; and his desire was then, as at all times, to promote amusements which were innocent and harmless in themselves, and cheering in their influence.

The rage for getting up bands soon became a kind of music mania. Thus would the members of a room yet unblessed with that costly acquisition put their melancholy case—'You see, sir, temperance is a very fine thing, and people who took the pledge ought to hold true to it—that we do n't deny; but why should n't one society have its band as well as another society?—and is it to be said that *we* are to have no music for a procession, or a soirée, or a meeting, or a walk out in the country on a Sunday?—and if Father Mathew comes to honour us by a visit, are *we* to be beholden to any other society for the loan of their band? No, sir; we must have our own band, whatever it may cost.' And with such sentiments on the part of a society, of course the getting up of the band was the next thing thought of; and until the instruments were actually in the room, shining in brazen glory on the walls, or were in the hands of the performers, and a master engaged, there could be neither peace nor contentment for that society. Subscriptions were frequently raised from the local gentry in the rural districts, or from the wealthier inhabitants of the cities and towns; but there was one unfailing resource for the society in want of a band—that was, in the exhaustless liberality of Father Mathew, to whom the appeal was usually made in this fashion, through a deputation headed by an elder of the room—'The truth is, your reverence, we can't get on at all without the music. We're afeard the members will be leaving us, and that would be bad, your reverence; for the poor fellows may be falling into temptation, and that's what none of us would like, your reverence, if we could help it at all. It will keep the members together to have the band in the room; and, your reverence, the boys and girls are so fond of the music, that it would be a pity to disappoint them, the poor things! Faith, sir, we'd be ashamed of ourselves if we wouldn't be able to play finely for you by Easter Monday. And, your reverence, we all greatly depend on you entirely; for sure, your reverence, you're our leader in the blessed cause. Our hopes are in you altogether, and we know *you* won't desert us, plaise God!' To an appeal of this kind, what could Father Mathew do but respond, as he always did, not to say liberally, but munificently? His reply to the deputation was sure to be in words such as these,—'I am very happy to see you, gentlemen, and to do anything I can for your excellent society. I am proud of your fidelity, and I trust you will always stand firm, and resist temptation, and that there will be no backsliders among you.' Here, of course, he was interrupted by a disclaimer, pronounced in tones of the most virtuous energy. There was not a man of that deputation but who, according to his own statement, was to remain faithful to his dying day. 'Very good, gentlemen,—very good, boys,—God bless you all, and enable you to keep your promise! You must have a band, of course, and I will assist you as far as I can. I hope to hear you play well when next I visit you. But, remember, be true and faithful followers of the Lord, and don't give scandal to others. God bless you, gentlemen; God bless you, boys!' 'Don't be afeard of us, your reverence; every man of us is true to the cause.' 'We are, your reverence, every one of us,' would the other members of the deputation chime in, in chorus. 'That's delightful to my ears, my dear children; and now, here is my contribution. Be faithful, like valiant soldiers in a good cause.' 'Thank your reverence! we're entirely obliged to your reverence. This will be great news for the boys and girls that are waiting for us.' And so, invariably, away would go the deputation rejoicing.

But this was not the last that Father Mathew had to do with the band to which he thus contributed, or, as the case may have been, which he thus established. If the big drum yielded to the merciless vigour of its lusty operator, whose conscientious performance was the pride of the room and the admiration of the neighbourhood, Father Mathew was probably consulted as to the condition and prospects of that much-aggrieved instrument; and, if it were hopelessly invalided, as it too often had every reason to be, a subscription from the President for the purchase of a new victim to the prowess of the 'great drummer' was expected; and, so long as he had a pound at his disposal, it was generally given by him.

If a considerable majority of the big drums that had to do duty during the Temperance campaign did not suffer dissolution, then I would be inclined to believe that the same Providence that watches over the fall of a sparrow must also have condescended to protect the Irish temperance drum; for, as a rule, that devoted instrument was entrusted to the ablest member of the room, a man of approved muscle and vigour; and rarely, I must frankly admit, was the confidence thus reposed in the energy of the performer ever betrayed. What was expected at the hands of this most important member of the temperance band may be indicated by the following little incident:—

It was on the occasion of an emigrant ship sailing from the harbour of Cork, with several hundred passengers, mostly the young, strong, and active—the very bone and sinew of the country. The emigrants had all taken the pledge from

Father Mathew, who had, as was his invariable custom in similar cases, presented them with cards and medals. Feeling a deep interest in the welfare of these poor people, Father Mathew determined on paying them a visit on board, before the ship left her moorings for her long voyage. Out of compliment to the President, and to give greater *éclat* to the proceedings of the day, one of the city bands, consisting of some six or eight performers, volunteered to accompany the party. Father Mathew and his friends embarked in a roomy whaleboat, which was in waiting for him at the usual landing-place; the band, with the exception of the drummer, finding accommodation for themselves at the bow. The ship lay about a mile and a half from the shore; and as soon as the boat was well under weigh, the premonitory tap on the drum assured us that we were to add the charm of music to the enjoyment of a lovely day in summer, waters dancing and sparkling in the sunshine, and the contemplation of that noble picture of maritime beauty which the harbour of Cork presents to the eye. The powerful fellow who pulled the stroke oar of the boat, and whose every dip in the water left after it what he himself termed the 'rale colliflower,' appeared, from the first, to take a marked interest in the drummer, who was perched on the stern, behind the coxswain. The band was really excellent, and was led by a musician of taste and cultivation. Here the drum, contrary to the established rule, was not only a useful but a subordinate adjunct; it marked the time, and enriched the harmony of the well-balanced instruments. The 'stroke,' who had taken me into his confidence, winked at me from time to time, and directed my attention to the drummer, by various nods, and an occasional nudge, whispering, 'Yea, listen to *him*, sir. Did ye ever hear the like of *that*?' His amazement deepened into the profoundest contempt, as the drummer was still contented with his shamefully subordinate and humiliating position; and most eloquently were the feelings of my friend the 'stroke' depicted on his expressive countenance. At length his disgust, long brimful, overflowed; and stooping over to me, he thus gave vent to his feelings—'Wisha, sir, he's a mighty poor dhrummer all out. I'd get a boy of ten year old in our room to bate him. He ought to be ashamed of himself, a great big fellow of his size! Ah, sir, if ye'd only hear *our* band, then you'd know what a rale dhrum is.' The critic was not perhaps altogether impartial, for he was the vigorous and most successful performer on the big drum of his own room; and, it must be added, no artist stood higher in the esteem of its members, or in the admiration of the small boys of the town. To use his own expressive words, 'he was the lad for knocking life into it, and no mistake.'

Though many years have passed since then, I have to this moment the liveliest recollection of the performance of a genuine village band, which had been established, as its patrons alleged, 'to cheer and delight the members with its strains of melody.' I had been requested by Father Mathew to accompany him to the 'Festival;' and as the carriage approached the door of the house in which the tea party was to be held, we were saluted by a startling outburst of complicated sounds that, on the whole, bore some resemblance to the air generally known as the 'Conquering Hero.' Had not the spirit of the horses been rather tamed down by a long pull, it would be difficult to say what might have happened; for the big drum was beaten by the village blacksmith, who was, to do him the barest justice, a powerful performer. Of course, there was a dense crowd assembled in a moment in front of the 'hall,' as it was proudly designated; and cheer after cheer welcomed the arrival of the world-renowned Apostle of Temperance. In a moment, and as if by impulse, a 'batch' was formed in a small semicircle, down on their knees in the street; and, for a quarter of an hour or twenty minutes, Father Mathew was hard at work administering the pledge in the centre of the little village.

At length we were enabled to enter the 'hall,' which was a moderate sized but low-ceiled room, whose walls were decorated with evergreens and garlands of flowers—for it was in the middle of June. The banner of the society occupied a conspicuous place over the chair, which was grandly upholstered with crimson merino; and on the wall, at the end, the words, '*Cead Mille Fealtha*'—in English, 'a hundred thousand welcomes!'—were painted in large yellow letters on a strip of green calico. At the top of the room, before the chair, was a mahogany table, lent for the occasion by some local patron of temperance; and this table was resplendent with tea-pots and coffee-pots, some of silver and more of grand 'Britannia,' also lent to do honour to Father Mathew. There was a goodly show of currant cake, a present to the society; and the whitest sugar and the richest cream showed the zeal of the members, and the liberality of the neighbouring gentry—not a few of whom were present, and occupied the place of honour. Two narrow tables, made of planks, knocked together for the occasion, ran down the length of the room, and sustained mountains of bread and butter, the slices of substantial thickness; also jugs of enormous size, and cups of liberal dimensions. At the tables sat young and old, from the grandmother to the child in arms. The *élite* of the village was there; and many a healthy decent-looking man, now sitting in quiet gravity in the midst of his family, was, not many years, perhaps even months, before, the tyrant of his home, and the pest of the neighbourhood. The elderly ladies rejoiced in snowy caps, with grand borders and flaring ribbons; and the young exhibited equal taste in the simple neatness of their dress, and the careful arrangement of their glossy hair. The appearance which the crowded but over-close chamber presented was a pleasing and a hopeful one indeed. On a raised and railed-off platform at the end of the room, the band had taken their position; and as Father Mathew entered, the 'Conquering Hero' was again given, in a style which would have impelled the 'Enraged Musician' to instantaneous suicide, had he been present at that merciless piece of instrumentation. But the audience, whose ears were in their hearts, could hear no discord whatever, and thought it the most ravishing harmony. And Father Mathew, looking as noble as a king, beamed with delight, his eyes and lips smiling in concert. Nor was he wanting in abundant praise of the performance, which, awful and nerve-shattering as it was to unaccustomed ears, was really wonderful, inasmuch as the greater number of the performers had never held a musical instrument in their hands a month previously to this grand exhibition of their proficiency. When the last bar was concluded, up rose Father Mathew, who, bowing with grace towards the orchestra, said—'Thank you, gentlemen! thank you very much, for your *beautiful* music!' The band was in a flutter of ecstasy at this public tribute from 'one of the greatest men in the world,' and not a member present but felt the compliment. 'I knew, sir,' said a village dame to me, 'that his reverence would be plazed. Faith, sir, I think the boys plays as well as the army, if not better.' The stewards are now bustling in and out, preparing the tea, which is being concocted in an adjoining room. The beverage is borne in in the enormous white jugs, from which ascend columns of steam in this hot June night. The tea 'for the Apostle and the quality' is also supplied; and just as the company are about enjoying themselves in that luxury, which cheers but does not inebriate, the tap of the drum is heard—then another tap—and, at the third, your whole nervous being is assailed with a crash of sounds such as to bewilder you for the moment. Shriek and squeak, bur, and roar, and clash, with a blending of all, and an occasional predominance of some—this is the band executing 'Love not!' an air which, at that time, owed much to the energy of our national musicians. The tumult is awful. The walls, you imagine, must shortly yield to the stupendous reverberations created by the big drum, which is under the able hands of the muscular blacksmith. The performers proudly persevere, their master beating time, and swaying his head from side to side, with a gravity worthy of the bandmaster of the Coldstreams. The members are in a state of rapture, and reward the musicians with a loud clapping of hands and stamping on the floor. 'Very beautiful, indeed!' is heard again from the President, whose commendation, honest and sincere, is by no means endorsed by the occupants of the upper table. The members of the band — Dinny and Ned and Larry and Tom and Billy — are invited by their delighted friends and relatives to seat themselves at the tables, and 'make much of themselves, poor boys;' and the largest cups and the thickest slices are awarded to the performers, as some faint expression of gratitude and admiration. The big drum has a place of special honour, for his labour has been mighty, and he now wipes the accumulated moisture from his manly brow.

When the band have done themselves justice, they again proceed to the 'orchestra.' Some whispered consultation is seen to be carried on; and, shortly after, a member of that important body makes his way through the crowded room to where Father Mathew is seated, and announces his message, which resulted in the following dialogue:—'Plaze your reverence, the gintlemen of the band would like to know what chune your reverence would prefer.' 'Oh, my dear, anything the gentlemen please themselves.' 'Your reverence, they'd like to lave it to yourself.' 'Well, my dear, "God Save the Queen" is a very fine air, and so is "Patrick's Day."' 'I'm afeard, sir, we're only learning them chunes; but would your reverence like the "Conquering Haro?"' 'Had n't we that before, my dear?' 'Well, you had, your reverence. Perhaps your reverence would be after liking "Love not?"—that's a mighty sweet thing.' 'It is indeed, my dear, a very nice air; but had n't we that also?' 'Well, you had, your reverence; but the gintlemen of the band thought you'd like to plaze yourself.' Father Mathew, of course, understood the limited nature of the band's *repertoire*, and so he gravely called for the 'Conquering Hero,' and expressed a hope that it might be followed, in the course of the evening, by that delightful air, 'Love not.' The band felt the more proud at having paid this graceful compliment, and they executed the doomed pieces of music several times that night with unabated vigour and undiminished discord.

In six months after, one could not have recognised that village band; for then they played air, and waltz, and march music, with harmony and precision. It was it's first night's public performance that so long haunted my memory.

I have listened with a kind of amused horror to the first performances of a temperance band within the walls of a reading-room, or temperance hall; but a more bewildering aggregation of sounds was to be enjoyed by the musical epicure on those occasions when Father Mathew gathered round him the societies of the districts within some miles of the city, for a special jubilee. I remember one of these. It was a kind of monster meeting at Blarney, a well-known locality, famous in song and legend, about five miles distant from the city of Cork. The meeting was held in a beautiful valley encircled by hills, on the sides of which many hundreds of well-dressed people were scattered in picturesque groups. Banners of all hues and shapes floated and fluttered from every prominence and vantage ground, and more than twenty bands sent up their blended dissonance to the skies. As no one band was allowed to have precedence of the other, and as each was desirous of exhibiting its proficiency, of course no one band would give way to the other; therefore all should be heard alike; and all were heard alike, to the greatest general advantage. One can scarcely realise, even to the wildest imagination, the sublime discord of twenty bands, each playing a different air, with twenty vigorous and athletic 'big drummers' energetically rivalling each other, and the surrounding hills multiplying while reverberating the complicated and torturing medley of sounds. Were nymphs and dryads still haunting sylvan solitudes, one could suppose them flying in dismay from such fearful discord, and never again returning to their sunlit dells and pleasant shades. But the day was beautiful, the sun shone brightly, the banners fluttered gaily, the people were happy, and Father Mathew was in ecstasy.

But Father Mathew had to pay for the music of that and similar popular festivals. Had to pay is not, perhaps, a correct mode of putting it; *did* pay, is more accurate. Many of these young men had come a distance of a dozen miles, or more, to do him special honour, and they had a dozen miles, or more, to travel before they reached home. As a rule, too, they were of the humblest class, who had but little to spare even for a day's festivity. Father Mathew was not the man to be insensible to the devotion or the sacrifices of his followers; and so his secretary was ordered to pay them such a 'compliment' as sent the poor fellows home rejoicing.

It did now and then happen that misunderstandings occurred in temperance rooms, and that the members of the band occasionally thought too much of themselves—that the cornet-a-piston sent in his resignation, that the flute gave up in disgust, or that the big drum refused to strike. Such things did happen; for it must be borne in mind that teetotallers were human, and not angels. When these little difficulties arose, it sometimes, though rarely, happened that the band was broken up, that the instruments were parted with, and that the room was abandoned; and that, when the moment of repentance came, and the society gathered together again, and the band was to be reorganised, and all things were to be set right as before, an urgent appeal to Father Mathew was inevitable. And to respond effectively to an appeal of the kind, Father Mathew would willingly have parted with his last shilling. Through the contention of that village society the President was pained; in the back-sliding of its members the Apostle of Temperance was scandalised. And what sacrifice would he not make—should he not make, he thought—to restore peace to that little society, and protect its members from folly and from danger? Thus it was that the bands, while useful to a certain extent, and a source of intense gratification to the people throughout the country, were to Father Mathew not only the cause of considerable anxiety, but of constant expense.

CHAPTER XIII.

Danger from insecure Platforms—The Catastrophe of Minane Bridge —His Defence of the Bands—The dead Drum-major.

ON several occasions Father Mathew was placed in serious jeopardy by the insecurity of temperance platforms ; but there was one adventure of the kind to which he rarely desired to allude, but to which his brother Charles now and then slily referred, to the momentary annoyance of the priest. Father Mathew had consented to preach for an old friend of his, the pastor of a parish distant from Cork about ten miles ; and, as usual, the opportunity was availed of by the friends of temperance to hold a meeting, and promote the spread of the cause in the village and the adjoining districts. The first thing to be done was to erect a platform, from which the speakers were to address the expected assembly ; and the rural architect, when he surveyed his work on the Saturday night, believed in his soul that a finer, safer, or more ingenious construction than his grand platform was never devised. Sunday arrived, and with it the Apostle of Temperance, who preached the promised sermon for his reverend friend. From the chapel the congregation proceeded to the place of meeting, and the numbers were increased by people flocking in from all the neighbouring districts. The platform presented a very imposing appearance, it being seven or eight feet from the ground, and decorated with laurel branches, and with banners, which floated from the four uprights on which the entire structure rested. A question of grave importance had arisen in the meanwhile—namely, which of the two bands present—the band from Cork, or the local band—was to have the place of honour? Courtesy to the strangers, who might have been regarded in the light of guests, would perhaps have suggested to the local society that their band should gracefully yield the occupation of the platform to the band from the city; but the local artists were proud of thei performance, and sensitively jealous of their rights—therefore, and as a matter of principle, they stationed themselves on the platform, and hailed Father Mathew's arrival with a grand burst of music, repeating the jubilant strain at least half a dozen times, the better to impress the gentlemen from the city with a notion of what 'boys from the country,' were capable of doing 'in the line of playing.' Upon the termination of the last bar, the chair was taken, and the proceedings of the day commenced. The band on the platform were constantly on the watch for the conclusion of a speech; and scarcely had the orator finished his concluding sentence when the music struck up. Indeed an occasional rumble of the drum, or squeak from one of the other instruments, would indicate the impatience of the musicians, and their decided preference for their own performance to the most glowing oratory or heart-moving pathos. The numbers on the platform had been gradually increasing, in spite of the remonstrances of one or two gentlemen, who had not the most implicit faith in the stability of the structure. The architect, it must be remarked, listened to such warnings with sublime disdain, or replied to them with withering contempt. Since the Tower of Babel there was no structure equal to this platform, for ingenuity of design, perfection of detail, or solidity and endurability. 'People ought to confine their observations to matters with which they were professionally conversant, and not meddle with subjects above their comprehension.' So thought and said the insulted architect of Minane Bridge.

Father Mathew had not been speaking longer than a few minutes, and had just commenced a new sentence with the words—'We have met here to-day, my dear friends, for'—when, lo! as a trick in a pantomime, or as a house of cards, the solid platform, which had been built for posterity, vanished in a second, leaving but the four posts, or uprights—to one of which Father Mathew was seen clinging, as a sailor would to a mast, his polished boots glittering in the sun! First there was a cry of horror, then a dismal wail, then a general sigh of relief. Fortunately, the platform, which had been built on a steep elevation, had fallen backwards against the hill, and not forwards—but, had it so fallen, the accident would have been probably attended with disastrous results, as many persons were then standing under it in front. No one had been seriously injured. Shins and knees were contused and scraped, coats and trowsers were torn and fractured, and an odd black eye or an ensanguined nose imparted variety to the catastrophe of the day. But the band!—the luckless local band! that would stand on its rights, and that would n't give up the platform to the strangers! Sad was their plight, miserable their condition, bitter their unavailing self-reproach. The flute had suffered from a compound fracture of a hopeless character; the cornopean was twisted into strange contortions, its wide circular orifice flattened into the resemblance of a cod's mouth; and as to the drum—the big drum—that noble instrument which had been the glory of the village, and the admiration of the country for five miles round—one might enjoy a comprehensive view of the landscape through its shattered sheepskin. It was not ruin, but chaos. Father Mathew applied an effective salve, in the shape of a crown-piece, to the slight wound of a poor old woman who for a time resolutely proclaimed that she was 'kilt entirely;' but it required a much more costly plaister to heal the deep wound inflicted by that fatal accident on the feelings as well as the instruments of that unhappy local band, whose sufferings were rather embittered than otherwise by the gay and joyous manner in which the Cork musicians played the people from the place of meeting to the gate of the chapel, where the proceedings were resumed. The architect had vanished with his platform, and was not seen for some days after. The writer often thought of that rural genius with no slight disgust ; for, having been one of the occupants of that treacherous erection, he bore, in a complicated abrasion of both knees, and corresponding but fatal fractures of his best black trowsers, more enduring than pleasing memorials of the day at Minane Bridge.

It had been often alleged against the temperance bands that they played during the hours of Divine Worship on Sundays ; but if they so transgressed, it was very rarely, and in direct violation of the positive injunctions of Father Mathew, that his followers should abstain from every cause of offence to those who differed from them in religion, and whose feelings might be wounded by sounds not certainly suggestive of devotional emotions. In a letter addressed to Richard Allen of Dublin, and written on the 7th of April 1842, Father Mathew, while alluding to the progress of the temperance movement, thus vindicates it from the charge of its being sectarian in its character, and defends the bands against their assailants :—

Be not alarmed, my dear Mr. Allen, temperance is not retrograding. At this moment I am honoured by more than seventy pressing invitations from the Roman Catholic prelates and clergy, to administer the total abstinence pledge in different parts of Ireland. Give me but time, and, with the aid of the Great Jehovah, we will wave our pure and spotless banner over the length and breadth of the land.

There are difficulties which cause me more pain than the assertion of Sir Robert Peel,—the insidious efforts to give to our society a political colouring, and to invoke a gloomy fanatic cry against us. The great body of teetotallers, it is true, is composed of Roman Catholics ; but that is from the great bulk of the people being Roman Catholic, and not from anything exclusive in our society. A hostile disposition has been excited on this account in certain localities; and I must also complain, with the deepest sorrow, that many who, from rank and station, possess great influence, have not, to use the mildest term, exercised it in favour of our society. I utterly disclaim any political object; my ardent desire is to promote the glory of God, by drying up the fruitful source of crime, and the happiness of His creatures, by persuading them to the observance of temperance.

Our musical bands, too, and our processions, are rocks of offence to many. If it was allowed to any to object to them, surely it should to the members of your society, who reject music and parade, in every case; yet you have all magnanimously cooperated with me, despising this paltry pretext. I respect the religious feelings which disapprove of music and processions on the Lord's day—I would not, on any account, offer violence to tender consciences; but we, Roman Catholics, after in general devoting the afternoon of Saturday, and the forenoon of Sunday, to religious observances, do not deem it a desecration of the Sabbath for such as have been earning their bread by the sweat of their brows during the week, to recreate themselves innocently during the remainder of the day. We should be allowed to enjoy our Gospel liberty—we regulate our conduct by what we interpret to be the spirit of the Gospel, and not by the letter of the Levitical Law. Oh! that the sweet and beneficent spirit of the Gospel, that thinketh no evil, was diffused from pole to pole, uniting all mankind as one family, and making a world happy. The earth would be then, indeed, a delightful habitation, in which each man could enjoy, in charity, the blessings of this life, especially through the Lord Jesus Christ, the blessed hope and glory of the great God. Lovers of God, and of His everlasting ordinances, should be to our failings a little kind.

Let them contrast the shocking spectacles which presented themselves heretofore on the Lord's day, with the calm decorum that at present universally reigns. The bacchanalian yell (that made hideous the Sabbath's early morn) is heard no more,—the Temples of the Living God, crowded with sincere worshippers,—the taverns, bridewells, and brothels empty,—the awful blasphemy,—the false oath, and dire imprecation, no longer insult the attested majesty of the Deity. It is my religious conviction that one sin of drunkenness, or one of the black deeds to which men are prompted when inflamed by intoxicating drink, outrages more the sanctity of a jealous God than all the music of the three hundred temperance bands on the Sabbath day.

Belonging to one of the best bands of Cork was an elderly man, a pensioner, who had seen good service in his day. Having no practical knowledge of music, he could not do duty as an instrumentalist; but he impressed his brother-members with the necessity of obtaining a grand-looking and imposing drum-major, who would make a splendid appearance on all public occasions. Of course, he himself was the grand-looking and imposing personage, who was to fill this conspicuous position. The idea was favourably entertained, and immediately acted upon; and soon the local public were startled by the appearance of this fine old fellow strutting majestically at the head of the band, wearing a hairy cap of prodigious dimensions, and swaggering a genuine drum-major's staff, with resplendent nob, in the truest style of military art. There was not a prouder man in her Majesty's dominions than that drum-major of the temperance band. The cheers of the little boys offered the sweetest incense to his harmless vanity. But even drum-majors are not proof against the assaults of time; and the mornful day came when our drum-major was compelled to lay aside his astounding chako, and surrender his glittering staff. In a word, he died. The members of the room sincerely mourned the loss of their faithful comrade, and the band was disconsolate at their bereavement. It was determined to bury him with suitable pomp and solemnity—with a grand procession, muffled drums, and military music. Unhappily, in their grief, the band forgot that they did not know a single note of the 'Dead March,' without which a public funeral was not to be thought of. What was to be done? It was plain there was only one thing to be done—namely, not to bury the drum-major until the march was learned. And so the drum-major was kept above ground for a week longer, during which the band were hard at work practising the march; and had it not been for the interference of the police, the drum-major might not have been consigned to the dust for another week, as the band were somewhat uncertain in their execution of that indispensable piece of music. There was, however, no help for it, as the neighbours had become greatly alarmed at the longer continuance of the drum-major above ground, and the police would not listen to the urgent plea for further practice ; and so the funeral came off with distinguished success, the band far exceeding their own hopes, and the chako and staff, which were placed on the coffin of the departed veteran, producing a striking effect.

The temperance cause had many friends, but not a few enemies ; and among the latter were those who sought to raise a cry against the teetotallers for holding their open-air meetings on the Sabbath, and who were so far carried away by their prejudices as not to consider that the promoters of such meetings were really engaged in furthering a great moral movement—indeed, if rightly understood, a great religious work ; and that working people could not conveniently, or without injury to their families, assemble on any other day than Sunday. Father Mathew thus replied to this unreasonable accusation :—

I pity (said he) the man who could contemplate in our meeting nothing but a profanation of the Sabbath day. We are not, it is true, under the fragile roof of a cathedral ; but we are assembled under the glorious canopy of heaven, to worship the Almighty God. Our work is on high—we are assembled to pay to the Lord the homage of pure hearts, and to inculcate the practice of the great cardinal virtue of temperance. Men point at us the finger of scorn, as the Pharisees did at our Lord, and say, 'They violate the Sabbath—the teetotallers assemble and hold temperance meetings on the Lord's day;' but these persons, my friends, are secret enemies of our glorious cause—they well know that, if we do not assemble on the Lord's day, we could not hold our meetings at all ; for the great majority of those composing our society are from among that useful and virtuous body, the operatives, who on every other day labour from the rising to the setting sun, and could not come to hear our doctrines inculcated—the principles and maxims of true sobriety laid down. The temperance cause is the work of the Most High God, and it is admirable in our eyes.

Scarcely anything connected with Father Mathew's temperance mission was more remarkable than the extraordinary rapidity of his movements. Heard of in the North one day, his arrival in the South was recorded in a day or two after ; and this, too, at a time when railways were almost unknown in Ireland. Thus, in October 1841, he was in Newry ; and in a couple of days after, having passed through Cork, he was administering the pledge in Tralee. An instance of this extraordinary celerity of movement was displayed in July 1842, and is recorded, not because it is more than usually remarkable, but that it happened to attract the writer's attention. After a successful visit to the county of Limerick, he arrived in Cork on Friday the 8th of July. He left Cork on Saturday, and held a meeting near Bantry on Sunday ; he returned to Cork on Tuesday, visited Tralee on Friday the 15th, held a meeting near Kenmare on Sunday, returned to Cork and remained until the 23rd, and then started for Castletown Beerhaven, where he preached and administered the pledge the following day, Sunday the 24th.

The two following paragraphs, taken from a Cork journal, will afford a further idea, not only of the rapidity of his movements, but of the tremendous labour to which he voluntarily subjected himself. As both these paragraphs appeared in 1844, it must be evident that he had then in no way relaxed in his wonderful exertions :—

Father Mathew left Cork, on Saturday, August 10th, for Newmarket, where he was to preach yesterday, the 11th, and afterwards to administer the pledge. On to-morrow, the 13th, he will take his departure for Esker, in the county of Galway, where he is to preach, and administer the pledge on Thursday, the 15th. He has arranged to visit Blanchardstown, near Dublin, on the following Sunday, the 18th, and Carlow on Wednesday, the 21st. He will return to Cork on the 23rd, in time for the great temperance demonstration, which will take place at Carrigtwohill, on Sunday, the 25th instant.

The Apostle of temperance left town by this morning's (Friday, November 22nd) Dublin mail, for Boyle, in the county of Roscommon, where he is to preach and administer the pledge on Sunday and Monday. He will return to Cork on Wednesday.

It was during this trying campaign that the splendid constitution with which he was endowed received its nrst injury, and that the germs of painful disease, from which he suffered severely in a few years after, took deep and lasting root in his system. Travelling, however wearying, was not that from which he suffered most ; but the continuous and incessant labour of addressing vast assemblies in the open air, and administering the pledge to many thousands in the course of a single day, standing frequently for six hours together, and not being allowed one moment either for rest or privacy during all that time. From the moment it was known that Father Mathew had arrived in any place, the whole population was in a ferment of excitement, and crowds rushed after him wherever he appeared. A rather comical cause of embarrassment arose, on one occasion, from the extraordinary anxiety of the people to catch even a glimpse of 'the great Apostle.' He had arrived in the dusk of the evening at the house of a parish priest in a remote part of the county Galway, where he was to preach in aid of the funds of a school, convent, or chapel, and afterwards administer the pledge. The best room in the house was prepared for the honoured guest, who was conducted to it by his host. The room was on the ground floor, and was lighted by a large bay window, which was without blind or curtain of any kind. Father Mathew, whose bedroom in Cove Street was as plain and simple as this apartment, only thought of preparing himself, by a good night's rest, for the labours of the following day ; and turning his face to the wall, and his back to the window, he soon fell into a deep slumber. Awaking, as was usual with him, at an early hour in the morning, he opened his eyes, blessed himself, repeated a prayer, and turned towards the window. But imagine his dismay, when he beheld a crowd of people—men, women and children—in front of the blind-less and curtainless bay window, and at least a score of noses flattened against the glass, the better to enable their respective proprietors to obtain a peep at his reverence. A more modest man did not exist than Father Mathew; and great was his embarrassment at this indication of his popularity. He glanced at the head of the bed, and at the table near him, to see if a bell were in reach; but such a luxury in the house of a priest, in a mountain parish of Galway, was not to be thought of. No help, therefore, from that quarter. There was something resembling a bell-pull at one side of the fire-place; but if it were a real bell-pull, and not a mockery and a delusion, it might as well have been twenty miles away, for any practical advantage at that moment; for it would be difficult to say what *would* induce Father Mathew to quit the shelter of the bed-clothes, and walk across the room to grasp that tantalising cord. The crowd outside was momentarily on the increase, and the deepening murmur of their voices testified to the animation of the conversation carried on. Occasionally might be heard such as the following:—'Do ye see him, Mary, asthore?' 'Danny, agra, lave me take a look, an' God bless you, child!' 'Where are you pushing with yerself?'—hould off ov my foot, will ye?' 'Oh, wisha! there's the blessed priest!' 'Honest man, would ye be plazed to lift off ov our back—one 'ud think 'tis a horse I was.' ''Tis a shame for ye to be there—what curosity is in yes all!' 'Mammy, mammy! there he is!—I sees his poll!' 'Whisht, an' don't be after wakin' him.' Father Mathew ventured another peep; but the slightest movement on his part only evoked increased anxiety outside; and it seemed to him as if the window-panes were every moment accommodating a larger number of flattened noses. The poor man felt himself a prisoner, and listened with eagerness for any sound which gave hope or promise of deliverance; but it was not till after three mortal hours of his guest's comical captivity that the considerate host, who would not 'disturb' his guest too early, entered the appartment, and thus became aware of the presence of the admiring crowd, who, it need scarcely be said, were quickly dispersed, to Father Mathew's ineffable relief.

For no result did this good man so earnestly labour as for the moral elevation of the youth of Ireland. In them was centred all his hopes. If he could only bend the green twig as he pleased, he knew the tree would correspondingly incline There were blessings, and carresses, and praises, and holidays, and medals, for the boys who took the pledge; there was the fondest affection and the most devoted friendship for the youth who adhered to it faithfully. Wherever Father Mathew went through the country, he was delighted at the improvement which he witnessed in the dress, in the manner, and in the bearing of the children of the humbler classes; and his heart was gladdened by the accounts which he received from the clergy of town and country of the daily increasing numbers on the school-roll. The improvement in the youth of the higher classes was equally striking. At one of his meetings he thus gave expression to his exultation at the progress which he witnessed with so much delight :—

Oh, I predict glorious things for the young and rising generation! My heart warms and expands as I conjure up before me all that is in progress for the advantage of and the improvement of the young minds of Ireland. Not alone in the arts and sciences how great will be their advancement, but indications of talent of every kind, of comforts hitherto unknown amongst us, of future peace and happiness, are making themselves manifest, and my aspirations are becoming more and more realised every day for the improvement and amelioration of the condition of my native land. Yes, heretofore, to be sure, individuals of talent and abilities occasionally arose and appeared; but, like the meteor flashes, they illuminated all around for the moment, and became the transitory ornaments of their native land; but the young men of the present day, oh! how can I describe them? Seem they not like the fixed stars in the clear and cloudless Heaven, shining on, shining on in their glory and their purity to the end. Oh! you cannot know how it cheers my heart to find how the young mind of Ireland is now progressing, not slowly, but surely, steadily, and successfully, and not alone in Cork, but in every part of the kingdom. Daily I receive accounts from the various parts of the country which are truly gratifying to the heart, of the fidelity of my dear teetotallers.

Father Mathew's style of speaking was simple and unafected, but it was earnest and impressive. He availed himself of any incident or event which had occurred, to illustrate his temperance discourses, and render them more forcible through the influence of example. The following, though spoken many years since in the village of Blackrock, a short distance from the city of Cork, is applicable at this moment, not to one locality, but unhappily, to almost every locality ; and its good sense is as apparant now as it was then :—

Were you, my friends, to remain in my house where I administer the pledge, from morning to night, while I am in Cork, you would see examples before you of the fearful consequences resulting from the use of strong drink, that would congeal your blood in your veins. Is it not awful even to think on the numbers, once respected members of society, degraded and ruined—all the victims of one besetting habit? I was going to call it a passion, but it is no passion. It is no passion arising from our nature—for we have no natural propensities that could make us delight in the use of intoxicating liquor. It is merely a habit, brought on by ourselves, like any other bad habit, like the habit of smoking tobacco, or taking snuff. This very morning, a young man came to my house from a remote part of North Tipperary. I saw him only a few weeks ago, sober, respected, and happy. He came to me a miserable object, capable of exciting compassion in the hardest heart—he was but a wreck of what he had been a short time ago. He had broken his pledge—spent in a few weeks the fruits of many years' saving—and left behind him a young wife and a helpless family. He returned there this morning, setting out on his journey without a coat to shelter him from the rain, and was obliged to beg for money to support him on his way. Will any one tell me that it was better for him to drink, to beggar his family, to run the risk of losing his life from the inclemency of the weather, to which he is this day exposed? No, my friends, do not let any one thus deceive you. It is not better for any one, either man or woman, to drink intoxicating liquors—it is far better for all to be total abstainers. Show me any one in the wide circle of your acquaintance, who was ever benefited, either in body or in soul, by the use of intoxicating liquors.. I allow there is some enjoyment—some sensual gratification—to be found in the use of those liquors; but what is that enjoyment to the frightful risk that is encountered? Ought any man blight his prospects in life, and those of his family, for the sake of that wretched indulgence? How many are there whose fathers, had they been teetotallers, would have been able to have given them the blessings of a liberal education, and who might now fill some of the highest situations in the land. There are many who, twenty or thirty years ago, were in the receipt of large sums of money, who are now miserably poor, and whose children are in rags—idle, and straggling, like vagabonds, through the streets; and all this owing to the criminal neglect of their parents, who spent in intoxicating liquors the money which should be expended in properly training and establishing their children in life. Show me the man who ever advanced in life, who was addicted to the use of intoxicating liquors. some may have risen high in life, who were not actually total abstainers, but they were invariably men who had a constitutional dislike to strong drinks, and were examples of temperance; but show me any man addicted to habits of intemperance who ever gained an advanced position in life.

It is not necessary to follow the temperance leader step by step through his extraordinary labours, or to weary the reader by descriptions of scenes which, from their very nature, must partake not only of the same general features, but even of similarity in detail. I prefer to say something of the results of those incessant labours, and the beneficial effects which followed from the more extended adoption of the temperance pledge.

Those results and effects were public as well as private, alike influencing the community and the individual. They were to be seen in the diminution of crime, and the improved moral tone observable throughout the country, notwithstanding the frequent pressure of severe poverty, and the existence of provocations to outrage arising, in a great measure, from various circumstances and conditions of the law, which do not properly enter within the scope of this work. Judges, in their opening addresses to Grand Juries, congratulated the counties which they visited upon the spread and progress of temperance, and distinctly attributed the lightness of the criminal calendar to the sobriety of the mass of the population. Many such valuable testimonies might be quoted, as proofs of the good accomplished by one man. Baron Richards was not content with a public reference to the fruits of Father Mathew's mission; but having heard that he was then—in July 1842—holding meetings in the county Kerry, he sent his registrar specially to him, to express his congratulations on the great success which attended his disinterested labours, and on the improved condition of those who had taken the temperance pledge. Indeed such was the estimation in which sobriety was now generally held, and the disgust which habitual intemperance excited, that the appearance of a medal on the breast of a witness in a court of justice had no small weight with judge and jury in favour of its wearer. The medal was of its self *primâ facie* testimony to his good conduct and trustworthiness.

As a conclusive proof that the diminution of crime was one of the necessary consequences of the spread of temperance among those classes of the community most liable to be tempted to acts of violence or dishonesty, some few facts from the official records of the time may be quoted here. They are taken from returns of 'outrages specially reported by the constabulary,' from the year 1837 to the year 1841, both included. The number of homicides, which was 247 in 1838, was only 105 in 1841. There were 91 cases of 'firing at the person' reported in 1837, and but 66 in 1841. The 'assaults on police' were 91 in 1837, and but 58 in 1841. Incendiary fires, which were as many as 459 in 1838, were 390 in 1841. Robberies, thus specially reported, diminished wonderfully—from 725 in 1837, to 257 in 1841! The offence of 'killing, cutting, or maiming cattle' was also seriously lessened; the cases reported in 1839 being 433, to 213 in

1841! The decrease in cases of 'robbery of arms' was most significant; from being 246 in 1837, they were but 111 in 1841. The offence of 'appearing in arms' showed a favourable diminution, falling from 110 in 1837, to 66 in 1841. The effect of sobriety on 'faction fights' was equally remarkable. There were 20 of such cases in 1839, and 8 in 1841. The dangerous offence of 'rescuing prisoners,' which was represented by 34 in 1837, had no return in 1841!

Without entering further into detail, the following return of the number committed during a period of seven years—from 1839 to 1845—must bring conviction home to the mind of any rational and dispassionate person, that sobriety is good for the individual and the community :—

Year.	Total Number.
1839	12,049
1840	11,194
1841	9,287
1842	9,875
1843	8,620
1844	8,042
1845	7,101

The number of sentences of death and transportation evidenced the operation of some powerful and beneficial influence on the public morals. The number of capital sentences in eight years—from 1839 to 1846—was as follows :—

Year.	Number of Sentence.
1839	66
1840	43
1841	40
1842	25
1843	16
1844	20
1845	13
1846	14

The sentences to transportation during the same period—from 1839 to 1846—exhibited the like wonderful result :—

Year.	Number of Sentences.
1839	916
1840	751
1841	643
1842	667
1843	482
1844	526
1845	428
1846	504

The figures already quoted are most valuable, as they prove, beyond the possibility of doubt, that national drunkenness is the chief cause of crime, and that national sobriety is, humanly speaking, one of the best preservatives of the morals of a people. The figures which are to be now given exhibit the marvellous change effected by father Mathew's preaching in the drinking habits of his countrymen. These figures show the number of gallons of Irish spirits on which duty was paid, and the amount of duty, from the year 1839 to the year 1844, both included :—

Year.	Gallons.	Duty.
1839	12,296,000	£1,434,573
1840	10,815,709	1,261,812
1841	7,401,051	936,126
1842	6,485,443	864,725
1843	5,290,650	904,908
1844	5,546,483	852,418

It has been seen that, even in the year 1842, the consumption of Irish spirits was reduced to one-half of what it had been in the year 1839. And though the Famine, which had its origin in the partial failure of 1845, and was developed into frightful magnitude by the total failure of 1846, produced a baneful effect on the temperance movement, by impairing its organisation, closing the temperance rooms, and inducing the people to seek in false excitement a momentary forgetfulness of their misery ; still the consumption of spirits did not recover from the effects of Father Mathew's mission, and for years exhibited the result of his influence, as the subjoined returns will show :—

Year.	Gallons.	Duty.
1845 . . .	6,451,137 . .	£860,151
1846 . . .	7,605,196 . .	1,014,026
1847 . . .	7,952,076 . .	1,060,276

The figures which we have quoted exhibit, it is true, most important results ; but an extract from the trade article of the *Freeman's Journal*, for February 1842, will indicate, in an equally striking manner, the happy influence of the temperance movement upon the comforts of the Irish people. The writer says :—

The people, we have abundant proofs, are happier and better, and the nation is more intelligent and prosperous. Perhaps the best proof which can be given of the former is the increase of the Customs revenue, more particularly as regards those articles which are especially consumed by the people. The increase in the Customs revenue of Great Britain and Ireland during the past year was £148,000, of which the increase of those duties levied in the port of Dublin alone was £77.000, or more than one half of the entire increase. The whole amount of this revenue from this port in the past year was £984.000, or very close upon one million. But the articles from which this large amount of increased revenue has been received are those the humbler classes consume most largely ; the increased consumption of *tea and sugar* producing in this port, within that period, an increased revenue of 10 per cent. In the duties on tea and sugar in this port of Dublin alone, the increase amounts to £55,000, or over one-third the whole amount by which those duties in the present exceed those of the past financial year.

The writer adds that the result would appear more striking were not duty paid in England on much of the sugar used in Ireland. The revenue on tobacco decreased to the amount of £3,000 within the year.

Father Mathew made frequent allusions to the injury he had brought upon members of his own family by his advocacy of temperance; and the following words, spoken in December 1842, come appropriately in this place:—

I do not know but that there are distillers or brewers listening to me. I have such in my own family. One member of my family in Cashel, a distiller, now manufactures, I am glad to say, as much in a week as would supply his customers for a year. That is a great falling off from other days. I am rejoiced at this; for when the glory of God is in question, we should not mind the ties of flesh and blood.

A member of Father Mathew's family, connected with him by marriage, thus writes in March 1843:—

Every teetotaller has gained morally and physically by the movement; but my immediate family have been absolutely and totally ruined by Father Mathew's temperance mission.

A writer in the *Dublin Review*, in an article devoted to the temperance movement in Ireland, has the following, in reference to the unselfish and disinterested conduct of Father Mathew:—

We need not, therefore, remark how little consistent with considerations of a worldly nature are the present occupations of the Apostle of Temperance. The brother and relative naturally wrote to him, and said, 'If you go on thus, you will certainly ruin our fortunes.' His answer is, 'Change your trade; turn your premises into factories for flour; at all events my course is fixed. Though heaven and earth should come together, we should do what is right.' This language is worthy of the Messiah.

CHAPTER XIV.

Important Testimonies to the Progress and Beneficial Effects of the Movement—Lord Morpeth—Maria Edgeworth—Cardinal Wiseman—Dr. Channing—Other Testimonies—Their effect—Temperance Speeches—Tim's Oration.

LORD MORPETH, when Irish Secretary, thus referred, at the annual dinner in the Mansion House, in Dublin, to the beneficial effects of the mission of Father Mathew, and the hopes and aspirations to which it gave rise :—

I have already adverted to the gradual diminution of crime; but when I look for the source of this most striking developement in this ameliorating process, I own I am rather pleased not to have to refer for it to the acts of policy of any government of the day. It was my lot, in the House of Commons, to hear an humble but sincere tribute to the wonderful efficacy that attended the exertions of Father Mathew; and although I fear, at this moment, we present rather too convivial an aspect for his entire approval, yet I am glad to speak in the presence of so many who, from their personal observation, can confirm the marvellous effects his mission has had in extending--nay, increasing habits of temperance throughout the land. He needs not, and looks not for, our praise—higher motives impel him, and higher agencies befriend him. I will not go into the details of this transformation; but I will ask, considering this pure and lofty renovation of a nation's virtue, is there anything which seems too large to hope for, or too bright to realise? This change which has passed over the people seems to have been anticipated by the poet of a former day, who is never so much at home as when he celebrates heroic or holy actions:—

The wretch who once sang wildly, danced, and laughed,
And sucked in dizzy madness with his draught,
Has wept a silent flood—reversed his ways—
Is sober, meek, benevolent—and prays.

Maria Edgeworth, the celebrated novelist, whose descriptions of humble life in her own country are the happiest because the most natural ever written, thus exhibits, by the testimony of her village of Edgeworthstown, the practical effects of the temperance reformation on the habits, manners, customs, and comforts—in a word, on the daily life of the Irish peasantry. Miss Edgeworth's letter was written in reply to one addressed to her by Mr. Allen of Dublin, with a view to elicit so valuable a testimony in favour of the cause. The distinguished writer says:—

In our village of Edgeworthstown the whisky-selling has diminished *since* the pledge has been taken, within the last two years, so as to leave public-houses empty, and to oblige the landlord to lower house-rent considerably. This we know to our pecuniary loss, I *need not add* to our moral satisfaction.

The appearance of the people, their quiet demeanour at markets and fairs, has wonderfully improved in general; and to the knowledge of this family many notorious drinkers, and some, as it was thought, confirmed drunkards, have been completely reformed by taking the pledge.

They have become able and willing to work, and to take care of their farms and business—are decently clothed, and healthy and happy, and now make their wives and children happy, instead, as before their reformation, miserable and half heart-broken. I have heard some of the strong expressions of delight of some of the wives of the reformed drunkards. One wife said to me, 'Ma'am, I 'm the happiest woman now that can be: sure *he* says he is wakened from a dream, and now *he* goes about his business so well—and, ma'am, he can eat more, and he can bear the noise of the children, which he never could formerly.'

I have heard of many instances where the health has been improved even where the 'total abstinence' began late in life, and after habits of daily intemperance.

I have not known of any in which the health has suffered. Very few, scarcely any, instances of breaking the pledge have as yet come to our knowledge. But some have occurred. The culprits have been completely shunned and disgraced, so that they are awful warnings to others.

So long as public opinion is upheld in this manner, and so continues to act, we may hope that this great power—this inestimable moral blessing to Ireland in particular—will continue; and most earnestly I hope and pray that it may.

Beyond all calculations—beyond all the predictions of experience, and all the examples from the past, and all analogy—this wonderful crusade against the bad habits of nations, the bad habits and sensual tastes of individuals—has succeeded and lasted for about two years.

It is amazing, and proves the power of moral and religious influence and motive beyond any other example on record in history.

I consider Father Mathew as the greatest benefactor to his country, the most true friend to Irishmen and to Ireland.

The following additional testimonies to the great reformation accomplished by one individual were borne by two distinguished men—Cardinal Wiseman and Dr. Channing. The former was then the Catholic Bishop of Birmingham; and it was on the occasion of the consecration of St. Andrew's Chapel, Dublin, that, in his dedication sermon, Dr. Wiseman thus referred to Father Mathew's preaching, and its marvellous results:—

Long ago, a Pilgrim came from the East, and described the sufferings of the Christians under the galling Infidel yoke, and beseechingly called upon their brethren to relieve them; his words sank deep into the hearts of many, and numbers of rich and poor put on their breast the Cross of the Church, and devoted themselves to the rescue of the Holy Sepulchre. The resolution and harmony with which so many obeyed his call, and the unspeakable success of his mission, seemed to give it a Divine sanction, and his cause was declared to be the cause of God. Actuated by motives as inspiring, an humble son of St. Francis has travelled your land, preaching against a vice which was the greatest bane of your domestic happiness and spiritual welfare; calling upon you to take up the Cross of the Church and place it in your hearts, and not on your garments. How has this mission succeeded, and how was that call obeyed? It has been obeyed beyond all human calculation; and the adhesion, not of thousands, but of millions, has proved the *authority* that sanctioned it. Has God not thus extended his blessing even to the most despised amongst you? Yes, my brethren, and when you see the reproach of intemperance, formerly, and perhaps not unjustly, cast upon you, now removed—when you see the humble family that was cold and helpless now warm and comfortable—when you see the children of the poor not neglected, not illiterate, and destitute of clothing, but decently clad, and educated and supported, and the young people sober, and industrious, and virtuous; and when, in fine, you see the happy and contented family sitting round a well furnished board, do n't forget him who, through God, has given those blessings, and blessed the peasant as well as the prince, the cottage as well as the palace. Those blessings will soon be the familiar words of the country ; the traces of your feuds will soon be extinguished, education will be brought to every home, the prevalence of temperance will open new ways of industry for honourable ambition ; and the period is not far distant when the neighbouring nations will point to you as a country God has specially favoured, and munificently blessed. Peace and prosperity are in your path.

In a discourse delivered in Boston, Dr. Channing describes that marvellous moral revolution which was being then accomplished at the other side of the Atlantic :—

At the present moment, it is singularly unreasonable to doubt and despair of the improvement of society. Providence is placing before our eyes, in broad light, the success of efforts for the amelioration of human affairs. I might refer to the change produced among ourselves within the last few years, by the exertions of good men, for the suppression of intemperance, the very vice which seems the most inveterate, and which, more than all others, spreads poverty and crime; but this moral revolution, in our own country, sinks into nothing when compared with the amazing and almost incredible work now in progress on the other side of the ocean. A few years ago, had we been called to name the country of all others most degraded, beggared and hopelessly crushed by intemperance, we should have selected Ireland. There, men and women, old and young, were alike swept away by what seemed the irresistible torrent. Childhood was baptized into drunkenness; and now, in the short space of two or three years, this vice of ages has been almost rooted out. In the moral point of view, the Ireland of the past is banished—a new Ireland has started into life; five millions of her population have taken the pledge of total abstinence ; and instances of violating the pledge are very, very rare. The great national anniversaries, on which the whole labouring population used to be dissolved in excesses, are now given to innocent pleasures. The excise on ardent spirits has now been diminished nearly a million sterling. History records no revolution like this ; it is the grand event of the present day. Father Mathew, the leader in this moral revolution, ranks far above the heroes and statesmen of the times. However, as Protestants, we may question the claims of departed saints, here is a living minister, if he may be judged from one work, who deserves to be canonised, and whose name should be placed in the Calendar not far below the Apostles. And is this an age in which to be sceptical as to radical changes in society, as to the recovery of the mass of men from brutal ignorance and still more brutal vice?

This beautiful passage was first called to the attention of Father Mathew by the Rev. Mr. Hort, a venerable Presbyterian minister, then—in January 1842—dwelling in Swansea, who writes to his reverend friend in a strain honourable to both :—

Every day of my life I offer, at the throne of grace, my prayer for continued support to your soul and body in your labours of Christian love—for continued efficacy to be imparted to your glorious and benevolent efforts; and I think I know you well enough to be sure that you will not esteem as presumptuous that prayer and blessing of a very aged fellow-disciple of the Saviour, trembling and tottering on the brink of the grave. I rejoice most sincerely in that honour with which God has been pleased to crown you; and in the reputation, so well sustained and so widely extended, which envelops you as a white and lustrous robe of real dignity. As a testimony of the extension of the report of the wonderful work of divine grace which is now being carried on by your efforts, I take the liberty of sending you a transcript from a late publication of the illustrious American writer, Channing, pointed out to me by Mrs. Huxham, daughter of mine, living in the vicinity, who, together with Mrs. Edgar, in Cork, share their father's respect, admiration, and high esteem for you.

The two additional testimonies to the practical benefits conferred on the community by Father Mathew's mission belong to the year 1842. The one was spoken by Lord Louth, the other was written by a Catholic priest.

The following brief report of his lordship's speech at a temperance festival in the assembly-room of Tallanstown, and at which many of his tenantry were present, is taken from an Ulster newspaper :—

Lord Louth complimented the members of the teetotal association, and said that, in whatever clime or country he should travel, he would be ever found the staunch advocate of the teetotal system. He had seen many societies, but a pleasanter sight he never saw than the present, where all was sobriety, harmony, and cheerful good order. He knew they had many enemies, who would rather have them fighting, cursing, and breaking each other's heads. As a magistrate, what had he or the bench to perform? scarcely anything except fining the poor people for their animals (pigs and goats) trespassing on the road; and the police had nothing to do than to watch them, and right glad would they be to catch them—for they had no other employment. A teetotaller never was brought before him accused of crime; and he was sure none of the present company would take one hundred guineas and break their pledge. He concluded by stating that, wherever he would be, he would be happy to see such a sight.

The writer of the pregnant note now given was then officiating in the parish of SS. Peter and Paul, in the city of Cork, and has been for several years parish priest of Blackrock, the beautiful peninsula which forms so fine a feature in the scenery of the Lee. Writing to Father Mathew on the 9th of April 1842, the Rev. Mr. O'Sullivan says:—

I hope your journey will be productive of much good in the parish of Killavullen. The change already effected there by your apostolic labours is almost miraculous. Quiet and order prevail in the little town, which two years since was the continued scene of riot, drunkenness and blasphemy.

Testimonies such as the foregoing, which might be multiplied, had a most beneficial effect upon the mind of the country. They assisted to impart to the public feeling of the nation a higher moral tone, and to inspire disgust and hatred of the vice which had neutralised so many fine qualities, and entailed so deep, if not so deserved a reproach upon the character of a whole people. If strangers, too, thought so much of what had been done, and what might still be accomplished—if those from a distance described in such glowing colours and in such lofty terms that moral revolution which was making Ireland famous throughout the civilised world—why should not her own children feel proud of the virtue and self-denial through which those great things were achieved, and of that bright and glorious vista opened to the aspiration of the moralist and the patriot? These testimonies, so full of generous sympathy, had, upon a susceptible and impulsive race, the effect of a trumpet blast—they stirred the heart, roused the spirit, and strengthened the resolution of the leaders as well as the more intelligent of the rank and file of the army of temperance. They also tended to deepen into something akin to idolatry the feeling of mingled respect, veneration, and affection, in which Father Mathew was held by the mass of the Irish people. The speeches, the addresses, the poetic effusions of that day, partook of a character which would seem absurdly inflated and exaggerated, if one did not make fair allowance for the circumstances of the hour, and the hopeful exultation of the ardent and the eloquent—who perhaps had been themselves rescued from danger or misery through the agency of Father Mathew, and who thus spoke from the fervent gratitude of the heart.

Comical, too, were many of the speeches delivered from the platform, and at 'festivals,' as tea-parties in the temperance rooms were usually termed. Here the members were occasionally induced to narrate their own experiences, and describe, for the advantage of the younger portion of the audience, the miseries which drunkenness had entailed upon themselves and their families, and the benefits, to mind and body and worldly interests, which sobriety had conferred upon them. Frequently, such addresses were full of homely good sense, of heart-moving pathos, and also of genuine humour; and to a more favourable or sympathetic audience than an assembly of Irish teetotallers, who had just enjoyed a plentiful but simple meal of true temperance fare, it would be almost impossible for an orator, practised or unpractised, to address himself. They were always in good humour and good temper; and neither a flash of wit, or fun, or humour, nor a happy bit of description, nor a brilliant sentence, nor an animated appeal, failed to elicit the appropriate response—a hearty laugh, or a rousing cheer. But if the orator had no experience to narrate, no lesson to inculcate, or no moral to draw—in that case he had only to indulge in unlimited praise of Father Mathew, and he was sure to succeed. That name was never referred to without applause following its mention; and with any assembly of teetotallers, praise of Father Mathew would alone have been sufficient to impart vivacity to dullness, or interest to the most rambling and inconsequent nonsense. The love of the people for their 'moral leader,' as they so often heard him termed, was intense, and manifested itself at every possible opportunity. The more grandiose orators heaped upon him all kinds of attributes, and ransacked history, both sacred and profane, for names which they might befittingly apply to him. Moses and Maccabæus, Judith and Joshua, as well as Julius Cæsar, Brian Borhu, and the Great Napoleon, were not rarely impressed into the service of the ambitious orator; and the innocent people applauded, and Father Mathew beamed with benevolence, while the speaker proved, to his own satisfaction, and most generally to that of his audience, the happy fitness and appositeness of the most outrageous 'parallel.'

The writer remembers an occasion on which a village schoolmaster, of high repute for a style of eloquence lofty and incomprehensible, but not the less prized on that account, compared Father Mathew to a 'solicitous mother holding up her tender babe to her lacteal bosom.' Eloquence of that sublime order required a somewhat specially cultivated audience to appreciate its merit; but a narrative like the following, delivered with appropriate gesture, and comical winks and nods, was sure to bring down the house.

After such really clever and brilliant speeches as were heard on these occasions from the accomplished and scholarly lieutenants of the temperance leader, droll addresses had all the effect of broad farce after genteel comedy. Tim ——, the orator whose speeches were at all times received with delight, especially by the younger portion of the audience, had an incorrigible propensity for pronouncing 'this,' 'that,' or 'the,' as if it were spelled 'dis,' 'dat,' or 'de,'—and this tightening process was applied by him to every other word that admitted of its application.

After much persuasion—for he, at first, affected the bashful—Tim was induced to step into the narrow space left for the speakers. Having bowed to Father Mathew, nodded to the rest, and taking one or two prefatory scratches at his red poll, Tim thus delivered himself:—

Yer reverence, ladies and gentlemen, de dickens a one of me knows how to make a speech at all; so ye all must excuse me, if ye plaze; but it would be a mane ting in me to be after denyin' de goodness of God; an' shure 't is I was de boy dat see de two sides of de shillin'—de bad an' de good. I 've nottin' to boast of in de way of hoight; an' dough I say it that should n't say it, dere were few boys ov my inches dat would bate me in hurley or football—dough dat is n't neider here nor dere—but, small as I am, I could put a gallon of porter out of sight wid de best ov 'em; and as for whisky, why 't was like mudder's milk to me—I 'd lap it as de cat laps crame. Ov course, dere ar'nt people standin' in de middle ov de road wid pints ov porter in dere hands, sayin', 'Good man, will ye be plazed to drink a drop dis hot day, or dis could mornin'!—for wheder 't is hot or could, 't is all de same—one drinks to be could, and anoder drinks to be hot—an' 't is mighty could it is in de end. No, yer reverence, an' ladies and gentlemen, little ye gets for nottin' in dis world—and fait' 't is myself had such a druthe upon me, dat 'twas just as if I swallowed a lime-burner's wig. I had n't aise or pace so long as I was n't turnin' the bottom of a pint or a naggin' to the ceilin'—an' so long as I had a fardin', I melted it in drink. Dere are many here dat knows me, an' knows dat I was a good hand at earnin' money; but if one tinks of nottin' but drinkin', de divil a good 't would be to him if he had de bank of Ireland to call his own, an' de banker houldin' on be the raipin'-hook up in de moon, like Daniel O'Rourke. So you see, ladies, de poor wife soon had n't a fardin' to bless herself wid, and de childer, de craychers, often went to bed could, and me blackguardin' and gladiaterin' about de town, drinkin' here an' drinkin' dere, until one 'ud tink I'd burst, savin' yer presence; for de dickens a one ov me knows where I put it all—I was like a punchin on two legs. Yer reverence, I 'm puzzled entirely to understand why one does n't take half nor quarter de tay dat one does ov porter or punch; but if de tay we had here dis evenin' was punch, an' I in de ould times, 't is n't de tay cap, but de big jug, dat 'ud be my share dis blessed night. Well, ov coorse, dis kind ov ting could n't go on widout bringin' me, 'an de poor wife and childer, to sup sorrow. I first drank my own clothes into de pawn—den I drank my wife's cloak off ov her back—den I drank her flannel petticoat and her gound—den I drank de cups and de sawcers out ov de cupboard—den I drank de plates and dishes off ov de dresser—den I drank the pot an' de kittle off ov de fire —den I drank de bedclothes from de bed, and de bed from under meself an' me wife,—until, de Lord bless us! dere was n't a mortial haport dat was n't turned into gallons ov porter, an' glasses ov whysky, an' dandies ov punch! Well, what brought me to my sinses at last was de could flure, and de empty belly, and de poor childer cryin' 'Daddy, daddy, we 're hungry.' I remimber de last night ov my blackguardin', dere was n't a bit to ait, or a sup to taste, for de poor little tings, an' I tould dem to go to bed, an' to hould dere whisht, an' not bodder me. 'Daddy, daddy, we 're hungry,' says de biggest fellow, 'and our mudder did n't ait a bit all day, an' she gave all she had to Katty and Billy!' 'Daddy, daddy,' says de littlest of the boys—dat 's Billy—'I can't go to sleep, I 'm so could.' 'God forgive yer onnateral fader!' says I; 'for 't is he 's the purty boy intirely! wid his drinkin' and his blackguardin'. Hould yer whisht,' says I, 'an' I 'll make ye comfortable;' an' wid dat, savin' yer presence, ladies, I takes me breeches—'t is no laughin' matter, I tell ye—an' I goes over to the craychers, an' I sticks one of de childer into one of de legs, an' anoder of the childer into de oder leg, an' I buttons the waistband round dere necks, an' I tould dem for de life ov dem not to dare as much as sneeze for de rest ov de night—an' dey did n't, poor childer. But be cockcrow in de mornin', Billy, who was a mighty airly bird, cries out, 'Daddy, daddy!' 'What 's de matter?' says I. 'I want to get up, daddy,' says he. 'Well, get up, an' bad scran to ye,' says I. 'I can 't', says de young shaver. 'Why can 't ye, ye kantankerous cur?' says I. 'Me an' Tommy is in de breeches,' says he. 'Get out ov it,' says I. 'Daddy, we 're buttoned up,' says de little fellow, as smart as you plaze. So up I got, an' unbuttoned the craychures; an' I says to meself 't was a burnin' shame dat de children ov a Christian, lave 'lone a haythin', should be buttoned up in a breeches, instead ov lying in a dacent bed. So I slipped on de breeches on my own shanks, and off I goes to his reverence, an' I takes de pledge; an' 't was de crown-piece dat yer reverence, God bless you! slipped into de heel ov my fist, dat set me up again in de world. Ladies and gentlemen, me story is tould; an' all I have to say is dis—dat I've lost de taste for whisky an' porter, an' for dandies of punch too. An' dough I do n't be for standin' trates or takin' trates, still, an' all, if a friend comes in de way, he 's welcome as de flowers ov May; and, glory be to de Lord, and tanks to his reverence, dere 's a clane place to resave him, an' a good leg ov mutton an' trimmins on de table, and *cead mille failtha* into de bargain. Dat is what I calls de two sides ov de shillin'—de bad an' de good,

The reader may imagine the applause amid which Tim, proud of his oratorical success, retired to his former corner, where he was received by his blushing but happy wife, and listened with complacency to the congratulations of his friends. Father Mathew heartily enjoyed Tim's description of the novel use to which he applied his small clothes.

CHAPTER XV.

Father Mathew an Advocate of Law and Order—Warns the People against Secret Societies—Denounces Blood-spilling—His Rage for making 'Converts'—The Victim of Lemonade—The Deserters.

FATHER MATHEW was not only the preacher of temperance, but also the most earnest advocate of law and order. Those crimes which occasionally startled the public mind, and brought odium and disgrace upon the country, were denounced in unsparing terms by the good priest, to whose kindly and generous nature cruelty and violence were peculiarly abhorrent. Against secret societies, those pestilent nurseries of outrage, he constantly raised his voice, oftentimes with the happiest result. On several occasions, for instance, in the year 1842, he availed himself of the occurrence of some remarkable outrage to address the most salutary warnings to masses of the peasantry throughout every district of the country.

At Lucan, near Dublin, he thus referred to the machinations of the secret societies, and called upon his hearers to beware of their villainous emissaries. This was in June 1842:—

I am sorry to hear, from a respected clergyman, that emissaries are in the habit of going into the coffee-rooms where teetotallers meet, for the purpose of ensnaring them into becoming members of Ribbon Societies. My dear friends, I caution you not to join them, whatever name they bear. If any of those emissaries address you, at once disclose the matter to your clergyman, or to the next magistrate; for these bloodthirsty wretches only seek to betray you, and, having effected their object, they would then go to a foreign land, there to live on the blood-money.

In the following month, at a meeting held in the county Tipperary, he again warns the people against the snares of those wicked organisations :—

I have seen with the deepest regret, that it has been imputed to the district of Newport that secret societies exist there. This I am afflicted to hear—that any district where the temperance cause has been established could harbour such societies. I have always, earnestly, perseveringly, emphatically, cautioned the people against those societies, because they are filled with danger, with vice, with iniquity—because they cut at the roots of social order—because they are the blight and bane of social happiness. I hope most earnestly that the people of Newport will use their best efforts to eradicate such societies, if any of them yet remain, and that they will persevere until every trace of them is obliterated. The authors and concoctors of those societies have no good object in view; they only think how they can ensnare the unsuspecting into their hellish toils, and then they sell their victims to the offended laws of the country for the wages of iniquity. Beware of these wolves in sheep's clothing—they steal upon their intended victim under the disguise of assumed friendship; but they are only thinking of the blood-money at the time. My venerable and respected friend, Dr. Healy, who was the first of the clergy of the Archdiocese to join the standard of temperance, has at all times cautioned his people against those societies; and I trust, most confidently, that the words of that exemplary priest will be listened to with attention, and that his warning voice will be heard amongst them.

In December of the same year, and in the presence of a vast multitude assembled in the same county, Father Mathew impressively enforced respect for the laws, and denounced, in the strongest language, two atrocious murders perpetrated but a short time before, at Kileacle and the Silver-mines.

The perpetrators of these red-handed murders (said he) cannot escape the just anger of God. Though the brand of Cain on their brow may not be apparent to the eyes of mortals, to the eye of the Eternal it is as plain as the sun at noon is to us. Let them hide in the solitude of a cavern, or even in the bowels of the earth, or though the waves of the sea rolled over them, the eye of Heaven pierces through every gloom, and marks out the wretch who has shed his brother's blood—who, with impious hands, has taken away the life of a fellow-creature. The murderer may escape the arm of man's justice; but so surely as he quits this world, and stands trembling before the judgement seat of God, so surely will he have to account to the Eternal Judge of the living and the dead, for the crime of which he was guilty in this life. Crimes such as these, my dear friends, bring a curse on the land. Oh, in the name of God! hold fast to the temperance pledge, and shun, as you would the plague, the company of those who would seek to entrap you into secret and illegal associations, which are the authors of every wickedness. Listen to the voice of your clergy, your faithful and devoted friends, and they will warn you against the wretches who go about, like roaring lions, seeking whom they may devour.

Father Mathew was too wise to condemn those who did not join the temperance society, or who enjoyed the use of wine and other stimulants in moderation. He employed every art to obtain followers and converts, but his advocacy was always within the bounds of reason and good sense. He thus expressed his opinion upon what was then a vexed question with the advocates of total abstinence :—

While I laud temperance, and call on all to join its ranks, far be it from me to pass censure on those who use strong liquors in a moderate way. I no more condemn them than did St. Paul condemn the state of honourable wedlock; but I say that every motive that could influence a Christian to adopt any line of conduct calls on us to warn others to abstain. There is no gratification worthy of a Christian that cannot be enjoyed without tasting intoxicating liquors.

But having thus defended himself from the imputation of holding an opinion or advocating a doctrine which would have a tendency rather to repel than to attract, he, in a few vigorous words, described the consequences, both temporal and eternal, which were brought about by habitual drunkenness :—

Oh! my friends, if our bridewell, our lunatic asylum, or our prisons, or even Hell itself, were to trace on our adorned walls the history of the desolation, the agony, and the eternal ruin wrought by drunkenness, as did the mysterious hand upon the wall of the Court of the King, Balthazzar, the reading of it would cause our hearts to die within us, and our spirits to faint away.

In his zeal for making 'converts,' no man ever surpassed Father Mathew. Neither age, nor sex, nor condition, was a protection against his seductive arts. The venerable grandfather in his arm-chair, or the toddler drawing his 'go-cart'—the master or the man, the mistress or the maid—the porter, the clerk, or the merchant—the policeman or the prisoner—the priest at the altar or the boy wearing the alb—the schoolmaster and the schoolmistress, or the scholar with the jacket and the scholar with the frock—the nurse in the hospital or the patient in the sick ward—the gentleman of wide estate or the lodge-keeper at his gate—the editor of the newspaper or the 'devil' besmirched with ink—the nobleman or the sweep—the fine lady or the street-scavenger—all were alike to Father Mathew, who never allowed slip an opportunity of adding a new follower to his standard.

'Did you see Father Mathew lately?' said one friend to another, whom he happened to meet travelling in the South of Ireland. 'I did,' was the reply. 'And I'll engage he made you take the pledge?' 'He did, indeed. But did you see him lately?' 'To be sure, I did.' 'And did he make you take it, too?' 'That he did.' 'There is no escaping him; but I am not sorry for it.' 'No, nor I, neither.'

Many a young fellow, who had as much notion of taking the pledge as he had of jumping over the moon, was caught, snaffled, bound hand and foot, before he knew where he was. 'My dear child, I know you wish to oblige me?' would be murmured in the softest and most winning accents of the practised entrapper of unsuspecting youth. This was one of his most deadly hooks, and seldom failed in its effect. 'Indeed, I would, Father Mathew—you *know* that, sir,' the intended victim would incautiously reply. 'Well, my dear, I assure you, you would greatly oblige me if you would join our society, and give me the benefit of your influence.' 'But, Father Mathew, I assure you I have no occasion for it—I was never drunk in my life.' 'Of course you were not, my dear; and therefore it will be *no sacrifice to you*—you have nothing to give up, as others have; and you will enjoy the consciousness of having afforded a good example to others. My dear child, do n't refuse me this favour.' And before the victim knew where he was, he found himself on his knees, repeating the words of the pledge; and on rising up, he was a Mathewite, enrolled in the ranks of temperance, with a silver medal hanging round his neck—the same medal which his captor had worn a moment before. Meet him in a coach or train; meet him in the street; visit him, or be visited by him; it was all the same—there was no escape, even for those who, to use their own words, 'did not require the pledge,' or 'had no occasion for it.' In flight alone was there protection from the wiles of one who was as well versed in the arts of the recruiting sergeant as in the duties and responsibilities of a chief and leader. Numbers of innocent boys and girls gladly did as he required of them, for the enjoyment of a holiday, or the possession of a picture-book or a doll; and if it were said that there was not much value in converts of this class, Father Mathew would reply, 'I prefer them to all others. Besides, they will be men and women one of those days. It is on the youth of the country I place my chief dependence.' And thousands of silver medals, and hundreds of thousands of the ordinary medals, did these young teetotallers cost him who valued their accession so highly.

For his young lady friends he had an appeal which was generally irresistible:—'Surely, my dear child, *you* cannot refuse to do glory to God? You know not what may be the salutary influence of your example in preserving poor weak creatures from misery and crime. To save others from temptation, is to do glory to God; and surely, my dear, *you*, who were so religiously brought up, cannot refuse to do that. Down on her knees went the young girl thus appealed to. And in this manner did the temperance leader swell the ranks of his society, and extend its influence amongst the educated and wealthy classes of the community.

'Once a teetotaller, for ever a teetotaller,' was Father Mathew's declaration and policy. No miser ever clutched his golden coin with a more eager grasp than did Father Mathew his teetotallers. It was with a positive sense of pain that he became conscious of the desertion or back-sliding of a single follower. He mourned over the loss of a stray sheep, and never rested till he had followed it into the wilderness of temptation, and brought it back, and placed it safely in the fold. There was one infallible mode by which the good man's temper might at any moment be ruffled. That was by returning him the card and medal, thereby formally seceding from the society, and renouncing the practice of temperance. He could retain his composure against open attack or malignant imputation, and no human being ever so readily forgave his enemies as he did; but to lay down the medal, and tell him that you no longer intended to adhere to 'temperance'—which meant total abstinence—was an offence for which he had no patience, and scarcely any forgiveness.

A gentleman called on him one day, at his house in Cove Street, and no sooner did Father Mathew hear his well-known voice than he hurried down stairs to welcome him. 'My dear sir, I am delighted and proud to meet you, and glad to see you looking so well.' 'Indeed, Father Mathew, I am not at all so well as I appear to be,' replied his friend, in dolorous tones. 'I am very sorry to hear it, my dear sir; perhaps you work too hard?' 'I do, sir, work pretty hard; but it is not that that injures me; the fact is, Father Mathew, it's the—lemonade.' 'The lemonade, my dear!—what lemonade?' 'The lemonade, sir, that I drink after dinner,—it does n't agree with my stomach 'Well, my dear, then do n't drink it. You can have coffee instead ; and good water is wholesomer than anything else.' It then appeared that the gentleman had come to resign his pledge ; at which intelligence the grief of Father Mathew was excessive, for he dreaded the influence which this example might have on others. He entreated and implored 'his old and much-loved friend, whom he had known from childhood,' to take back his medal, and 'not abandon the good and holy cause ;' but the much-loved friend was inexorable, explaining, at the same time, his conscientious belief that, from the peculiarly delicate nature of his constitution, and, in fact, intricate construction of his stomach, he required the mild stimulant of at least one tumbler of punch in the twenty-four hours. 'Then, sir, you may go and drink a bucket-full of it every day of your life,' said Father Mathew, losing all patience, and turning his back upon the victim of lemonade. For months after Father Mathew could not afford a civil word to the backslider, for his fall was as the fall of a tower ; but the indignation died away in time, and the deserted leader could even laugh pleasantly at the sad effects of ærated beverages upon a delicate constitution.

The writer had dined and spent the evening with Father Mathew, and, at nine o'clock, was about leaving his house, being escorted to the door by his polite host ; but just as he was bidding him adieu, there appeared in the door-way a great strapping fellow, more than six feet in stature. 'Let me see who this is,' said Father Mathew. 'Well, my dear, what is it you want ?' said he to the countryman ; 'perhaps you desire to take the pledge. If so, you will do a good work, and God will bless you for avoiding temptation. No good ever came from strong drink, my dear, either to body or soul.' The poor countryman seemed terribly embarrassed, and fumbled something between his fingers. 'Kneel down, my dear, and repeat the words of the pledge after me,' said the priest. ''Tis n't that I want, yer reverence—'tis to give it up.' 'Give it up!—you surely do n't mean to break your solemn pledge, and to become a drunkard!' thundered the indignant temperance leader. 'No, yer reverence; but I 'm not well in my health, and the docther says I 'm better be after giving up the pledge—and here 's the kard and middle.' Saying this, the countryman flung them both on the table in the little parlour, and made a rapid movement towards the door; but before he had reached the door, Father Mathew seized him by both shoulders, and treated him to a downright hearty shake, saying, 'Go away—go away—you great big booby! What a shame to think that a man of your size can 't do without strong drink! Do n't tell me of your doctors,—I know better,—you do n't want whisky or porter—I do n't want them. Go, sir! you will be one day sorry for your foolishness.' And he shoved the recreant into the street, down which the poor fellow fled, as if the dogs of remorse were yelping at his heels.

There might sometimes be seen a flying pledge-breaker, pursued by one of the clerks or by a volunteer, rushing down Drinan Street,—which was immediately opposite the well-known dwelling in Cove Street,—or down Cove Street, and Father Mathew watching the chase from the window or the street door. It occasionally happened that a head was popped inside the parlour door, and that a clink of some hard substance on the floor followed the words,—'There 't is for ye—I 'm done with it anyhow;' and a rush towards the street door would bear witness to the fact that an audacious deserter was about escaping, having, as it were, flung down his firelock before the face of his commander. Away the brave Donnelly would rush in pursuit, aided, perhaps, by some sturdy son of temperance who happened to be in the parlour at the time; and if the culprit were overtaken and captured, and Father Mathew in the way, speedy repentance and prompt pardon were the result; but it as frequently occurred that the plan of escape had been too well matured, and that means had been taken to baffle pursuit, and prevent the possibility of capture. There was also a more simple and less perilous mode of giving up the pledge, which was largely availed of. This was by slipping the card or the medal under the hall door, or into the letter-box, or even sending it through the post-office ; and to this safer mode of abandoning the cause, and 'taking to strong drink,' the dread of meeting Father Mathew, and encountering his anger, induced many to have recourse. But when, wretched and woe-begone, with tattered clothes and pale faces, the deserters returned after a week's debauch, there was no anger to dread,—they knew that compassion and tenderness were always awaiting the poor penitent prodigal. Truly, there was more joy in that parlour at the return of one drunkard than at the enrolment of ninety-nine sober, who had never fallen.

The original pledge did not contain a clause against 'cordials ;' and ere long, the evil of the omission was made apparent in a very injurious manner. A new trade sprang into existence, under the shadow and protection of the Temperance Society, and the practice of cordial drinking became but too general.

'Pat,' said a gentleman to his servant who was oscillating on his legs in a strange manner, 'you have been drinking. Why, the man *is* drunk !' 'Me drunk, sir ! and I temperate these four years !' said Pat, in a wronged and reproachful tone. 'Well, if you *ar n't* drunk, I never saw a drunken man in my life,—that 's all.' 'Sir, I 'm temperate,' said Pat, who had at the same time to clutch the edge of the sideboard, to save himself from an upset. 'Tell me, Pat, my poor fellow, *what* have you been taking that *disagreed* with you so ?' enquired his master, with an air of intense solicitude. Well, then, sir, I 'll tell you no lie, 't is them cordials—the divil's curè to them for cordials !—indeed, I 'm sure and certain there 's poison in them, for I can't ketch a hoult of anything that it does n't slip out of my hand ; and it gives me enough to do to manage my legs, that 's going under me, all the same as if I was a cripple. Bad luck to you for cordials!'

Now, poor Pat was the type of many others, who—though nothing could induce them to break the pledge, by taking the forbidden articles, whisky, porter, ale, or other 'strong drink'—freely indulged in what, after all, was much the same thing; for whisky was the base and chief ingredient of these 'cordials, fruit liquors, and the like,' against which Father Mathew now protested with all his energy. At a meeting near Blarney, in the year 1842, he referred to this too common practice of cordial drinking, and also to the medical dispensation in the original pledge—which, as his own statement proves, was liberally availed of by not a few of his followers:—

> There is one subject which I must particularly call your attention to, and I caution you against making use of those snares of Satan, temperance cordials, for they cannot be manufactured or compounded without the aid of whisky of the worst description; and, as Colonel Titus said to Oliver Cromwell, 'Shall we who fought the lion (whisky and porter) allow ourselves to be devoured by the wolf?' I would sooner a man would break his pledge openly, for he then would be a base pledge-breaker; but a man who drinks those cordials is not only a base pledge-breaker, but also a hypocrite. There was a dispensation placed in the pledge, that the use of spirits would be allowed for medical purposes. but when I introduced that clause I had no idea that a man in perfect health would have a doctor's certificate in his pocket, and then consider himself authorised to take wine and punch at his dinner; but my intention was that he should bring his prescription to an apothecary or druggist, and anything he wished to give him he was perfectly welcome to take. I have now in my possession a certificate from a doctor, not forty miles from where we are at present, given to a pig-jobber, who could not do his business without a glass, and also another given to a carman, who wished to take a glass in the morning and another in the evening every day he went to Cork.

Thenceforward, Father Mathew might be heard announcing at the very top of his voice, and high above the heads of kneeling crowds, that the pledge included 'cider, cordials, fruit liquors, and the like'—the latter comprehensive word being rather sung than spoken, and pronounced as if it were spelled 'loike.'

Relapses and backslidings were among the trials to which the temperance leader was subjected, and which, for the time, had a most depressing effect on a mind that, always sensitive, was occasionally sad. But he had his hours of consolation as well. Thus his heart rejoiced within him as he received accounts of the progress of temperance in distant parts of the world—in America or in India—or when he received invitations from Scotland and England, and also from the United States, expressed in the most flattering language, and giving glowing evidence of the spread and triumph of his beloved cause. The following letter from the Right Rev. Dr. Fennelly, Catholic Bishop of Madras, was one of that class of communications which were sure to have a cheering effect upon his mind:—

Catholic Cathedral, Madras:
November 22, 1842.

VERY REV. AND VERY DEAR FRIEND,—The little zeal I was supposed to entertain, while I was in the Island of Saints, for the prosperity of that great society for which the Almighty has raised you up as an Apostle, was wafted to the coast of Coromandel, by a shorter and more expeditious way than the Cape of Good Hope, and long before my arrival was noised abroad in Madras. I was not well landed here, when a large party of Her Majesty's 57th Regiment, with the Rev. Mr. Gorman at their head, fell upon their knees before me, begging to be enrolled in Father Mathew's Society. I was pleased to find them fully acquainted with the nature and extent of the pledge, particularly when they informed me, that their minds were made up for several weeks to the perpetual abandonment of all intoxicating liquors. When I expressed a hope before sending them away, that they would never dishonour Father Mathew, one of them cried out, 'Of course we will be as good as our countrymen at home.' He was an Irishman.

The Catholic soldiers at Poonamalla and St. Thomas's Mount were not behind their brethren of Fort St. George, when opportunity offered to consecrate themselves to the same glorious cause of Temperance

The good clergyman at St. Thomas's Mount, the Rev. C. Murphy (is not that a Cork name?) profited of the good example which was given him by the Rev. Mr. Gannon, and, to the great edification of his flock, he took the pledge likewise.

Nor was Father Mathew, humble and modest as he was, at all insensible to the eloquent praises of a well-written address, a gracefully-penned letter, or a happy speech. It was not his vanity that was flattered—it was his heart that was touched. Never was testimony so acceptable as when it did justice to his motives—for there were, alas! too many who questioned their purity and disinterestedness, notwithstanding that he, with his own hand, had struck down the prosperity of his own family. Coming from those who differed from him in religious faith, these testimonies were still more acceptable to his harassed mind, which naturally sympathised with his jaded frame. Thus, for instance, writes Sir Francis Le Hunte, a Protestant gentleman :—

The body of Christians to which the revered father belongs may well praise God for having raised up among them such a man; of him Ireland may well be proud; but human love, quickened by love divine, knows no bounds; properly speaking, *our dear Friend* belongs not *exclusively* to any party, to any country; his sympathies are co-extensive with human joy and woe. All the kindreds and nations of the earth will claim Theobald Mathew as their own—all will equally love and revere him, for *his* love extends over all.

The letter from which the above is quoted was followed by an address, to both of which Father Mathew thus replies :—

My dear Sir Francis, your kindness has caused the full measure of obligation to overflow. I glory in being your fellow-labourer in this fruitful vineyard of the Lord, though only hired at the ninth hour. I would have sunk under the weight and heat of the day, were I not cheered on and invigorated by the soul-stirring address forwarded to me in the far south by you and my other generous Brother Teetotallers of Wexford.

Thackeray, who certainly is no hero-worshipper, bore a just and discriminating testimony to the character of Father

Mathew, whom he happily hit off in his 'Irish Sketch-Book.' The age of Father Mathew at the time he was sketched by the authority of 'Vanity Fair,' was not two-and-forty, as he supposed it was, but two-and-fifty. The difference was in the reality, not in the appearance; for he did not look a day older than the age then attributed to him.

On the day we arrived at Cork, and as the passengers descended from the 'drag,' a stout, handsome, honest-looking man, of some two-and-forty years, was passing by, and received a number of bows from the crowd around. It was Theobald Mathew, with whose face a thousand little print-shop windows had already rendered me familiar. He shook hands with the master of the carriage very cordially, and just as cordially with the master's coachman, a disciple of temperance, as at least half Ireland is at present. There is nothing remarkable in Mr. Mathew's manner, except that it is exceedingly simple, hearty, and manly, and that he does not wear the downcast, demure look, which, I know not why, certainly characterises the chief part of the gentlemen of his profession. He is almost the only man, too, that I have met in Ireland, who, in speaking of public matters, did not talk as a partisan. With the state of the country, of landlord, tenant, and peasantry, he seemed to be most curiously and intimately acquainted; speaking of their wants, differences, and the means of bettering them, with the minutest practical knowledge. And it was impossible, in hearing him, to know, but from previous acquaintance, whether he was Whig or Tory, Catholic or Protestant. His knowledge of the people is prodigious, and their confidence in him as great; and what a touching attachment that is which these poor fellows show to anyone who has their cause at heart, even to anyone who says he has! Avoiding all political questions, no man seems more eager than he for the practical improvement of this country. Leases and rents, farming improvements, reading societies, music societies, he was full of these; and of his schemes of temperance above all. He never misses a chance of making a convert, and has his hand ready and a pledge in his pocket for sick or poor. One of his disciples, in a livery-coat, came into the room with a tray: Mr. Mathew recognised him, and shook him by the hand directly; so he did with the strangers who were presented to him; and not with a courtly popularity-hunting air, but, as it seemed, from sheer hearty kindness and a desire to do everyone good. When breakfast was done (he took but one cup of tea, and says, that, from having been a great consumer of tea and refreshing liquids before, a small cup of tea, and one glass of water at dinner, now serve him for his day's beverage) he took the ladies of our party to see his burying-ground, a new and handsome cemetery, lying a little way out of the town, and where, thank God! Protestants and Catholics may lie together without clergymen quarrelling over their coffins.

Invitations flowed in upon Father Mathew from various places in England and Scotland—from Catholic bishops, from temperance societies belonging to all sects, and also from private individuals of station and eminence. Early in the year 1842, he received a gratifying address from the ladies of Edinburgh, signed by 2,000 fair petitioners, who prayed him to commence his promised mission in Scotland in its capital. Invitations from many other places in Scotland were received likewise about the same time; to one of which—from Greenock—he replies :—

The only regret I feel is in consequence of the impossibility of my fixing at present a period for my journey to Scotland. It would afford me great pleasure to hasten the time; but I must first heal the deep and festering wounds of the Irish people.

CHAPTER XVI.

Desires to keep free of Politics—O'Connell a Teetotaller—The Easter Procession of 1842—The Liberator and the Apostle—Tom Blewitt's Speech—The Stranger's Evidence—Characteristic Incident—Father Mathew's Considerateness.

TO keep the temperance cause free from the slightest connection with the politics of the day, was one of Father Mathew's most anxious desires; and we doubt if, among the many anxieties consequent upon his position, as the leader of a great movement, there was one which pressed so heavily upon him as that which he felt upon this head. To those who remember the period, from 1840 to 1845, it is well known that it was one of intense political excitement, when the public mind of Ireland was in a state of constant activity, and during which were held, in almost every part of the island, meetings and demonstrations unsurpassed in their magnitude and significance. Father Mathew had, on a hundred different occasions, proclaimed, and most truly, that his society was unsectarian and unpolitical, and that temperance had nothing whatever to do with polemics or politics; though he well knew, at the same time, that nearly the nine-tenths of those who had taken the pledge at his hands were Repealers, more or less advanced in their opinions, and that there was another man in Ireland who divided their admiration and affection with himself—and that that man was Daniel O'Connell. If Father Mathew were ever so much inclined to interfere with the political belief or action of his followers, he was too prudent to think of carrying his inclination into practice; for he could not fail to be conscious of the fact that, however great and deserved was his influence, and however much he was loved and venerated by the mass of his countrymen, still, if he attempted to impose restraint or check upon their free action, they would have burst the bonds of allegiance to his moral leadership, and openly disregarded his admonitions, or even his commands. What he could do, in a matter so full of delicacy, and indeed of peril, he did—namely, to induce the members of the temperance reading-rooms to refrain from turning their rooms into political meeting places, and to withold their bands, if possible, from being present at political gatherings. In the former, he very much succeeded ; but with the bands his task was far more difficult, and much less successful. Father Mathew never supposed that a man was to relinquish his natural interest in politics merely because he relinquished strong drink, or that the fact of his wearing a medal was to change his whole nature. He was well aware that, in their homes, in their workshops, and in their rooms, his followers read other than temperance speeches ; and that there were few, among those who received him at all times with such genuine demonstrations of respect and affection, whose blood was not stirred by the fiery accents of that great Tribune, whose voice was so often heard with delight by his countrymen.

Though taking no part whatever in politics, Father Mathew was still proud to know that his influence was felt in the political agitation of the day, and was thoroughly appreciated by O'Connell, for this reason—that enormous multitudes of people, who assembled at the call of the political leader, were held in perfect restraint by the controlling influence of the moral leader ; and that many thousands of the full-grown population of Ireland met together, in various places and at different times, in all seasons and under all circumstances, and that no one instance of outrage or riot ever justified the interference of the watchful and jealous authorities

Large bodies of men, young and old, came from long distances to the places of meeting, and returned to their homes and occupations with a peaceableness and good order that were among the most striking features of that wondrous political agitation, which seemed to rouse the whole manhood of at least three provinces of the kingdom. If O'Connell were enabled to keep in check an excitable and ardent people, whom he had inflamed to the highest point, by visions of future prosperity and happiness, of glory and grandeur to their country, as the result of that legislative independence which he assured them, and which he no doubt at the time believed, they could obtain—it was through the aid of Father Mathew that he did so; for though O'Connell might have successfully imposed total abstinence from all kinds of intoxicating drink upon his countrymen for a week, or for a month, as was done during the Clare Election, on which Catholic Emancipation mainly turned, it would have been impossible for him to have imposed it upon them for any considerable time. And had he to deal with a people liable to drunkenness, and therefore rife for disorder and tumult, he never could have guided his followers for so many years within the narrow paths of obedience to the law, respect for the sacredness of property, and undeviating adherence to the doctrine of 'moral force.' It was to Father Mathew that O'Connell was mainly indebted for the peace and good order which so signally marked those great gatherings, that inspired the apprehension of the Government of the day, and the wonder of those who regarded them with the interest or the curiosity of strangers. Independently, then, of the good which temperance conferred on the people in their individual capacity, and of the greater industry and higher morality which it promoted, O'Connell cherished it as a means to his own ends—the accomplishment of the object which required a thoroughly obedient and docile people to lead. And only in a country elevated and purified by Father Mathew's preaching, could the political tribune have found that thoroughly obedient and docile people. Hence O'Connell aided, so fai as he could, the moral movement of the day.

That O'Connell was impressed, even at an early period, with the gravity of the movement, and the hold which temperance had taken upon the minds of his countrymen, we have an interesting evidence in the fifth volume of Guizot's 'History of My Times.' At a dinner party at the house of Mr. and Mrs. Stanley (now Lord and Lady Stanley of Alderly) on the 8th of April 1840, the French Statesman met the Irish Tribune; whose conversation he thus records :—

> He spoke much; he detailed the progress of temperance in Ireland; the drunkards were disappearing by thousands—the taste for regular habits and more refined manners advanced in proportion as inebriety receded. No one expressed the slightest doubt. I asked him whether this was a mere puff of popular humour, or a lasting reform! He replied gravely, 'It will last; we are a persevering race, as all are who have suffered much.' He took pleasure in addressing himself to me—in calling me to witness the improved fortune of his country, and his personal triumph. I retired towards midnight, and was the first to go, leaving Mr. O'Connell surrounded by four cabinet ministers and five or six ladies of rank, who listened to him with a mixture, somewhat comic, of curiosity and pride, of deference and disdain.

O'Connell was really sincere in his advocacy of temperance; and the best proof of this sincerity is the fact that, for a considerable time, he gave up altogether the use of wine, which he had enjoyed in moderation. And it was not until he had been ordered by his medical advisers to resume his former practice of using wine, as a stimulant necessary in his case, that he did so.

Perhaps O'Connell thought he was conferring a signal favour on Father Mathew, when he publicly announced, at the usual weekly meeting in Conciliation Hall, in Dublin, that on the following Monday—Easter Monday, the 28th of March 1842—he was to join the temperance procession which was to take place in Cork on that day. But Father Mathew, though he may have regarded the visit of the Lord Mayor of Dublin as a compliment, certainly did not look on it in the light of a favour ; and if he could have prevented the announcement of the visit by any sacrifice on his part, he would willingly have made that sacrifice, and simply for this reason—that he was honestly sincere in his desire to keep the temperance movement free from the least connection with politics, and that he felt that O'Connell's presence on such an occasion, and in so marked and conspicuous a manner, would seriously compromise his personal reputation, and injure the cause in certain quarters from which he had received valuable countenance, and even practical assistance. If Father Mathew could, by any possibility, or on any pretence, have adjourned the procession, or got rid of it altogether, he certainly would have done so ; but Easter Monday was the day specially devoted to such demonstrations, and the temperance societies, throughout an extensive district of the country, had already made their preparations for taking part in it. There was no help for it now, and therefore the best thing to be done was to put a good face on the matter ; which he accordingly did.

Whatever the feelings with which Father Mathew received the announcement of O'Connell's intended presence on Easter Monday, the delight of the people was excessive: they thought only of the pleasure of beholding their beloved 'Liberator' on an occasion so full of joy and exultation. The idea of seeing the two men whom they most loved and admired walking together in the same procession, gratified their attachment to their political leader, who had emancipated their altars, and to their moral leader, who had brought happiness to their homes. Great then was the joy which the announcement of O'Connell's intended visit spread through the now blended ranks of Temperance and Repeal.

O'Connell arrived in Cork on Saturday the 26th of March, and, on the following morning, he edified the congregation of the church in which he performed his devotions, by his fervour and piety; for O'Connell was profoundly attached to his faith, and complied with its solemn obligations with the most devout reverence.

The great event of the following day was described the same evening in a local newspaper; and as the sketch was written at the moment, it will now—twenty-one years after—afford the reader a more vivid picture of what a temperance procession was in those days, than any description which memory could supply. We omit a long list of the different societies, with local descriptions and allusions, which could not be understood by the general reader; and it is only necessary to say that the societies, 57 in number, were accompanied by 41 bands, and that the strength of these societies ranged from 50 members, the lowest, to 700 members, the highest. The average number was from 150 to 200—making, on the whole, about 10,000 persons actually walking in procession. With this statement, we shall allow the writer of the following sketch * to describe one of the most remarkable, and certainly one of the most memorable, of the temperance demonstrations of that period:—

From an early hour in the morning, which was rather threatening and inclined to rain, the city was thronged with numberless groups of people, either anxious to behold the anticipated spectacle, or about to fall in with the several societies that were to walk on the occasion. Every road, street, lane, and avenue, leading into Cork, echoed to the sound of music, as hundreds and thousands poured in from neighbouring towns and districts of the country, or even from places so far distant as thirty or forty miles. Long before the time appointed for starting, the vast area of the Corn Market was densely crowded with various societies, each headed by its band of twenty or even thirty musicians, the members dressed, with scarfs, blue, pink, or green, of Irish manufacture, and holding a long white wand decorated with coloured ribbons or laurel. Before the several societies was borne a flag or banner, generally with the name of the particular room to which they belonged; some having painted on them an appropriate

* From the *Cork Examiner* of the same day.

device, or allegorical representation, and, in many cases, a full-length figure of the Apostle himself.

At the hour of eleven, the procession began to move slowly from the Corn Market, over Anglesea bridge, down the South Mall, along the Parade, and up Great George Street, the Western Road, and so through the entire rout settled on some weeks previously. When they had proceeded as far as the County Club-House, they were met by the Lord Mayor of Dublin, who came to join Father Mathew. Their greeting was warm and affectionate.

The scene which followed, it might be possible to imagine, but is certainly impossible to describe. Who could tell of the wild joyous shout that rent the very air as the two great men of Ireland, the political and the moral emancipators of her people, met together! The eagerness—the exclamations of delight—the rushings forward to snatch a look at both—the rapture and enthusiasm of that moment—are beyond our poor powers of description. In a short time after, Thomas Lyons, our own Mayor, accompanied by several respectable gentlemen and merchants, joined the procession. Another shout welcomed his arrival. Father Mathew then walked, with the Lord Mayor on one side, and the Mayor of Cork on the other. Every window was crowded with brilliant groups of fashionably-dressed ladies, who waved their handkerchiefs as the splendid array filed before them. Every roof, hall-door, balcony, balustrade, wall, and projection was literally covered with a mass of eager and delighted beings, who cheered with all their might as the Liberator or Apostle came in view. As the procession was passing the house of Dr. Bullen, on the South Mall, in a window of which sat the Right Reverend Doctor Murphy, the leaders halted, whereupon every man raised his hat, in respect for our venerable and beloved Bishop, while loud and continued cheers echoed from ten thousand voices. His lordship, who seemed visibly affected at this testimony of affectionate respect, blessed the thousands before him, and bowed with an appearance of great feeling. No language can at all do justice to the tremendous crowd of people, who did not form part of the regular army, but who lined the streets on both sides, and who required all the exertions of the vigorous stewards to keep them from breaking the line of march. In whatever street there was a temperance reading-room, there was an arch of green boughs spanning its breadth from house to house. Banners, emblems, garlands of flowers, paintings of various kinds, busts of Father Mathew, and allegorical devices, decorated the walls and windows of the several rooms before which the procession passed.

The Lord Mayor separated from the procession at the end of Lancaster Quay, when he knelt down and received the blessing of Father Mathew amidst the rapturous cheerings of the countless spectators. His lordship then departed in company with the Mayor of Cork.

After marching through the various streets marked out by the arranging committee, the vast body of people arrived at the terminus, the Corn Market, about three o'clock, when, after having cheered several times, they quietly separated with the most admirable order.

Thus terminated the demonstration which inspired Father Mathew with so much anxiety ; but his labours might be said to have commenced with its termination—for during the remainder of the day, and until an advanced period of the night, he was unceasingly at work, administering the pledge—vast numbers of people, from the country as well as belonging to the city, having been influenced to join the society, as much through the excitement of the day, as by the practical lesson taught in the good clothes, healthy appearance, and happy countenances of those who walked in the procession.

The pride and exultation of the teetotallers themselves will be best expressed in the words of a working man, a prominent member of one of the most famous temperance rooms of the city. The excellent man who spoke these words at a meeting held in the Globe Lane Room on the same night, is now no more ; but, so long as he lived, he continued to be a staunch supporter of the cause, from which he derived much personal benefit and no little fame—for Tom Blewitt was a welcome guest at every 'festival' held in Cork. On this occasion he was dressed in the handsome uniform of the band of the room of which he was a member. It may be mentioned that, among the bands that accompanied the procession of the day, there were several that wore really handsome uniforms—some, like that of the Globe Lane Room, purely military—others fanciful, with national colours or devices. Many a senator in St. Stephen's would be happy to possess Tom Blewitt's facility of speaking, and that, too, at a moment's notice, and without the possibility of preparation. It was thus that the working shoemaker of Cork responded to the call of the chairman :—

My dear friends, I will not trespass on your time by making excuses about inability, but will at once say, that I never felt so proud in my life as I do at this moment. I feel proud when I recollect the splendid spectacle of this day—I feel proud of my present companions, and I feel proud when I think that I have been one of the humblest instruments of raising my fallen country to that proud position intended for her by nature and by nature's God. Is there anyone, I ask, who possesses a spark of true feeling, who thinks with the mind of an Irishman, or a Catholic, that will not lend his every energy to advance this cause, until all Ireland shall stand up in the ranks of regeneration? I hope that the pride which animates me this evening, will continue to animate me until the close of my earthly existence. On the hill which overlooks the City Jail, a trifling delay caused the procession to halt. I looked over the dark and massive walls of that prison, and then gazed on the countless thousands who filed beneath me in grand array, and I thought if it had not been for Father Mathew, and the noble work of his hands, how many of those whom I then saw before me in happiness, in virtue, and independence, would be solitary mourners in the cells of that period! I thought how many deserted wives and children would crowd around its door, weeping in bitterness and despair. I reflected, that were it not for temperance, how many would have been guilty inmates of its dungeons—how many would have rattled the convict's chain, or fallen bleeding victims to the offended laws of their country. I thought this, and I asked myself—was there man, woman, or child, who would put forth a hand to check this great work, that will eventually lessen the inmates of the prison and the work-house, banish the convict hulks, and close up our penal settlements? My friends, if you see such a person, mark him as an enemy to his country and his kind—one who, like a second Nero, would stab the womb that gave him birth!

On the following evening an interesting meeting took place, at which Father Mathew was present. It was held in the Church Street Room, on the occasion of a number of emigrants—240 in all—being entertained previous to their departure for New Brunswick, in the ship 'Clyde.' Father Mathew was surrounded, as he frequently was, by many of the leading citizens, and supported by his most zealous and eloquent assistants. Whether it was from weariness, or the necessity for reserve, he appeared reluctant to speak; and in answer to his own name, which was mentioned in glowing terms, and received with more than ordinary enthusiasm, he said but a few words, which are given principally to show how he had been employed during the whole of that day:—

It was unnecessary for him to allude to the encomiums that had been made; he knew that they had drawn them from their own hearts, pure and unrestrained. There were many there who had witnessed the progress of the temperance cause, from the time he had planted the grain of mustard seed, until it had grown into the mighty tree under which so many thousands had found repose. But if he alluded to the progress of the cause, he was so identified with it that anything he might say might be considered egotism. He would leave it then to other persons. He did not lay any claim to eloquence, nor had he had time to write a speech, for since half-past six o'clock that morning he had been occupied in administering the pledge, and whatever pleasure they might have enjoyed from listening to a prepared speech from him, he was certain that they would be better pleased to know that he had been so occupied.

William Martin came out with peculiar force on that occasion, and added the camel to his list of illustrious water-drinkers, which already included the race-horse, the lion, and the elephant. He again alluded to the feeling of personal relief which he experienced in April 1838, when he felt the load of the temperance cause lifted from off his shoulders and placed on those of 'his friend the Apostle'—for William, sober Quaker as he was, fell into the habit of the day, and called Father Mathew 'the Apostle,' just as others did. William declared that there was not a circumstance which happened on the previous day that could offend the most fastidious.

As a matter of course, the health of Captain PENTREATH, of the good ship 'Clyde,' was pledged in flowing cups—of tea; and his speech, short and sailor-like, is valuable as the testimony of a disinterested and unprejudiced witness:—

He could not (he said) allow himself to be seated without offering his opinion on the temperance movement. He came to the port of Cork, after being four years absent from it, and was not prepared to meet the change that had taken place. On coming into the harbour, he was boarded by a pilot, whom he invited to dinner; during the dinner, he asked him to take a drink of ale, but he said, 'he could not, for he was a teetotal man, and one of Mr. Mathew's society.' He (the captain) asked him was it possible that a Cork pilot could be a Mathewite? and he was told by the pilot that he was one, and for fifty guineas he would not drink ale. Next came the boatmen, who said, they would take me in for such and such a sum; and how different was their manner then, compared with when they used to drink the calamity water! It was a pleasure to come into the port of Cork under the present circumstances. On his landing he was not prepared to witness the sight he did witness; for though he had been in the five quarters of the world, he never witnessed anything of such importance as the procession of the previous day.

That procession was a costly one to Father Mathew. A considerable number of the societies and bands had come distances of 20, of 30, and even of 40 miles. As many as 700 people had walked in from Kinsale. Large numbers had also come from Dunmanway, from Millstreet, and from Mitchelstown. Now these people were almost exclusively of the class that lived by the labour of their hands; and the very effort which they made to dress for such an occasion, and to prepare for such a journey, was a severe drain upon their scanty resources. Humanity as well as policy would have suggested to any one in Father Mathew's position, that some consideration should be shown to these poor people; but the prompting of his own generous and thoughtful nature impelled him to a liberality towards them which might be truly termed munificent, but which, by those who did not thoroughly understand the man or appreciate his position, was designated as foolish and wanton extravagance. The temperance leader had in him much of the spirit of the knights of old. To him, as to them, money was the least of the goods of life; and no conqueror in the tournament ever scattered largess so profusely among the applauding commonalty as Father Mathew scattered silver and gold among his humble followers. Thus it was that these temperance demonstrations, which indicated the progress and the triumph of the cause, formed a serious item in his expenditure, and a heavy drain upon his exchequer.

It was about this time that the following rather strange incident occurred. Father Mathew had been invited to preach for some charity, and afterwards administer the pledge, in a certain locality. A gentleman residing in the neighbourhood, whose name has probably been since heard of in the Court of Encumbered Estates, invited him to his place, where he treated him with that hospitality and distinction which were alike honouring to the host and the guest. Father Mathew was to sleep at this gentleman's house, and to be driven next day in his carriage to the place of meeting. At the appointed time, on the following day, the carriage was at the door; and having taken his leave of the ladies of the family, he set out, in company with his host. The two gentlemen passed the time agreeably, as the well-appointed carriage rolled smoothly along, drawn by a pair of fine and spirited horses. They had arrived within a mile or so of the appointed place, when there was a sudden stop. Father Mathew at once looked out, and saw two or three rather poor-looking men, one of them as if holding the horses' heads, and the others at the side of the carriage. Believing them to be enthusiastic followers, who desired to anticipate his arrival by coming to meet him on the road, or poor fellows who wished to take the pledge thus early, in order perhaps to make no delay in the village, he opened the door of the carriage, and leaned out eagerly towards them, saying—'Good morrow, boys! Glad to see you. I hope we shall have a fine meeting. You wish to take the pledge?' 'No, yer reverence,' said a cunning-looking little man, with a peculiarly sharp eye, scratching the side of his head with an air of comical perplexity; 'we arn't going to be after taking the pledge now, an' I'm temperate myself these three year; 'tis on another little business we've come.' 'I am delighted to meet a faithful teetotaller like you, my dear. And can I do anything for you or for your friends?' 'We're much obligated to yer reverence, and a fine warrant you are to be good an' kind; but 'tis with the masther there we've a word to say,'—and he indicated the owner of the hospitable mansion, and the occupant of the luxurious carriage, with a nod of his head, and a significant shrug of the shoulders. 'Oh! I beg your pardon, my dear sir,' said Father Mathew, drawing back, so as not to prevent free communication between his travelling companion and his tenants, or workmen, as he supposed the three men to be. But, to his horror, he found that the cunning-looking little man was a bailiff, who had a writ to serve on his hospitable friend, and who was then and there about taking possession of his carriage and horses. The dismay and confusion of the unhappy gentleman, at this unlucky mischance, might possibly be imagined, but certainly could not be described; but the embarrassment and annoyance of Father Mathew, at witnessing the humiliation of a friend, was still greater. The amount, though not very large, was utterly beyond the capability of the gentleman to meet, at least on that occasion; but Father Mathew pressed his hand softly on the arm of his companion, saying, 'My dear sir, pardon the liberty I am going to take with you. Do allow me the gratification of relieving you from this annoyance.' And having ascertained the amount, he at once settled the debt, and added a douceur to the bailiff, such as, were he not a staunch teetotaller, 'for three year an' more,' would have afforded him the means of enjoying a protracted 'bat-ther,' as the man of law technically termed a systematic debauch, or drinking-bout. Away rolled the liberated carriage, while Father Mathew employed every kindly art to soothe the feelings of his humiliated friend, and to distract his mind from dwelling on a circumstance so peculiarly unpleasant.

CHAPTER XVII.

His Charity extends itself abroad—He visits Glasgow—His Doings in that City—Excitement in Cork—An Irish Ovation—Acknowledges the Welcome—His annual Holiday—The austere Teetotaller—Found in the Fact—The Tins—No Whisky in Father Mathew's Plum-Pudding.

HAVING now fully done his work in Ireland, he consented to think of other portions of the United Kingdom. His charity, while properly commencing at home, was now inclined to extend itself abroad. There were, besides, his own societies and his own country people thickly scattered over the manufacturing districts of England and Scotland; and from the Irish and their clergy, the most pressing invitations had been constantly addressed to him for more than two years, praying that he would visit them, even for a day, and representing the great and lasting benefit which he would thereby confer on the Irish populations of the Scotch and English towns, and the service which he would thus render to religion and to the country. Father Mathew well knew to what temptations the working populations of those great towns were of necessity exposed, and how habits of intemperance not only degraded the poor impulsive Irish, but altogether obscured those virtues which had full play whenever they were rescued from a brutalising and debasing vice. He longed, then, for the opportunity of coming to their rescue, and liberating them from a bondage which destroyed the individual, and dishonoured the country that gave them birth. To Glasgow, where there was a vast Irish population, he first turned his practical attention.

His brief visit to Glasgow was most successful, not alone on account of the service which he rendered to many thousands of his own country people in that great city, but of the influence which his presence and addresses had in breaking down prejudices, and extending his popularity amongst those of other communions. He had received many and pressing invitations from various parts of Scotland, and from various bodies; but that which he had formally accepted was from his friend the Catholic Bishop of Glasgow. He arrived in Greenock on Saturday, the 13th of August, 1842, and reached Glasgow the same evening. He was received with affectionate reverence by the good bishop and his clergy, the greater number of whom had come from Ireland, and who on that account felt a deeper interest in their honoured guest. On the next day, he preached in the new church of St. Mary, to an immense and overflowing congregation, and commenced, as soon after as possible, to administer the pledge, principally to those of his own country and faith. During the next day he was occupied for a considerable time in the duties of his mission; and the following day, Tuesday, his arrival in Scotland was formally celebrated by a public procession.

The staid and sober Glasgow papers of that day indulged in glowing descriptions of the imposing splendour of this demonstration; which descriptions were read in Ireland with gratified pride, and tended, if possible, to elevate the illustrious leader of the temperance cause still higher in the esteem of his own countrymen. When the carriage in which Father Mathew had joined the procession reached the hustings on the Green, it was found, to the disappointment of the vast assemblage, that he was not in it; the fact being, that, to accommodate the people from Edinburgh, who should return by a certain train, he had slipped quietly away to the

Cattle Market, and was there hard at work, administering the pledge to thousands.

At five o'clock, a banquet was given to him in the City Hall, by the Committee of the Scottish Western Temperance Association, which, as the Chairman of the evening stated, embraced nearly all the teetotallers of the West of Scotland. He added, that they were met from the east and from the west, from the north and from the south, to do honour to their guest, the most unwearied and devoted champion of temperance. An address, from the pen of Robert Kettle, was read to him by its author, amid the plaudits of an assembly consisting chiefly of members of the National Church of Scotland. It was highly eulogistic, but written with good taste, and thus concluded :—

May you be long spared, sir, as a blessing to your country, and a benefactor to our common humanity; and having already learned, may you long enjoy, 'the luxury of doing good!'

Father Mathew's reply, in which he, as it were, bares his breast, and discloses the feelings of his heart to his new friends, is too valuable to be omitted. In acknowledging the address, he said:—

He received with unbounded pleasure the address from the members of the Western Scottish Temperance Union. He felt very much indebted to the writers of this address that they had spoken the truth, and had not given him credit for qualities which he did not possess, or for services which he had not performed. On this head he might appropriately quote the words of sacred authority, and say that Providence always selected the foolish things and weak things of this world to serve his purposes, 'that no flesh should glory in his presence.'

He was convinced that, though differing in features, opinions, customs, or religion, they were the same people. He had seen nothing in Scotland to make him think that they were not natives of Ireland. At all events, they were the children of one common father—born to the same rights—redeemed by the same Saviour—believers in the same blessed gospel; and oh! that the sweet and beneficent spirit of the gospel of Jesus were diffused from pole to pole, uniting and making all happy, pure, and guileless. The world would then be a pleasant habitation, and its children worthy of heaven. Though naturally timid and desponding, he felt new vigour arise within him to see so many of different religious professions—for it was not likely that they could all have unity of faith, but they could all meet in unity of affection—banded together in behalf of so great and good a cause. However, he thought he heard some one saying, 'Now, Father Mathew, this is making fine speeches to delude the people of Glasgow: perhaps these are not your sentiments in your own country.' For five-and-twenty years he had entertained these views, and if any man could say that his heart had been shut against his neighbour because of differences in religion—if any man could say that the needy had been turned from his door in consequence of an opposite belief—that the tenant had been dismissed from his holding, or the servant from his place, because of a difference of religious belief—he would allow them to say that his actions did not correspond with his words. In that time he had done what lay in his power to reconcile and harmonise the warring principles of factions—to sweeten the cup of woe—to exalt the down-trodden and unfortunate, and if another voice were required at his hands, still he would repeat, 'A new commandment I give you, that ye love one another.' He ought, perhaps, to apologise for thus alluding to himself, but Heaven forbid that he should do so from a spirit of paltry egotism, but for the glorious cause in which they all laboured. It was for this purpose that he wished to exhibit to them the inmost recesses of his heart, and to show it glowing with love for the whole human family. This was a cause in which they should all unite; it was the cause of their common humanity, the cause of their common country, and the cause of God.

The *Argus* thus describes his operations in the Cattle Market, the principal scene of his labours; and let it be remembered that, whether it were a city in Scotland or a village in Ireland which was the scene of those labours, the amount of exertion, of hardship, of physical and mental wear and tear, was about the same in either instance:—

On Monday, Father Mathew administered the pledge to from 1,000 to 1,500; and on Tuesday, after the great procession was over, not fewer than 10,000 to 12,000 people were enlisted in the teetotal cause. Yesterday (Wednesday), however, the number of applicants was so immense that all attempts at calculation must be set aside. In the morning Father Mathew celebrated mass in the Catholic Chapel, Clyde Street, and afterwards proceeded to the Cattle Market, where a vast concourse of people were assembled. Indeed, the great square of the market was at one period of the day so crowded that it was scarcely possible for the most vigorous to push their way through; and many who ardently longed for an opportunity of kneeling before the great Apostle of Temperance, and taking the pledge from his lips, could not get even a sight of his face. Late in the afternoon, we saw females who had anxiously waited the whole day in the hope of being able to get near his person, but were disappointed; and we understand that great numbers were similarly circumstanced at the close of the proceedings. From ten o'clock A. M. till six o'clock, Father Mathew was laboriously employed in administering the pledge; and, as the day was excessively hot, his exertions must have been attended with great fatigue. Group after group was pledged during the whole of the day, to the number of many thousands; but as, from the pressure, it was impossible to keep any account, it is impossible, as we have already remarked, even to guess at the gross number. Such of the people as were previously in possession of tickets or medals put them into his hands, and he returned them, throwing the ribbons by which they were suspended over the necks of the owners. In the Catholic Chapel yesterday morning, he distinctly informed the audience that he arrogated to himself no miraculous power of curing diseases, and that anyone who approached him under such a delusion must be signally disappointed—the power of performing miracles belonging alone to the Supreme Being. He, however, stated that he was ready and willing to bestow his blessing on all who chose to seek it. Notwithstanding these disclaimers, however, crowds of diseased persons were taken to the Cattle Market. At the close of the proceedings yesterday, Father Mathew appeared to be quite exhausted by his labours.

The practical result of this visit, in the improvement of his own countrymen, is thus indicated in the 'Scottish Temperance Review,' of September 1848. The testimony is the more valuable, as coming from a clergyman of another creed:—

When distributing tracts after this on the Sabbath, amongst the prisoners, we seldom met with a person from Ireland, either charged with intemperance or theft. But the result of the good man's labours was still more visibly seen in the lower parts of the city. In the district we visited, for example, as a city missionary, there was a close off High Street which contained about eighty families, the majority of whom were Catholics. The people were so uproarious that they almost required a policeman constantly amongst them. On a Wednesday morning, however, most of the adults, and a number of the juveniles, set off in a body to the Cattle Market, and took the pledge from Father Mathew. From that day till may 1845, when we left the district, there was not a quieter close, considering the number of inhabitants, in the city. A number are still adhering to the pledge, and their orderly demeanour is an agreeable contrast to several of their tippling Protestant neighbours.

Before quiting Glasgow, Father Mathew presented a costly chalice to the Church of St. Mary. In acknowledging this act of thoughtful munificence, Dr. Murdoch said that that chalice would remain in St. Mary's long after its donor had gone to heaven, a memorial of his piety and generosity. But, save in whispered thanks and fervent blessings, there were no acknowledgments of the sums which he lavished on the many objects of his compassion during those few days in that busy and flourishing city.

The teetotallers of his own city were flung into a fever of excitement by the account of his doings in Scotland ; and that being the season of enthusiasm, and the spirits of the people being then high, it was determined, as if by an impulse, that the beloved leader should be received on his return as a moral conqueror fresh from his field of glory, and surrounded with the spoils of his bloodless conquest. It was resolved to meet him in grand procession, and to testify, by a suitable address, the exultation which his new achievements had inspired in the breasts of his own special followers, amidst whom the cause had had its first and perhaps greatest triumphs. Tuesday, the 23rd of August, was the day which Father Mathew had himself appointed for his return to Cork; and that day was accordingly fixed upon for his public reception by his fellow-citizens.

A few years more, and sorrow, and suffering, and death, too, were in the streets and highways of the same city which now resounded with cries of joy and shouts of welcome; and the population that now pressed on in happy crowds, confident in the present and thoughtless of the morrow, were soon to learn the true meaning of the terrible words, Famine and Plague.

The following sketch, written by one who was in the midst of the people, and had a part in the proceedings of the day, accurately represents this remarkable manifestation of popular enthusiasm :—

Short as was the notice afforded for preparation, the spectacle was really magnificent, not from decorations or trappings, but from the mighty masses who poured forth at a nearly hour from the city towards the appointed place of meeting the Apostle, and hailing him on his triumphant return from Scotland. The day was exceedingly beautiful, the air cooled by a gentle breeze, and the whole face of nature brightened under a glowing sun that shone upon many a rich garden, and many a field of golden wheat ripe for the sickle of the reaper. Every face looked happy, and every step was buoyant, as young and old, men and women, parents and children, cheered on by the strains of numberless bands, advanced to meet their best friend and benefactor. The road was literally alive with gay groups, with bands and banners, with carriages, gingles, low cars laden with well-dressed females, and with vehicles of every possible description. The members of the different Temperance Rooms wore either scarfs, sashes, or rosettes, together with their medals, and nearly all bore wands decorated with white or pink ribbons. Mostly all the bands were dressed in uniform, some remarkable for richness, others for lightness and exceeding taste; and many, especially those who received the advantage of good instruction, played the finest pieces of music in a manner which clearly evidenced the vast intellectual capability of the humbler and hitherto most neglected classes of the Irish people. But their gaiety, their good temper, and their excellent conduct were by far more delightful to behold. Long before the arrival of the Limerick mail at the appointed place, the different societies, headed by their bands, were formed into line of procession, and also the private and hired carriages, the cars, and other vehicles. As the time drew near, the excitement became intense; and a stranger hearing the eager and longing exclamations of the multitude, and seeing them rushin[illegible] forward to catch one glimpse of the Apostle, would be inclined eith[illegible] to think Father Mathew was returning after an absence of years, i[illegible] stead of days, or that he was one upon whose features and person they had never looked before. At length, from man to man the cry was passed—'He is coming!—he is coming!' And then there arose one wild outburst of feeling—one prolonged shout of joy, as the coach drove up, and, passing through a living lane of human beings, stopped at the usual place for changing horses for the last stage. Again and again did the heavens echo with the shout, as the Apostle descended from the coach, and, escorted by a number of gentlemen, entered the carriage of his Worship the Mayor. Mr. Mathew looked fresh, healthy, and untired as ever, and as if he had never encountered the wonderful fatigues to which his mission of charity and love so constantly exposes him. No sooner did the Mayor receive him into the carriage, than the people pressed forward with eagerness to see him, to touch him, or to hear his voice. The bands struck up with great spirit, and again the multitude sent up their cry of welcome to the moral emancipator of their country. After a few moments spent in necessary arrangement, the word to march was given, and gradually the several societies, with bands playing and banners waving, filed past the carriage in which stood the hero of the day.

The address was read amidst frequent bursts of applause, as its sentiments and expressions were ratified and endorsed by the approval of the mighty mass that thus took part in its presentation.

The address, after expressing the warmest congratulation and welcome, briefly referred to his labours at home, and thus proceeded:—

Having achieved so singular, so miraculous a change in five millions of the Irish nation, you have shown the world that your exertions were not confined to any particular clime, country, or religion—that you were the friend of mankind—in every grade—in every land—under every circumstance—that your mission was for the whole human family; and that where good was to be done, there was your station—every country being for you a field to sow the moral seed, no matter under what aspect, or with what degree of intensity, the bright and fostering light of Christianity shone upon it.

We were proud to witness your success amongst the religious and intellectual people of Scotland. It was gratifying to see one hundred thousand of that gifted nation assembled around you, and pledging themselves to you that they had the fortitude by restraining them selves and abandoning long existing habits to elevate still more the character of their country; and it has added to the interest of the great scene at Glasgow, to witness the railways—those mightiest achievements of art and science—employed to bring before you the populations of Edinburgh and other more distant towns.

Henceforth we shall look upon the people of Scotland as bound to us by other and peculiar ties. We cannot forget that both nations sprang from one common ancestry, and it increases the interest we have ever felt in that country to think, that as it was from Ireland the Scots first came, so it was from Ireland they obtained, through the Apostle of Temperance, a share in those lasting blessings which this moral movement has produced.

In conclusion, very reverend and esteemed sir, let us entreat of you to persevere and complete the glorious undertaking. You have always acted on the principle of considering nothing done while anything remained to be effected; and though many years of your less conspicuous life had been spent in the exercise of good works—in relieving the needy—in administering to the sick—in comforting the unfortunate—in spreading the mantle of charity over the distressed of every class, creed, and country—still an inward impulse prompted you to even higher, because more enlarged efforts, and we now see in you, our kind, mild, unostentatious fellow-citizen, the most remarkable man of the present day—whom no fatigues can tire—no opposition daunt—or no incense of praise, or human applause, change from being the humblest and meekest amongst you.

That you may continue for many years in the enjoyment of health and strength, perfecting your great work, and, in the fulness of time, that you may obtain the reward which alone you desire, is the ardent prayer of your sincere friends and devoted admirers,

THE TEETOTALLERS AND OTHERS,
INHABITANTS OF CORK.

Father Mathew's reply—which was brief, earnest, and brimful of affection to his adopted people, and of modest exultation at the success which had just crowned his labours in a new sphere of action—is part of the history of that day; and the manner in which his allusions were received represents the tone and feeling of those whom he addressed. The speech is therefore given here as it was reported on the occasion of its delivery:—

Mr. Mayor, brother teetotallers, and dearly beloved friends, citizens of Cork, I feel my bosom swell with rapture at this moment (cheers).

Feelings unutterable throb within my breast, not through the gratification of any personal vanity, but for the sake of the glorious cause in which my feelings are wrapped up (loud cheers); and for whatever toils (as this excellent address states) I might have undergone, or labours endured for the last twenty-seven years, that I have lived amongst you, as a humble minister of religion, I feel myself rewarded at the present moment—(loud cheers)—a reward far superior to any desert of mine (loud cries of 'No, no,' and renewed cheers that lasted some minutes). The feelings that fill my bosom at this moment are so great, that I cannot find language to convey them (cheers). The honour is so great and unexpected—for, until this very morning, I had no idea that such a spectacle as this would be presented to my eyes on my approach to the city, not of my birth, but of my adoption (tremendous cheering and waving of handkerchiefs). I should, had I been aware that such an address as this would be presented to me, be better prepared; however, you will receive the plain sentiments of my heart instead of eloquent language (loud cheers). I thank you for this welcome (loud cheers). I assure you that whatever may be my toil, my feelings are those of love for the whole human family (loud cheers). I have come from Scotland with a far humbler opinion of myself, and of my feeble efforts in the great cause, but with feelings far more exalted than before (loud cheering). I never witnessed such a sacrifice of self to the principles of true virtue, as was displayed by the people of Scotland (great and continued cheering). I felt proud, my friends, of the affection displayed (in my person) for the people of Ireland (loud cheering). I was in Scotland the representative of the people of Ireland (cheers), and, as such, received the great greeting of more than two hundred thousand persons on the Green at Glasgow (renewed cheering). We had persons assembled there from the most distant parts—Edinburgh, Ayr, Stirling, and distant Aberdeen, to swell the number on that great occasion (loud cheers). It is unnecessary for me to allude to the great effects that followed that day's proceedings—they speak for themselves (cheers). And here, the vast assemblage, the presence of the high, the moral, and the good of our city to grace this proceeding—speaks trumpet-tongued for our society (tremendous cheering). At this late hour of the day I will not detain you longer, than to renew my assurances of gratitude to you, and to tell you that I will devote the remainder of my life to your service, and to that of the community at large (renewed and repeated cheering). I have made it the study of my life, without distinction of creeds or politics, to do good to all (hear, hear, and cheers); for I never conceived why we should feel enmity to any man, no matter what his religion; I do not say this from any miserable egotism, but rather from a desire to bare the feelings of my heart before you, (hear, hear. hear). We may differ on controversial points; but we should all value the lesson of the holy Gospel—'A new commandment I give unto you, that you should love one another.' I trust that as temperance has made us a great people, that it will also—and I have seen an instance of it here this day—persons of all creeds and politics uniting—prove a bright and golden chain, uniting all persons in one bond of union, and by this means making all happy (loud cheers). Once more, I beg to thank you sincerely (cheers).

During the whole evening the city was in a state of happy commotion; and, to a late hour at night, thousands of people filled the streets adjoining the humble residence of the great man, who witnessed their innocent gaiety with delight, and heard with gratified affection the enthusiastic cheers that followed every mention of his name.

Which of us is there, from the schoolboy to the minister of state, who does not long for and enjoy a holiday? Father Mathew also had his annual holiday, to which he eagerly looked forward; but it was with him a holiday of the heart and of the affections. It was usually enjoyed in the midsummer, or early autumn, and always in his native Tipperary. For three or four days, scarcely ever for a week, his eldest brother John's house at Rathcloheen was his head-quarters; and the announcement of his arrival was the signal for gladness and feasting to his nephews and nieces, the children of his brothers and his sister. Nor was Father Mathew forgetful of the commissariat, as many a hamper and parcel and jar and box amply testified. The dining-room at Rathcloheen was spacious enough to accommodate the whole of the Clan Mathew, who presented a formidable number, as some five-and-twenty of the seniors sat round the great table, and some fifteen or more were disposed of at the side table. Father Mathew's orders were that *all* should be summoned to the feast; and all, save the infant in arms, were accordingly present. Good conduct, and capacity for managing a spoon with decent independence,—these were the only conditions necessary for admission to one of those grand family banquets, at which the Priest presided, as the acknowledged and honoured head. And, for the time, there did not breathe a happier man than the giver of that feast, as he sat at the head of that well-provided board, and saw round him those whom he loved most on earth, and in whose every glance he met reciprocal affection; or as he listened to the innocent prattle and the gay laughter of the merry occupants of that side table. In that delightful spectacle, in those joyous sounds, he lived over again the days of his own boyhood; and the ever-present image of his mother—his good and gentle and holy mother—rose more vividly upon his memory, filling his eyes with tears, but tears of chastened happiness. From his burdened shoulders and his weary spirit he flung his heavy responsibility and his grievous anxieties, and for these few brief days his spirits were the spirits of a boy. He played with the young people, entered eagerly into their sports, ran with them, romped with them, and promoted all kinds of novel and enchanting games.

The children were enthusiastic followers of their 'Reverend Uncle,' as they termed him, and cherished their silver medals with commendable pride. But it was not at all certain that the same enthusiasm was felt in the cause by some of the elder members of the family; still, while the Priest was in Tipperary, water was the only beverage that sparkled in the glasses on the dinner-tables of his brothers. John, the eldest brother, preserved a marvellous gravity when the subject of temperance was introduced, and was for some time held to be an austere convert to the cause.

On one of these visits, John Mathew was thus complimented by his illustrious brother:—'My dear John, really I must compliment you on your appearance. I never saw you looking better; your complexion is clear and healthy, and your colour is so youthful. Why, John, I could not have a better proof than yourself of the virtues of temperance. You have got a new lease of life. It is well known, by your appearance, that *you* drink nothing but water.' John made some modest remark about his brother's kindness, but did not seem inclined to prolong the conversation as to his own merits as an abstainer, and turned it, as soon as he could, to the weather and the state of the crops. 'How good of John,' Father Mathew, thought, 'to give up his little indulgence to please me.' Amiable delusion! Now, if there was a man in all Tipperary who had a conscientious respect for whisky punch, 'of course in reason,' John Mathew was that man. Like many others of the old school, he regarded it as a panacea for the cure of every ill to which the flesh is heir, from the lightest depression of spirits to the fiercest attack of the gout. Not finding it convenient to apply the elixir outwardly, he persistently applied it inwardly, but 'in moderation.'

The Priest invariably retired at an early hour, and silence soon after reigned in the house; and then John, the austere teetotaller, who had never taken the pledge, and who was determined never, 'with the blessing of the Lord,' to do so if *he* could help it, quietly indemnified himself for his forced abstemiousness at and after dinner. The polished brass kettle was placed upon the table, with the decanter, the glasses, the sugar, and the lemon; and John mixed his tumbler, drank the Priest's health, wished the whole world as happy as himself, and enjoyed his punch perhaps with the keener relish because of the concealment which he was compelled to practise, 'out of respect for poor Theobald's feelings.' It was on an occasion of the kind, when the door had long closed upon the retiring Priest, and when John, having finished his first tumbler, had just artistically fabricated the second, with the aid of water 'screeching hot,' that a well known step was heard upon the stairs. Awfully that footstep sounded to John's guilty soul in the stillness of that silent house. Nearer and nearer it came, till it approached the door of the dining room, which now reeked with the unmistakable odour of whisky punch. What was to be done?—would the roof obligingly fall upon poor John?—or, at least, would the ground open and swallow the now repentant Sybarite! Leaving on the table such damning evidences of his treason as the decanter, the glasses, the sugar, the lemon, and the kettle, John seized the hot tumbler, and, rushing from the table, made several ineffectual attempts to hide it away somewhere, anywhere—all the time being compelled to shift the glass from hand to hand. John was thus engaged, juggling with his tell-tale tumbler, and madly rushing here and there in the hope of concealing it, when the door opened, and the Apostle of Temperance walked in! The appearance of the Commander was not more astounding to Leporello than was this unexpected vision of his reverend brother to poor John. A desperate hope suggested itself to his mind, as he still clutched the tumbler, and then suddenly passed it to the other hand—perhaps the Priest walked in his sleep! But no, John; the hearty burst of laughter that smote your ear was a too convincing proof of the fact that the Apostle was wide awake, and that his eyes were now thoroughly open. Father Mathew made no remark, but quickly retired, having obtained a book for which he had been in search. It is not certain as to what manner John disposed of that luckless tumbler of punch, or whether he soothed his ruffled spirit with a third; but one thing is historically correct—that Father Mathew never again quoted John's improved looks as a signal triumph of total abstinence.

From his own house in Cove Street, the very temple of temperance, the arch enemy was not wholly banished. Thus, one day, at a dinner party in that most hospitable of abodes, the flavour of the water was, to say the least, rather suspicious. The more rigid of the guests looked puzzled, while the younger ones tittered, as they glanced at the little butler, whose nose was more than usually red, and whose eyes shone with a wild gleam. At last, Father Mathew put his glass to his lips, but at once placed it on the table, saying—'John, what a strange taste and smell the water has! What's the matter with it? You must have had spirits in the jug.' 'Oh, yes, sir, I had to polish the tins, and whisky is very good for brightening them. Unfortunately, I put it into this jug.' The younger guests audibly chuckled at the excuse; but Father Mathew only remarked that it was 'all right,' and that he would not then trouble his butler by requiring a more elaborate explanation of the 'accident.'

Father Mathew honestly believed that his plum-puddings were made without the slightest admixture of whisky or wine; and he was frequently heard to say, 'Now there are some people, and sensible people too, who assert that plum-puddings cannot be made without alcohol; but that is as fine a pudding as I ever tasted, and there is not a drop of whisky in it. Is there, John?' 'Oh, no, sir; not a drop,' was the invariable reply. But had there been a mirror in the room, by which the little man's face could be reflected, as he turned to the sideboard, a grin might be seen upon those puckered features, which would have cast some doubt upon the boastful assertion of his unsuspecting master.

CHAPTER XVIII.

The Key to the Father's Heart—The greatest Miracles of all—Red Denis—The Meeting in the Theatre Royal—The Man and the Cause—O'Connell's Speech—A monster Tea-Party—He pays for it—Death of his Brother Tom.

THE greater the success and the wider the triumph of the temperance leader, the more earnest he became in endeavouring to obtain new converts. The spectacle of the happiness of the family of the sober man was as much an incentive to increased exertion in spreading the cause of happiness, as was that of the misery suffered by the family of the drunken man an incentive to try, if possible, to banish that source of misery from the land. His belief that there was a key to every man's heart, if one could only find it, was one day touchingly exemplified. A Cork workman of the better class had fallen to a deplorable condition, in consequence of his drunken habits, and every day he seemed to sink deeper and deeper in the Slough of Despond. To render the calamity greater, he had a wife and a family of young children ; and the madness of the father stripped the clothes from the back of his poor wife, and starved his wretched infants. The wife did all that a good and virtuous woman could do to reclaim the man she had not ceased to love ; but a kind of devil had taken possession of him, and he became a savage as well as a confirmed drunkard. Twice, at her urgent entreaty, Father Mathew called at their miserable place, and used every effort to subdue the ferocity of the husband ; but all in vain. He did not, however, despair, but came a third time, and used every argument and tried every mode of persuasion; but the man was sullen and dogged, and even insolent. Nothing daunted, Father Mathew persevered—pointing out to him his sad degradation, the desolation by which he was surrounded, the misery of his wife, the spectral appearance of his innocent children. But to no purpose, save to inflame his anger. 'Father Mathew,' said he, 'you have no right to come to me. I am a Protestant, and you are not my clergyman. Don't dare interfere in my affairs—I don't want your advice—I can do without you or it—and the sooner you leave this, the better.' The wife was pale with apprehension, as the last plank of hope seemed to fail her; and the half-frozen and starving children cowered in a scared group, out of the way of their father. Seeing that further attempt would do no good at that moment, Father Mathew turned to leave; but as he was passing the children, he took one of them in his arms and kissed it, and patted its little head, and spoke kindly to it; and when he placed it on the floor again, he slipped a piece of money into its hand. This was done quietly, but the gleam of the silver caught the eye of the hardened man, who was looking wickedly in that direction; and no sooner did he behold what had been done, than a miracle was worked in him—his whole being was changed in an instant; and flinging himself on his knees, he cried out, amidst convulsive sobs, 'Oh, my God, pardon me! Here is this good man, who has acted more like a father to my children than I have ever done: he would feed them, and I have starved them. God forgive me! God in His mercy forgive me!' He then humbly besought Father Mathew to give him the pledge, the words of which he repeated with fervour. That man was saved, and his family were rescued from the work-house; for the key had been found to the father's heart.

A gentleman, speaking of Father Mathew, and referring to the popular belief in his power of working cures—a power which he took every means of repudiating—said, 'If there ever was a saint from heaven, he was one. But as to his miracles, the most striking were the marvellous reforms he accomplished in people's lives. Men who took their twenty, and even their thirty glasses of whisky in the day, giving it up at his request—these were miracles. And their keeping the pledge was a greater miracle still.'

Miracles of this kind were worked every day, and in every part of the country, to the amazement of those who had made up their minds that such cases were hopelessly incurable. One week, for instance, a tattered, dissolute-looking, and dirty fellow might be seen reeling through the street, growling out curses at everyone he met, or venting his brutal wrath on some poor child, or miserable dog, that crossed his path ; and the next week, a decent, well-dressed man might be seen passing the same street, his manner quiet, and his bearing to those he met kindly and considerate. This was but the exterior aspect of the transformation ; but that worked within doors was yet more marvellous. There, the furious brute, more devilish than human, was changed into a lamb of gentleness—the desperate spendthrift, whose only object in life appeared to be the indulgence of the one passion, became cautious, frugal, saving—the terror and curse of the neighbourhood was not recognised in the kindly and obliging man who was now ready to do everyone a good turn. And the children—what a transformation in them ! From sprawling in the gutter in their scanty rags, and learning all manner of evil in that worst of academies, the street, they might be seen comfortably dressed for their station in life, and going to and returning from school with unfailing punctuality ; for if their father were gentle instead of savage, and affectionate instead of cruel, he was also resolute and vigilant, and not to be deceived or 'come round,' as of old. Now these were the miracles which Father Mathew was working every day of his temperance mission ; and much did the world marvel thereat.

There was a porter in the service of a merchant of Cork, and the porter was both faithful and intelligent, but a drunkard of the first water. His entire thought was how to get money for whisky, and his sole enjoyment in life was in drinking whisky. Morning, noon, and night he was at his ruinous work. He was most necessary to his master, for no dealing with the country people could be managed without the aid of 'Red Denis,' as he was called, from the colour of his hair. Twice he was dismissed from his employment, and he was about being sent away a third time; but his master reasoned with him, and asked him to go and see Father Mathew. Matters were looking so serious with Red Denis, that he at last made up his mind to try what the Priest could do for him, and 'what bargain he could strike with him;' for total abstinence was altogether out of the question—an indignity to which Red Denis was determined never to submit. Father Mathew was delighted to see Red Denis, on whom he had often cast a longing eye. 'Thank God, you are come to me, Denis, and of your own free will too. A voluntary sacrifice is most acceptable to the good God. Kneel down, my dear child,' continued Father Mathew to the giant, who was scratching his red poll in great perplexity. 'Well, sir, the truth of it is, you must make a bargain with me,' said Denis. 'Bargain, my dear!—what bargain?' 'I 'm thinking, your reverence, of giving up the sperrets, but—' 'God will bless you for doing so, my dear It never did any one good, and it has slain thousands and thousands of immortal souls, too.' 'What you say, your reverence, is thrue enough, and I 'm going to give it up—but I must have a darby.' 'A darby, my dear!' 'Yes, your reverence, one darby a day. I 'll take the pledge if your reverence will only give me one darby a day.' 'No, no; you must give it up entirely, or I can't let you take the pledge.' 'Why thin, Father Mathew, your reverence, I tell you 'tis n't in the power of God Almighty to make me do without whisky entirely.' 'Shame, sir, shame! to use such language! You should not dare say what you have done. The power of God is omnipotent, and He can do much more than change the heart of a miserable drunkard,' said Father Mathew, with a severity not usual to him. 'Well, your reverence, I beg God's pardon and your pardon; but 'tis what I thought; for I never *can* do without the darby.' 'Go now, my dear, and come back to me in a week, and you may then be in a better state of mind.' When the week had elapsed, Red Denis was again in the parlour at Cove Street. ''Tis no good, your reverence, without you allow me the darby of whisky—I'm afeard of myself entirely.' 'Denis,' said Father Mathew, in his most impressive manner, 'kneel down this moment, and repeat the words of the pledge after me, and I tell you that God *will* give you strength to resist temptation for the future—I promise you that He will give you strength and grace to do so—I promise it to you in His name.' Denis was overpowered by the solemnity of the priest's voice and manner, and he knelt and took the pledge with great earnestness. He rose from his knees a confirmed teetotaller, as, from that moment to the last hour of his life, he never afterwards tasted whisky, or strong drink of any kind. To use his own words, 'a darby would choke him.'

The world had been long convinced of the fact that the Apostle of Temperance had gathered to himself the love and veneration of the great mass of the Irish people of his own faith; but it was now to be made aware of the no less important fact, that he commanded the respect and admiration of those who were not of his Church, and who belonged to and represented the very highest classes in the country. In every movement, whether to compliment an individual, to found an association, to promote a county ball, to get up a regatta, or to organise a political party, there is some one who takes the initiative, and is, in reality, the prime mover. In this case, it was Mr. Peter Purcell, the mail contractor, who had on more than one occasion exhibited a kindly feeling to Father Mathew, for whose worth and whose character he entertained the greatest admiration. Mr. Purcell's motive and object are best explained in his own words. Writing to the public press on the 4th of November, 1842, he says :—

> Having frequent occasion myself to witness the vast and beneficial change which Mr. Mathew's exhortation and example have produced among those employed throughout my own establishments, and deeply alive to the importance of rendering that change progressive and permanent among the people, I have, in conjunction with other gentlemen who entertain the same opinion as myself on this interesting question, thought it most desirable to ascertain the feelings and views of influential people connected with Ireland, as to the propriety and expediency of affording to the country an opportunity of testifying to the merits of the Rev. Father Mathew, in such a manner as would be at once complimentary to that most estimable benefactor of mankind, and, by supplying an evidence of the deep sympathy in which his exertions are held by the wise and the good, strengthen this noble cause to which his life is devoted.

When the letter was published, Mr. Purcell was authorised to mention the names, among others, of sixteen noblemen, who approved of and concurred in his project. A requisition was shortly after published, convening a public meeting in the Theatre Royal, Dublin, on the 26th of January, 1843. The requisition was signed by two Dukes, four Marquises, nineteen Earls, ten Viscounts and Barons, four Catholic Bishops, upwards of forty Baronets, thirty Members of Parliament, and an immense array of Clergymen of all persuasions, Deputy-Lieutenants, Magistrates, and gentlemen from all parts of the country. The meeting was in keeping with the requisition, the fine theatre presenting a splendid appearance, filled as it was with the rank and fashion of the Irish metropolis.

The chair was taken by the Duke of Leinster, who, in a few words, expressed the great pleasure he felt in presiding on the occasion, and the desire he had 'in every way in his power to show the respect and esteem which he entertained for the Very Rev. Theobald Mathew.'

Mr. Purcell was appointed secretary to the meeting, and, in an interesting speech, explained its object. In the course of his address he read a number of letters, and among others, the following from Surgeon Carmichael, which is of itself a testimonial to Father Mathew:—

Rutland Square: Jan. 22, 1843.

My dear Sir,—I send you a brief memorandum of the facts I accidentally mentioned to you the other day, respecting the cases of admission into the Richmond Surgical Hospital, before Father Mathew's happy influence converted the poor of this city from drunkenness to sobriety.

The hospital contains 130 beds, chiefly appropriated to surgical cases; and before the pledge was so generally taken by the poor of the city, we were never without cases of wounds, and broken heads and arms of women, the cruel inflictions of their drunken husbands; when, at the same time, it usually contained cases of infants and children half burned, or scalded to death, through the negligence of their drunken mothers. The hospital, I may safely say, was never without cases of delirium tremens, many of which ended fatally. Indeed, I know of no instance of any individual affected with this malady, arising from the abuse of ardent spirits, that did not ultimately die of the disease.

Now, if we contrast these facts with the records of the hospital, since Father Mathew has made us a sober people, we do not find a single instance of wounds, burns, or scalds *attributable to drunkenness!* and seldom or never is any case of delirium tremens admitted into the hospital.

The records of the hospital also prove that, since the great mass of the population of this city have become sober, the rate of mortality amongst all descriptions of patients is *considerably reduced*, a proof of the increased strength and powers of the lower orders in this mode, effectually resisting the influence of diseases, &c. &c.

My dear Sir, truly yours,

Richard Carmichael.

It may be well to afford the reader an opportunity of learning in what manner the Apostle and the Cause were spoken of on this gratifying occasion by the foremost men in the land.

The Marquis of Headfort, who took the lead, and gave the tone to the meeting, thus spoke :—

My lord duke, I have attended many public meetings to promote the honour, the liberties, and the interests of Ireland; but I know of none which is more calculated to promote those interests than that which I have now the honour to address. Were it possible for me, or had I language at my command, sufficient to pronounce an eulogium, most willingly and gladly should I do so: but, my lord, his merits are beyond all praise, and the result of his labours beyond any reward which the world can bestow. It is impossible not to look with pride and gratification to the present moral, social, and political state of Ireland. Twenty years ago, would the rev. gentleman have attempted what he has now succeeded in effecting, when the energies of the country were paralysed, and the people sunk in degradation? But these days have passed away, never to return. None of us can appreciate, my lord, the present state of amelioration in the condition of our country; but for my own part, I look forward to future generations with exultation, when those who shall come after us will require no pledge to persevere in the path of sobriety and industry, which alone lead to happiness. My lord, I shall not detain you further, but propose, with the greatest pleasure and gratification, the following resolution :—

'Resolved,—That the benefits resulting to society from the labours of the Rev. Theobald Mathew entitle him, beyond all living men, to the immeasurable gratitude and ardent admiration of all ranks and persuasions in the British Empire.'

The Marquis of Clanricarde concluded his speech, proposing the second resolution, in these words :—

No testimony of this meeting could discharge the debt of gratitude which Ireland owes to Father Mathew; but I hope I may say, that such a meeting as assembled here this day will evince a due sense of our gratitude, although we know that no praise or homage of ours can discharge that obligation. I know, and we all know, that the pure and high motives of that great man cannot be affected by any tribute of praise which his fellow creatures can bestow upon him; at the same time, I think I may say, it is impossible for any man not to feel some degree of self-satisfaction and consolation for the labours he has undergone, when he knows that these labours are understood and appreciated as they should be by the people of Ireland.

'Resolved.—That the friends and admirers of the Rev. Mr. Mathew will best evince their sense of the utility of his labours, by a public and enduring testimonial;

which, while serving to perpetuate the memory of the *man*, would not only conduce to the continued triumph of the *cause* to which he has so usefully and energetically devoted himself, but also aim at confirming the people in those habits of temperance, and, consequently, of industry and order, which have already made such amazing progress in Ireland; and which, if rigidly adhered to, cannot fail to render the population happy, prosperous, and contented.'

Mr. Wise, member for the city of Waterford, bore testimony to the wonderful reformation worked by Father Mathew:—

Here is a reformation not of words, but of deeds, through the regenerating influence of the Rev. Mr. Mathew. I speak not merely from the experience of those who hear me, but I can cite you from the eulogium of strangers who have visited this country from Germany and France. They have viewed with astonishment the alteration in the habits of the people, as compared with the accounts of former travellers. I have myself known one gentleman who visited Ireland ten years ago, and so great was the change he witnessed, so improved was the condition of the peasantry, that he could hardly recognise the same country as that he had been formerly in. I have also known cases where gentlemen came to Ireland, with the full conviction that the people were degraded; but who, on going home to their own country, were astonished at the general improvement which had taken place by one of the greatest moral revolutions ever witnessed in any part of the world. My lord, I came here to-day to express my sympathy, my full desire, my most zealous wish to co-operate in the objects of this great meeting, and to place this important movement in that point of view where it not only may be an incentive to persevere as we began, but may be an example to England and Scotland, as well as Ireland, and every part of the world.

Mr. Smith O'Brien, M P., said he came as the representative of the county which had been benefited more than any other by the labours of Father Mathew, and thus referred to the intended testimonial:—

Endeavour to ascertain what the amount of the funds may be; and then proceed to determine whether it shall be a work of art, to speak to all posterity, in the metropolis of Ireland, or some institution founded for the benefit of the afflicted and distressed. Whatever it shall be, will be best determined by the committee; but of this he was quite sure, that they could not erect any testimony so acceptable to him, or so glorious in its results, as an inviolate fidelity to the solemn engagement entered into, by the great mass of the nation, to that good man.

Daniel O'Connell, who was then at the very height of his popularity, came to bear his testimony to the merits and services of the man who divided with him the affections of the Irish people. If previous speakers were authorised to speak in the name of a class or a locality, no one was more entitled to speak in the name of the country than the greatest political leader of the age. To hear O'Connell address a popular assembly, was at any time an object of interest; but to hear the 'Liberator' with the 'Apostle' for his theme, was a matter not only of interest, but of some anxiety to the friends of the latter. A few passages from the speech of the most remarkable man of the day, on an occasion so remarkable in itself, could not properly be omitted from these pages. O'Connell's vindication of the character of the Irish people anterior to the advent of Father Mathew, exactly represented the feeling of a very large class of the community, who were offended by the natural and pardonable exaggeration occasionally indulged in by speakers at temperance meetings, when glorifying the achievements of their beloved leader, or describing the temperance reformation from their own point of view. After some preliminary observations, O'Connell thus proceeded :—

Now, though I am rather accustomed to public speaking, I have yet not come here to make what is called a speech, nor have I the presumptuous vanity to suppose that I am capable of making any speech that could compensate you one moment for delaying the expression of veneration and approbation which you entertain for that excellent man whose name has called us together here to-day. I would be ashamed of myself if I were capable of thinking that I could make any speech that would enhance his merits, or place his virtues or his utility in a more striking point of view than the simple enunciation of his name alone must command. The name of the Rev. Theobald Mathew is, in fact, a spell-word. It proclaims in itself the progress of temperance, morality, prudence, and every social virtue throughout the land. I have, as I already said, come here not to make a speech, but to bear my testimony to his indescribable merits. I could not stay away from such an assemblage as this; for though I felt how little importance my attendance here could be, still I owed it to myself to share in the testimony of the mighty moral miracle that has been performed, and to raise my humble voice in the declaration of my sentiments of admiration at his utility as a man, and his virtues as a clergyman, by joining in this demonstration of the gratitude of his country towards him. . . . . . . Having said so much, I ought now to retire, for I feel this—that it is not in language to describe, and that there is not rapidity in human speech to follow, the brilliancy of his career. There can be no wings given to words, to enable them to rise to his moral exaltation. You might as well think of looking the noon-day sun in face, without injuring the vision, as to place the merits of Father Mathew in a clearer point of view than they at present exist. No; and if witnesses are wanting of his utility, I call on four millions of teetotallers to come forward with their testimony. . . . . . . I have heard a great deal to-day—and I did not hear it for the first time—of the intensity of the useful work he has performed. I have heard of families reformed—of mothers and children redeemed from ruin—of youth brought up in virtue, and rising into manhood with honour, whose career would have been blighted, and their hopes blasted for ever, if the temperance pledge had not come to their rescue, and saved the individual from destruction, and society from a curse. I have heard much of eulogium on the Irish people as they at present exist, and I only felt some cause of regret that, in forming a contrast with their present state and that from which they had been rescued, there was some appearance of showing that they had been previously in a state of degradation, and that, in praising what has been done, there was too heavy a censure passed on the former condition of the country. Perhaps I am wrong, and that my anxiety arises from the jealousy with which I regard everything reflecting on the character of my country. It would appear as if, prior to the temperance movement, the Irish were a depraved people—emphatically a drunken population—and that it required some mighty Apostle of the Living God to rescue them from their depravity. Take notice that, in saying this, I do not mean in the slightest degree to detract from the great merits of what has been done by the Rev. Mr. Mathew. I admit that he has performed a mighty moral miracle; but at the same time utterly deny that the people of Ireland were at any time inferior to their neighbours, or to the people of any foreign country, in any part of the globe. While I have been speaking, a thought has just flashed across my mind, to which I must give utterance—it is, that the parliamentary papers furnish evidence on what I have been referring to. Do they show that Ireland was a drunken country? Quite the contrary. Taking the population of Scotland, with relation to the population of Ireland, what do we find? Now, Scotland is a country that everybody praises. You do not blame Scotchmen for praising Scotland as they always do; and it happens that Scotchmen always contrive to take care of each other, wherever they meet. But the parliamentary papers show that, after all, the Scotchmen are not really so good as they are represented. What is the evidence? I take up the parliamentary papers, and they show me the consumption of ardent spirits in Scotland and Ireland, before Father Mathew's mighty movement commenced. Now, I hope you do not think that the Irish drank more than the Scotch. But even that would be enough to rescue them from the charge of depravity, as they are not worse than a people who are so praised. But the fact is, they did not drink half so much. I have it from the parliamentary document, that for every pint Scotch that the Irish drank, the Scotchmen drank two pints, and what is called a 'tilla' into the bargain. And that occurred, too, during a period when there was very little illicit distillation in Ireland, and a great deal of it in Scotland; and if the illicit whisky was taken into account, it would make the balance one-third more against Scotland. I then say, that Father Mathew did not redeem a drunken people; but he did redeem a people who were predisposed to his mission. . . . . . . Whatever our politics may be—whatever our creeds may be—whatever our condition or avocation in life may be, we are all here of one mind, and that is how Ireland should express her sense of the merits and the virtues of Father Mathew. We are come here to pledge all Ireland to the working out of that measure, and to show that we are worthy of sharing in such a plan by the enthusiasm which you have shown in listening to his praises, and by the anxiety exhibited of trying who can praise him most.

I thank you, my friends, I need not tell you, for the kindness with which you have listened to me. I feel how inadequate I have been to the subject, for words are nothing when such a topic comes before the mind. There is no painting the rainbow, the ray that comes from the sun, or the angelic plumes that flutter round the throne of the Deity; and there is no angel more pure or worthy than the angel of public morality, dignified in the person of Father Mathew.

At a meeting held in Cork on the 23rd of March following, under the presidency of Sir William Wrixon Becher, Bart., for the purpose of promoting the same object, Mr. Fagan, M.P., referred to the fact of Father Mathew's embarrassments, the necessary consequence of his position, and gave expression to the general common sense feeling as to what form the testimonial ought to assume :—

> At the commencement, great talk had been made about the Apostle's making money by the sale of medals, and I felt it necessary to speak to him about the matter; but I can assert that, instead of making money, he is at the present moment embarrassed to some extent by his too liberal donations of 20*l.*, 30*l.*, and 40*l.* to different branches of the society. With regard to the testimonial, I am not for erecting hospitals, or laying out the money collected in any brick and mortar work. I am of opinion that it ought to be funded, or placed in the hands of trustees, to enable the Apostle to carry out to the fullest the object of the movement, and bear him free of expense; for I know that he is at this moment a poor and embarrassed man, by reason of the temperance movement.

Perhaps the most imposing and useful demonstration made by the followers of Father Mathew was that in Cork, on the 16th of February of this year, when he was publicly entertained in the Corn Market. At this monster tea-party over 1,700 persons, including many of the first citizens, sat down to tables well furnished with every requisite for an evening 'banquet,' as it was termed by its promoters. All classes, parties, and creeds were harmoniously blended on that occasion, which was one of unalloyed gratification to the good man himself; for he then saw, as he fondly believed, the cause gathering round its standard the worth of the middle and the influence of the higher classes of the community His blended feelings of exultation and anxiety were expressed in his address, from which one or two passages are given :—

> Cold and unsusceptible must he be who would not catch a spark of the etherial fire. I pity the man who could sit here without feeling an attachment to our cause, and who would leave us with a hostile heart. 'Hostile heart!' I think I hear some person say, 'who can

have a heart hostile to a cause whose object is the general good of society at large?' But with sorrow I confess that our cause has enemies, that there are many who would rejoice in the fall of our society, and who would hail the return of intemperance. Prejudice, interest, appetite, and drinking customs, and, in a few cases, political motives and sectarian feelings, are arrayed against us; but strong in the strength of the Almighty God, the cause is pursuing a right forward career, and every difficulty is yielding before it. Five millions of persons are enrolled under the banner! the mighty vice of intoxication is yielding, and, with the blessing of God, we will cast the 'pale horse and his rider' into the sea. With heart-felt exultation we can survey the present condition of the country, we can witness the happiness of the people in the smiling faces that surround us; but let us not forget that there are those amongst our fellow-citizens, thousands of whom are suffering from the evil consequences of intoxicating drink. Oh! if we could take in at one view the ravages occasioned by intemperance in this city, we would see the dissipated husband, the bereaved father, the disconsolate mother, the pining orphan, and the youth of high hope and fervent aspirations sinking into a shameful and premature grave. It is to oppose the progress of this great evil, to arrest this abomination, that the temperance movement has been established.

He concluded with the following earnest appeal to the representatives of the wealthier and more influential classes, for aid in his work :—

I call on the virtuous and temperate to assist us in this great work. By saying this, I mean no censure; and if the labours of the present humble workers of the cause have been so blessed by the Almighty God as to be the means of conferring happiness and blessings on thousands, a richer, greater, and better harvest may be expected when those persons who possess wealth, influence, and rank will cooperate with us for the benefit of the holy cause of total abstinence. I call upon all who love their species, their God, and their religion, to assist us in the accomplishment of this glorious work. It is true we are not commanded by any precept, human or divine, to abstain; but if the great springs of human action, hope and fear, have not lost their influence on our hearts, you will all obey the call, and assist us in reviving the era of Christian charity and love, and in making the world a glorious habitation, in which every man may sit down in peace, and in the enjoyment of the blessings secured through Christ; temperance binding all together in the strictest and sweetest bonds of Christian charity and brotherly love.

The expense incurred in getting up this monster tea-party was considerable, leaving a balance of little short of 100*l.* against the committee, who were about paying it out of their own pockets, when Father Mathew heard of the fact. He appeared amongst them one evening as they were settling their accounts, and placing a bag full of silver on the table, insisted that he alone should make good the deficiency. Remonstrance, and even refusal, were altogether unavailing; for he was a man who, when he had made up his mind upon any matter, would have things his own way.

In May 1843, his brother Frank died, and for a short time after Father Mathew was unable to prosecute his mission; but a sense of duty soon triumphed over the natural tenderness of his heart, and saved him from indulging without restraint in grief which, if given way to, would have impaired his usefulness, and prevented him from fulfilling engagements to which he was pledged. He could not, nor did he attempt, to stifle the sorrow which every recollection of that beloved brother inspired; but he resolutely kept it locked up within his breast, and pursued his mission with unabated energy. Frequently, however, he would steal an hour from his triumphant mission to weep and pray at that tomb; and when the same sepulchre held the remains of his brother Tom, who died shortly after, his visits were still more frequent. The act soothed his feelings as a man, and gratified his piety as a priest.

CHAPTER XIX.

He determines to visit England—Inducements to do so—Earl Stanhope's Letter—The Quaker's 'Hotel'—Reception in York—In Leeds—In London.

THE next great event of his life was his visit to England. That he had gone through the length and breadth of his own country previous to this visit to the sister country, we have from his own words. Writing from Cork to a friend in America, in February 1843, he says: 'I have now, with the Divine assistance, hoisted the banner of temperance *in almost every parish in Ireland,* and, in every instance, by the pressing invitation of the parish priest, whose guest I invariably was.'

Invitations to visit England had been pouring in upon him since 1840; and had he not kept steadily in mind the task which he had undertaken in Ireland, and the necessity of completing it, so far as it was humanly possible for him to do so, he might have yielded to the pressing entreaties addressed to him. These appeals were made alike by Protestant and Catholic, by English and by Irish, by individuals as well as by societies. The Christian concord which his presence would be sure to promote among men of different persuasions—the prejudices which he would break down—the good which he would do his country through the moral elevation of the poor Irish, who, from their poverty and their social habits, were exposed to the worst temptation of large towns,—these inducements, and a hundred other likely to impress a man of his sensibility, were constantly addressed to him; but whatever his impulse might prompt him to do, his strong sense of duty enabled him to resist these solicitations, so long as his work at home was not sufficiently accomplished. The announcement of his intention to visit England in the summer of 1843 was hailed with satisfaction by the friends of temperance, and with natural enthusiasm by the Irish populations of its great towns.

A letter from the late Earl of Stanhope well expresses the esteem in which Father Mathew was held by those who differed from him in religious belief, and the satisfaction with which the announcement of his intended visit was received:—

Chevening, near Sevenoaks: Jan. 26, 1843.

MY DEAR SIR,—I was inexpressibly rejoiced to learn by your letter that you propose to visit London in May next, and I fervently hope that nothing will occur to prevent your arrival, which will be hailed with extreme and heart-felt satisfaction by the friends of temperance, and will be of infinite importance to the cause; for I trust that Divine Providence will continue to bless and prosper your benevolent exertions in this country, as well as in your native land, and that you may have the happiness of conferring their benefits on many of those who in the metropolis have fallen through intemperance into a state of destitution and of moral degradation. Your presence in this country will to myself in particular afford the greatest happiness, as I entertain for you the sincerest veneration, as I am most grateful for your inestimable services, and as I have long and ardently wished to have opportunities of conversing with you, when you will find me most anxious to profit by your instructions. But I am only a very humble follower in the great cause. If your engagements should allow it, you would oblige me extremely by honouring me with a visit at this place, which at that time of the year is in great beauty.

Allow me again to assure you that I am, with the utmost regard and esteem, my dear Sir,

Most faithfully yours,

STANHOPE.

To the Rev. Theobald Mathew.

The pressure of his many engagements in various parts of the country did not admit of his leaving Ireland sooner than the 30th of June, when he left Cork to redeem his long-standing and oft-repeated promise.

It is not necessary that a detailed account should be given of Father Mathew's visit to England, nor to enumerate the towns through which he passed, the addresses he received, the replies which he made, the speeches which he delivered, or the numbers that he enrolled. It was a repetition of his visit to Glasgow; the same enthusiasm and excitement, the same processions and assemblages, the same respect evinced towards him by those not of his own communion, the same wild exultation and delight manifested by his own country-people—the same impression of the character of the man left upon the minds of all who saw him, spoke with him, or were in any way brought into contact with him. By the bishops and clergy of the Catholic Church he was received with affectionate reverence; and wherever he went, in his short but triumphant tour in England, he contrived to pay back the kindness of his reception by conferring, through his preaching, some solid advantage on the Catholic mission of each locality or district.

In Liverpool, in Manchester, in Salford, in Huddersfield, in Wakefield, in Leeds, and in a number of other places, his success was extraordinary, but not greater than ought to have been the natural result of his extraordinary labours. In Liverpool and Manchester, he preached and administered the pledge in all the Catholic churches and schools of those great towns. There was not a day, during his stay in either place,—in both of which there was then, as there is now, an immense Irish population,—on which he did not lecture on temperance, and administer the pledge for several hours, frequently from an early hour in the morning to a late hour in the evening. Then, on Sundays, he preached for some special object, and also addressed crowded congregations on the ever-present purpose of his visit to England. Vast numbers of Protestants and members of the various dissenting bodies came to hear him preach in the different places through which he passed; and the impression which was made on their minds added to his reputation as a Christian minister, and enhanced his popularity with the English people. The employers of labour, whether rude or skilled, soon began to appreciate the benefits which his mission conferred on themselves, through the improved habits of their workpeople; and few there were, indeed, save the interested or the foolishly-bigoted, who did not wish God-speed to the good work so modestly and unostentatiously performed. Wherever he went, he received the most pressing invitations to take up his residence in the houses of his friends and admirers; but, to avoid giving trouble, and also to maintain, as much as possible, his personal freedom, he preferred remaining at hotels. Writing to a friend in London of the invitation which he had received to York, he says:—

The Right Rev. Dr. Briggs has condescended to invite me to be his guest during my stay in the archiepiscopal city. I prize the honour he has conferred on me, but I have most respectfully declined it, as it would not be compatible with the nature of my mission to be in a private mansion. I must be free to see all persons, rich and poor, at all hours.

This determination induced a respected member of the Society of Friends to resort to an ingenious device to obtain the honour of Father Mathew's company during his stay in Wakefield. The Quaker invited him to stay at his house, and received the usual reply, that he was to stop at the hotel, for the convenience of those who required to see him at all hours. The Friend would not be put off, but intimated that his house was a hotel, whereon Father Mathew gladly consented to 'put up' at it while in Wakefield. A board, with the word 'Hotel,' was placed on the outside of the mansion, and the private residence became, for the time, a most comfortable inn. Father Mathew was greatly pleased with the quiet and order, the wonderful neatness and simple elegance, which pervaded the entire establishment; while the agreeable manners of its master, which combined the cordiality of a friend with the politeness of the most gentlemanly host, filled him with astonishment. The servants of the house were also different from the usual class to be found in ordinary hotels: they were kindly, attentive, and respectful; and though they seemed to anticipate his every wish, they were neither fussy nor obtrusive. Then the bells of this Quaker hotel were singularly quiet; so that the 'boots,' and the chamber-maids, and the waiters must have known by intuition when and where their services were required. Truly, it was a model establishment, which any visitor might leave with very natural regret. The kindly device was not discovered until the time of his departure drew near, when the master of the house, no longer fearing the abrupt departure of his guest, appeared in his true character—as a generous and thoughtful host.

Father Mathew's reception in the fine old city of York was not only most flattering, but most significant. A grand procession of the temperance societies from the surrounding districts, accompanied with banners and bands, received him on his arrival, and escorted him through the city to his hotel. The venerable Bishop Briggs—who, in a few years after, displayed such practical sympathy with the starving poor of Ireland—Lord Stourton, Sir Edward Vavasour, and other distinguished Catholics, witnessed from the windows of a private residence this public manifestation of respect for the Irish Friar by that vast concourse of people, of various religious creeds, and of strong prejudices—in a city, too, where, as some of the party said, were a Catholic priest to have made a similar entry some years before, he would have been rather roughly treated.

In Leeds his reception was equally gratifying, and his success even more striking. Demonstrations of all kinds were got up in his honour, such as processions, soirées, meetings, and addresses. In one of his speeches in this important place he thus rather humorously vindicated the Temperance Society of Ireland from the charge of being a political body :—

It is imagined in England that the teetotallers of Ireland, as such, have mixed themselves up with the great agitation that at present prevails in that country. Why, to be sure, when nearly all the population have taken the total abstinence pledge, it is not very likely that 300,000 persons could assemble without a few teetotallers being amongst them.

Father Mathew's appearance, and the impression which he made upon the English people who beheld him for the first time, were well described in the 'Leeds Mercury' of that date :—

That in which the attraction of the procession centered was the carriage in which stood erect, with uncovered head, the great Apostle of Temperance, Father Mathew—the object of ten thousand greetings from the vast number of spectators who thronged the windows and every spot of vantage ground in the streets through which the procession moved. . . . . . His manners are simple and unassuming; and the kind and hearty reception which he gives to all who approach him (whether brought into his presence through curiosity or respect) is such as strikingly manifests him to be a true philanthropist, whose love and affection for his fellow-men overstep the narrow sphere of benevolence in which moves the mere kindred, party, or sectarian benefactor. Hitherto his least-recognised excellence by Englishmen has been as a public speaker; but his addresses at Leeds, York, and other parts of England prove that in this capacity his merits have not been duly understood or appreciated. His voice is mostly shrill and feeble, and his speeches, in general, are simple as his attire; they are always short, pointed, and harmonious,—often clothed in interesting similes, drawn from surrounding or familiar objects, and invariably appropriate and well selected. His addresses, however, are never distinguished by the gaudy ornaments of rhetoric; their elegance and force are more consistent with the language natural to an enlarged, fervid, and virtuous heart, than with a studied nicety of arrangement, or a lofty figurative style. Many public speakers are more eloquent, —most more tedious; yet few were more sincere, pleasing, and effective, and fewer in all things more charitable. Such is Father Mathew, the moral regenerator of Ireland.

After having made a successful tour of most of the principal places in Lancashire and Yorkshire, Father Mathew visited London, where his services were much required. And here, during several weeks, he underwent an amount of labour which very few men could have gone through with impunity, but for which his missionary labours of the previous three or four years had well prepared him. He commenced his good work in the poorest districts of the metropolis, in which the Irish principally dwelt, and where he was received by his country-people with all the enthusiasm which his character, his sacred office, and his nationality excited in a warm-hearted and affectionate race. His success was proportionately great, as was soon evinced in localities which up to that time had been the scene of constant brawl and confusion, of stupid quarrel and of savage conflict. Bishop Griffiths and the Catholic clergy lent their willing aid to one who accomplished so much for their flocks, and who, wherever he went, left after him proofs and evidences of his good work in the improved tone and habits of those who submitted to his influence. But others of a different faith zealously assisted the efforts of the Irish Priest to prosecute a mission which had the good of all for its object.

Nor during his stay in London was Father Mathew to be found only in the midst of the poor—appealing to the wretched drunkard to abandon the cause of his misery, and affectionately exhorting those of his own race and country to allow fair play to the many virtues which distinguish them when sober and self-respecting. He was also to be seen in the mansions of the aristocracy, with whom he was a welcome and an honoured guest. It was while London was yet 'in town,' and he was the lion of the hour. His table was covered with cards and notes of invitation to all kinds of entertainments, including the fashionable breakfast and the late dinner. Father Mathew was as much at home in the gilded saloon of the noble as in the modest parlour of a brother priest; so that, if *gaucherie* or restraint were expected from the Irish Friar in the presence of the great, the mistake was at once apparent; for in ease of manner, and quiet dignity of bearing, few surpassed Theobald Mathew. But there was superadded, in his case, the charm which springs from the purest benevolence and goodness of heart; and this, with the *prestige* of his world-wide fame, and the thought of the wonderful work which he had accomplished, invested him with extraordinary attraction in the eyes of those who beheld him for the first time, and who were pleased to find in the celebrated Apostle of Temperance a thorough gentleman. By the members of the Catholic aristocracy, at whose houses he visited, he was received with affectionate reverence, due alike to his personal character and sacred profession. To many he had been known before, either personally or as a correspondent; but in every case his welcome was as cordial and sincere as it was respectful.

The late breakfasts and the late dinners were very trying to him, from the manner in which the hours of almost every day were filled up. He rose, as usual, at an early hour, and invariably celebrated Mass in one of the chapels of the city; after which he was occupied with the poor until half-past ten, the ordinary hour of his fashionable appointment for his first meal. As soon as he could well leave the party that had been invited to meet him, he proceeded to the place fixed for the public meeting of that day, and there he remained, exhorting and administering the pledge, so long as there was a chance of obtaining an additional disciple. He then returned to his hotel, where he wrote letters or received visitors; and at eight, or half-past eight, when the hour for dinner arrived, he generally found a large party, that had been invited to do him honour. His breakfast was invariably but a moderate repast; so that the dinner, which he partook of at this, to him, unseasonable hour, might be said to be his only meal during the entire day. To those who were not aware of the long fast to which he had been subjected, his vigorous appetite must have excited admiration, and probably it was attributed to the beneficial influence of total abstinence. At ten o'clock he contrived to slip away from his grand party; and in his bed-room at his Temperance hotel he concluded the good work of the day, by the devotional exercises which his office prescribed, or which his piety inspired.

If he received encouragement and support, he also met with opposition and insult. In Ireland, from one end of the kingdom to the other, the Apostle of Temperance never received insult or incivility in any instance, even from those whom he injured most. With Protestant and Presbyterian, as with Catholic, the purity of his motive and the benevolence of his character protected him from every attempt at open opposition or personal indignity; but, availing themselves of the stupid prejudice against 'the Popish priest,' which was felt most strongly by the lowest class of their besotted customers, some crafty publicans in Bermondsey, in Westminster, and in other parts of the metropolis, who were afraid of losing their unhappy slaves, organised several attempts to interrupt the proceedings of his meetings, to upset the platform, or to create disturbance and confusion. In some instances, the attempts were successful, and the proceedings were abruptly terminated; in others, the assailants suffered for their folly, having been soundly drubbed by the indignant Irish, who resented the insult to their country and their religion in the person of Father Mathew. The presence of the police at other times kept the publicans, who came on the ground with beer for sale, as well as their noisy and half-drunken myrmidons, in check, and prevented the rioting which had been evidently intended; but on one occasion, where drink had been distributed gratuitously and in abundance by the alarmed sellers of the locality, a mob of drunken 'roughs' was bearing down on the platform with mischievous intent, and Father Mathew was compelled to escape from the back of the platform, where there was a cab in readiness to receive him. A scene of this disreputable character took place on his visit to Bermondsey, which was thus described in the 'Morning Chronicle' of the following day :—

Father Mathew arrived about half-past twelve o'clock, at which time there were about 2.000 persons assembled, and on his appearance on the platform he was met with shouts of disapprobation, mingled with cheers. Finding this was the case, the reverend gentleman dispensed with making any address, and simply called on those who wished to take the pledge to come forward. This call was met with derisive laughter ; and in order to frustrate the labours of the apostle, a large body of fellows, chiefly dockmen and apparently labourers in the tan-yards, took possession of the space within the barrier, and refused to leave it. Mr. Hart, one of the temperance advocates, went amongst them to remonstrate, and was shamefully treated, one of the ruffians striking him in the face. Father Mathew proceeded to administer the pledge to a few persons who had got in front, and on the platform. The greatest confusion and uproar continued to prevail, and it was ultimately deemed necessary to send for a body of the M division of police, who, on their arrival, endeavoured to clear the barrier, but were met with the greatest resistance, and in several instances they were violently struck in the execution of their duty. The removal of the parties from within the barrier in no way tended to the preservation of order without, for the yells and hootings continued rather to increase than diminish, and whilst Father Mathew was administering the pledge to some females on the platform, stones were thrown at him from the back of the crowd. One of them, which struck a gentleman standing very near the 'apostle,' was shown to him. It was a large-sized flint-stone, which evidently, from its shiny appearance, had been in a person's pocket some time. The police, in order to prevent a recurrence of so disgraceful a proceeding, and to deter the parties, distributed themselves among the crowd. Shortly after, a gang of the dastardly ruffians were discovered in the rear of the platform, making preparations to cut the ropes fastening its cross supporters to the uprights ; and, had this been effected, the most serious consequences, if not a large amount of loss of human life, must have resulted, the stage of the platform being unusually high, and at the time crowded with people. Four or five of the delinquents were, it is stated, secured, and given into custody.

An address was about to be presented to Father Mathew, from the Bermondsey and Rotherhithe Total Abstinence Association, when one of the most disgraceful and extraordinary scenes which can be imagined took place. A great noise was heard proceeding from one of the arches of the railway, and immediately after a body of the anti-teetotallers, who had left the spot a short time previously, made their appearance in procession. They were about sixty or seventy in number, followed by three times the number of boys. Some of them had staves, and were decorated from head to foot with hop-leaves. Each of them bore a quart or pint pot in his hand, and in the centre the men carried large cans, containing each at least four or five gallons of beer. They were forcing their way to the hustings, evidently with a determination to take possession of it, when they were met by the police. A general conflict then took place, in which a considerable quantity of the beer was upset. The 'Malt and Hops' gentry were compelled to retreat, but immediately after rallied, and mounted a large pile of bricks in one corner of the field, where the most gross language was indulged in, and from which the pots and cans were held up in derision. An additional body of police having arrived, tne rioters were driven from their position, but not before they had thrown some of their beer into the faces of their assailants. The ground was at last cleared of these gentry; and Father Mathew, in returning thanks for the address, regretted that any men should be so lost as to attempt to disturb proceedings of the kind they had met to carry out; more especially when it was for the good of those very poor men who had done so.

Opposition of this nature had the contrary effect to that which its foolish authors intended ; for it not only excited the indignation of well-thinking people, but it made the Irish residents of London more willing to take the pledge, and more resolute in keeping it.

In the account given, in the 'Times,' of one of his visits to Westminster, is the following :—

After giving the pledge to the second batch, Father Mathew said that while he was below he had heard one person say to his neighbour, 'What a shame it was that a Protestant should receive a blessing from a Catholic priest.' Now, since he had been in England, he had everywhere received the blessings of the Protestants, and he was proud of it If a blessing did them no good, surely it could do them no harm. Since he had been in this country he had got half a million of blessings from the Protestants. He was daily saluted with 'God bless you, Father Mathew!' 'God speed you, Father Mathew!' and such like earnest expressions. There certainly could be no evil in a blessing, come from whom it would.

CHAPTER XX.

A Rare Occurrence—A Noble Convert—The Press and the Peerage—Lord Brougham—Characteristic Incident—The Great Duke and the Apostle of Temperance—Welcomed by the Bishop of Norwich—The Bishop's noble Eulogium—Father Mathew's Good Work in England.

IT was a rare circumstance with Father Mathew to hesitate as to giving the pledge to any one, or to pause to ascertain from the postulant who knelt before him whether he had fully made up his mind as to the step he was about to take. Marvellous as the fact must have seemed to himself, when he thought of it afterwards, he did hesitate in one instance—perhaps the only one that could be recorded of him. It was on the occasion of his holding a meeting in Golden Lane, Barbican, which was attended by a great concourse of people, chiefly Irish. He had been addressing himself specially to the working classes, and earnestly impressing on them the necessity of renouncing the cause of so much misery; and when, at the conclusion of his address, several hundreds knelt to receive the pledge, Father Mathew, on looking round him, found the future Duke of Norfolk, then Lord Arundel and Surrey, also on his knees. Anxious as he was to obtain so illustrious a 'convert,' Father Mathew was of opinion that the young nobleman had yielded to a sudden impulse, and was about to take the pledge unreflectingly; and however ardently he desired to add him to the number of his followers, he was apprehensive of the evil which would follow were he to abandon the cause which he impulsively joined. So, before administering the pledge to the hundreds who were waiting to take it, he spoke privately to the earl, and asked him if he had given the subject sufficient reflection. 'Ah! Father Mathew,' replied his noble convert, 'do you not know that I had the happiness to receive Holy Communion from you this morning at the altar of Chelsea Chapel? I *have* reflected on the promise I am about to make, and I thank God for the resolution, trusting to the Divine goodness for grace to persevere.' Tears rolled down his cheeks as he uttered these words, with every evidence of genuine emotion. He then repeated the formula of the pledge. Father Mathew embraced him with delight, pronounced a solemn benediction 'on him and his,' and invested him with the medal which he took from his own neck. This scene was witnessed with the most intense interest by the vast assemblage, by whom the earl was hailed with cheers, as he rose from his knees a disciple of the Apostle of Temperance. The example thus given had the effect of adding many hundreds to the ranks of the society on that day. This act, publicly performed, was regarded by the good and pious nobleman as one of no ordinary gravity; for he long continued faithful to the pledge thus voluntarily taken; and it was not until many years after, that, at the command of his medical advisers, he substituted moderation for total abstinence.

Father Mathew's rare self-denial on this almost solitary occasion was amply compensated by his zealous efforts to enlist recruits from the influential ranks or professions. It would be difficult to say whether he prized more, as a convert, a newspaper editor or a peer of the realm. 'Oh,' exclaimed he one day at a meeting in Chelsea, which was attended by several members of the aristocracy and representatives of the press, 'if I could only induce some of my noble friends and my young friends of the press to join, I should be most happy, for I know how powerful their example and influence would be.' The reporters of the daily papers were here placed in the same category as the scions of nobility, and no man better knew than he did the service which the former could render to his cause. But an editor of an influential journal was a prize equal in value to a prime minister. His estimate of the value of the support which he received from the public press was expressed on various occasions in Ireland; but while in England he also proclaimed his obligation and gratitude to that powerful agent. At one of his meetings in London he said :—

I have often taken occasion to say that, next to God, to the support I have met with from that most mighty moral power on this earth, the public press, do I attribute the success which has attended the great moral movement, total abstinence. In Ireland, with one solitary exception, the whole press has been in my favour; and in London you all know the support I have reeeived from the public press of all shades of opinion; and I thus publicly tender my grateful thanks to those who have the control of every metropolitan daily journal, not so much for the kindness they have accorded to me personally, as for the good they have done for the cause of morality, by sustaining my humble efforts to arrest a great evil.

During his stay in London, Father Mathew met the most distinguished men of the day, who had been invited to meet the great moral reformer. He created no small amusement to a large party at the hospitable mansion of an Irish nobleman by his attempts, partly playful, but also partly serious, to make a convert of Lord Brougham, who resisted, good-humouredly but resolutely, the efforts of his dangerous neighbour. 'I drink very little wine,' said Lord Brougham: 'only half a glass at luncheon, and two half glasses at dinner; and though my medical advisers told me I should increase the quantity, I refused to do so.' 'They are wrong, my lord, for advising you to increase the quantity, and you are wrong in taking the small quantity you do; but I have my hopes of you.' And so, after a pleasant resistance on the part of the learned lord, Father Mathew invested his lordship with the silver medal and ribbon, the insignia and collar of the new Order of the Bath. 'Then I will keep it,' said Lord

Brougham, 'and take it to the House, where I shall be sure to meet old Lord —— the worse of liquor, and I will put it on him.' The announcement of this intention was received with much laughter, for the noble lord referred to was notorious as a persistent worshipper of Bacchus. Lord Brougham was as good as his word; for, on meeting the veteran peer who was so celebrated for his potations, he said: 'Lord ——, I have a present from Father Mathew for you,' and passed the ribbon rapidly over his neck. 'Then I tell you what it is, Brougham; by ——! I will keep sober for this night,' said his lordship, who kept his vow, to the great amazement of his friends.

The Marquis of Clanricarde, who was the noble entertainer, accompanied his distinguished guest to the hall, where he was surprised by seeing him go eagerly towards one of the servants in waiting, and shake him warmly by the hand. This was an English servant, who, afraid of losing his situation, had taken the pledge, some two or three years before, when Father Mathew visited Portumna Castle, the seat of the noble marquis in Ireland. Father Mathew, whose memory for persons was extraordinary, at once recognised his follower, and, in the presence of several members of the aristocracy—who were not a little amazed at what the witnessed—treated that servant with manly respect.

Father Mathew and the 'great Duke'—the two most distinguished conquerors of the age, though in widely-different fields of glory—met on one of these occasions. The duke was singularly gracious to his brother hero, for whose character and services he entertained well-known respect. 'I ought to claim your Grace as one of ours,' said the priest to the soldier. 'How can that be, Father Mathew? I am not a teetotaller, though I am a very moderate man,' replied the duke. 'Oh, but you are a temperance man, your Grace; for if you had not so cool a head, you would not have been the illustrious Duke of Wellington,' was the quick rejoinder.

'Father Mathew,' said a gentleman one evening to the lion of the party, 'you must have felt rather embarrassed in your visits to the north of Ireland; the people are so much colder than your warm-hearted countrymen of the south, and so prejudiced against your Church.' 'Far from it,' replied Father Mathew; 'I felt quite at home among them from the first, and they were most kind and hospitable. In Fermanagh, I was nobly received and entertained in the mansion of Captain Archdall, one of the leading Orangemen of that county.' Even if Father Mathew had any other story to tell, he would have remained silent, rather than say a word disparaging to the character and good feeling of his countrymen.

Perhaps the most gratifying circumstance connected with his visit to England was the manner of his reception by the late Dr. Stanley, then Bishop of Norwich. The bishop had been invited to Cambridge, to meet Father Mathew in that city; to which invitation he sent the following reply, addressed to Mr. E. Walker:—

Palace, Norwich: August 18, 1844.

SIR,—I regret that I cannot comply with your request that I should attend at Cambridge on the occasion of the Rev. T. Mathews's visit. If, however, he comes to Norwich, I shall think it my duty to sanction a meeting, and pay every respect to an individual to whose zealous exertions, in recovering so large a portion of the community from the degrading and ruinous effects of intemperance, men of all religious persuasions and parties owe a debt of gratitude.

I remain, yours faithfully,
E. NORWICH.

The friends of temperance in Norwich were much gratified at the publication of this testimony to the merit of the apostle of the cause; and his lordship was soon made acquainted with the fact that Father Mathew had accepted an invitation to visit Norwich on the 7th of September. The English Protestant bishop then addressed the following letter to the Irish priest:—

Palace, Norwich: Sept. 2, 1844.

REVEREND SIR,—I have just been informed that it is your intention to visit Norwich on Thursday next, Sept. 7, on which occasion I shall feel it my duty as well as my inclination to give you the cordial welcome due to one who has so zealously and so effectually devoted himself to a cause in which Christians of all denominations may cooperate. I purpose therefore attending an evening meeting, which I understand will be held in St. Andrew's Hall on the day of your arrival, and I take the earliest opportunity of expressing my earnest hope that you will favor me with your company either to dinner or breakfast, at any hour that you may name most convenient to yourself. I should be obliged by a line in reply.

I remain, yours faithfully,
E. NORWICH.

The Rev. Theobald Mathew,
Hart's Temperance Hotel, 159 Aldersgate Street.

Father Mathew received the bishop's letter with feelings which may be well imagined, when it is considered that one of the objects of his life was to cultivate the kindliest intercourse with his Christian brethren of every denomination, and to reciprocate that fraternal charity which ought to exist among ministers of the Gospel, notwithstanding differences of doctrine. That letter, written in a fine bold hand, was preserved by Father Mathew to the hour of his death; and it is from that letter, now nearly twenty years written, that the above has been transcribed by his biographer. The bishop fully redeemed his promise of a cordial welcome, not only by his elegant hospitality, but by a noble eulogium, which was honourable alike to the speaker and to its grateful object. In the face of a crowded assembly, the bishop thus addressed the man whom those thousands had met to honour and to hear:—

And now, Reverend Sir (addressing Father Mathew), you, my friend and brother from another island, I meet you not here as a Roman Catholic priest; I differ from your creed—I will candidly tell you I am even hostile to it; but I meet you here in a nobler, in a more comprehensive character than that of a priest,—I meet you as a man like myself, as a Christian brother, as a Christian brother on neutral ground, where Christians of all denominations delight to meet and congregate together. Sir, I have watched your proceedings for many and many a year. I remember, many years ago, that I censured you in public; nay more, may I not add, abused you. I believed those public reports spread, I scarcely know how, save by malign and foolish misrepresentation; nevertheless, I thought it my duty, as a man of candour, to apply to you as a gentleman, a Christian, and a man of honour, to tell me how the case really stood. You answered me in a manner that did you credit, and I turned over a new leaf—I abused you no more; and now I rejoice to meet you here as a friend. I am not one of those who will not believe a Catholic on his oath; I acted more courteously; I believed you on your candid and honest affirmation; and I am satisfied that you did not deceive me. I have watched over your character; I have had every resource in my possession, and I have endeavoured to ascertain precisely what it was. I will say, and I think it my duty to say, it is embodied and written in print. I will read you the character which I believe Mr. Mathew entitled to, and which describes that character and estimation in which he is held by those who know him better than I do. Here his lordship read the following eulogium: 'He is a gentleman by birth; for 24 years he has devoted his energies to the service of the poor; and so far from being actuated by sordid or pecuniary motives, he has applied his private property to religious and benevolent purposes. As to politics, notwithstanding insinuations to the contrary, it is a fact that he has never, during his whole life, attended one political meeting, or mixed with any political agitation; and though entitled to the franchise, he has never voted.' My friends, I believe it; and I may say that the good sense and the good feeling of the aristocracy of London have borne me out in the opinion I entertain of this worthy man. When in London, he was visited and most hospitably received by men of high rank, high character, and high station; they knew his worth, and they bade him go on and prosper, knowing well that they should receive the advantages, if not directly, indirectly, of his invaluable exertions. But, sir, your cause was not an easy one; it was not altogether over a Macadamised road you had to pass; but you had thorns and brakes and briars in the way. You were assailed in turn by those who, while their disapprobation and censure was eulogy, sunk them in deeper degradation. . . . Men of Norwich! citizens of this ancient city! I appeal to you, and I trust that my appeal shall not be in vain—receive this wanderer on a sacred mission from a distant country—receive him and give him a Christian welcome, for he has come on a Christian mission.

This was the crowning triumph of a visit which had done so much, not alone for the cause of temperance, but for the promotion of Christian charity amongst men of different creeds and churches.

It was computed that 600,000 persons had taken the pledge during this brief but successful campaign, which added much to the popularity and *prestige* of the apostle. It is a matter of little difficulty to compute the numbers who knelt before Father Mathew and received the pledge at his hands; but it would be a difficult task indeed to tell the good which he accomplished, the fallen whom he raised, the erring whom he brought back to virtue, the despairing whom he comforted, the hungry and the naked whom he fed and clad. For many years after, the blessed traces of that mission of peace and good will to England were not erased; and to this day—nearly a quarter of a century after the Apostle of Temperance preached in the highways of its great towns and famous cities—there are many sober and self-respecting men, and many families too, who treasure in their hearts the remembrance of that auspicious visit. It is true there are very many more who have reason to mourn in bitterness over the folly which induced forgetfulness of his advice; but even to this hour the broad foot-prints left by the Apostle of Temperance on the soil of England are not altogether obliterated.

A writer in the 'Globe' of that date thus accounted for the admitted success of his English mission:—

> The secret of his success consists chiefly in the fact that he has wholly abstained from doing what his opponents have accused him of. He has avoided making his labours subservient either to religious or political objects; and it is by this singleness of purpose—this determination to make temperance his chief and only object—that he has been able to achieve so much for the cause he has undertaken.

CHAPTER XXI.

Return to Cork—The Mathew Tower—Mr. O'Connor's Motives for its Erection—Again in Harness—His Visitors—Midnight Labour —His Correspondents—Strange Epistles.

GREAT was the joy in Cork at the return of Father Mathew from England. It was his first prolonged absence from his own country, and the deepest interest had been excited and kept alive, in the minds of his friends* and followers, by the varied events of his triumphant English tour. For a week after his arrival the parlour in Cove Street was crammed almost to suffocation, from morning

* To the impression made upon the mind of his personal friend, the late Mr. William O'Connor, merchant tailor, of Cork, by the reception given to Father Mathew in London, are the lovers of the picturesque indebted for the erection of the Mathew Tower, which forms so striking an object, from its lofty sight on the hill-side, on the Glanmire bank of the Lee. The foundation-stone was laid on the 30th of October, 1843; and at the fête with which its completion was celebrated, its spirited founder explained the motives which impelled him to an act of such signal munificence. He said:—

'I have not the least regret for the motives which actuated me in building this edifice; for though many said it was an expensive undertaking, yet with the same views I then and still entertain, I would not consider ten times the expense misapplied for such a purpose; and if I could raise the tower to ten times its present height, it would still be unequal to the dignity and moral grandeur of the services of him of whose labours it is commemorative. A greater impression was never made on an individual than upon me, at witnessing the kindly reception Father Mathew met with from all classes of society in London, and I resolved, on my return to Ireland, to commemorate it in some manner; and soon afterwards, when walking over the grounds you are now on, it struck me that the site would be a most eligible one to build a tower on, which would perpetuate Father Mathew's fame, and, at the same time, signify my gratitude for the reception he had met with in London: and I feel assured that it is only necessary that the people of both countries should know each other better and more intimately, to create more kindly feelings between both.'

to night. There were straying sheep to be taken back into the fold, prodigals to be welcomed and forgiven, backsliders to be pardoned; there were petitions to be presented, disputes to be settled, difficulties to be smoothed down; there were deputations to be received, and applications to be answered; there were whispered communications to be made in the corner of the little room, by some poor creature who had counted, with trembling eagerness, every day and hour till the good man's return; and there were interviews to be held at the foot of the stairs, or in the sitting-room. And amidst all this bustle and excitement, Father Mathew was in his element, having a word for every one, and an ear for all. He would break through the recital of some complicated tale of a misunderstanding between the leading members of a favourite reading-room, to receive a tattered drunkard, in whose tangled locks, pale cheeks, blood-shot eyes, and trembling limbs, a useful lesson might be read. Others might have shrunk from contact with that poor degraded human being, but not Father Mathew, who would exclaim, in a cheery voice, 'Welcome, my dear!—welcome!—it is never too late to do a good work. We never should despair of the mercy of the Lord. God help you, my poor child; you have been too long the slave of strong drink—it is time for you to rise up against your greatest enemy. Kneel down, my dear, and pray of God to give you grace and strength to keep the promise you are about to make.' No sooner was the poor fellow sent away happy, perhaps with half-a-crown slipped into his hand, than Father Mathew would again plunge into the complicated perplexity of the misunderstanding. Arriving rapidly at the real merits of the question, he would offer a few words of earnest advice, or, if necessary, interpose his authority; but his usual plan, when the statement was *ex parte*, was to appoint a time when both sides were to be heard He would then turn to a 'batch,' which had been forming in the interval; and after having administered the pledge, spoken a kind word to each, heard the whispered tale of some who were more wretched-looking than the others, and ordered medals to be given to the children, he would receive an address from a local society, and reply to its splendid hyperbole and magnificent metaphors in a manner which would flush the earnest faces of his followers with proud happiness—which reply was certain to be repeated to the assembled members, on the same evening, by the deputation, without the loss of a single word. Then would come an appeal for a personal interview of 'only half a minute.' This would be acceded to unfailingly, and soon Father Mathew's hand might be seen to dive into that deep pocket of his, and then brought into contact with the hand of the person to whom he was speaking; and then there might be heard a deep murmur of thanks, mingled with prayers, as the person retired rapidly, and with a much relieved air. Father Mathew would then go to the hall door—which, as a matter of course, was always open—to see and speak with some peculiarly cherished beggar, whom, perhaps, the rest of the community regarded as a confirmed impostor; and having made that fellow-creature happy for the day, he would return to the parlour, to receive another deputation, patch up a difference, accept an invitation, or give or promise aid towards the formation of a new temperance band, which, according to the solemn assurance of the spokesman, was essential to the social and moral salvation of the district.

Just as the salvation of the district had been satisfactorily secured, at the expense of Father Mathew's pocket, a strange voice might be heard at the door, enquiring, 'Is it here Mr. Mathew resides?' and a more familiar voice replying, 'If ye mane does his reverence Father Mathew live here, this is his house, sure enough, and God bless him every day he rises.' This was an English or American stranger who had come to pay a passing visit to the Apostle of Temperance;

but whether the stranger came with or without an introduction, he was always certain of receiving a cordial welcome from Father Mathew, whom the world's applause had not robbed of his genial and unaffected manner. The stranger would perhaps venture into the parlour, glance curiously at the groups around, examine the pages of the register, read over the last name recorded, with its corresponding number, and remain for a short time, till he had witnessed the administration of the pledge ; then he would accompany the master of the mansion to his grand reception room, which was as simple in its appointments as the cell of a monk. The interview, however brief, would be sufficient to impress the stranger with the shrewdness, sagacity, and worldly knowledge of a man whom he had most probably regarded as an enthusiast—something between a Howard and a Peter the Hermit.

But just as some new topic had been started, Father Mathew, who, from the window, which commanded the opposite street, had seen a critical case approaching, would apologise for his momentary absence, and, rushing down stairs, arrive at the door in time to hail the arrival, and secure the prize before there was an opportunity or possibility of escape.

There were visits to be paid, cases to be hunted up, obdurate sinners to be pounced upon unexpectedly ; there were friends and strangers to be entertained at dinner ; there were temperance rooms to be called in upon ; there were leaders in the cause to be consulted or advised with.

But with these various engagements the duties and labours of the day did not terminate. There was the heaviest task of all to be still undertaken—there was the correspondence to be read, and to be replied to. And what a pile of letters had accumulated during his absence in England ! Why here was work for half a dozen active secretaries. Letters from India — letters from America — letters from England and

Scotland—letters from all parts of Ireland—letters from every class of society, and on almost every imaginable subject. Here was a communication concerning the interests of his order, from the superior of an Irish house, or a high official in Rome; next, was a document with an enclosure—the document, a letter giving sundry cogent reasons why the writer relapsed to whisky-punch—the enclosure, the surrendered temperance card of the logical seceder. Next came an anonymous production, in which Father Mathew was affectionately besought to abandon his sinful Church, and to lead a new Reformation. Then a letter full of praise and congratulation from some English nobleman, who expressed his regret that the illustrious Apostle of Temperance had not honoured his house by his presence. Then a letter from a female writer, imploring his prayers for the object which she specified; and one from a more impetuous and imperative correspondent, who insisted on obtaining his blessing 'by return of post.' Here was a land agent, soliciting his influence with an overholding tenant, to induce him to give up a dwelling peaceably; and here a coaxing missive from a poor fellow, who found the temperance martingale too tight for his virtue, and who was satisfied to remain a devoted and enthusiastic follower of the cause till the day of his death, if he would only be allowed an occasional 'dandy' for the sake of his delicate stomach, and a moderate allowance of ale or porter wherewith to supply exhausted nature.

That the reader may see there is no exaggeration in this description, or rather indication, of the varied character of the correspondence to which, spent and wearied by a long day of incessant exertion, Father Mathew had to devote his attention during the hours of night, when all around him were enjoying their natural repose, a few extracts and letters are given, as a sample of the rest.

Here, for instance, was a letter that clearly admitted of no delay in reply. It bore a number of signatures, and was written in a style at once grand and forcible. It complained of some individual who had '*the avaricious audacity*' to withhold, and still retain, 'the 10*l.* given by your reverence for instruments for our band;' and it thus concluded :—

But the motto of Horace suits this person, we think, admirably—that is—*semper avarus eget.* The question now is, shall we get our instruments, or shall we not? shall we continue a Temperance Band, or shall we not? shall we, must we (*after all*) be ***driven to give up our pledges.*** or shall we continue Temperate, OR NOT? On your reply in the affirmative we still have reliance.

The reader may not clearly comprehend the connection between the 10*l.* and the pledge, or between the band and sobriety, but Father Mathew did; and the answer was of course a second donation, but not forwarded through the medium of the party whose 'avaricious audacity' was the occasion of the correspondence.

His immediate attention was called, in the next, to a tremendous feud raging between two societies, which preferred equal claims to his acceptance of an invitation to their respective rooms. But, unhappily for the innocent advocate of one of the rivals, and for the cause he pleaded, he added this fatal postscript, which he believed to be a clincher:—'And, your reverence, the Society must not omit to tell you, that their band amuse the people by their music on every occasion, *and played Mr. O'Connell into town when he had his Repeal meeting here.*'

Here is the joint production of man and wife, two servants, who evidently had a desire to fall into temptation with a free conscience, and whose plea for release is plausibly urged. It is given exactly as it was written :—

Dublin July 23.

REVD SIR—I beg leave to inform you that this is the second time i have wrote to you on this occasion an has Got no answer which makes my mind very aneasey it is in consequence of me and me wife taking the pledge from your Reverence for a few months Mereley to induce two friends of ours to take it as the were living a very anhappy life all from drink an as the would not take the pledge unless we did we a greed to do so but neither Me or me wife never had any occasion to do so only on their account as we always lived very temperate an never took any drink to injure us Eather soul or body and as our friends is living a very hapy life Ever since Both me an me wife is determined to give up our pledge but would not wish to do so till we would acquaint your Reverence and as I mentioned in the other letter that I sent to your Rev about a month agoe that it is not in Regard of drink But we feel a dread on our minds that we never felt before which makes us very aneasy an as we are both Servants an going from one place to another to earn our bread there is Great temtations Every where we goe it is for me wife she has confined herself to the house Ever since afraid of Going into any society lest any thing might attempt her She is not near so well in health as She was before an whether it is that is the occasion of it or not we cannot say but she thinks it is as her mind is very aneasey But if we thought that it would make such an Impression on our minds as it has done or that there was any diffecuty in Giving it up we would never have taken it but as your Rev Said in the Royal Ecchange that any person after two or three months was at their own free will to Give it up if the wished So on them terms we took it for our friends Sake it is now better than three months an as we have made up our minds to give it up we beg of you in honor of God to leave us your Blessing we Remain Most Revd Sir your very obt an humble Servants Mary an Abraham * * * *

at Mr * * * *
Carlisle Buildings dublin

we wait most anxcious for your Revnce answer before we Give it up

The following is thus comprehensively addressed :—

To
The very revd. theobald
town
Mathew of Cork or elsewhere.

The writer is evidently bent on the recovery of his freedom, and resolves to be free, whether Father Mathew should give him permission or not ; still a liberative line from his reverence would be a triumph over the less formal deserters, who turned their back upon their flag, and did not lay down their arms and surrender their commission with dignity, as this Wexford man desired to do :—

April 20th.

REVEREND SIR—I write thise few lines to you hopeing to find you in good As this leaves me at present thanks be to god for it, Dear Sir I Wrote thise few lines to you hopeing that your reverence Would be so kind as to take the pledge from me, As i Would wish to give it up, Dear Sir it is not to become a Drunkard that i am going to give it up but as temtation is so great and that the greater part of people that has taken the pledge is after brak throug it and i Would Not Wish to break the pledge that way Without geting liberty to do so and i hope that your reverence Will be so kind as to take the pledge from me, and if you dont i Will break it, for my part I did Not want a pledge at all for i never was a drunkard at all Nor i Wont take any more glass of Sperrits or a pint of beer, so reverend sir i hope you will be So Kind as to grant me my request.

Dear Sir I Would be very glad that you Would Write me a few lines to let me know What you would do about it if it was not to much trouble for, and if you write derict your letter to James * * * *
Taghmon Co Wexford

So i remain your most obegant and humble Servant James * * * *

Here is a very different kind of letter, which painfully illustrates those unhappy cases in which the husband or the wife, the father or the mother, implored the interference of Father Mathew :—

VERY REV. DEAR SIR—With grief and sorrow I address you. My poor wife has ruined herself and me, and nearly brought disgrace on our darling children by the unfortunate habit of drinking. It has gone on for a long time, and shame compelled me to keep it secret; but it would be a crime to let it rest longer. She promised me this morning she would take the total abstinence pledge, but would not be induced to go over to you; in fact, she is not able, she has brought herself to death's door with it. She has not been out of bed since Saturday last till this morning. You never did a greater act of charity than to call on her. She promised me she would tell you all.

Very respectfully and gratefully,

The prescription in the following elaborate appeal to Father Mathew's finer feelings is too valuable to be lost. It will be seen, however, that the patient who may be inclined to adopt the prescription should take his medicine in a pious state of mind, as otherwise its efficacy might possibly be neutralised :—

Ballyhooly, May ye 2nd.

VERY REVD. FATHER—Its with much pleasure I have to announce to you, that I am a Loyal member of Yr. Society, now, nearly Six Years. And During that time I not only kept from any kind Spirituous liquors, but in one of the Visits Yr. Very Revd. person, paid one of my Neighbouring Villages, I renewed my Pledge Against Any of the other Stuffs that I frequently Saw teetotallers make use of, Such as Soda, Peppermt. Ginger ale, cordial, lemonade, &c. &c., and all such things. I Entirely avoided them one, and all. I happened last winter, through Excessive labour, to Get a very heavy fit of Sickness, which both Emaciated, And Debilitated me, Very much. I had as good Nourishmt. as Any Poor man in my Sphere of life, could have, And all was not serving me. I was ordered by a friendly Neighbour of mine, to Drink, a large tumbler of Punch, that would be hot, Strong, and Sweet, with a large lump of Butter melted on it, and take it sitting in my bed, before I'd Settle myself to Sleep, this was, in order to remove the Pains out of my bones, which at the Same time, I was very bad with, then, tho bad I was, I did not do it until I'd See more about it. I got a Stick, And walked with its help, down to my Priests House, (for I considered leave was very light,) and told him all as I have here stated, And what he told me, was, to drink Some whey, that it was Very Good ; and that I, at that hour of the Night, or Even Season of the Year, had no more Getting of whey, nor anything to make whey of, than I had of Spanish wine, in the miserable Street of Ballyhooly, or its Vicinity. I then returned home, Not pleased at my Disappointmt. he feared, I suppose, that I'd return to drink again at my Six Years end, like a Dog to his Vomit, but I do assure both him and You, that I'd do no such thing, but Sir, when I came back from my Priest, I acted my own Physician, I sent for a Noggin of Spirits, made punch of it, mixed my butter with it, And Drank it off, in God's name. And whether it was occasioned by I being in the latter end of my fit, or the Drinking of the punch I know not, but thank God, I slept that night very sound, perspired much, and was relieved next morning, And Since, this is a clear and true confession.

Now Sir, I took my pledge, July 19th 1839, And at that time, the No. was 14,449. And my name is John O' * * * *. All this you'll find in Yr. Book. Now, in consequence of age, hard labour, & fatigue and Dejection of Spirits, I'd want Some additional nourishmt. and I trust on this application Yr. revce. will be pleased to allow me Some two or three. Pints Glasses, tumblers, or Dandies, (not Cider) And I'll continue temperate, but not a teetotaller, otherwise if you dont comply with this request, I'll Decently convey the tokens to Cork, but I'll never Drink, without your Permission, while I have them, I Expect an Affirmative answr. to this, by return of Post, I remain with Every Possible mark of respect, And with all the ceremony of complemts. Yr revces. Very Obedt. Humble Servt., a teetotaller yet,

John O' * * * *

The following is a strange epistle, and is given literally as it was written :—

REEVD SIR,—I beg you will Look on a Foolish and Almost insane young Man the only thing I Reqeire from yoor Revde is a an Enterview for 10 Minutes as I dred Suciede and that I shall Get yoor blessing to Protect or if not I Fear I will Full Fill the words of the Scriptuer that is to Say that I Shall Die as I have Lived For the Last 3 Months

I am obed yoors
Veery Humble Patrick * * * *

Here is a joint resignation, most formally worded :—

Wexford, August 10.

REVD. SIR,—As our business requires us to take a little spirits occasionally we have come to the resolution of giving up the pledge—yours most respectfully

Nicholas * * * * and
Pat * * * *

PS Please send an answer by return of Post to Mr. * * * * at Mr * * * * Corn Market
Wexford

An anonymous correspondent thus invites him to cover himself with glory in a new mission :—

Dublin : Nov. 19th.

SIR,—I beg to be excused for sending you the letters of Ronge, which have been lately published in this city. You ought seriously to inquire *in your closet*, where you are not so likely to be led away by the breath of popular applause, whether if you can in your conscience *support* the corruptions denounced by Ronge, or whether you can in silence look on while others practise such delusions on the people. The movement of Ronge has penetrated the whole of Germany—the Papal power is shaken to its centre, and if you look to the first article in the last *Quarterly Review*, you will perceive that France is ready for a similar movement, and that it will shortly break out in an open way, as it has done in Germany.

* * * * * * * *

Take a bold step, follow the noble example of Ronge and disabuse the people's minds of their false notions, you would be followed by so large a party that in one year Ireland would become as beautiful and prosperous as any other part of the empire, instead of being pointed at as the land of blood and murder. If you delay, there is no doubt that in a year or two the work will be done without you; but it may fall into the hands of those who may teach infidelity instead of religion.

I am with great respect
a Sincere Well-wisher to my Country.

And a Scotch philosopher benevolently suggests a mode of settling for ever the question of Irish distress :—

Edinr.

FATHER MATHEW,—I feel quite at a loss to address an Eminent Stranger.

I have been reading a Travelers account of your great work, to soften, the misery to the populace of Ireland. He very naturally questions, can, it, continue? Few mortals are so gifted, for such an undertaking, either in Body, or mind. I have speculated, to find, a plan if possible, to prevent the cause of it, too incident only, to Ireland, of the Early Marriges. If some patriot, or wealthy Gentleman, on, promising, a gift, to those who would bring a *Certificate* of the Man's Age, above 25, and the woman turned of 20 years, (I would suppose furniture to their little dwelling) it would be a worthy use of Riches in the cause of virtue, and humanity—To bring a Family into Life, to suffer as now, is worse than Cattle. A Cow, has its grass cooked to eat a warm Coat, and a Comfortable Bed to lie on.—perhaps,—Dr Sir, as, you have done *more*, you may be able to persuade some kindred Heart, and Head, to try the Experiment The good fashion might spread, as, great events often arise, from small beginings &c.

I avoid being Tedious and hope you will excuse my Letter. I have only ventured to write these few lines, relying on your belief it is a frail chance of Doing good.

By the post mark you will see it is from Scotland, but it is of no value to give my Name. With much Esteem

Decemr 1845 Your wellwisher ——.

no address, I, presume is necessary.

The land agent of a well-known gentleman writes an urgent letter, imploring Father Mathew to use his influence with an overholding tenant, to give up a dwelling-house belonging to the agent, 'without,' as the writer continues, 'putting me to the cost, trouble, and inconvenience of seeking the possession from a court of law.'

One would be inclined to say, from the samples given, that Father Mathew's correspondents occupied no small portion of his time and attention.

From necessity, he was compelled to devote to hard work those hours which, in justice to himself, ought to be more properly devoted to sleep; but he also availed himself of any favourable moment, during the day, to pay off some instalment of his accumulated debt to his correspondents. He was free from interruption during the silent hours of night, whereas during the day he was liable to be interfered with by his domestic tyrant—his servant John. The attachment of this austere servitor, however gratifying to his master's self-love, assumed, very frequently, most inconvenient opportunities for its manifestation. Thus, while Father Mathew was at work at his ink-spattered desk, the floor covered with the results of his precious labours, John would take a fit of troublesome cleanliness; and, after elaborately flapping the more prominent features of Lord Morpeth's bust with a duster, proceed to remove ideal specks and imaginary stains from the sideboard or the table; and after he had satisfactorily performed this important task, he would then direct his best energies to the picture frames, reserving his special solicitude for the work of high art in worsted, for the merits of which he entertained an exalted opinion. Gradually would John invade the neighbourhood of the desk, and even crumple beneath his feet the leaves of manuscript which, after having hastily dashed them off, his master had thrown upon the ground. If he dared do it, John would have submitted the ink bottle to a general cleansing, and given the desk itself a comprehensive wipe of his duster; but his audacity was usually limited to abortive efforts at opening a conversation respecting the habits and customs of the English aristocracy, and the innovations lately adopted in the science of laying the dinner cloth in grand houses. Now Father Mathew was a man of exemplary patience, and could, without murmur, endure as much as most men; but to be thus interrupted, perhaps in the middle of a subject of great moment, and to feel your coat subjected to an elaborate dusting process as you were commencing a new paragraph, or rounding a sentence with grace, was something beyond the limit of mortal endurance. And just as John had reached this point, his master would start from his chair, and, looking down at the startled culprit, who now feared he had been pushing matters too far, would hurl this awful threat at his domestic,—'John, if you continue to go on in this dreadful way, *I declare I must leave the house!*' This tremendous threat never failed in its effect; and John invariably hid himself for a time in the darkest recess of his pantry.

CHAPTER XXII.

Father Mathew's pecuniary Liabilities—His Unhappiness—The Medal Delusion—His Arrest—Items of Expenditure—Vindicatory Statement—How the Money went—Silver Medals—The enduring Memorial—An edifying Balance-sheet—Valuable Testimonies—The Soldier's Gratitude.

THERE was, however, a trouble far less difficult to bear than the pressure of hard work, or the intrusion of a favourite and indulged domestic; that trouble arose from the daily increasing amount of his pecuniary liabilities. At times, the shadow of debt darkened the very sunlight, and haunted him like a spectre in his solitude. There was a period, yet to come, when the tyranny of the ever present idea of his obligations became insupportable, and crushed him to the earth; but, though in his fifty-third year in the year 1854, he still possessed the physical energy and vigour of ordinary men of thirty-five or forty, and the tone and strength of his mind were yet unimpaired. He could, therefore, resist a painful impression, at this period of his life, better than in half a dozen years after, when his constitution had received many severe shocks. Still the slavery of debt could not but have been keenly felt, at any time, or under any circumstances, by a man of his extreme sensibility and high notions of personal honour. There was also an additional bitterness imparted to this sufficiently bitter feeling—this arose from imputations as unjust as they were galling.

At the very moment when his liabilities amounted to a sum of 7,000*l.* it was asserted that he was in the possession of enormous wealth, and that he had enriched the very family whom his mission had almost impoverished. If the writers of these stupid calumnies could have known how they were wounding that sensitive heart—how they were rendering his nights wakeful and his days unhappy, by their monstrous accusations, it is only fair to believe they never would have made them.

At a festive meeting in Cork, held on the evening of St. Stephen's day, the bitterness of his soul found vent in these mournful words:—'Although your excellent chairman has wished me the enjoyment of many happy days, I must say I enjoy very few moments of happiness. *My heart is eaten up by care and solicitude of every kind.*' These words fell upon that joyous assembly, consisting mostly of the young and the light-hearted, with an inexpressibly saddening effect, and a murmur of sympathy evinced the feeling which they had awakened in every breast.

The calumny against him was based upon the wildest assumption. Because Father Mathew had administered the pledge to so many millions of persons, therefore he had sold so many millions of medals, and therefore he had received 50,000*l.* for every million of followers; and further, that if he had given the pledge to only three millions of persons, he had sold three millions of medals, and received 150,000*l.* If he had given the pledge to four millions of persons, of course he had received 200,000*l.*! This was actually put forward in one of the most influential of the Irish newspapers; and the writer even went the length of asserting, that if this number of medals were *not* sold, and this amount of money *not* received, the alleged number of followers was a gross delusion. The whole thing was based upon the utterly groundless supposition, that everyone who took the pledge also purchased a medal; whereas not more than *one in ten*, if so many, of those who did the one also did the other. Even if they had the inclination to purchase the medal, they were too poor to do so.

Father Mathew's chief success was amongst the humblest classes in the community ; and at the very time when this imputation was made, it was admitted, on official authority, that there were two millions and a half of people in Ireland little above the condition of absolute destitution. Few medals were purchased by this class ; and yet, happily to a large extent, they had taken the pledge, and thereby preserved themselves from deeper misery.

Father Mathew's arrest, while publicly administering the pledge in Dublin, rudely dissipated the belief entertained by those who accused him of the possession of fabulous wealth. He was arrested for the balance of an account due to a medal manufacturer; and the bailiff to whom the duty was entrusted knelt down among the crowd, asked his blessing, and then quietly showed him the writ! It may be mentioned, as an instance of Father Mathew's presence of mind, that he did not falter even for an instant, but continued to administer the pledge, as if nothing had happened. This self-possession was fortunate for the bailiff, whom not even he could have saved, had that treachery been made known at the moment. This painful circumstance dissipated calumny and slander into thin air ; but it also aroused the liveliest sympathy throughout the country, and galvanised into activity those who had been talking of a colossal bust, or some such other 'testimonial,' as a fitting type of the nation's gratitude to its great benefactor. People then began to consider that it was far more wise to free Father Mathew from his embarrassments than to carve his effigy in stone or marble, and to enable him to prosecute his work rather than erect some benevolent institution in his name. And the more the question of how to act, and what to do, came to be discussed, the more honouring was the result to the character of one of the most disinterested and generous of men. How his liabilities grew upon him was now a matter of easy explanation. The readers of these pages have already seen sufficient to satisfy their minds upon the subject; but a few additional particulars may not be here out of place.

This fact should be distinctly borne in mind,—namely, that upon one man, and one man alone, rested the responsibility of one of the most remarkable movements, and the support of one of the most extensive organisations, of modern times. Father Mathew was the centre of all, the one on whom the success or failure of the movement, and the stability of the entire structure, depended. Without Father Mathew, the movement would never have been what it was; deprived of his exertions, his labours, his zeal, his self-sacrifice, his munificent liberality, it could not have progressed as it did. We may see a department of state exclusively engaged in undertakings less onerous, and with details less complicated or extended, than were involved in the mission to which Father Mathew voluntarily devoted his energies. What we witness every day done by large and well-endowed associations, with numerous and highly-paid officials, and a thoroughly efficient staff, Father Mathew undertook and accomplished single-handed. He had to provide and pay a sufficient staff; to print and disseminate handbills, tracts, and placards; to aid in the establishing of temperance reading-rooms, and the formation of bands; to prevent local societies from falling into decay, and to supply funds towards their revival; to defray the principal expenses attendant on those demonstrations which were considered necessary as an example or an incentive; to meet the heavy charges for travelling with one or more attendants, and for hotels; to contribute the most generously to the very charities whose claims he came to advocate,—in fine, to satisfy the demands hourly made upon his compassion or his generosity, and which were of necessity multiplied in consequence of the very nature of his mission and the prominence of the position it entailed.

Thus, for instance, he was in debt to the amount of 1,500*l.* before he made a single visit to any part of the country, or before he quitted the city of Cork, the first scene of his mission. As has been described in the appropriate place, poor people came daily to him in great numbers, not merely from the surrounding country or the adjoining counties, but even from remote districts of Ireland, to receive the pledge at his hands; and he would as soon have thought of turning away a penitent unshriven from his confessional as of not relieving the wants of a weary and foot-sore pilgrim, who had walked thirty or fifty miles with an intention that excited his gratitude almost as much as it did his sympathy. The amount of his debt at that time—in the year 1839—does not in any way represent the sums so distributed; for Father Mathew was then in the receipt of a considerable income, the result of his popularity as a clergyman; and this income he dispensed wholly in charity of one form or another.

His printing account, from the commencement of the movement in April 1838, to the summer of 1844, amounted to 3,000*l.* The average charge for this indispensable outlay was from 8*l.* to 10*l.* a week. It is scarcely necessary to defend the good policy of this item of expenditure, which has its like in every movement, association, and organisation, of whatever nature or character. If a remarkable testimony were borne to the value of temperance, either by speech or by letter, it was immediately published by Father Mathew. In the evidence which he gave for Charles Gavan Duffy, in the early part of 1849, he mentioned that he had struck off 30,000 copies of a speech which Mr. Duffy had made in Newry in the year 1841; a fact which shows the importance attached by Father Mathew to whatever tended to promote the cause of temperance.

It is not necessary to go through the other items of expenditure, to prove how inevitably they arose out of the circumstances in which he was placed. The idea of the sale of medals did not originate with Father Mathew. The practice was introduced into Ireland by a temperance lecturer from

England—John Hockins, known popularly as 'the Birmingham Blacksmith.' This person brought a quantity of medals with him from Birmingham, and profitably disposed of them to the Irish teetotallers. His example was followed, on his own account, by James McKenna, the first secretary to the society, who was subsequently taken into Father Mathew's service in the same capacity.

At a meeting held in Westminster, in August 1843, Father Mathew referred to the origin of his sale of medals :—

It has again been asked, what becomes of the money paid for medals? I have answered such questions over and over again, and am sorry that I feel it to be an act of justice to myself to repeat it. For a long while after I commenced administering the pledge of total abstinence, I did not sell medals at all, but presented them gratuitously to every one who took the pledge. At length my secretary informed me that I was 5,000*l.* in debt, and most earnestly requested permission to sell the medals. After a little consideration I acceded to that request; but I can assure the meeting, that since I have been in this country, the amount I have received for medals has not half paid the expenses attendant on my mission. I have never received money from any one for my own benefit, and never will. Only this day a lady at Hammersmith begged of me to accept a considerable sum towards my expenses, but I have declined its acceptance, and sent it back. It is painful to me thus to be obliged to vindicate myself, and I hope I shall not again be called upon to do so.

The absurd notion that every person who took the pledge also purchased a medal is thus disposed of in Father Mathew's words, spoken in Dublin in June 1842, and frequently repeated in subsequent years :—

I deny, in the strongest terms, that I am, as it is alleged by certain parties, making money of cards and medals, and I declare that I am a poorer man this day than the first day I gave the pledge, for *out of several thousands who take the pledge, not as many hundreds take a card or medal*, so that the allegation is totally false. This is a fact well known in Cork and elsewhere; for, if I have any money, I give it to feed the hungry, and clothe the naked.

Not only was it the fact that not more than one in every

ten—if so many—purchased a card and medal, but that Father Mathew distributed the medals with a profusion which his secretaries regarded as reckless. Thus, up to the time when his difficulties became publicly known, he had given upwards of 100,000 medals to the children of the schools throughout the country. From policemen, soldiers, and emigrants, he never received payment for them; and no poor person ever asked for a medal in vain. Nay, he has been frequently known to arrest the hand even of a comfortable farmer, when he was about to pay the person who had the sale of the medals, and say—'No, my dear, you shall not pay—it is not your money I want, it is yourself. Take the medals for yourself, and your wife and daughter; all I ask you is to be faithful to the cause.'

The accusation of his making money of this traffic was a source of constant bitterness to a man of his proud and sensitive nature. He writhed under it as under a lash. To be accused of interested and selfish motives in the promotion of a cause which, while it benefited many, injured not a few, was torture to his mind; and the very disregard of money which he constantly exhibited might, in many instances, have been influenced by the sting of the taunts levelled against him either in ignorance or in malice.

These accusations were likewise a source of pain to his friends, by whom his character was thoroughly understood, and to whom his fair fame was as dear as their own.

An important meeting was held in Cork, in November 1844, with the view to organise some effective means of relieving Father Mathew from the pressure of his embarrassments, and at that meeting the writer of this biography, who from his boyhood had enjoyed the advantage of the good man's friendship, was personally authorised by him to make a statement of the causes of his embarrassments, and in vindication of the charge of having realised a fortune by the sale of medals. A passage from that statement, made with the sanction of Father Mathew, and upon information principally derived from the same source, may tend to throw further light on this medal delusion :—

Permit me to tell you a few more facts about medals, and prove to you that, even when there was sale, there was no corresponding return, and therefore no profit. When the desire to obtain medals was most general, Father Mathew received orders from various parts of the country for thousands and thousands of medals; which medals were sent, and sold or distributed, but for which medals Father Mathew never received a single shilling. This I have from the lips of Father Mathew. I impute nothing to the secretaries or patrons of the societies from whom no return was given; it may have been from neglect, apathy, or forgetfulness, that all the medals ordered were not sold, or that the persons who received them were not themselves paid for them; but it is certain, that hundreds of thousands of medals have not been accounted for. I give you one fact, which may in some measure account for this non-return. A few days ago, Father Mathew received back two boxes, containing 1,400 of the ordinary medals, and 20 of the silver. They had been ordered, but forgotten; and it was not until the present excitement had awakened the recollection of the party who had ordered them, that they were thought of. How many such 1,400 medals, how many such 20 silver medals, may we not suppose are now lying forgotten, without recompense or benefit to Father Mathew? It is also a notorious fact, that in many parts of the country Father Mathew could not sell his medals, even to the smallest amount, and for this sufficient reason—that the patrons of societies in those districts had themselves ordered medals, exactly similar to those issued by Father Mathew, from the manufacturer in Birmingham, and had, of course, disposed of them for the advantage of their peculiar society. . . . .

A few evenings since, I, with other gentlemen whom I now see around me, attended a meeting in a small room in Market Street. I there alluded to the fact that Father Mathew had presented silver medals, to a large amount, to persons who belonged to his society, and I said that the large medal which I exhibited had cost the sum of fourteen shillings. Its real value is not more than six shillings; but at first the sum charged by the manufacturers was fourteen shillings. What will you think when I tell you that in that small room, not more than fifteen or sixteen feet square, and where there were not above thirty or forty persons assembled, there were as many as twenty persons present who had received similar medals of silver from Father Mathew?

Extracts might be multiplied to disprove the charge of money making, and to exhibit the manner in which whatever profit was received was afterwards expended. A very few will suffice as an illustration. In the 'Belfast Vindicator' of February 1842 we find this paragraph :—

An error prevails respecting the amount of money received for medals. Of the thousands enrolled many had been previously supplied with medals, and were satisfied to receive them from the hands of Father Mathew. *To all who intimated, in the most distant manner, their inability to purchase* (and the numbers were *very considerable*), *he instantly gave gratis the requisite quantity.* He not only gave 40*l.* to the Rev. D. Murphy, P.P., Moira, and 15*l.* to Mr. Duffy, for the teetotal library, *but appeared to many inconsiderate in the extent of charity to mendicants*, who uniformly resort to such scenes —some true objects of relief, some practised impostors.

In the same paper it was stated that a number of children of the National Schools took the pledge, and that Father Mathew gave 100 medals to the teachers for them.

The same month, a correspondent of the 'Limerick Chronicle,' writing from Kilrush, adds this postscript to his letter :— 'Although Father Mathew gave an immense sum before, he now gave 5*l.* for the poor of the town, and 2*l.* to compliment the little band.'

Another paper mentions, in the same year, a munificent contribution of 20*l.* to the Catholic church at Miltown Malbay, and of various sums of money distributed in the surrounding parishes.

Father Mathew's outlay for silver medals was something considerable, and without any return worth noticing. As a rule, these medals were presented, not purchased. In his memorable visit to Maynooth, in 1840, he distributed medals of this material to the value of 200*l.*; and at the date of the appeal made for him in 1844 he had presented to his followers in the United Kingdom silver medals for which he had paid the sum of 1,500*l.* The amount paid by him for this class of medals up to the year 1851 was more than double that sum.

The reader, who remembers the great meeting held in the Theatre in Dublin in January 1843, may be curious to know what became of the fund raised on that occasion. Mr. Purcell, in a letter published on October 1844, makes this extraordinary statement :—'Not one twentieth of the grand folks who signed the requisition *paid* a farthing.' This is not over creditable to the 'grand folks,' but it may be fairly assumed that many of them atoned for their forgetfulness by contributing to the fund raised subsequently with a more practical object. But as for the 'public and enduring testimonial' itself, it eventuated in something very much approaching to a job. If public opinion had not coerced even a tardy winding up of this grand result of a grand demonstration, which had been sanctioned and assisted by the highest aristocracy in the land, the balance in hand would have been small indeed. As it was, the difference between expenditure and balance was rather fractional in its amount, as the following edifying and instructive balance-sheet will fully display :—

		£	s.	d.
	Sum Collected	2,118	8	0
	EXPENDITURE.			
1844. Dec. 5.—*By*	*Postage* . . .	93	8	0
	Advertisements . .	397	1	2
	Printing . . .	56	13	0
	Clerks . . .	114	6	0
	Rent . . .	104	12	0
	Hire of Furniture . .	15	15	0
	Servant's Wages . .	6	2	0
	Secretary . . .	125	2	0
	Coals and Candles . .	2	1	5
	Sundry small Articles .	0	8	0
	Use of Theatre . .	50	0	0
	Ironmongery . .	1	16	5
	Stationery . . .	1	4	10
		968	8	0
	Balance . .	1,150	0	0
		£2,118	0	0

That a man of sanguine temperament should have expected much from a movement commenced under such auspices, and with such parade, was only natural. Father Mathew imagined that the sum to be then raised would have been so great as, after erecting a statue or other memorial, to have left a large balance, which he could apply to the further promotion as well as permanence of the cause. But the balance-sheet now given will suggest how grievous must have been his disappointment at the reality, which was indeed a most lame and impotent conclusion to so grand a beginning.

The meeting in Cork was held on the 11th of November 1844, and in a few days after the statements there made, Father Mathew was gratified at receiving, both in the public press and through private communications, expressions of sympathy and respect, together with the liberal offers of assistance.

'Punch' had the following characteristic bit in its racy pages :—

> Now, Mathew the martyr brought his fortune into the market to buy up vice; to bribe wretchedness into comfort; to purchase, with ready money, crime and passion, that he might destroy them. He has laid out all his means, that he might make temperance alluring to an impulsive whisky-loving people; he counts his tens of thousands of proselytes, and then, taking his purse, he counts nothing. He has triumphed, but he is a beggar. Taught by his temperance lessons, the peasant and artificer—aye, thousands of them—have made their homes more worthy of human creatures, and the teacher himself is shown the way to a gaol. Mathew is arrested for the price of the medals with which he decorated his army of converts—we know few orders, home or foreign, more honourable, if sincerely worn—and, unless Ireland arise as one man, the reward of the great preacher is the county prison.

From the numerous letters addressed to Father Mathew at this time—November 1844—two or three may be selected. They are valuable as testimonies, but in a different way The first is from Dr. Lyon Playfair :—

Royal Institution, Manchester: Nov. 16, 1844.

VERY REV. SIR,—I beg to enclose a small sum towards the subscription for defraying the expenses which you have incurred in promotion of the Temperance Movement. I am not a member of a Temperance Association; but I have had so many opportunities, as one of her Majesty's Health of Town Commissioners, of seeing the great moral, as well as sanitary effects which appear in certain districts after your visits, that I cannot refrain from offering my mite, as an indication of my respect for your character, hoping at the same time that you will not measure my esteem for you by the small value of the gift.

I have the honour to be, Very Rev. Sir, your very faithful servant,

LYON PLAYFAIR.

The second is from a priest who is long since numbered with the dead, but who was one of the most distinguished ornaments of the Catholic Church of Ireland. As handsome in person as he was dignified in manner, Father Justin M'Namara combined in a singular manner talents of the highest order with strong good sense and practical wisdom. He was as remarkable for his eloquence as a preacher as for the indomitable energy with which he discharged the duties of his ministry. His testimony is the more valuable, as for the greater part of his life he had performed the duties of a working curate in the parish of SS. Peter and Paul, in the city of Cork, and had been brought into daily contact with his friend Father Mathew. Father Justin had been for some years parish priest of Kinsale, and one of the vicars of the diocese of Cork. The letter bears date November 28:—

I always considered it cruel and unjust that you, dear Sir, should have been burthened with the enormous expense necessarily attendant on an undertaking of such vast extent and magnitude, for its machinery should have been worked out from the beginning by benevolent funds, not by your individual resources. I long anticipated that you could not continue to sustain such an immense, unequal pressure, and I therefore regard our present interference in your affairs as an honest repayment of a debt you incurred on the part of the public, obviously for the beneficial interest of all, and also, I may say, as the recognised agent of every man that loves his country, and feels a concern for the moral and social improvement of her people.

One happy result from the unavoidable exposure of your circumstances is the decisive evidence it affords to all, even to your captious enemies, that you never trafficked in temperance, or engaged in such a glorious cause for any selfish, lucrative, or unworthy motive. I trust you will be placed, by the gratitude of the empire, in an independent position, not for any advantage to yourself, but that being freed from pecuniary difficulties you may be enabled in future to consecrate all your undivided energies to the great apostleship to which you have been so providentially deputed. Kinsale is a locality that, equally with a thousand others, owes you many obligations, which its parish priest and people will hold in lasting and grateful remembrance.

I remain, dear Sir, yours very sincerely and respectfully,

JUSTIN F. M'NAMARA.

To the Very Rev. Theobald Mathew

The third letter is from a poor soldier, whose heart is afflicted at the picture which he conjures up—of his benefactor lying in a prison, the companion of the vilest criminals. Father Mathew cherished the honest fellow's letter, which is worth preserving :—

Parkhurst Barracks, November 8th, 1844 A.D.

REVD AND DEAR SIR,—your Reverence will Excuse Me for thus addressing your Reverence but Sir it is one that has Partook of your Bounty in Glasgow in 1842.

and Dear Sir—it was with Pain That I saw in the Publick Prints that your Reverence was arested for giving all you had in the World for our Benefit, and to Say we that Shared of your Goodness would not do sumthing for you When in Bondage. Yes, Revd. Father, I will not, for one, Stand alone and See you Draged to Preson for doing all of us Poor Creatures—all the good in the World—yes, Dear Sir, I am Proud to acknowledge you as the Second Moses in these our days— — —

Wee, Sir, Would be Liken unto the Wicked People of Pharo who was all swallowed up in the Red Sea. Wee would be all Drowned in the Gulph of intemprence, only you was chosen to be a Moses in our behalf, and Worthy did you do your Duty boath for God and Man, and it would be ill My Part not to Come forward at the Present Time when you are in Dangers and in the Hands of the Enemy but you Shall not be Suffred to be Cast into Preson Like a Common Fellon, no you Shall not be in the same Den with Thefes and Robers—Dear

Sir, I am Most Happy to be one to Put My Mite into the Box—and I Beg you will Except this small Token of my Reguard towards one has done Me Good—to Harm they self. no Dear Father I will never suffer such a Stain on My Name.

I am Dear Father on the Eve of Embarkcation for India, and Perhaps I would not have the opportunity of Tesfying My Respects to your Good Services to Me.

I Shall Ever Remember you as Longe as theirs Life in My Body—May I beg of your Reverence to Enclose Me your Blessing before I out to India. I go in a fuw days, so I beg Most Respectfully you will send me your Blessing.

I am with Great Respect
Your Reverence Humble and Obt Servant
James Murray
Corporal Depot
71st Regt
Isle of Wight.

A most gratifying and important testimony was borne to Father Mathew, by Lord John, now Earl, Russell, at a meeting held in Exeter Hall on the 19th December in the same year. This speech was in the highest degree creditable to the noble lord, who spoke as follows :—

To make a great impression upon a whole nation—to bring them at once from a habit in which they were too apt to indulge, to the practice of those virtues by whieh their domestic happiness may be increased, and their moral and religious conduct improved, must, I say, have called for no ordinary diligence; no common exertions would have sufficed for such an object. But we all know the extraordinary eloquence, the untiring energy, the disinterested forgetfulness of all selfish objects, which did enable Mr. Mathew to accomplish this moral miracle, and, by his exertions, to effect a change in Ireland which was surprising to the whole civilised world. But, gentlemen, although Mr. Mathew was endowed with this zeal and energy, and although he felt it as a great reward to be able to effect such a change in the conduct of his countrymen, unhappily he did not accompany his course with that prudence which a person whose soul and heart were less engaged in the cause might have been able to follow. Hence his difficulties; and let me assure you, that from all the inquiries which I have made, the stories that have been circulated as to any wealth amassed by Mr. Mathew, or any one belonging to him, of immense sums being poured into his hands, are entirely without foundation.

In numbers of cases—when I say numbers, I believe that in hundreds and thousands of instances—the medals obtained by persons who took the pledge were given gratuitously by Mr. Mathew to those who received it. In many other instances nothing was received whatever, and no medal was carried by those who took the pledge. Mr. Mathew also became involved in expense by the journeys which he made in promoting the cause which he had so much at heart, and by the career in which he engaged with a zeal and enthusiasm with which worldly prudence was not compatible. What, then, should be the conduct of that country to which he belongs, and of this country which is closely, and, I trust, perpetually united with it? What should be our conduct, but that, if we have not shared in this merit—if we have not undergone the fatigues which he has endured—if we have not achieved that great moral victory which Father Mathew has obtained, we should at least have the satisfaction of contributing something to his success by relieving him from some of his present difficulties, and enabling him to start afresh in his most glorious career. The fact is, a man oppressed by pecuniary difficulties and embarrassments cannot persevere in such a career with that vigour and that disregard of worldly considerations which he would be able to evince if relieved from his incumbrances, first by the generosity of the people of Ireland, and afterwards by his countrymen in England. I say, therefore, let us embrace this opportunity of being sharers in the glory of Father Mathew, by contributing in this country, and in the sister country, to promote the cause of temperance; and let us have the satisfaction of thinking that we have done something that will be grateful in the eyes both of God and of man.

At the special request of the Cork Committee, the authorised statement made by the writer of these pages, at the meeting of the 11th of November, was published for circulation in a pamphlet form: and as the preface, which was appended to it, expressed what the friends of Father Mathew felt as to the disposal of the funds which were certain to be raised in response to the appeal originating in the Cork meeting, it may not be out of place to quote the following extract therefrom :—

The Cork Committee are in possesssion of Mr. Mathew's entire confidence, and are actuated only by two grand motives—a wish to relieve him from his present difficulties, and an earnest desire to advance and render permanent the temperance reform.

To effect the first object, in the best manner, they wish that all persons who are anxious to subscribe towards the present fund, SHOULD FORWARD THEIR SUBSCRIPTIONS DIRECT TO CORK, either to their Treasurers—the Mayor, and Alderman Thomas Lyons; or, if persons should prefer it, to Father Mathew himself. Every sum received by either party, shall be acknowledged in the public prints; and, if received by one or other of the Treasurers, immediately handed over to Father Mathew, who, the Committee rightly think, is the *only* one who should have the disposal of the funds for an object so peculiar and so delicate.

Then, as to the surplus—the large surplus—which they confidently hope may remain after discharging all the pecuniary obligations of Father Mathew, they are also of opinion that, as no man is so well acquainted with the working of the temperance movement as its successful leader, *he alone* should be entrusted with the funds placed at his disposal by the gratitude and wisdom of the Nation.

The Committee are well aware that no movement, and more particularly a vast one, can be carried on without a liberal command of money upon the part of him who leads or directs it; and while they are anxious to place the pecuniary means of carrying on the temperance reformation in the hands of its illustrious Apostle, they would jealously guard him from even the semblance of control—which the entrusting of the funds to other hands, in trusteeship or otherwise, would undoubtedly be. They have unlimited confidence in the wisdom and prudence of Father Mathew, being satisfied that whatever funds are placed at his disposal by the nation, will be expended for the benefit of the nation. They, above all things, repudiate the notion of any body of men attempting to fetter the movements, or control the disbursements, of one who must be free to be powerful, and liberal to be useful.

Father Mathew, though not caring for the possession of money on his own account, appreciated its value as a means of prosecuting his great work; and he was naturally disappointed at not having been left by Lady Elizabeth the large legacy which, on several occasions, she had expressed her intention of bequeathing to him. Between Lady Elizabeth and the priest the most affectionate relations subsisted through life. The love which she lavished on her little *protégé*, the engaging child, she never withdrew from the man. She was proud of his fame, and of the veneration in which he was held by all classes of his countrymen ; and so far as she could promote the cause by personal encouragement, and the influence of her position, she cheerfully did, as much, indeed, to afford pleasure to her 'good Toby,' as to assist a great and useful work. Lady Elizabeth was not eminent as a letter writer, though she continued to keep up a rather extensive correspondence with her friends. Several of her letters, yellow with age, lie before me. Some are addressed to Father Mathew himself, and others, though written to third persons, are full of allusions to him. The few extracts given are only valuable as indications of the interest which the early protectress of 'little Toby,' took in the great work of the moral reformer of the age, and of the affection which nearly half a century had not power to weaken or alter. Thus her ladyship writes to a friend :—

The dear Viscount* leaves me to-morrow. Mr. E——— stays some time longer. I gave a great teetotal party on St. Stephen's day, to three hundred teetotallers. They danced until seven in the morning, and I gave them plenty of beef, cakes, apples, tea, coffee, lemonade, &c. &c.

I had yesterday, *three priests* to dine with me—Dr. ———, Mr. ———, and Father Mathew.

I went to Tipperary to hear Father Mathew preach. He preached most beautifully, and he gave the pledge to 14,000 persons.

Her ladyship, who was a kind-hearted woman, and indulgent to her domestics, adds—'I gave the upper servants a Ball, and they danced till morning. C——— danced *Jim Crow.*'

Alluding to a subsequent visit from Father Mathew, Lady Elizabeth announces that 'Toby Mathew is to dine with me on that day.'

While in Dublin, she writes, 'The good Father Toby is to dine with me this week.' And subsequently, 'Toby Mathew has been here, and has promised to get C——— to be a teacher in a school in Dublin.'

* Viscount de Chabot, the present possessor of the Llandaff property.

Her ladyship could evidently do a little speech-making on her own account, for she tells her friend, 'I am going on St. Patrick's day to give a great tea party to the teetotallers, and I am going to give them a fine speech. I expect the great man (Father Mathew) here in a few days.'

The mode of designating her distinguished namesake was, as may be seen, rather varied. Thus, she says, 'Lord Glengall gave a great party in compliment to Father Toby, who dined at the castle;' and she winds up another letter with, 'we expect our good Toby in a few days here.'

There is a letter addressed to him, commencing with 'My good friend Toby,' and terminating with, 'I remain, my good Toby.' Another commences and ends with 'My dearest friend.'

Lady Elizabeth had always given Father Mathew to understand that she would provide for him in her will; and this assurance she repeated within a day of her death, which was quite unexpected. She thought she had time enough to carry her intention into effect, but it was fated to be otherwise. The very day before her sudden death, which occurred in Dublin, she was accompanied by her beloved friend to have her likeness taken, and it was he who selected the bonnet in which she was to sit for her picture. 'You will see, Toby,' said she to him that day, 'that I have not forgotten you, and that I have kept my word.' But the friends never saw each other again in this world. To each of Father Mathew's sisters—Mrs Dunbar and Mrs. Hackett—to whom she was much devoted, she left the sum of 1,200*l.*; but the as many thousands which she had allowed their brother to believe was to be his share, never came to him or his family. The disappointment which he naturally felt was in no way on his own account. He had no reason to suspect that the oft-repeated promise was not to be realised; and when incurring debts, solely with a view to promote the temperance cause, he, not unfairly, had in his mind the certainty of receiving a large legacy, at one time or other. Referring to this disappointment, in many years after, he said, 'If I had to begin life over again, and to go through what I have done, I never would depend on the promise or expectation of a legacy.'

Father Mathew's embarrassments were now for the moment wiped out; but, as the reader will see, new and more pressing claims were created, and in a great measure by a calamity, in the presence of which prudence and calculation would have been, at least in his eyes, a crime against humanity. We must not, however, anticipate. The sad story of the Irish Famine is yet to be touched upon, not told, in these pages. The pen of the historian is required to picture for posterity the awful horrors of that period, which indeed tried the souls of men, but out of which the fame of Theobald Mathew came purer and brighter, glowing, as it were, with a holier lustre.

CHAPTER XXIII.

The Parish Priest of Blarney—The Water-party at Blarney—Father Mat's ingenious Device—The Antiquaries—The Ogham Valentine—The enchanted Stream—Death busy with the Antiquaries—Killarney—Fidelity of the Boatmen.

THE two most remarkable meetings attended by Father Mathew during the year 1844, were held in the parish of Blarney, and amidst the matchless beauty of Killarney. To mention Blarney, and not to refer to its famous parish priest, the Rev. Mathew Horgon, or 'Father Mat,' as he delighted to be styled, would be a treason to friendship; for the writer knew and loved the simple-minded priest, and stood by his grave in the humble parish chapel while his coffin was covered with the sacred mould.

Father Mat, whose name was known to every Irish scholar of the three kingdoms, was as homely in his appearance as he was simple and kindly in his manner. Innocent as a child in the ways and wiles of the world, he was also as credulous in his guileless vanity. He regarded himself as the highest authority on all questions appertaining to the science of agriculture; and, without disparagement of any other man, he held himself to be possessed of a more thorough and comprehensive knowledge of the principles of architecture, sacred as well as secular, ancient as well as modern, than any architect of any age or country. He was as conversant with the Cyclopean as with the Phœnician style—with the fire-pillars of the Persian, as with the cavern temples of the Egyptians.

From various styles, he derived a new style of his own, which might be termed Horgonian. Father Mat was not content with being a theorist; he was a practical propagandist as well. As ready to superintend the erection of a cathedral as the building of a school-house, he was ever on the look out for the opportunity of undertaking one of those great works, through which the name and fame of the erudite and accomplished Pastor of Blarney were to be transmitted to future ages. I cannot pretend to say how many are the now existing proofs of the architectural genius of Father Mat; but there is, still extant,* a church which he was permitted to adorn externally, by the addition of an excrescence, partly of the nature of a tower, and partly of the nature of a spire, which has scarcely its equal in the world for elaborate incongruity and perplexing novelty. It is one of those marvellous works which bewilder the mind. Of this sublime effort of his inventive genius Father Mat would speak with intense enthusiasm; but it was on another work—his Round Tower—that he proudly rested his claim to the imperishable gratitude of posterity. This was his darling work, the very apple of his eye. The enraptured tourist may behold it as the train passes the village of Blarney. This rival of the fire-pillars of the Persians was partly erected with his own hands; for Father Mat would lay aside the eloquent pen, with which he had encountered Vallencey, Petrie, or O'Brien, in refutation or in defence of some hated or cherished theory, respecting the origin and use of the Round Towers of Ireland, in order to don the apron and assume the trowel of a mason. As this hideous structure rose, course above course, so did Father Mat's exultation swell in proportion. This monster of stone and mortar was his child—the offspring alike of his reverence and his enthusiasm—which was to refute false theories, convince the

* Happily, the entire structure is doomed. Ere long, a noble church will be erected its on site.

sceptic, and confound the scoffer. This 'celestial index' was to endure for ages, as the most splendid evidence of the antiquarian faith and erudition of the priest of Blarney. It has been irreverently, but not inaptly, described, no doubt by people without faith, as 'an architectural churn;' and really, if the great people with whom Gulliver was made acquainted in his travels, could have seen it, they might possibly have appropriated it to the humble use which the name implies. The shallowest impostor could wind Father Mat round his little finger, were he to speak of the Horgonian Spire of Queenstown, or the Round Tower of Blarney, with becoming admiration.

Father Mat was the soul and essence of hospitality. To behold the 'little boys and girls'—meaning thereby full-grown men and women—enjoying themselves, either at dinner or dance, was to him an indescribable pleasure. In his esteem, money was but dross. 'What good is it for money?' said Father Mat. What good, indeed, but in giving it away to those who want it, and spending it in entertainments to one's friends. When his exchequer was at the lowest ebb, then his state of mind was most serene; but when a 'fat wedding,' or a good christening suddenly swelled his coffers, Father Mat began at once to suffer from a state of extreme excitement. The pound notes burned his pocket; they lay on his breast at night like a nightmare; in the day they assumed all manner of fantastic shapes, and danced before him as he walked abroad; they robbed his hand of his cunning, as he assisted his masons on the immortal 'index;' and they spluttered his pen, and confused his ideas, as he toiled at one of those tomes, which he truly believed were to find an honoured place in the public libraries of all civilised countries. The money was a disturbing demon; and the way in which it could be exorcised most effectually, and its evil influence got rid of, was by its speedy transmutation into rounds of beef, legs of mutton, plump turkeys, loaves of sugar, and jars of the best Cork whisky. When that process had been gone through, the fever left Father Mat, and he was at peace with all mankind. Summonses were then sent out to town and country, to gentle and to simple. The barn—his brother's barn—was converted into a spacious banqueting-hall; and the tables, which were borrowed or knocked together for the occasion, were arranged in mathematical symmetry, under Father Mat's superintendence.

Resolving to do special honour to his dear friend the Apostle of Temperance, the Parish Priest of Blarney invited him to administer the pledge to his people, and to a grand banquet, with which the proceedings were to be fittingly concluded. The dinner was to be on strictly temperance principles. Not the faintest odour of Wise or Murphy, Hewitt or Daly,* was to offend his guest. Water, and nothing but water, was to be the order of the day; and, as will be seen, care was taken that there should be no lack of that pure and wholesome element. Now Father Mat's own ideas on teetotalism, personal and in the abstract, may be gathered from the speech which he delivered at the meeting, and which was marked by his characteristic quaintness of style:

I always patronise temperance wherever I am; and it is no matter at all whether poor old Father Mat is a Teetotaller or not, but he is a sincere friend to the cause. Oh, I am never so happy as when I have a score of the fellows about me, they are so religious, and so loyal. There are a thousand blessings in this temperance. There is one thing I cannot help being proud of, and that is, that no matter what character strangers may have given our country, still no one ever asserted that the females of Ireland were ever guilty of excess. How could it be!—for if they were guilty of excess, how could they be such good mothers, such good wives, and such good daughters? Let all girls be teetotallers, and then the men will be so happy (laughter). I am delighted that you all laugh at my speech, for I am then certain that you like it greatly; for wherever the people

* Eminent Cork distillers.

look like so many philosophers when a body is talking, you may be sure that he is making but a poor hand of it. I also recommend my people to stick to the honest, decent industry, and always to wear the work of their own hands.

The welcome hour of dinner arrived, when the proud host conducted the great man to the banquet hall, whose rude walls were shrouded beneath a verdant drapery of laurel, to which the demesnes of the neighbouring gentry had contributed. A goodly company followed in the wake. Town and country had about equally supplied the guests; and sects and parties were fully represented, as well as harmoniously blended, at the hospitable board. The majority present patronised teetotalism somewhat in the fashion of their host, and were rather dismayed at the formidable array of huge water-jugs with which the tables were adorned. Father Mathew was in his glory. It was the kind of public entertainment he had so longed to see—abundant, substantial, and no description of strong drink whatever.

The first chill of disappointment got over, the guests did full justice to the good things so lavishly provided. During the repast, the ears of the fastidious citizens were regaled with the most vigorous efforts of a local band, whose merits, at that period of their existence, were entirely of intention. The host was naturally proud of his accomplished parishioners; and the Temperance Leader, who, as we already know, had 'no ear,' was quite enchanted with this performance; but the greater number of the strangers would have preferred that the musicians were ten miles off. In the mean time, the great jugs were in constant requisition, and soon the cry of 'more water' was heard on every side, to Father Mathew's inexpressible satisfaction. Every precaution had been taken by the considerate host to supply this want; for, along the side of the wall, might be seen a row of churns, tubs, and crocks, which, before dinner, were full to the brim. Those who never in their lives drank more than one glass of water in the four and twenty hours, now consumed several—'out of the mere habit of drinking something,' as they afterwards apologetically explained, when talking of this innocent debauch. Of course there was abundant speech-making, in which strong drink was vehemently denounced, and nature's wine, which had been so profusely supplied from the well, was lauded with corresponding enthusiasm. In sheer desperation, the non-teetotallers called lustily for additional jugs of the pure element, which Tim, and Biddy, and Norry, supplied from the now failing churns. Some of the speeches were delivered under circumstances of extreme difficulty; for the cocks crowed, and the ducks quacked, and the geese gobbled, and the cows lowed—and one calf, gifted with a fearful contralto, stationed itself on the grassy roof of a neighbouring shed, and indulged in a series of performances which were terribly embarrassing to the orator, utterly destructive to flights of fancy, and absolute death to every attempt at poetry or pathos. A mournful and disconsolate animal was that calf, and most persistent in its lamentations. When the guests rose from the tables, the water vessels had been drained to the bottom; it being computed that no fewer than *nine churns* of the refreshing beverage had been consumed by a company, the majority of whom best liked the fluid when it was used as a mild dilutent of a stronger liquid.

The temperance party was at an end. But, having done all possible honour to his illustrious guest, the hospitable host was determined to indemnify his more select friends for their long abstinence and compulsory libations. It was rather too delicate a matter for him to say roundly—'Come, boys, let us have a little drop of good whisky punch,' so soon after the departure of the Temperance Leader; therefore, as a little tact was necessary in introducing the subject, Father Mat had recourse to an ingenious expedient, which saved him from the grave inconsistency of *asking* any one to take punch, and thereby desecrating the close of a day which had been specially dedicated by himself to the honour of the great Apostle, and the promotion of the sacred cause. Turning suddenly to his dearest friend, the learned and accomplished Windele, the chosen companion of many an antiquarian ramble, and the one who treated his theories on the Round Towers with the greatest tenderness, Father Mat enquired —'John, what are you looking at me so hard for?' 'Looking at you, Father Mat!—I assure you I am not looking at you at all,' replied his friend. 'I know you are, John,' rejoined Father Mat. 'I assure you I am not, Father Mat.' 'I tell you, John, I know better; and, more than that, I know what your look means, too,' persisted Father Mat. 'Well, Father Mat, I can't help you, if you don't believe me; but'—'Oh don't tell me, man; sure I know what's in your mind as well as you do yourself.' 'Then if that be so, what did that look of mine mean?—as you *will* have it that I was looking at you.' 'I tell you what it meant. It meant to say—"Father Mat, there is a little key in your left-hand breeches pocket, and that key opens the door of the side-board, and there is a jar of the finest Cork whisky in that side-board; and if you would only tell the little girl, she'd get the glasses and the kettle, and we could have a decent tumbler of punch, after all that cold water, and their long speeches in praise of it."' 'Oh! I see,' said the now fully convinced friend—'that is what I must have meant; and as so ardent a promoter of temperance as you are, would never think of *offering us* a glass of punch, why Father Mat, we must rob you of that key, and get the materials for ourselves.' Father Mat submitted to the larceny of the key with the cheerful composure of a philosopher.

Surrounding the erudite Parish Priest of Blarney, was a group of zealous antiquaries, who devoted many a leisure hour to pleasant excursions—to the exploration and inspection of ruined abbeys, Danish Forts, Round Towers, cairns, Ogham inscriptions, and matters of similar interest. Their more serious labours were diversified by social intercourse of the most agreeable kind, in which were drawn forth the convivial talents and harmless peculiarities of the learned brotherhood.

Amongst them was Windele, the author of more than one work of merit, and one of the safest authorities on all subjects connected with the laws, customs, literature and history of ancient Ireland.

Then there was Kelleher, the Librarian of the Cork Library, whose chief interest in antiquities lay in the amusement which the enthusiasm of his friends afforded him, and the opportunities for ridicule, and fun, and practical joke, of which their discoveries and speculations were the constant occasion. The 'fort,' which the other members of this society approached with interest, and penetrated with awe, was, according to him, an abandoned fox hole; those mysterious writings on slabs or blocks of stone, through which Father Mat or Windele, or other illustrious pundits, read the epitaph of a hero or a bard, or the record of some striking event in the annals of a royal race, were, with the irreverent Librarian, nothing more wonderful than milk-scores; and those upright stones of great size, which were pronounced to have been 'Druidical altars' by the most famous Celtic scholars of the day, were, in the esteem of the unbelieving Kelleher, conveniences considerately erected for the gratification of cattle, to enable them to enjoy the luxury of a good scratch.

But there was one member of the body, whose good nature, gaiety, and childlike simplicity, rendered him the delight of his learned brethren. This was Abraham Abel, a Quaker of literary tastes and antiquarian tendencies. Abraham was far advanced in years, but as lively and agile as a boy. His neat dapper little figure, and his vivacious temperament, gave one the idea of a mercurial gentleman of thirty ; but Abraham had approached his sixtieth year. In the matchless simplicity and the marvellous credulity of this guileless human being, his waggish associates possessed a never-failing source of enjoyment. The wonderful discoveries to which Abraham stood godfather, would, if proved authentic, have upset the theories and speculations of all the great writers on Irish antiquities ; but such discoveries were invariably the result of some well laid plan of his friends, to whom his exultation at these fortunate elucidations of long existing causes of perplexity, was a delicious treat, of which they never tired. Abraham Abel once received a Valentine written in Ogham (oum) characters ; at which his wonder was very great. He immediately brought the prize to his friend the Librarian, for the benefit of his translation of characters which, to the object of the epistle, were a profound mystery. 'My dear William,' said Abraham, in a whistling voice, and wagging his little chin, on which grew a small pointed beard, 'I never received a Valentine in all my life before. And is it not most strange that the first should be written in Ogham!' The document was gravely investigated by the Librarian, while his little friend stood by, in a fever of expectation. 'You are a happy man, Abel,' began the learned decipherer ; and thereupon he favoured him with a free translation of the Valentine, which disclosed a burning, long-concealed, and unrequited passion, expressed in language of so intense a character as to suffuse the face of the venerable bachelor with blushes, and even make him question his identity. 'Dear me, dear me! Poor creature, poor creature!' was the sole commentary of the commiserating Abel ; but it was almost enough to give the translator an attack of apoplexy, from his efforts to control his laughter; for, of course, the precious document was the result of a deliberate conspiracy. It might be added that the translator knew as much of Ogham as he did of Sanscrit

A more amusing hoax was practised on the little man's

credulity, and with the aid and co-operation of an innocent-looking countryman. This artless peasant, to whom Abraham Abel was well-known from his frequent excursions to Kilcrea Abbey, which was periodically visited by the brotherhood, came to Cork to see the Quaker on special business —to tell him something of the most extraordinary nature. 'Faith, sir, I declare I do n't know if your honour will believe me, but 'tis the quarest thing that ever come across me.' 'What is it Daniel?—is it a new discovery?' 'Discovery, sir, indeed!—Faith then, it's a discovery entirely, such as you and me never heard of before.' 'Dear me, Daniel, what can it be?' 'Well sir, here is the way of it. You know the little strame that runs through my farm?' 'Of course I do, Daniel—I saw you jump across it the other day.' 'True for you, sir. But what would your honour say if you could'nt hear a person spakeing at the other side of it?' 'You do n't say so, Daniel! Why it is not above eight or nine feet broad.' 'There's where all the wondher is, sir. To make a long story short, I must tell your honour, I went down a few days ago—by the same token, it was a Friday, of all the days in the year—to call the boys into their dinner, for the praties were biled. Well, sir, I come down within a couple of spades of the little strame, and I says—"Jerry, the dinner is ready—tell Paddy and Mick." But, saving your honour's presence, the divil a one of Jerry appeared to notice me, though he's a fine warrant for the "pink eyes." I thin come nearer to the brink of the wather, and I says, "Jerry! do you hear me, ye omadaun?" But it was the same as if Jerry hadn't an ear in his head. "Bad cess to ye, ye bosthoon," says I, "I'll make ye hear me;" and with that, I takes a running jump, and I clears the strame. "Jerry," says I, "what the dickens ails ye?" "Me, masther?" says he. "Oh you can hear me now, can you? but how come you not to hear me before?" says I. "Sorra a wan of me ever heard ye, sir," says Jerry "What do you mane," says I, "saying ye couldn't hear me, and I standing on the other side of the little river?" Then out it come that the man was telling the born truth, and that a body can't be heard across it.' 'Daniel, you literally amaze me. Can this be true?' said the philosopher. 'True, sir; I wish I was sure of having a hundred pounds in my fist to-morrow next day,' said Daniel, with an air of great sincerity. 'It is very marvellous, indeed. But, Daniel, have you told any one of this phenomenon?' 'Phee what, sir?' 'This strange occurrence, Daniel?' 'No sir, not to mortial man.' 'Well, then, Daniel, keep it a strict secret, and I will go with you early to-morrow morning to the place, and we can then severely test the thing ourselves.' 'Nothing better, sir,' said Daniel.

On the following morning early, Abraham and the farmer were on the ground, each standing on the opposite side of the rivulet. The farmer opened and shut his mouth, and gesticulated and waved his hands wildly, and, as Abraham was convinced, made the most desperate efforts to render himself heard; but not a sound crossed the stream! 'Most wonderful!—most astonishing!' said the philosopher. The farmer continued to make mouths and gesticulate, until, overpowered by his unavailing efforts to render himself audible, he at last sank exhausted on the bank! Abraham was in an ecstacy of amazement. Here was a discovery! Here was something to communicate to his friends!—to Father Mat and the scoffing librarian. Here was matter for the *Gentleman's Magazine!*' 'Daniel, *can* you at all account for it? what *do* you think of it?' enquired the enraptured *savant*. 'Well, faix, if the ould monks of the Abbey hav' n't something to do with it, it would go hard with a poor man like me to tell a scholard like your honour, who knows everything.' 'The monks, Daniel?' said Abel with a look of enquiry. 'Why, sir, I've heard tell that the monks used be taking their walks up and down the banks at both sides, and repeatin' their prayers to themselves—and they dar'nt as much as say "Good morrow, Father Bernard," or "God save you, Father Pat." 'Tis the pennince the holy men would be doing, sir.' Singularly enlightened by this attempt at an explanation, off rushed the delighted Quaker; and as soon as he reached Cork he proceeded to the house of a friend, who had often characterised Abraham's discoveries in rather strong language, and who, indeed, was an infidel on all matters connected with Irish antiquities. 'Well, Joseph, now you will be convinced,' began Abraham, who then told his tale of wonder. His friend looked at him in amazement, believing him to have suddenly gone mad. But no; Abraham was perfectly collected, and undoubtedly sober. 'Joseph,' said he, 'if I did not *see* it with my own eyes, perhaps I would not believe it.' 'Faith, you would, Abraham.' 'Well, Joseph; but I *saw* the man speaking, and I could not hear the slightest sound.' As a personal favour, Abraham besought his friend to accompany him to the charmed stream; and as a pleasant drive of nine or ten miles on a fine day was a thing rather agreeable than otherwise, Joseph consented to accompany the philosopher, 'in order to be convinced.' Joseph took his position on one side, and Abraham on the other. 'Now for it!' thought Abel, as, lifting himself on tiptoe, and raising his voice to the highest pitch, he cried out, 'Joseph? do you hear me?' 'To be sure, I do, you goose. I tell you what it is, Abraham Abel, you are a downright fool. Do *you* hear that?' 'Indeed, I do, Joseph,' meekly replied the little man, who was rather crestfallen at the failure of the experiment, but who got out of the difficulty on two suppositions—either that there was something peculiar in the atmosphere on that particular day; or that it not being Friday, the day on which, according to Daniel, the monks were enjoined to silence, the charm would not work. As to any notion to the prejudice of his 'trusty and honest friend' the farmer, no such thing ever entered the head of Abraham Abel.

For a time, Abraham stoutly maintained the theory that at an early period of the world man went on all-fours ; and on one occasion he displayed remarkable agility in illustrating his theory by practical experiment. A field near Blarney was the scene of this illustrated lecture on the antediluvian mode of human progression.

It was upon this innocent and guileless little man that Father Mathew fixed his hungry eye, determined to have him as his own. Not that Abraham had, to use the phrase of the day, any occasion to take the pledge, for, had the rest of the world been like him, there would have been no necessity for total abstinence ; but Father Mathew liked and respected the amiable and kindly Quaker, and longed to invest him with a silver medal. Father Mathew took every opportunity of working on Abraham's susceptible feelings, and Abraham was much inclined to yield ; but when this alarming state of things became known to his friends, through casual observations which he let fall, as to 'people being bound to afford an example to their weaker brethren,' and 'to make a sacrifice of their own inclinations for the public good,' they took him resolutely into their own hands, and watched over him, as one would over a pet pigeon when a hawk was on the wing. On the day of the Water Party at Blarney, Father Mathew was several times seen in dangerous propinquity to Abraham, who was much impressed by the proceedings of the open air meeting ; but his vigilant friends were constantly on the watch, and ready to interpose and effect a diversion, when strategy became necessary. Indeed, at one moment things had gone to such a length, that Abraham was within a hair's breadth of enrolment, when one of his guards, rendered desperate by the prospect of losing the very life and soul of their pleasant society, boldly dashed in between the moral mesmeriser and his victim, saying, 'No, Father Mathew, Abraham Abel does not require the pledge : there is not a more temperate man living. You have sufficient in your society, and you will have many more; but we can't let you have our Abraham.' Poor Abraham fluttered back to the protection of the Antiquaries. But Father Mathew turned away in high dudgeon, and it was not for many months after that he quite forgave the 'uncalled-for interference' which robbed him of one who would have followed such a leader with the most devoted enthusiasm.

Few, indeed, of that cheerful band are now left. The Quaker, the Librarian, and the Parish Priest of Blarney, have all passed away, as well as the Apostle of Temperance; and those who survive are advancing far into the vale of years. Father Mat died on the 1st of March, 1849, in the seventy-third year of his age, and the forty-sixth of his ministry, thirty-four of which he devoted to the duties of parish priest of Blarney and Whitechurch. At his death a sum of *three shillings* was found after him, as his sole earthly possession. It was his wish to be buried in his beloved Round Tower, and he left elaborate directions for this ceremonial; but the wish was disregarded, and he reposes at the foot of the altar at which he long and faithfully ministered. His friend Mr. Windele, when lately editing a metrical legend written by Father Mat in Irish, and translated by Edward Kenealy, thus truly describes the good old man:—

Although humble and unpretending, with a character of great simplicity and naïveté, he was no ordinary man, and whilst he lived filled a great space in the affectionate regards of a large and discriminating public; truly was he 'a man to all the country dear.' One more racy of the soil and more singularly lovable seldom existed; a warm and sincere patriot, an enlightened friend of civil and religious liberty, he was an advocate of whatever tended to advance and benefit his country and promote the welfare of the people. He was foremost in every movement calculated to better their condition. Although no teetotaller, for his genial and hospitable nature would not suffer him to shackle his social tendencies, yet no man advocated the cause of temperance more earnestly. He preceded his flock in every procession, lectured the people in their places of assembly, and was foremost in their soirées and réunions, addressing and encouraging them. In all their innocent gaieties and amusements he participated. No man better knew or understood the 'dulce est desipere in loco.' His hospitality was unbounded and almost indiscriminate. His doors were ever open to his friends without distinction of sect or party, and his reputation procured him the visits of many of the celebrities who from time to time visited his world-renowned neighbourhood of Blarney.

In the same pages Mr. Windele touches off with quiet humour the character and habits of his lost friend Abraham Abel, who died on the 12th of February 1851, in the sixty-eighth year of his age. The following, however, will suffice to exhibit some of the harmless peculiarities of the innocent mortal whom Father Mathew so earnestly desired to secure as a follower:—

His toilet was peculiar. He commenced by cleaning his own boots and shoes, performing the operation in a condition of entire nudity. Then he sponged and brushed his body, after which, ascending an isolated stool, he threw in as much electricity, by the friction of a silk handkerchief on the heels, as sufficed for the day.

Occasionally he fasted the whole twenty-four hours to keep down corpulency, to which he had no tendency; but his father had been a remarkably obese man. On one occasion his left arm vexed him by evincing rheumatic symptoms, and he determined to chastise the insubordinate limb. He said the fellow was a sinecurist and waxed wanton, whereupon he made him work, imposing the duties of brushing clothes, shoes, &c., until he found the beneficial consequences. When in business he sometimes sat at his desk with a cat at either side of him, and frequently with a favourite tom-cat on his back; their friendly purring, he would say, made a cheerful music to soothe him in his labours.

Beautiful is Killarney at all times, under all circumstances, and at all seasons of the year. Beautiful, when the glittering peaks of the snow-clad mountains rise above the brown woods that clothe their rugged sides. Beautiful, when the tender green of early summer softens the stern aspect of those guardian giants, beneath whose shadow sleep the lovely lakes. Beautiful, when autumn flings its varied hues over the foliage of that favoured clime. Beautiful, when not a breath of air stirs the leaf, and the water resembles an unbroken mirror, in which every charm is doubled by reflection. Beautiful, when the surface of the Lower Lake reminds one of an inland sea, and the waves roll and pitch, and the white-horse exhibits its angry crest; for then the wind-driven clouds fling their changing shadows over land and water, mountain and lake, tree and shrub, thus producing a succession of effects such as delight the eye of the beholder, but baffle the utmost art of the painter to reproduce on canvas. Even when the rain descends in torrents—which it often does in Killarney—and volumes of mist shroud the lofty Toomies or the jagged Reeks, and float along like mighty spectres,—even then this region of beauty is not divested of charms. But it is when the storm has passed, and the blue sky looks out from the riven clouds, and the sun flings a slanting beam over the mountain side, lighting up the moistened leaves till they glisten like emeralds, and the waters catch a stray sparkle, that the witchery of Killarney is most potent; for then the torrent dashes and foams over its stony bed, the cascade springs from its rocky ledge in mightier strength and with bolder leap, and every hill-side is musical with the murmur and the gush of tiny rivulets. Killarney is then as a beautiful but passionate woman after the storm of emotion has passed over her fair brow, and tears still glisten in her eyes, veiling the brightness of her glance.

Such was the day, in June 1844, when a grand excursion on the lakes was given in honour of Father Mathew, who, amongst his other miracles, had worked a complete moral reformation in Paddy Blake's Echo. Fortunate was the tourist who beheld the gay flotilla leave the pier at Ross Castle, and shoot out into the waters of the Lower Lake, amidst joyous shouts and strains of music. Banners of silk floated from bow and stern of each of the boats of the little fleet which accompanied the stately eight-oared barge of the Church Street Society, in the stern-sheets of which Father

Mathew was seated. There were gentlemen with the Apostle, who, residents of the locality, could fittingly introduce him to every fairy islet and enchanting bay, and pour into his ear the legends with which each spot was deathlessly associated. The fleet first steered for 'Sweet Innisfallen,' the loveliest isle that gems the Lower Lake; and, landing, the party roamed over its velvet turf, and enjoyed from various points unrivalled glimpses of the glorious panorama. Embarking again, the joyous company were borne across the lake to Glena Bay; where, when the waters are at rest, they sleep most calmly, and where the arbutus assumes its brightest tint. Round by Dinis' Island steered the flotilla, which then entered Torc Lake, deemed by many the loveliest of the sister lakes. The band was unusually good; but no language could give an idea of the magical effect of its music, as the boats slowly glided by those spots consecrated to Echo. The sounds were caught up by the spirit of the mountain, and were given back upon the enchanted ear from different points, in murmurs faint and more faint, until melody expired in the sweetest sigh that ever reached the ear of mortal. And what thunders the peals of the drum awakened amid the mountains! From hill to hill, from peak to peak, the sounds crushed like volleys of artillery, as if a hundred guns had been hurling their iron rain upon an enemy. After paying a visit to 'O'Donoghue's Wine Vaults,' and casting a pitying glance at the wave-washed semblance of the enchanted butler, the party quitted Torc Lake, and again rowed out on the island-studded bosom of the Lower Lake. It had rained occasionally during the day, with sufficient intervals of bright weather to allow of Father Mathew visiting many places storied in wild legend, or charming for their intrinsic beauty. But just as the boats were well out of Glena Bay, the rain burst from the clouds which had been gradually enveloping the mountains as in a shroud, and poured down in a glorious deluge. Fortunately, however, the capriciousness of the spirit of the mountain and lake had been calculated upon, and precautions had been abundantly taken; otherwise the excursion might have partaken too much of the character of a genuine water party. About six o'clock, the boats reached Castle Loch, a ruin-crowned promontory, the extreme point of the demesne of Denis Shine Lalor, who then resided in a mansion which has since been converted into the Castle Loch Hotel, and who was on this occasion the hospitable entertainer of Father Mathew and a numerous company.

At another time a grand entertainment was given to Father Mathew on the Island of Innisfallen. Here, indeed, the Apostle of Temperance might be supposed to have enough of water; it surrounded him on every side, and no other beverage sparkled on the board save that which sprang from its home in the mountain. A stag-hunt was also arranged for his gratification; but, though the music of the hounds, as it swelled in sublime chorus, or was faintly heard from the depth of a lone valley, was a glorious treat for those who heard it for the first time, Father Mathew was not happy so long as the chase lasted, and only enjoyed real pleasure when the gallant stag plunged into the lake, and was saved from the fangs of the hounds. The stag was not the first, as William Martin might have remarked, that saved himself by 'taking to the cold water.'

In no part of Ireland was the triumph of the temperance leader more complete, than in this region of lake and mountain, as many a tourist has had good reason to appreciate since then. 'I was pleased,' said an English lady, speaking of a visit to Killarney, in 1862, 'to find that our boatmen and our guides were all teetotallers, and to learn from them, that the greater number of their class practically remembered their great benefactor.'

It was at Waterford that Father Mathew gave the following popular definition of the term 'gentleman'—one which was certainly justified by the conduct and bearing of those who had made a practice of sobriety :—

The spectacle this evening should be, indeed, gratifying to every human mind. All parts of society are here represented, the high and the low ; the chasm which used to separate the classes is filled up ; the poor are made worthy to sit among the princes of the people. Now when the intoxicating cup is dashed away, every man is fit to associate one with another. EVERY FAITHFUL TEETOTALLER IS A GENTLEMAN.

CHAPTER XXIV.

The Riots in Philadelphia—Promises to visit America—The Temperance Institute—The oratorical Catastrophe—'Old Dan Tucker' The Mesmerist—'Boo—boo—boo!'—The Tipperary men—The crowning Indignity—His Reception of the Fugitive Slave.

IN the following letter, Father Mathew gave expression to the horror with which he read the account of the terrible riots in Philadelphia, of which his fellow countrymen and co-religionists were the principal victims:—

Cork; June 4, 1844.

MY DEAR FRIEND.—Your very kind letter found me reading, my eyes suffused with tears, the fearful accounts from Philadelphia.

The name of that polluted city should be Aceldama. Blessed Jesus! whose dying legacy was peace, peace—whose darling precept was 'my dear little children, love one another,' can such deeds of horror be perpetrated by Thy followers, Thy eternal Gospel in their hands? Horror congeals my blood, my heart dies within me, at the fearful details from blood-stained Philadelphia. 'By this,' says our Divine Redeemer, 'shall all men know you are my disciples, that you love one another.' Delightful words! Though repeated a thousand and a thousand times, they must still charm every humane, every Christian breast. We may apply the words of holy Job, to the day and night, when the cry of brother's blood, and the smoke of the burning temple of the living God, ascended to Heaven: 'Let that day be turned into darkness; let a darksome whirlwind seize upon that night; let them not be numbered in the months.' If fraternal charity, if civil and religious liberty have resting-places upon earth, these should be the breasts of the citizens of America. Well may the mighty population of the States exclaim 'that there was never such a thing done in Israel, from the days that our fathers came up out of Egypt, until this day;' and all your Israel, from Dan even to Beersheba, should gather together as one man, and vindicate your selves before the nations of the earth, and solemnly covenant, to secure for evermore, within the boundless extent of your once envied Union, the rights, property, and lives of men. O Philadelphia, thou city of brotherly love, how art thou fallen!

Under existing circumstances, I must postpone for a few months my intended visit to the States, and I feel confident that you will approve of my resolution. To you and the proprietors of the 'Ashburton,' I feel deeply indebted for your great kindness, of which I shall ever cherish the remembrance. I have looked forward with anxious expectation to the happiness of making a Temperance Tour through the States, and of being privileged to be instrumental in diffusing more widely the blessings of Total Abstinence from intoxicating drinks.

The disapointment is indeed a bitter one; but it would be uncandid of me, were I to attribute it solely to the dismal doings at Philadelphia. The claims of my own poor country to another year of my labour, had partly determined me to remain in Ireland for that period. I am now firmly resolved to devote the ensuing twelve months to the consolidation of our glorious society in my dear native island, and then, God permitting, the United States will be my destination, where I confidently hope for a continuance of the Divine Blessing.

I am, with high respect, my dear Sir, yours sincerely and devotedly

THEOBALD MATHEW.

Thurlow Weed, Esq., Albany.

Father Mathew had always contended, that he sought rather to multiply and enhance the pleasures and enjoyments of his followers, than to lessen or diminish them. He encouraged innocent amusements and harmless recreation of every kind, and promoted whatever had a tendency to improve and elevate his followers, especially his young friends of the middle classes of his own city. With this object in view, he established the Temperance Institute; an institution at cnce social and intellectual—in which tea-parties were given, meetings were held, music was studied, books were read, and debates on literary and other subjects were encouraged. The rooms were elegantly and tastefully embellished; and the library, presented by Father Mathew, was well stocked with books suited to all capacities. In the principal apartment of the Institute were frequently given the most agreeable parties, to which many of the leading citizens were invited; and very few of those who so readily availed themselves of these invitations, that did not enjoy the entertainment provided for them on such occasions. The speeches were short, and few in number; but the music, both vocal and instrumental, was really excellent, and the proceedings were invariably wound up with the pleasant dance, into which the young people entered with never-failing spirit. The nominally responsible committee were at times rather troubled to know how to make the receipts meet the expenditure; but difficulties of the kind were dispelled by Father Mathew's thoughtfulness and liberality. 'It is all right, my dear,' he would say to the perplexed Chancellor of the Exchequer, as that functionary was bewildered in his unavailing attempts to strike a satisfactory balance in favour of the Institute, after some more than usually brilliant and successful soirée. 'It is all right, my dear—you must not be responsible in any way; you did your best, and I am more than satisfied. And the creditors would at once be settled with, and all liabilities wiped off.

A flourishing debating society arose in the Institute, under Father Mathew's auspices; and there are now at the press and in the professions, many who were then members of that Institute, and of that society. Others are scattered over every region of the globe; and not a few, like their loving and beloved President, sleep the sleep that knows no waking. This Institute was, in Father Mathew's esteem, the apex that crowned the pyramid erected by his hands. In the improved material comforts of the mass of the people, he recognised the practical advantage of sobriety; but here were elegant accomplishments and intellectual pursuits grafted upon the moral training of the youth of the middle and higher classes —and those who saw his work, congratulated him upon its success.

A little incident that occurred at a very critical stage in the existence of the debating society, comical as it may appear, is mentioned as a proof of the good sense and tact for which no man was more remarkable than the Apostle of Temperance. It was on the night of a grand debate, when a subject of special interest was to be stoutly contested by the crack speakers of the Institute. Great things were expected from the encounter of the rival orators, whose admirers and backers had assembled in full force, to support and cheer their respective leaders. Nor were grace and beauty wanting to crown the conqueror in the intellectual tournament. In the chair sat Father Mathew, his handsome face beaming with pleasure, as he glanced around his young followers, the parents of most of whom had been his earliest friends. The debate was opened with marked success by the appointed member, amidst the applause of his exulting partisans. Then rose his oponent, who proceeded to show how utterly deficient in historical information, and how destitute of the slightest claim to common sense, was the honourable and learned gentleman who opened the debate. The spirits of the orator's partisans exhibited a marked improvement as the hits told on the opposite party, who seemed to stagger under their weight and rapidity. But as the speaker was delivering a trenchant blow, his memory suddenly failed him, and though the sword was held aloft to strike, he could not strike. Was it an oratorical artifice?—was the blow suspended for a while only to descend with deadlier force on the casque of his oponent? Alas! no, it was an intellectual paralysis of the most hopeless kind. A mocking cheer greeted the speechless one, and his dismayed partisans; and a decided titter was heard from the ladies' gallery. Then followed a dead pause. The torture of the poor bewildered orator was at its height, when Father Mathew interposed, to the relief of the vanquished party, by saying, in a cheering voice—'Ladies and gentlemen, perhaps our young friend Mr. James Traynor would favour us with a song, as an agreeable variety, after those admirable speeches?' The suggestion meant a command, to which Mr. James Traynor promptly responded; and very soon both sides of the house were united in harmonious efforts to do full justice to the lively chorus of 'Old Dan Tucker.' It was, no doubt, a somewhat incongruous feature in a grand historical debate; but it solved the difficulty of the moment, and saved a young fellow from poignant humiliation—which was quite sufficient justification, in Father Mathew's opinion, for even a more daring innovation than the refrain of 'Clar de Kitchen!'

Detesting anger and bitterness, and suppressing every attempt at a sneer or a sarcasm, which he termed a 'gibe,' he appreciated wit and humour with the keenest relish, and enjoyed honest fun with the delight of a child. And no scoool-boy relished a practical joke more thoroughly than he did, always provided that no one was injured or seriously pained thereby. The writer was present when an instance of this kind occurred. Some dozen of his young friends dined with Father Mathew one day in 1845, on which occasion John's soup and coffee merited and elicited the highest encomiums, which that grim individual received with lofty satisfaction. The dinner was excellent, the sweets were from the first artiste in the city, and the dessert was choice and abundant. The guests enjoyed the good things, to the intense gratification of the host, who also enjoyed their 'good things;' for wit, and jest, and pleasant anecdote, and sallies of humour, lent a charm to a repast which did not require the stimulus of wine to heighten its pleasures. The youthful spirits of the party were quite sufficient for that. The coffee was being discussed, when the conversation happened to turn on mesmerism, and much discussion arose as to its claim to scientific recognition. One of the party stoutly asserted his full and entire belief in the truth of the science, and the extraordinary nature of its phenomena; and he concluded by saying, that he had himself performed wondrous feats as a mesmeriser. 'Try what you can do with me, then' said another of the party. 'Bravo, bravo!' cried the delighted youths, who, so they could elicit some amusement out of the experiment, little cared whether it succeeded or failed. The challenge was accepted. The subject of the intended operation seated himself in a chair, which was surrounded by the entire party—Father Mathew among the most interested of all. The operator proceeded to go through the usual process, making 'passes' according to the established rule, and doing everything with all the gravity and solemnity of a regular professor. 'Faith, you have him, my boy! There he goes off!' said one of the youngest and most impulsive of the group. 'Hush!' remonstrated the mesmeriser in a solemn whisper, as he multiplied the passes, and, as he thought, overwhelmed the patient with the mesmeric fluid. The patient did certainly seem to be overcome—his eyes became heavy, and as if sightless, and the muscles of his face assumed a strange rigidity. 'Didn't I tell you, sir! exclaimed the mesmeriser, addressing himself with triumphant disdain to a confirmed sceptic. 'I do n't believe a word of it. Let me stick a pin in the fellow,' said the sceptic. 'No, my dear,' said Father Mathew, 'we must not try experiments of that kind.' The patient now appeared to have fallen into a state of coma, and to be no longer conscious of anything passing around. 'Now I shall raise his arm, and stiffen it like a bar of iron,' announced the operator, who did what he said—the limb being stretched out, like a pump-handle or a finger-post. 'God forgive us!' cried John, who firmly belived that the watchful enemy of mankind had an active share in the enchantment. The spectators became really impressed with the conviction that there was truth in the science, that it was wrong to doubt the evidence of one's senses, and that the operator knew his business thoroughly. 'Observe me!'

said the operator, 'while I relieve him from the overpowering influence of the fluid.' The profoundest interest was now felt by the hushed and awe-struck spectators, who followed every movement of the great magician with breathless attention. But just as the interest was at its height, and the silence became almost painful, the patient winked several times with extraordinary rapidity, screwed his mouth to a most unnatural shape, and cried 'Boo—boo—boo!' in the very face of the mesmeriser, and finished his performance by jumping from the chair of operation, and dancing the first bar of the Sailor's Hornpipe. The company roared with delight at the amazement and confusion of the discomfited operator; but not one of the young people enjoyed the joke with greater relish than Father Mathew, who sank on a chair literally exhausted with laughter. The mesmeriser had a capital voice, of which he was not a little proud; and in the hearty plaudits with which his best song—for which his host specially asked—was received, he was fully compensated for his failure as an operator.

Father Mathew was not always as successful in satisfying his guests as when he thus entertained his chosen followers, as an instance will prove. Two old friends from his beloved Tipperary having business in Cork, paid him a visit, and readily accepted his warm invitation to dinner. These worthy gentlemen admired temperance in the abstract, and were proud of the fame of their illustrious countryman. But at this point they stopped. 'Temperance,' according to their opinion, 'was a fine thing for people who could not control themselves; but so long as a man could enjoy himself in moderation, and take his five or six tumblers of whisky-punch without turning a hair, surely no one would be fool enough to say that such a man required to take the pledge.' That was their doctrine, and they did not care who knew it. These respectable individuals were received with the utmost warmth by their host, with whom they had a pleasant talk about

Tipperary and their mutual friends. There were but four at the table—the two strangers, one of the lieutenants of the temperance leader, and the host. The dinner was excellent, as usual, and the gentlemen from Tipperary enjoyed it thoroughly, having been much about the town during the day. But they thought it rather strange that they were not asked by the servant if they preferred porter or ale to water, which they conscientiously detested. They were however too polite to make a remark, or to ask for their favourite—indeed their invariable—dinner beverage ; and they sipped the 'Lady's Well' water with as decent a show of relish as they could possibly affect. It was also strange, they thought, that there was no wine on the table ; but they supposed it was reserved until the cloth should be removed. 'Here it comes now,' thought they, as a fine dessert replaced the dinner, and the host desired John to 'bring in the tray.' In Tipperary, in the hospitable homes of the two gentlemen, to bring in the tray at such a moment meant the advent of 'materials ;' but their disgust was unbounded when they found that coffee was the substitute for 'honest whisky-punch.' They looked at the sideboard, to discover if any hope lay in that quarter, but in vain. They glanced at John, who returned the glance with a vicious gleam from his bright little eyes, and then they looked at each other in blank despair. In vain their host helped them to the most delicious fruits of the season ; in vain they were urged to try another cup of the fragrant coffee—in vain were old friends referred to, and early associations conjured up by their kindly host. There was but one indignity remaining which could be inflicted upon the martyrs, nor was that long wanting ; for, seeing that his guests did not relish the coffee, their host suggested in the most persuasive manner—'Perhaps, my dear sir, you would prefer tea ?' 'No, no !—many thanks to you, Father Mathew,' replied his friend, with a look of horror. 'Then, perhaps, gentlemen, you would like a little lemonade after your dinner?' Lemonade! That was the crushing blow, the crowning indignity. The Tipperary men rose, as if by an impulse, and muttering some kind of apology, in which the words 'pressing engagement,' and 'lawyer,' were alone audible, they literally rushed from the room; and betaking themselves to the nearest public-house, they amply indemnified themselves for the outrage done to their palates by the coffee, and to their nationality by the hateful suggestion of lemonade. Five tumblers formed the lowest standard of their notions of rigid moderation; but after such a trial as they had just passed through, eight or ten they considered to be a fair and reasonable allowance. When these worthy men had occasion to visit Cork again, they, to employ their own expressive words, 'gave Father Mathew and his house in Cove Street a wide berth.'

As a host, and as the temperance leader, it afforded Father Mathew a double gratification to know that his guests enjoyed his abundant but simple fare, and did not feel the want of the customary wine and the orthodox whisky-punch to be found either on their own tables, or the tables of their friends. His gratification was still greater when he elicited the admission from one who thoroughly enjoyed 'the good things of this life,' that the dinner was all the better without the stimulant. 'Now, B——,' said he, one evening, to a jovial friend, whom the pledge would have robbed of half his jollity, 'do 'nt you feel much more comfortable without your usual tumbler of punch than if you were taking it?' This was asked in the most persuasive tone of voice, and with the most benevolent expression, as he laid his hand softly on B——'s shoulder. 'Then, indeed, Father Mathew, to be candid with you, I do not; for I have a most extraordinary feeling without it,' was B——'s honest reply, which, as was invariably the case, was wound up by a pleasant laugh. 'Oh, B——, you are incorrigible; I can make no hand of you, was all that Father Mathew could say to his good-humoured friend.

The advocates of social reforms and humane ameliorations of the law found a ready and influential supporter in Father Mathew, who sympathised in whatever tended to render their hard lot in this life more tolerable to the poor and the afflicted. In like manner did he hold in abhorrence the idea that one man could possess property in his fellow-man; and the expression of this feeling, which he did not conceal, was to him, as the reader will see in time, the source of much anxiety, and no small embarrassment, during his tour in the United States.

Frederick Douglas, known as the 'Fugitive Slave,' describes in a letter to the 'Boston Liberator' his reception by Father Mathew, whom he visited in Cork, in October 1845. Men of the highest rank and greatest eminence constantly visited at that humble house in Cove Street; but neither to noble nor to statesman, to poet nor to orator, to painter nor to sculptor, did Father Mathew offer a heartier welcome than to the Fugitive Slave, who thus records his impressions of that reception:—

On the 21st inst., Father Mathew, the living saviour of Ireland from the curse of intemperance, gave a splendid soirée as a token of his sympathy and regard for friend Buffum and myself. There were 250 persons present. It was decidedly the brightest and happiest company, I think, I ever saw anywhere.

Everyone seemed to be enjoying himself in the fullest mannner. It was enought to delight any heart not totally bereft of feeling, to look upon such a company of happy faces. Among them all, I saw no one that seemed to be shocked or disturbed at my dark presence. No one seemed to feel himself contaminated by contact with me. I think it would be difficult to get the same number of persons together in any one of our New England cities without some Democratic nose growing deformed at my approach.

On the morning after the soirée, Father Mathew invited us to breakfast with him at his own house—an honour quite unexpected, and one for which I felt myself unprepared. I however accepted his kind invitation, and went. I found him living in a very humble dwelling, and in an obscure street. As I approached he came out of his house, and met me about thirty yards from his door, and with uplifted hands, in a manner altogether peculiar to himself, and with a face beaming with benevolent expressions, he exclaimed, 'Welcome! welcome! my dear sir, to my humble abode;' at the same time taking me cordially by the hand, conducted me through a rough uncarpeted passage, to a green door leading to an uncarpeted stairway; on ascending one flight of which, I found myself abruptly ushered into what appeared to be both drawing and dining-room. There was no carpet on the floor, and very little furniture of any kind in the room; an old-fashioned sideboard, a few chairs, three or four pictures hung carlessly around the walls, comprising nearly the whole furniture of the room. The breakfast was set when I went in. A large urn stood in the middle, surrounded by cups, saucers, plates, knives and forks, spoons, &c. &c., all of a very plain order—rather too plain, I thought, for so great a man. His greatness, however, was not dependent on outward show; nor was it obscured from me by his plainness. It showed that he could be great without the ordinary attractions, with which men of his rank and means are generally anxious to surround themselves.

Upon entering the room, Father Mathew introduced me to Mr. William O'Connor, an invited guest; though not a teetotaller, an ardent admirer of Father Mathew.*

This gentleman complained a little of his severity towards the distillers of Cork, who had a large amount invested in distilleries, and who could not be expected to give their business up to their ruin. To which Father Mathew replied, in the natural way, that such men had no right to prosper by the ruin of others. He said he was once met by a very rich distiller, who asked him, rather imploringly, how he could deliberately plot the ruin of so many unoffending people, who had their all invested in distilleries? In reply, Father Mathew then told, with good spirit, the following excellent anecdote: 'A very fat old duck went out early one morning in pursuit of worms, and after being out all day, she succeeded in filling her crop, and on her return home at night with her crop full of worms, she had the misfortune to be met by a fox, who at once proposed to take her life to satisfy his hunger. The old duck appealed, argued, implored, and remonstrated. She said to the fox—You cannot be so wicked and hard-

* The merchant-tailor who erected the Mathew Tower in commemoration of his reverend friend's reception in London in 1843.

hearted as to take the life of a harmless duck, merely to satisfy your hunger. She exhorted him against the commission of so great a sin, and begged him not to stain his soul with her innocent blood. When the fox could stand her cant no longer, he said—Out upon you, madam, with all your fine feathers; you are a pretty thing to lecture me about taking life to satisfy my hunger—is not your own crop now full of worms? You destroy more lives in one day, to satisfy your hunger, than I do in a whole month!'

CHAPTER XXV.

His Speech on Capital Punishment—The Oriental's Question—His distinguished Visitors—Innocent Festivities—Protestant Sympathy—Sacredness of the Pledge.

AT a meeting held in Cork, in 1845, Father Mathew expressed his views on the question of Capital Punishment, which the promoters of the meeting sought to abolish. It will be seen that he availed himself of the opportunity thus afforded him to urge upon his fellow-citizens the wisdom and humanity of arresting crime by the protection and reformation of the young. In proposing the resolution which he had been solicited to propose, he said :—

I deemed it my duty to take part in your proceedings this day; and if my humble advocacy can in any way tend to ameliorate the condition of the most degraded member of the human family, I consider the violence which I offer to my feelings in thus presenting myself before you to be amply compensated. The resolution handed to me requires no preface; it is simply the enunciation of a great principle, agreed to by all persons—that the prevention of crime and the reformation of the criminal, not vindictive justice, should be the object of all governments. The ministry to which I have been called, and to which I have devoted myself so many years, has given me great knowledge and experience of human nature. I have been for nearly thirty years a calm observer of passing events. Guilt in all its various gradations has appeared before me; and I have very seldom found a case where, by kindness and winning his confidence, I did not succeed in the reformation of the criminal, by holding out to him a pardon through Christ.

Indeed such were the numbers of persons of that description that came to me, that often the finger of scorn was pointed at me, as the sinners' reproach. But I was proud to be calumniated in such a way, for my Divine Master was similarly reproached. I speak not for the purpose of magnifying myself, but to prove that I came not here for the purpose of propounding a beautiful theory, but to give you the result of my own experience. I have seen vindictive justice grasping the lash, and exhibiting the gibbet, in vain. Such exhibition may tend to make juvenile culprits more cautious, but the old offender smiles at the threats of the law; and I have found such to be the case invariably. Threats of vengeance and punishment I ever have found to be most inefficient; nothing but a religious education can be an effective remedy. The law may hold back the ruffian's hand, but it is religion alone that can heal the cankered heart. It is my conviction, and I have long studied the subject, that even the crime of murder should not be punished with death. I do not now wish to enter into the discussion of the permission given by the Almighty in the words that 'he who sheds man's blood by man shall his blood be shed;' but from the consequences that have followed the punishment of murder by death, I am convinced that the amount of crime is increased, because the public mind becomes brutalised by the frequent repetition of executions; and I am further convinced that if the punishment of death were done away with, we would have no murders at all. I never found that the apprehension of punishment by death held back the murderer's hand; and it has often occurred that the person punished was considered the person murdered, and his punishment therefore produced the contrary effect to that intended. I have strayed from the subject of the resolution, to implore your sympathy and compassion for the juvenile offenders of this city. I do it with all my heart, for I mourn over them; and I should say that it is your own neglect of the youthful culprits that is the unhappy cause of the frequency of the perpretration of such crime. They are wretched beings, the offspring of poverty, who learned nothing save the low artifices of thieves: they are sent to jail and confined; but so far from being reformed, they become worse, and as they grow up they advance from the petty thief to the blood-stained murderer. I would therefore suggest the necessity of having moral and spiritual training for the juvenile classes, instead of jails and prisons. It is not my wish that murderers should escape with impunity. I think they should be confined, and brought up to useful trades, and kept in prison until, by their labour, they paid not alone for their own maintenance, but also repaid those to the last farthing whom they robbed or injured. I would not give the culprit a *bonus*, and send him back upon the world; I would make him pay the penalty to the last farthing. I call on the mayor, and those present, to turn their attention to the number of poor creatures I see daily about the streets, and crowding the quays and markets, led on by their wretched parents, serving, as I might say, an apprenticeship to robbery. These are the parties that should be looked to, as they are likely to become inmates of a prison, or to fill the harlot's shameful grave. There should be something done to compel the parents to give them instruction and education; and if they have not parents, the law should interfere to protect them. I am aware that the whole subject is encompassed with difficulty. I have never been able to bring myself to the full conviction, nor could I discover, that the Almighty has given any power over the life of man. He has reserved vengeance for himself, for— Vengeance is mine,' said the Lord. From all I have observed and read, I am convinced that the infliction of capital punishment has been a fatal source of the frequent murders that disgrace and stain the land. It is a difficult subject; but the object you have in view is a glorious one—the good of society, and the amelioration of the condition of the people. Stopping the shedding of human blood is an object worth contending for, no matter what the difficulties are. We have the good fortune to be born in a glorious era; floods of light and life are pouring on us; and I am sanguine that I shall live to see the day when capital punishment will be done away with, and abolished from the code of these realms.

Among the visitors attracted to Cove Street by the fame of the Apostle of Temperance, was a genuine oriental, rejoicing in the name of Meer Shamet Alli, a descendant of the original Mogul race. He was a grand-looking Mussulman, highly accomplished, and spoke more than one European language with facility. Father Mathew, to whom he had a letter of introduction, invited him to breakfast, and—that the stranger might have the pleasure of hearing his own language spoken in a place so far from his own country, he also asked his friend Captain (now Colonel) Gamble to join the party. Father Mathew took the illustrious stranger to various places, and showed him several institutions—among others, the Ursuline Convent at Blackrock, within some two miles of Cork. The institution is a very noble one, and eminent for its success as a school for young ladies of the middle and higher classes. Meer Alli was received with distinction by the ladies of the community, and shown everything of interest. Father Mathew's presence acted as an 'open sesame,' and every door flew open before the approach of the stranger, who examined and admired with a quiet gravity peculiar to his race. While Father Mathew's attention was otherwise engaged, the Meer asked confidentially of a gentleman near him, who formed one of the party—'Are all these ladies his wives?' The rather Eastern idea had arisen in his mind, chiefly from the air of mingled respect and affection with which the good nuns treated their Spiritual Superior, which office Father Mathew then held. When Father Mathew was afterwards told of the oriental's query, he was considerably amused at its strange proposition.

Meer Shamet Alli was not the only distinguished oriental who made the acquaintance of the Apostle of Temperance. Dwarkanauth Tagore, the great Calcutta Merchant, expressed in the following letter the admiration and esteem in which he held him:—

Brighton.

MY DEAR FATHER MATHEW.—Do not think, from my silence, that I for one moment forget my promise of writing to you. But on my arrival here I had so many visitors, to give them an account of my travels, and afterwards obliged to go to Southampton and the Isle of Wight, on a visit to some friends, that I have had no time until now to write. I avail myself of a leisure moment, free from all interruptions from visitors, to dictate this from Brighton; in the first place, to thank you for all the kindness and attention I received from you during our too short acquaintance, and which I shall never forget as long as I live; secondly, to express my congratulations in having fallen into your society, which has enabled me to judge of the real character of the lower classes of Irish, and to remove those prejudices which I formerly held; and through your efforts this wonderful improvement in their morals must be attributed. So you have done and are doing more good to Ireland than all the political excitement of others. I have not only expressed this to the First Minister in England, and to others, but have written the same to my friends in India. I only wish that I could have remained a few more days in your company, or that I can at some future period meet with you somewhere. I have in my possession the valuable present you bestowed on me, which has been seen and admired by everybody. Think that I went to pass a few days with the Lord Chancellor at his country house, and Lady Lyndhurst wanted me to give up your medal; as she only lives upon water, and never touches wine, she said she had a greater right to it than myself. So you see how much I am envied in having such a gift. I can only say it will go as an heirloom to my family as a remembrance, and remain in my possession as long as I live. If I am not so fortunate as to meet you somewhere in England, you may depend that, if I am alive, I will some day next year do so in your own country. My Irish friends insist that your portrait must be painted in Dublin, though I had wished it to be done here, for two reasons; first, that I should have the gratification of meeting you, and second, it would have been painted by a first-rate artist. However, if I am to agree to my Irish friends, Mr. Gresham will arrange everything; it must be a full length, and in the position of giving your blessing to the people, whilst giving the pledge. If the artist could introduce a *Hindoo* with his turban, standing by your side, it would increase the interest as commemorative of an event which can never be obliterated from my mind. With great respect,

I remain,
My dear Father Mathew,
Yours very sincerely,
DWARKANAUTH TAGORE.

Father Mathew did not altogether confine his attentions to his visitors and strangers of the male sex; he occasionally displayed great courtesy to the gentler sex, and even afforded them hospitality, either at his own house, or at Lehenagh —arranging, of course, in case his own house was the scene of the entertainment, that members of his family should join the party. The Countess Ida Hahn-Hahn thus acknowledges the kindness and hospitality which she had received at his hands :—

London, Octbr, 17, 1846.

DEAR SIR,—I am about to leave England, and feel compelled, before doing so, to express to you my best thanks for your kindness and hospitality. The hours which I did spend with you shall not be forgotten. I was prevented from accepting your invitation at Killarney by a want of full-dress, and I thought myself not fit to appear in an evening party, and amongst ladies, in my travelling dress; so I lost the opportunity of seeing you once more. But I saw you in moments of higher importance to my feelings, and they are perhaps the most gratifying in my whole journey.

God bless you, dear sir, in the grand and noble work you carry on, and God bless your people with wisdom in the stormy trials hovering just now over them.

Yours with true and warm admiration,

IDA CTSS. HAHN-HAHN.

Mrs. Asenath Nicholson, a lady from New York, made a pedestrian tour through Ireland in 1844-45, for the purpose of becoming personally acquainted with the condition and character of its people. She generally lodged in the cabins of the peasantry, and distributed tracts among them as she went on. In a work which she published on her return, entitled 'Welcome to the Stranger,' Mrs. Nicholson gave a description of her interesting tour. Her impressions of Father Mathew—whom she first saw at Roscrea, and whom she afterwards visited at Cork—are admirably given in the book, and are the more valuable from the writer being of another faith. A single extract from its pages will be read with interest, as the testimony of a clever and appreciative stranger. Her sketches are also true pictures of the extraordinary movement of the day. She thus describes her first impressions of its leader:—

At 8 o'clock the next morning, Father Mathew gave a stirring scriptural discourse on the importance of temperance, proving from Scripture, as well as from facts, the sin of using ardent spirits. The concourse was immense, so that 'they trod upon one another.' At 12 o'clock he gave another address. His simple unaffected manner carries that evidence of sincerity and integrity with it, that no one can doubt but he who loves to doubt. His unabating zeal is beyond all praise; yet, at this late hour, do I hear his name traduced by his countrymen, who are ascribing his object to a political one. Yet among all his traducers not one can be found who is an abstainer, whether he took the pledge from him or some other one; and I should not hesitate to say that in Ireland, he has no enemies among the tee-totallers, few among the drunkards, but many, many among the moderate drinkers.

Father Mathew's visits to the Blackrock and other convents, both in Cork and Dublin, were the occasion of much rejoicing to the young ladies, who generally enjoyed a holiday and a feast in consequence. He delighted in witnessing their innocent merriment, and received their graceful tributes of affection—usually in the form of a pretty poem, descriptive of his triumph as the great moral regenerator of his country—with the utmost gratification. He treasured up these poetical effusions with care; and many a mildewed poem, written carefully, and in the neatest hand, on embossed card or satin paper, were found in the recesses of his ink-spattered desk. But a little drama, in which the mission of the Apostle was illustrated by its influence upon the life and fortune of a family, and which was admirably played by the pupils of the Convent of Loretto, Dublin, was a testimony of which he was especially proud. It was written by one of the nuns, and was assisted in its general effect by the introduction of national music and graceful dances, in which the younger children took a conspicuous part. No one could appreciate better than Father Mathew the efforts of these innocent young people to please and do him honour; and they, in their turn, were proud of his praise.

Between Father Mathew and several dignitaries of the Established Church a strong feeling of friendship existed. Even where prejudice was entertained against his creed, it was disarmed by the charm of his manner, and the conviction of his real goodness of heart; but where genuine liberality took the place of prejudice, and he became known to a man of his own stamp in the Protestant Church, the acquaintance soon ripened into friendship, and esteem invariably warmed into enduring affection. That this sentiment was felt to-towards him by the late Venerable Tighe Gregory, Rector of Kilmore, the words of that liberal-minded man will attest:—

Paget Priory, Post Town, Kilcock:
June 6, 1846.

MY VERY REVD. FRIEND,—By the merest accident I have this moment heard that you are to be in Maynooth to-morrow. An additional weight of duty, consequent upon the day, renders me unable to drive over and wait on you; but I trust your arrangements will not clash with your favouring me by naming a day, before your return to the south, on which I shall have the pleasure of welcoming you to Paget Priory, where there cannot, I assure you, be a more valued or welcome guest.

I have had a note from my right revd. friend Bishop Cantwell, promising to partake the humble hospitalities of my poor parsonage, on his approaching visitation of this district, as his lordship kindly did on his last progress.

I would that you could meet on the occasion. Polemics and politics are forgotten in the good ship Harmony, as she placidly sails in the bay of Concord; 'tis the vessel which Jesus pilots—may it never be wrecked.

It would, I well know, have given my son great delight had you been induced, when in Norfolk, to extend your progress towards Lyme Regis, and paid him a visit at his glebe in Hunstonton, eighteen miles east of it, from the pulpit of which his heart warmed towards his 'dear, his native land,' as he fearlessly advocated the claims of the Apostle of Temperance; and as the worthy and enthusiastic Mr. Hansard observed, it was cheering to recognise father and son, separated by seas, and unknowing of each other's intent, embarked in the same cause. It is, indeed, a cause which presents a neutral ground on which all should and could cooperate. Every day gives evidence of the blessings of temperance, and I never saw it more fully exemplified that last Easter Monday in my own churchyard, where an ill-conducted terrorist of the Clarendon Lodge found his safety (and impunity too) in the exemplary sobriety which caused the meritorious forbearance of the numerous Roman Catholics present, whom, in drunken bigotry, he audaciously stigmatised and insulted, in spite of his pastor's stern reproof.

They talk of panaceas for Ireland's ills, and say 'all attempts to find one are utopian.' I deny it. *Temperance* is the *panacea—on* it domestic peace, public order, morality, industry, meakness, mildness, and Christian charity are reared; and family broils, riot, tumult, violence, dissipation, idleness, intolerance, and bigotry are *crushed beneath* it.

The instance I have just recounted—almost at the time, and but six miles from the place where you will probably be administering the pledge when you receive this—forms a great and striking proof that in temperance this panacea is to be found; and with heart and hand ALL should therefore promote its growth. I was charmed to find my son, and my friend the Bishop of Norwich, acting the noble part they did, in presenting you at the Shire Hall. Persevere and prosper.

Accept, very reverend and dear friend, the assurance of the enduring esteem of,

Yours faithfully and truly,

E. TIGHE GREGORY, D.D. and LL.D.
Rector and Vicar of Kilmore.

The Very Revd. Theobald Mathew, &c.

It has been seen that Father Mathew, in the belief that he was acting most wisely with a religious people, imparted as much as possible a sacred character to the pledge. This practice was the occasion of considerable controversy, even between members of his own Church; those who objected to it contending that, when the pledge was violated, after having been so taken, its violation inflicted the additional injury of degrading the person in his own esteem, making him feel as if he had been guilty of perjury. On the other hand, it was urged that the more solemnly the pledge was administered, the more binding was it rendered, and that the introduction of the religious element was wise and beneficial. Of this latter opinion was the Vicar of Yardley, who thus expressed it in a letter to Father Mathew:—

Vicarage, Yardley, Birmingham:
Nov. 27, 1845.

MY DEAR SIR—I hear, with gratitude to God, of your doings in Ireland to promote total abstinence from all intoxicating drinks as a beverage. I rejoice in your abundant and successful labours, and wish you 'God's speed' with all my heart.

I find, and probably you do so too, that when true piety attends or follows the temperance pledge, there is stability, and there hope and almost confidence may be entertained; but that, when this is not the case, the fairest promises are often broken, and the brightest prospects blasted.

I admire, in your pledge, the acknowledgement of the need of *Divine assistance*, and, in your blessing, a prayer for ***grace* and *strength*** to keep the promise.

This is your rock of strength. Go on, my brother, and prosper, till Ireland and the whole earth be converted to your holy principle of temperance. I am glad that I have a spark of the temperance fire that glows in your heart; and may I have your prayers and your blessing, and you shall continue to have that of, my dear sir,

Your faithful but unworthy
Brother and fellow-labourer,
HENRY GWYTHER,
Vicar of Yardley

CHAPTER XXVI.

The Famine—Its Effects and its Causes—Ireland before the Famine—The Blights of 1845 and 1846—Father Mathew's Correspondence with the Government—Timely Appeal—The Famine setting in.

TOO soon, alas! arose a state of things which, while materially influencing the Temperance movement, brought about a social revolution of the greatest magnitude, and the gravest results. The history of the Irish Famine is yet to be written; and no event of modern times more requires an able and impartial pen than that terrible calamity, which filled the land with horrors for which a parallel can only be found in the pages of Boccaccio or De Foe—which counted its victims by hundreds of thousands—which originated an emigration that has not yet exhausted the strength of its fatal current—which caused twenty-three millions' worth of property to change hands, called into existence a new race of proprietors, and swept into poverty, banishment, and oblivion, many a once opulent family, and erased from the bead-roll of the Irish gentry many a proud and distinguished name. That history is yet to be written, and will be best written when time shall have brought with it a more impartial spirit and a cooler judgement than exist at this moment, while the memory is still too vivid, and the sympathy too keen, for a task so grave and so important. Fortunately for the writer of this biography, his duty compels him to treat that terrible event merely as an episode in the history of Father Mathew's career, and as a means of exhibiting, in a more striking manner, a character which the misfortunes of the country, and the sufferings of its people, developed into a still brighter and purer radiance.

To understand properly the condition of Ireland immediately preceding the famine, one has but to turn to the Report of the Devon Commission, which was appointed in December 1843, and prosecuted its enquiries in every part of the country during the subsequent year; and in its pages will be seen more than sufficient evidence to prove to what extent misery and wretchedness had prepared the way for the ravages of blight and plague. A single passage, descriptive of the condition of the labouring class, will suffice for the present purpose:—

> A reference to the evidence of most of the witnesses, will show that the agricultural labourer of Ireland continues to suffer the greatest privations and hardships; that he continues to depend upon casual and precarious employment for subsistence; that he is still badly housed, badly fed, badly clothed, and badly paid for his labour. Our personal experience and observation, during our inquiry, has afforded us a melancholy confirmation of these statements; and we cannot forbear expressing our strong sense of the patient endurance which the labouring classes have generally exhibited, under sufferings greater, we believe, than the people of any other country in Europe have to sustain.

Upon the ill-paid labour of his hands, and the produce of a patch of potato ground, which he rented at a high rate, or for which he mortgaged a considerable portion of his working days, the Irish labourer exclusively existed. This patch of ground was either let to him manured and planted, by the farmer, at an enormous rent; or, out of the proceeds of his own labour, he prepared and planted it himself. If the crop turned out abundant, everything went well with the poor labourer: it fed himself and his family, and it fed his pig and his poultry; it freed him from debt and liability, and it enabled him to purchase, in the nearest town or village, those necessaries which were required by his condition in life. But if the crop—the one and only crop—failed him, then misery, and debt, and hunger, and sickness, were the lot of the Irish agricultural labourer.

The class above the labourer—namely, the small farmers, holding a few acres of land on a tenancy at will—were but little better off than those who were 'badly housed, badly fed, and badly clothed.' This class had no capital other than their own labour, or that of a miserable dependent, to whom they let out a patch of ground in con-acre, for a potato garden; and having neither lease, nor security of any kind, to protect the fruits of their industry, the small farmers were generally satisfied with raising a scanty crop from the soil, and content with the poorest fare, and the meanest dwelling —the principal result of their hard toil being absorbed in the rent, which was too often exorbitant in amount. A large proportion of this class of small farmers held, not directly from the landlord of the estate, but under middlemen, who, having obtained long leases at easy rents, lived as gentlemen upon the toil of the wretched serfs whom they called their tenants, and among whom the land was cut up into small holdings.

The landlords of Ireland where then—just preceding the famine—suffering as well for the sins of their predecessors as from their own extravagance. As a rule, the landed property of Ireland was crushed under an accumulated load of debt and encumbrance; and many of the finest estates in the country were well-nigh ruined, and almost laid waste, by the destructive litigation and still more destructive management of the Court of Chancery.

Thus there was an embarrassed gentry, a harassed or discouraged tenantry, and a labouring population whose very existence depended upon the chances of the seasons, and the success or failure of a delicate and susceptible tubor. Manufacturing industry was limited to a few counties, and a few large towns in these; and commerce did not extend its beneficial influence beyond the sea-board, principally that facing the western shores of England. No country, in fact, could be worse prepared to meet the coming danger, or ride out the storm which so soon darkened the heavens. And when the storm broke forth in its fury, helplessly the poor ship laboured in the trough of the angry sea, no vigorous hand at the helm, and water entering at every yawning seam.

From 1817 to 1839, there had been repeated failures of the potato crop in Ireland, some partial, and some more general in their destruction; and each failure was attended with the invariable results—famine and pestilence. Those whom the hunger spared the typhus smote, and the red hue of the rural graveyard gave fatal evidence of the consequences of a potato blight. In 1822, an abundant harvest was gathered in and stored; but the potato rotted in the pits, on account of the wetness of the growing season, and it was not until an advanced period of the year that the unhappy people were conscious of the calamity that had befallen them. The most energetic efforts were made to mitigate the distress, which was felt in its worst form in the provinces of Munster and Connaught. Large subscriptions were raised, and local committees formed, throughout Ireland; and the people of England, whose liveliest sympathy was excited by the sufferings of their Irish brethren, raised a sum of nearly 200, 000*l*. for their relief. Of the 44,000*l*. then raised in Ireland, 41,000*l*. were subscribed in the distressed provinces of Munster and Connaught, and but 3,000*l*. in Ulster and Leinster, which had escaped the calamity. The entire amount, either voted by Parliament, for public works or other modes of relief, or raised by individual subscription, was somewhat over 600,000*l*.

In 1832, severe distress was felt in Galway, Mayo, and Donegal, from a partial failure of the potato the year before, the result of violent storms and heavy rains. In this instance, private benevolence, partly assisted by government aid, was sufficient to meet the necessity; and a plentiful harvest soon obliterated the traces of local suffering. England contributed 74,410*l*. to the relief of Ireland on this occasion: and Ireland raised, by voluntary effort, the sum of 30,000*l*. The Government advanced 40,000*l*., which was partly expended in public works, and partly in the purchase and distribution of food.

On occasions subsequent to 1831, and previous to 1845, the potato partially failed, but not to any extent requiring notice.

The blight, which was the precursor, but not the actual cause, of the famine, first appeared in 1845, in the autumn of that year. It had appeared the previous year in North America, and again in 1845 and 1846—its second appearance being the most destructive to the plant. The disease manifested itself in Ireland in the late crop, the early crop having been comparatively untouched. Late in the autumn, it was found that the potato was rotting; and among the first to apprise the Government of the fact was Father Mathew, whose frequent journeys through all parts of the country rendered him thoroughly acquainted with its condition. Mr. Richard Pennefather, the then Under Secretary in Dublin Castle, gratefully thanked him for the information which he afforded, and the suggestions which he made. The announcement of this calamity excited considerable apprehension, and the Government appointed a Commission to enquire into and report upon the causes and extent of the disease. Dr. Playfair and Mr. Lindley specially reported, on the 15th of November 1845, 'on the present scarcity of the potato crop, and on the prospect of the approaching scarcity.' They say :—

We can come to no other conclusion than that *one half* of the actual potato crop of Ireland is either destroyed, or remains in a state unfit for the food of man. We moreover feel it our duty to apprise you, that we fear this to be a low estimate.

The Commissioners of Enquiry, in their Report, dated the 20th of January 1846, fully corroborate this statement.

It appears (they say), from undoubted authority, that of thirty-two counties, not one has escaped failure in the potato crop; of 130 Poor Law Unions, not one is exempt. . . . .

The poor-houses will, without doubt, be found a most important means of relief, and we consider it a most providential circumstance, that such an extensive resource is available against a calamity more widely extended, and more serious in its nature, than any that has affected the Irish people since the year 1817.

In the end of November 1845, the ovens in the naval dock-yards were set at work, making biscuit for storing, to be used in case of necessity; and in the following month the Government arranged with Messrs. Baring for a supply of Indian corn and meal, to the extent of 100,000*l*., to be shipped from the United States, and transmitted to Cork, there to be kept, as in a central depôt. The fact of this order having been given was kept secret from the trade as long as possible.

Father Mathew was met, in the course of his mission, by an officer of the Government, who obtained from him much valuable information, as the following extract from that official letter will show :—

COMMISSARY GENERAL HEWETSON TO MR. TREVELYAN.

Cork : Jan. 10, 1846

I have passed through several counties, and travelled with some intelligent men, both landlords and farmers, and with Father Mathew from Clonmel; they estimate the loss by disease as one-third of the potato crop. Father Mathew, who has been travelling through the country for the last four months, said he hoped the majority of the people would yet be able to hold a sufficient number of good potatoes for seed; but it is impossible to judge, at present, how far they will turn out in the pits. . . . Father Mathew, who is well acquainted with the country and the habits of the lower orders, gave me a good deal of interesting information, and among other things, touching the working of the Poor Law Unions. . . . The father looked upon me as a gentleman travelling on his own affairs, seeking, at the same time, information as a stranger.

Commissary Hewetson was stationed in Cork, and was thenceforward in frequent communication with Father Mathew. Writing on the 24th of February, 1846, he says :—

Father Mathew has been with me to-day. I gave him your letter to read; of course he felt gratified by your remarks. He fully agrees with me, that the meal, *once* ground, with the light corn sifted, according to a sample I sent you, is the proper meal for the classes who need it.

Fortunately, the grain crop of 1845 was unusually abundant; and though a considerable proportion of the potato crop was destroyed, there still remained enough to last the people for some time. So that, although the distress was severe in many localities, it in no instance assumed the dreadful features which were soon to be almost universal throughout the country. A blight, however partial in its character, was far from being a fortunate preparation for the entire destruction of the principal food of a nation.

The Irish are a sanguine and a devout people; and implicit trust in the mercy of Providence is one of the beautiful forms in which their piety is manifested. Not that they, in this instance, blindly relied upon Providence, without adopting every human means of endeavouring to secure success in their industry; for the partial failure of 1845 only incited the people of Ireland to make greater efforts to till, and sow, and plant, for the harvest of 1846. How terribly their hopes were disappointed, we may best describe in the affecting words of Father Mathew, who thus writes to the Secretary of the Treasury, Mr. (now Sir Charles) Trevelyan:—

REV. THEOBALD MATHEW TO MR. TREVELYAN.

Cork: August 7, 1846.

I am well aware of the deep solicitude you felt for our destitute people, and your arduous exertions to preserve them from the calamitous effects of the destruction of the potato crop last season. Complete success has crowned your efforts. Famine would have desolated the unhappy country were it not for your wise precautions.

Divine Providence, in its inscrutable ways, has again poured out upon us the vial of its wrath. A blast more destructive than the simoom of the desert, has passed over the land, and the hopes of the poor potato cultivators are totally blighted, and the food of a whole nation has perished. On the 27th of last month I passed from Cork to Dublin, and this doomed plant bloomed in all the luxuriance of an abundant harvest. Returning on the 3rd instant, I beheld, with sorrow, one wide waste of putrefying vegetation. In many places the wretched people were seated on the fences of their decaying gardens, wringing their hands, and wailing bitterly the destruction that had left them foodless.

It is not to harrow your feelings, dear Mr. Trevelyan, I tell this tale of woe. No, but to excite your sympathy in behalf of our miserable peasantry. It is rumoured that the capitalists in the corn and flour trade are endeavouring to induce Government not to protect the people from famine, but to leave them at their mercy. I consider this a cruel and unjustifiable interference. The gentlemen of the trade have nothing to do with Indian corn; it is, I may say, a creation of the Government, a new article of food wisely introduced for the preservation and amelioration of the people of Ireland. Insidious efforts were even made to prejudice the people against this new food. Thank God, they were in vain, and it is now a favourite diet; and ten thousand blessings are hourly invoked on the heads of the benefactors who saved the miserable from perishing.

I am well aware of the vast expenditure incurred in providing Indian meal as a substitute for the potato, but I humbly suggest a cheaper and more simple plan. I have already laid it before Mr. Reddington, our excellent Under Secretary. If Government would purchase in America, and lay up in stores in the several sea-ports of Ireland, a supply of Indian corn, unground, and sell it at first cost to all who will purchase it, it would be soon bought up by the country millers and farmers, and the unholy hopes of the corn speculators and flour factors would be completely frustrated. . . . . I am so unhappy at the prospect before us, and so horror-struck by the apprehension of our destitute people falling into the ruthless hands of the corn and flour traders, that I risk becoming troublesome rather than not lay my humble opinions before you.

I earnestly entreat of you to look with compassion on the poor of this country, and to exert your justly powerful influence to save them from unutterable wretchedness.

Not only was the potato crop utterly destroyed, but oats and barley were deficient, and wheat was a barely average crop.

In subsequent letters, during the same month, Father Mathew urged his views upon the Government, and pleaded in moving accents for his myriad clients, who knew not that the good man who had devoted so many years of his life to rescue them from the evils of intemperance, was now employing his well-earned influence to try and save them from the horrors of impending famine. The letters, of which the following are extracts, were addressed to the same official:—

Cork: August 22, 1846.

. . . . I unqualifiedly assent to your opinions, and hope they will become the rule of action. In defiance of the sophistry with which it is attempted to lull the Government into a false security, I would not entrust our—soon to be foodless—millions to affected sympathy. Desperate cases demand desperate remedies. More than 2,000,000 acres of potatoes, valued on the average at 20*l.* the acre, are irrevocably lost; besides, the unhappy cultivators are all in debt to the small country usurers, the loan funds, or the cruel sellers on time of seed potatoes and seed corn, at a profit of cent. per cent. I hail with delight the humane, the admirable measures for relief announced by my Lord John Russell; they have given universal satisfaction. But of what avail will all this be, unless the wise precautions of Government will enable the toiling workman, after exhausting his vigour during a long day to earn a shilling, to purchase with that shilling a sufficiency of daily food for his generally large and helpless family? The bonds of blood and affinity, dissoluble by death alone, associate in the cabins of the Irish peasantry, not only the husband, wife, and children, but the aged parents of the married couple, and their destitute relatives, even to the third and fourth degree of kindred. God forbid that political economists should dissolve these ties! should violate these beautiful charities of nature and the Gospel. I have often found my heart throb with delight when I beheld three or four generations seated around the humble board and blazing hearth; and I offered a silent prayer to the great Father of all, that the gloomy gates of the workhouse should never separate those whom such tender social chains so fondly linked together.

Cork: August 25, 1846.

. . . .

This country is in an awful position, and no one can tell what the result will be. For the sake of our common humanity, I anxiously hope that Her Most Gracious Majesty's Government will adopt the wise precaution of providing as large a supply as possible of Indian corn, to protect the wretched people against famine and pestilence. With Indian meal at a penny per pound, we could, with the Divine blessing, set both the one and the other at defiance. At the present price of Indian corn, the Government loss would be trifling.

In a letter of the 30th of September, Father Mathew justly takes credit for the effect which the spread of temperance had in maintaining order and tranquillity under circumstances most likely to lead to disturbance and outrage :—

Cork : September 30, 1846.

. . . .

The measures of Government to provide remunerative employment are above all praise, yet have not been accepted with gratitude. The treasury minute directing that the rate of wages should be lower than that paid by the farmers, has afforded a pretext for much discontent. But no rate of wages will save the people from extreme distress, unless the price of provisions be kept down. A shilling a day, or even one and sixpence, is nothing to a poor man with a large family, if he is obliged to pay twopence per pound for Indian meal. At present it nearly averages that price in the country districts. If I may presume to give an opinion, it appears to me to be of more importance to keep down the price of Indian or other meal, than to provide labour. There are so many opinions as to the amount of blighted potatoes, and consequently of the required quantity of corn as a substitute, it would be of advantage to ascertain the number of acres that were under that crop throughout Ireland. In one week the constabulary force could supply the most accurate information on that important subject.

It is a fact, and you are not to attribute my alluding to it to vanity, that the late provision riots have occurred in the districts in which the temperance movement has not been encouraged. Our people are as harmless in their meetings as flocks of sheep, unless when inflamed and maddened by intoxicating drink. If I were at liberty to exert myself, as heretofore, no part of Ireland would remain unvisited ; but the unavoidable expenses of such a mighty reformation are now an insurmountable obstacle. Were it not for the temperate habits of the greater portion of the people of Ireland, our unhappy country would be before now one wide scene of tumult and bloodshed. Thank God, temperance is now based on such a firm foundation, nothing can weaken its stability! Intemperance, with the Divine assistance, will never again be the national sin of the Irish people.

If possible, dear Mr. Trevelyan, *have the markets kept down*, and thus save from woe unutterable our destitute population.

In the following timely appeal, Father Mathew appears more in his character of the temperance leader, interposing to protect the most helpless of his followers from a snare of the worst description :—

REV. THEOBALD MATHEW TO MR. TREVELYAN.

Cork : November 20, 1846.

Concluding that you now enjoy a little relaxation of your excessive labour, I presume to address you on a subject of, in my estimation, the highest importance. I am not called upon to give an opinion as to the utility of the public works now in progress ; necessity gave them birth, and they must be executed. But it afflicted me deeply to find the benevolent intentions of Government frustrated, and the money so abundantly distributed made a source of demoralisation and intemperance. Wherever these benevolent works are commenced, public-houses are immediately opened, the magistrates, with a culpable facility, granting licences.

The overseers and pay clerks generally hold their offices in these pestiferous erections ; even some of these officers have a pecuniary interest in those establishments.

It often happens that the entire body of labourers, after receiving payment, instead of buying provisions for their famishing families, consume the greater part in the purchase of intoxicating drink.

The same deplorable abuse takes place on the different railway lines.

As I have the honour to address you, I feel pleasure in stating that the non-interference of Government in the purchase of corn, though productive of much suffering, has eventuated in an abundant supply of grain. Prices are rapidly declining ; and I confidently hope that our population will enjoy a comfortable and a comparatively happy Christmas.

If Indian meal can be had by the poor for a penny a pound, all danger of famine would be at an end.

We still follow Father Mathew, whose letters, assuming darker colours as he proceeds, will afford the reader an idea of the deepening horrors of the famine, which had now really set in. In the next month he thus writes :—

THE REV. T. MATHEW TO MR. TREVELYAN.

Cork: December 16, 1846.

Since last I had the honour to address you, I have been in several parts of this wretched country, remote from and near to Cork. I am grieved to be obliged to inform you that the distress is universal, though the people are more destitute in some districts than in others. Where the rural population is dense, and was accustomed to emigrate during the harvest to other parts of the empire, to reap corn and dig potatoes, no understanding can conceive, no tongue express, the misery that prevails. The money earned during the autumn enabled these 'spalpeens,' as they are called, to pay the rent of their potato gardens, and supply themselves and families with clothes and other necessaries. This resource has utterly failed, as well as their own stock of provisions, and they are now wholly dependent for their means of existence on Public Works.

The amount of loss sustained by the peasant whose acre of potatoes has been blighted, has not been sufficiently estimated. Bread stuffs to the value of 30*l.* would not supply the loss. . . .

The present exorbitant price of bread stuffs, especially Indian corn, places sufficient food beyond the great bulk of the population. *Men, women, and children, are gradually wasting away. They fill their stomachs with cabbage leaves, turnip-tops,* &c. &c., *to appease the cravings of hunger.* There are at this moment more than five thousand half-starved wretched beings, from the country, begging in the streets of Cork. *When utterly exhausted, they crawl to the workhouse to die.* The average of deaths in this Union is over a hundred a week. . . . I deeply regret the total abandonment of the people to corn and flour dealers. They charge 50 to 100 per cent. profit. Cargoes of maize are purchased before their arrival, and are sold like railway shares, passing through different hands before they are ground and sold to the poor.

We are establishing soup shops in all parts of the city, to supply the poor with nutritious and cheap cooked food.

After this long and painful detail, allow me, honoured dear sir, to thank you for your successful interference with respect to the temptations held out to the labourers on the public works. When I assure you that the few lines you addressed to the Board of Works accomplished more good than if I had written volumes on the subject, you will pardon me for having added to your multitudinous and most laborious duties.

Towards the close of the year 1846, the condition of the

people throughout the country was becoming frightful. and no doubt could be any longer entertained, even by the most sceptical, that a calamity unparalleled in its magnitude had befallen the people. Death was already striking down its victims in every direction, and masses of the wretched peasantry were flinging themselves into the cities and large towns, in the desperate hope that there food was to be found. And as they fled from their desolate homes, they carried with them, in their miserable clothing, if such it might be called, the infection of disease and the seeds of death. A few instances of the state of things in the more remote districts of the county Cork, in the beginning of December 1846, will prepare the reader for the appalling horrors of 1847.

In the neighbourhood of Beerhaven, a gentleman visited several cabins, in which he saw their famishing and despairing occupants stretched on beds of damp and broken straw, abandoned by all hope, and bereft of all energy. Their eyes were closed, and their voices feeble and tremulous. He besought them to rise, offered them money, spoke to them cheerily, and endeavoured to rouse them to some exertion; but in vain. Theirs was a mental and bodily prostration beyond human aid, and they continued to lie still and apathetic, evidently welcoming the death whose shadows were fast closing around them.

In Crookhaven, the daily average of deaths was from ten to twelve; and as early as the first Sunday in December, a collection was made to purchase a public bier, on which to take the coffinless dead to the grave—the means to provide coffins having been utterly exhausted in that locality.

In Skibbereen numerous cases occurred, in November and December 1846, of the dead being kept for several days over ground, on account of the want of coffins; and even at so early a period, there were instances of the dead being consigned to the grave in the rags in which they died. Ere long, the name of Skibbereen became the representative of the worst horrors of the Famine. That desolate district was one of the longest to suffer, and the slowest to recover, for in none other was there a greater destruction of human life. Throughout the entire west of the county Cork, it was a common occurrence to see from ten to a dozen funerals in the course of the day, during the close of 1846.

CHAPTER XXVIII.

The Society of Friends—Their Reports on the Condition of the Country and State of the People—Frightful Mortality.

THE Society of Friends in Ireland commenced their beneficent labours in December, 1846, and sought the cooperation of their brethren in Great Britain and throughout the United States. Their appeal was attended with the best results in both cases, but with extraordinary success in the United States. The account of their operations is recorded in a most interesting volume, published in 1852, the Report being from the able pen of Mr. Jonathan Pim. From the Appendix, which contains a number of highly valuable documents, I shall select some extracts, which will exhibit, in simple and unexaggerated language, the sad condition to which the mass of the population was reduced.

The Friends in London deputed certain members of their body to visit the distressed districts of Ireland, and to report upon the actual state of things in that country. Joseph Crosfield, writing from Roscommon on the 3rd of December, 1846, says:—

. . . The total number receiving pay from Government in the county of Roscommon is not less than 40,000. Many of these people rent land from one to five or six acres each; but from their crops of potatoes having failed, they are in no better condition than the common labourers. The price of provisions is extremely high in this part of the country, the poor paying 2*s*. 9*d*. per stone of 14 lbs. for meal, and, when they buy it in smaller quantities, 3*s*. 4*d*. per stone for it; so that a man who has a wife and family of five or six children to support out of 8*d*. per day, is scarcely removed from starvation.

From Boyle he writes on the 5th of the same month:—

The condition of the poor previously to their obtaining admission into the workhouse is one of great distress; many of them declare that they have not tasted food of any kind for forty-eight hours; and numbers of them have eaten nothing but cabbage or turnips for days and weeks. This statement is corroborated by the dreadfully reduced state in which they present themselves, the children especially being in a condition of starvation, and ravenous with hunger.

From Carrick-on-Shannon, he writes on the 6th:—

Our first visit was to the Poor-house; and as the Board of Guardians were then sitting for the admission of applicants, a most painful and heart-rending scene presented itself; poor wretches in the last stage of famine imploring to be admitted into the house; women, who had six or seven children, begging that even two or three of them might be taken in, as their husbands were earning but 8*d.* per day; which, at the present high price of provisions, was totally inadequate to feed them. Some of these children were worn to skeletons, their features sharpened with hunger, and their limbs wasted almost to the bone. From a number of painful cases, the two following may be selected. A widow with two children, who for a week had subsisted on one meal of cabbage each day; these were admitted, but in so reduced a state, that a guardian observed to the master, that the youngest child would trouble them but a very short time. Another woman with two children, and near her confinement again, whose husband had left her a month before to seek for work, stated that they had lived for the whole of this week upon two quarts of meal and two heads of cabbage. Famine was written in the faces of this woman and her children. . . . A great number were necessarily refused admittance, as there were but thirty vacancies in the house. . . . .

Throughout this journey, it was William Forster's observation, that the children exhibit the effects of famine in a remarkable degree, their faces looking wan and haggard with hunger, *and seeming like old men and women.* Their sprightliness is entirely gone, and they may be seen sitting in groups by the cabin doors, making no attempt to play, or to run after the carriages. . . . . . . To do the people justice, they are bearing their privations with a remarkable degree of patience and fortitude; and very little clamorous begging is to be met with upon the roads.

William Edward Forster thus describes the town of Westport, and other places, as he saw them on the 18th, 19th, and 20th of January, 1847:—

The town of Westport was in itself a strange and fearful sight, like what we read of in beleaguered cities, its streets crowded with gaunt wanderers sauntering to and fro with hopeless air and hunger-struck look; a mob of starved, almost naked women, around the poor-house, clamouring for soup-tickets; our inn, the head-quarters of the road-engineer and pay-clerks, beset by a crowd of applicants for work.

Early next morning we proceeded to the small village of Leenane, where we found a large body of men engaged in making a pier under the Labour-rate Act. This village appeared to me, comparatively speaking, well off, having had in it public work for some weeks, and the wages at pier-making being rather better than those earned on the roads. Still, *even here*, the men were weak, evidently wasting away for want of sufficient food.

Bundorragha, the village of which we had heard so bad an account the previous evening, being on the other side of the harbour, I took a boat to it, and was much struck by the pale, spiritless look and air of the boatmen, so different from their wild Irish fun, when I made the same excursion before.

Out of a population of 240, I found 13 already dead from want. The survivors were like walking skeletons; the men stamped with the livid mark of hunger; the children crying with pain; the women in some of the cabins too weak to stand. When there before, I had seen cows at almost every cabin, and there were, besides, many sheep and pigs owned in the village. But now all the sheep were gone, all the cows, all the poultry killed; only one pig left; the very dogs which barked at me before had disappeared; no potatoes, no oats. We ordered a ton of meal to be sent there from Westport, but it could not arrive for some time. I tried to get some immediate help for those who were actually starving; there was hardly enough of meal in the village to fill my pockets, and I was compelled to send a boat four miles to Leenane, to buy a small quantity there.

I met here with a striking instance of the patience of these sufferers. The Bundorragha men had been at work for three weeks on the roads, and the men at the neighbouring village for five weeks; owing to the negligence or mistake of some officers of the works, with the exception of two of the gangsmen, who had gone themselves to Westport the end of the previous week, no wages had until this morning been received. While I was there, the pay-clerk sent a messenger over, but still only with wages for a few; and it was wonderful, but yet most touching, to see the patient, quiet look of despair with which the others received the news that they were still left unpaid. I doubt whether it would have been easy to find a man who would have dared to bear the like announcement to starving Englishmen. . . .

We learned that their wages did not average, taking one week with another, and allowing for broken days, more than 4*s*. 6*d*. per week; in fact, for the most distressed localities of Mayo and Galway, I should consider this too high an average. To get to their work, many of the men had to walk five, or even *seven Irish miles!* Four and sixpence per week thus earned, the sole resource of a family of six, with Indian meal, their cheapest food, at 2*s*. 10*d*. to 4*s*. per stone! What is this but slow death—a mere enabling the patient to endure for a little longer time the disease of hunger? Yet even this was the state of those who were considered well off—*provided for;* and for this provision the people were everywhere begging as for their lives. In some districts there were no public works; and even where they were, we found that though the aim was to find employment for one man to every five or six souls, it really was not given to more than one man in nine or twelve.

Writing from Clifden, on the 20th of January, Mr. Forster says:—

On arriving at the small town of Clifden, we heard of four cases of death there from want, within the last three or four days. One woman, who had crawled the previous night into an out-house, had been found next morning *partly eaten by dogs.* Another corpse had been carried up the street in a wheelbarrow; and had it not been that a gentleman, accidently passing by, had given money for a coffin, it would have been thrown into the ground merely covered with a sheet. Of burials without coffins we heard many instances; and to those who know the almost superstitious reverence of the Irish for funeral rites, they tell a fearful story.

Of the village of Cleggan, a near point of Clifden, he says:—

The distress was appalling, far beyond my power of description. I was quickly surrounded by a mob of men and women, more like famished dogs than fellow-creatures, whose figures, looks, and cries all showed that they were suffering the ravening agony of hunger. . . . . . I went into two or three of the cabins. In one there were two emaciated men lying at full length on the damp floor, in their ragged clothes, too weak to move—actually worn down to skin and bone. In another, a young man lying ill of dysentery; his mother had pawned everything, even his shoes, to keep him alive; and I shall never forget the resigned uncomplaining tone with which he told her that *the only medicine he wanted was food.*

Writing from Galway on the 25th of January, Mr. Forster says, 'It was comforting to observe how cordially Roman Catholics and Protestants both lay and clerical, were uniting together in common efforts to save their poor neighbours.'

In the Claddagh, a district of the city of Galway exclusively inhabited by the fishermen and their families, he witnessed the following example of the charity of the poor to the poor, the destitute to the destitute:—

> In one small wretched hovel, in which were huddled together three families, I saw a young mother, whose rags were really no covering, much less a protection against the weather; but even here I found an instance of charity that would shame many a wealthy home. A poor blind woman was crouching upon the floor; and my companion told me she was no relation to the other inmates, but that they supported her and gave her house-room out of kindness. Even the very nets and tackling of the poor fishermen were pawned.

Writing of the general impressions of his melancholy tour, Mr. Fórster says:—

> When we entered a village, our first question was, how many deaths? '*The hunger is upon us*,' was everywhere the crý, and involuntarily we found ourselves regarding this hunger as we should an epidemic; looking upon starvation as a disease. In fact, as we went along, our wonder was not that the people died, but that they lived; and I have no doubt whatever that in any other country the mortality would have been far greater; that many lives have been prolonged, perhaps saved, by the long apprenticeship to want in which the Irish peasant has been trained, *and by that lovely, touching charity which prompts him to share his scanty meal with his starving neighbour*. . . .
>
> Like a scourge of locusts, '*the hunger*' sweeps over fresh districts, eating up all before it. One class after another is falling into the same abyss of ruin.

From Burncourt, near Clogheen, county of Tipperary, the Friends are informed that deaths from starvation were of daily occurrence, and that corpses were buried at night without coffins. From Cork county the reports are even worse. The report of the Cork Auxiliary Committee, written from the city of Cork, and addressed to the Central Relief Committee in Dublin, dated February the 20th, 1847, has this true picture of the effects which the general starvation, and the terrible familiarity with death, produced upon a people who, above all others, are most remarkable for their reverence for the dead:—

History records some affecting instances of the disruption of social relations, and the severance of domestic ties, in the depth of a nation's extremity; and it is truly humiliating to witness, in one day, the blighting effects of this calamitous visitation in the character and habits of our afflicted peasantry; no mourning for the dead, and in many instances but little attention paid to the dying; whilst funerals —once the noted occasions of their humble display—but rarely attract the interest of surviving relatives and friends.

Skibbereen is described as '*one mass of famine, disease, and death,*' the poor rapidly sinking under fever, dysentery, and starvation. Here, so early as the first week in February, 1847, there was constant use for a coffin with movable sides, in which the dead were borne to the grave, and there dropped into their last resting-place. But as weeks and months rolled on, the mortality was multiplied. Skibbereen, which had sent large quantities of agricultural produce to other markets, in the year before the fatal blight, now depended altogether on foreign food for the daily support of its inhabitants.

A gentleman writing from the county of Armagh on the 23rd of February, shows that things in that county were as bad as in other parts of Ireland. In the parish of Tartaraghan, he saw 'the living lying on straw by the side of the unburied dead, who had died three days before.'

From Ballyjamesduff in the county of Cavan, this terrible statement is made:—

The report of one dispensary doctor this day (February 28) is, that 200 persons in this district are dying of destitution, and that fifty of them are so far gone that little hope remains of their recovery. Many deaths from destitution have already occurred. At first, this sad fact was verified by the verdict of the coroner; but now he is seldom sent for, *as it would entail unnecessary expense on the county.*

Richard D. Webb, of Dublin, addressed a series of interesting letters to the Central Relief Committee whilst on a visit of inspection to Erris. Writing from Belmullet, Co. Mayo, on the 28th of May, he says:—

Many who saved money for no other purpose, were careful to preserve a hoard to defray their funeral expenses. Few of the popular customs appeared more firmly rooted than this; but it has been swept away like chaff before the wind. . . . Funerals are now rarely attended by more than three or four relatives or friends; they excite little attention, and apparently less feeling. Whole families are exterminated by dysentery, fever, and starvation; and this catastrophe has been so common in the west of Connaught, that it excites no more notice than would have been occasioned two years ago by the death of an individual.

On a retrospect of the misery I have witnessed among thousands of our fellow-creatures, who at this time never enjoy a full meal, and cannot tell to-day where to turn for sustenance to-morrow, I am surprised at the absence of outrages amongst them. Between to-day and yesterday, I saw the corpses of a girl, a man, and an old woman, who died of hunger. This day I saw a woman sinking into a faint, while I was giving out relief to some peculiarly wretched families. I saw thousands to-day of the most miserable people I have ever seen.

In Erris whole families were swept away by starvation, or fever, or both. In one cabin I saw six children lying heads and points on their miserable beds on each side of the turf fire, while the father and mother, wasted and emaciated, sat crouching over the embers. In another cabin I saw the father lying near the point of death on one side of the fire-place; over the ashes sat a wretched little boy wholly naked—and on the opposite side of the hut, beneath a ragged quilt, lay the body of an old woman, who had taken shelter there and died. As she belonged to nobody, there was nobody to bury her; and there had been *many instances of bodies lying five or six days unburied,* before anyone could be induced by threats or rewards to bury them. I saw many graves made within a few yards of the cabin door. In some places, bodies have been interred under the floors on which they died; and in others they have been covered by the ruins of the cabins they occupied; this mode of burial being resorted to as the least hazardous, troublesome, and expensive.

The following extracts from the correspondence of Father Mathew with Government officials, while indicating the deplorable state of things in his adopted city, evince his cease less efforts to mitigate the horrors of the famine, and protect the lives of the people:—

To Mr. Trevelyan.

Cork: February 4, 1847.

. . . .

The soup kitchens are affording very great relief, and have lightened in an unexpected degree the pressure upon the corn and flour markets.

We are in a deplorable state in Cork from the influx into the city of more than 10,000 foodless, homeless people, young and old, from several counties around us. I am in a horror whilst I walk the streets, and I return to my besieged dwelling in sadness and hopelessness. The workhouse has been closed, and there is no refuge for these miserable creatures. . . . .

As I have been much through the country latterly, I can assure you, and with great pleasure, that agriculture has not been neglected. The quantity of wheat sown is as large as usual. . . . . In the fond hope of preserving a supply for seed, the poor con-acre peasants allowed the potato gardens to remain undug. . . . . . I would gratefully accept from you one of your improved querns, as a model for the instruction of our mechanics. . . . . . It should be incumbent on soup committees to introduce flesh-meat, fish, or milk, into their soup; otherwise it will not be fit food. The multitudinous deaths in the workhouses, especially amongst children, are to be attributed to the want of animal food.

I fervently pray that the Lord may grant you every spiritual and temporal blessing.

To Sir R. Routh.

Cork: February 5, 1847.

For the last six months I have been distributing soup to the destitute, having proved its permanent utility during former periods of partial scarcity. We find beans, peas, and biscuit the best ingredients to add to thel iquor of flesh-meat. Occasionally, and always on Friday, we use salt fish. If this latter were given twice a week to the inmates of the different workhouses, it would be a great advantage to our, I may term them, infant fisheries.

I am delighted with Lord John's measures, and I shall have no apprehension about the future fate of the Irish people when once they come into operation. Independent of the beneficial effect the distillery laws will produce, by promoting temperance, I rejoice in it for the sake of humanity, on account of the immense quantity of grain it will save from destruction.

To Mr. Trevelyan.

Cork: March 4, 1847.

. . . .

To encourage our soup committees to give gratuitous food to be consumed on the premises, now that our workhouse is closed against admissions, I have presumed to give to them the three boilers you so considerately presented to me. Mr. Bishop has promised to give me a very fine copper cooking apparatus, with which I expect to be able to rival M. Soyer. My great anxiety is, to teach our unhappy simple people to manage to advantage their scanty means. The potato deluge, if I may so term it, during the last twenty years, swept away all other food from amongst our cottagers, and sank in oblivion their knowledge of cookery.

Last week I travelled to Limerick, and returned yesterday; and you will be gratified to hear, that in all directions the plough is at work, and oats, barley, and potatoes, are being sown in large quantities. . . . . I am full of hope, and rely with unbounded confidence in the mercy of God. We are in His Almighty hands, and not in the hands of men. He will in due season reward, with abundance, the resignation to His Divine will of the most patient and religious people on the face of the earth.

The famine now raged in every part of the afflicted country, and starving multitudes crowded the thoroughfares of the cities and large towns. Death was everywhere—in the cabin, on the highway, in the garret, in the cellar, and even on the flags or side-paths of the most public streets of the city. In the workhouses, to which the pressure of absolute starvation alone drove the destitute, the carnage was frightful. It was now increasing at a prodigious pace. The number of deaths in the Cork workhouse, in the last week of January 1847, was 104. It increased to 128 in the first week of February, and in the second week of that month it reached to 164—or 396 in three weeks! During the month of April, as many as 36 bodies were interred in one day, in that portion of Father Mathew's cemetery reserved for the free burial of the poor; and this mortality was entirely independent of the slaughter in the workhouse. During the same month, there were 300 coffins sold in a single street in the course of a fortnight, and these were chiefly required for the supply of a single parish From the 27th of December 1846, to the middle of April 1847, the number of human beings that died in the Cork workhouse was 2,130 ! And in the third week of the following month the free interments in the Mathew Cemetery had risen to 277—as many as 67 having been buried in one day.

The destruction of human life in other workhouses of Ireland kept pace with the appalling mortality in the Cork workhouse. According to official returns, it had reached in April the *weekly* average of 25 per 1,000 inmates; the actual number of deaths being 2,706 for the week ending the 3rd of April, and 2,613 in the following week. Yet the number of inmates in the Irish workhouses was but 104,455 on the 10th of April—the entire number of houses not having then been completed.

More than 100 workhouse officers fell victims during this fatal year to the Famine Fever, which also decimated the ranks of the Catholic clergy of the country. Mr. Trevelyan gives the names of 30 English and Scotch priests who sacrificed their lives to their zealous attendance on the immigrant Irish, who carried the pestilence with them in their flight to other portions of the United Kingdom.

The pestilence likewise slew its victims in the fetid hold of the emigrant ship, and, following them across the ocean, immolated them in thousands in the lazar-houses, that fringed the shores of Canada and the United States.

In meal, and coffins, and passenger ships, was the principal business of the time. A fact may be mentioned which renders further description of the state of the country needless. The Cork Patent Saw Mills had been at full work from December 1846 to May 1847, with twenty pairs of saws constantly going from morning till night, cutting planks for coffins, and planks and scantlings for fever sheds, and for the framework of berths for emigrant ships.

CHAPTER XXIX.

The People rush from the Country into the Towns—Instances of the Destruction of Life amongst them—An awful Spectacle—Father Mathew in his Element—He warns the People against Intemperance—America sends Food to Ireland—The public Measures of Relief—An honourable Testimony.

THE destruction of life amongst those who rushed into the towns, scared by the naked horrors of the starved country districts, was almost beyond belief. A single instance will afford an idea of this frightful carnage.

In a small house in one of the lanes off Clarence Street, a crowded thoroughfare of Cork, some two or three families from the country had sought refuge. The writer was in the company of another gentleman of the city, when his attention was directed to this wretched abode of famine and pestilence. A tall man, of once powerful frame, stood leaning against the door-post, and apparently indifferent to everything in this world—even to the moans and cries which proceeded from a kind of closet, a few feet from where he stood. Every trace of expression, save that of blank apathy, had been banished from his face ; and the skin of his face, neck, and breast—for his discoloured shirt was open in front—was more of the hue of a negro than of a white man. It was the dark colour of the famine. In the front room, lay, stark and stiff, stretched on the bare floor, the dead bodies of two of his children—one a girl of thirteen, the other a boy of seven ; and in the closet, on a heap of infected straw, raving and writhing in fever, lay the dying mother of the dead children, and wife of the dying father and husband who was leaning against the door-post. Sixteen human beings sought an asylum in that dwelling, and in less than a week *eleven* were taken out dead!

One or two other facts, witnessed by the writer during the month of April 1847—not in the midst of some wild mountain district, but in the heart of a populous city—will afford a further idea of the *reality* of the famine. The writer, accompanied by a friend, as in the preceding instance, entered a wretched house in the same district, a room of which was occupied by a destitute family, who had also come in from the country. On opening the door of the apartment, a miserable sight presented itself. On the floor was the dead body of an infant; on a kind of bed—a bundle of straw, on which was thrown a man's coat—lay the mother of the child, tossing and moaning in the delirium of fever, with another infant, in the last stage of the disease, lying collapsed by her side; and, crouching over the scanty embers of an almost empty grate, were a great gaunt man, and a little girl, her head resting upon his lap. The man, on whose shoulders was some kind of female garment, was nearly speechless, and could with difficulty articulate a word, or indeed be induced to notice that he was spoken to. The air of the apartment was thick and deadly, and the odour intolerable. Fever—the true Famine Fever—was here in all its malignity. The mother was removed to the nearest hospital, whose wards were then crowded with the victims of the terrible typhus, and relief was administered to the other members of that afflicted family. When the door of that chamber was opened a few days after, the consummation of the tragedy was then beheld. In the middle of the floor, his face turned to the boards, the father was stretched—a corpse. He had evidently fallen in that position, and died where he fell. On the straw which had been recently occupied by the poor mother, lay one of the children, also dead; and crouched up under the grate, with its little arms crossed on its bosom, was another dead child. Of that family of seventy-five children and their parents—there was but a single survivor.

If it were thus that the Famine and the Famine Fever slew its victims in the very midst of large populations, one may imagine, though faintly, the awful horrors of the country districts.

Among many others who suffered the penalty of their devotion to the relief of suffering humanity, was a respectable gentleman of the city,* a member of the Society of St. Vincent de Paul—a society which, having its origin in Ireland with the Famine, has since then become the most important charitable organisation in the south of Ireland. The funeral, from the character and position of the deceased, assumed somewhat of a public nature, and was attended by the local bodies and the society of which he had been a member. Father Mathew was among the clergymen who marked their respect for the virtues of this martyr to charity. As the procession reached the church of St. Anne Shandon, a cry of horror was raised at the spectacle which was there beheld. Under a kind of open shed, attached to a guard-house which has since been removed, lay, huddled up in their filthy fetid rags, thirty-eight or forty human creatures—men, women, children, and infants of the tenderest age—starving and fever-stricken—most of them in a dying state—some dead—and all gaunt, yellow, hideous, from the combined effects of famine and disease. Under this open shed they had remained during the night, and until that hour—about ten in the morning—when the funeral procession was passing by, and their indescribable misery was beheld by the leading citizens of Cork, including the Mayor, and several members of the Board of Guardians. The odour which proceeded from that huddled-up heap of human beings was of itself enough to generate a plague. On their return from paying the last mark of respect to the

* Mr. John Lynch.

deceased member of the Society of St. Vincent, the authorities sent for carts to convey the unfortunates to the workhouse ; but before they were placed, carefully and tenderly, on the straw with which the carts were supplied, the necessary precaution was taken of sprinkling their clothes plentifully with chloride of lime, which was also profusely distributed over the place on which they had lain during the night. It was a sad sight to behold those helpless and unconscious creatures borne off to almost certain death ; for, in all probability, by the end of the week, there were not five out of the entire number that had not found a shallow grave in the choked cemetery of the Union.

The public mind became familiarised with the horrors which were of daily occurrence. A little group clustered round some object in the street : you enquired what was the cause of the apparent interest, and you found it was some one who had just 'dropped from the hunger ;' or, perhaps, it was an emaciated human being who was actually drawing his last breath on the public highway of a populous city. I have myself witnessed more than one awful occurrence of the kind. I have beheld women, in scanty rags, that did not reach much below the knee, whose legs had no more flesh on them than there is on the leg of a crane. From knee to ankle, there was nothing but bone and shrivelled skin—not the faintest indication of the ordinary calf. Literally, the streets swarmed with walking skeletons. In every face was care ; on every brow was gloom ; in every heart was sorrow and depression. The healthy hue seemed to have been banished from the countenance even of youth ; the brightness of the eye was dimmed, and the once gay laugh of a light-hearted people was hushed. The very atmosphere was charged with sorrow and suffering and death. It was indeed a sad time for that stricken people.

But although there was no class in society that did not feel the terrible pressure of the hour, either through positive loss of income or the multiplied burden of taxation, there existed a noble feeling of charity pervading the whole community. Few indeed were there hard-hearted enough to refuse the application of a suffering neighbour, or to turn the wandering beggar from the door, notwithstanding that infection was disseminated by the starving beings who had rushed in from the country, and that in every fold of their wretched rags and filthy blankets the deadly typhus lurked.

It was a time truly in which to try the souls of men; and at no period of his career did the character of Theobald Mathew shine out with a purer and holier lustre, as in this terrible crisis. He was the life and soul of every useful and charitable undertaking; and there were many such at a moment which called into activity the best feelings of our common nature, and united those who had been previously opposed, in fraternal and Christian concord. Industrial schools, clothing societies, relief associations, visiting committees—these and similar efforts sprang from the necessity of the time and the compassion of the good; and there were few of these that did not derive aid and strength from the cooperation or countenance of Father Mathew. What influence he could employ, he brought to bear upon those whose interest it was to make a profit of the great necessary of life, upon every ounce of which depended the safety of a fellow-creature; and by his lavish and unbounded charity—for the excess of which he was afterwards to endure many a moment of mental torture—he supplemented the public relief, and thereby rescued thousands from an untimely grave.

Between Father Mathew and the Irish people no ordinary bond of sympathy and affection existed. He was their leader in a movement such as the world scarcely ever before witnessed, and they were his obedient and devoted followers. If no such link had united them to him, they would have equally claimed his best services in their behalf, and he would have spared no effort or sacrifice for their relief; but as their leader, who had shared with them the joy and exultation of happy days, he felt bound, in a hundred-fold degree, to stand by them in their hour of mortal peril. In a letter addressed to an American corespondent, we find this feeling strongly expressed :—

Cork : January 30, 1847.

DEAR MR. ALLEN,—There is no desire more ardent in my breast than to visit the United States, that great and glorious Republic. Obstacles, not of great magnitude, impeded my wishes heretofore. Now, there is an insurmountable impediment in the Famine that desolates our stricken land. It would be inhuman—it would be a flagrant act of baseness, to abandon, in their hour of sorrow, my dear, my dying countrymen—men who, in the pride and joy of their hearts, enrolled themselves, at my word, under the banner of Temperance, and who now, though tempted to violate the pledge, to drown their agonies in drink and die, cling to their sacred engagements with desperate fidelity, braving every temptation. A brighter day is dawning. Our Government and the benevolent people of England are liberally contributing to save us from destruction. Your happy land, through its length and breadth, sympathises in our sufferings, and is making mighty efforts for our relief. Ten fold more effectual would American aid be, if, out of your abundance, breadstuffs were shipped for Ireland, instead of money. We are in the deadly grasp of corn monopolists, who compel starving creatures to pay 19*l.* a ton for what could be purchased in your country for little more than one-third of that famine price.

When it will please a Merciful Providence to stay the hand of the Destroying Angel, and bless with plenty old Ireland, I shall gladly avail myself of the opportunity, and gratify the dearest wish of my heart.

Again thanking you for your great kindness, I am, with high respect, dear Mr. Allen, your devoted friend,

THEOBALD MATHEW.

Not only did Father Mathew expend his last shilling, and involve himself in new difficulties, to relieve the starving, but he availed himself of every opportunity to warn the people against the sin and madness of intemperance at such a moment. Thus he continued to accept invitations to preach for local charities in many parts of the country, because, independently of his desire to assist his brother clergymen in promoting works of charity or advancing the cause of religion, it afforded him the occasion of addressing their flocks upon his great theme. One of the happiest of his addresses was delivered in the commencement of the Famine, at Lisgoold, a village some miles from Cork. It was spoken from the altar of the Catholic Church, and produced a profound impression upon a congregation whose faces wore a sad and anxious expression; for '*the hunger*' was already in many a home in the parish. An extract or two from that admirable address will be found appropriate in this place :—

Thousands upon thousands now pine in want and woe, because they did not take my advice; to them the horrors of famine and the evils of blight are aggravated, while tens of thousands of those who listened to me and adopted my advice, are now safe from hunger and privation, because they had the virtue to surrender a filthy sensual gratification, and the wisdom to store up for the coming of the evil day. Thousands are now perishing, who, if they had not the folly to spend their hard-earned money in drink, in riot, and in debauchery, would now be safe from danger, and enabled to assist, by their charity, creatures who are now without a friend to comfort or assist them. The prison and the poor-house are opening wide their doors for many who have wilfully brought ruin on themselves and their families, and who, had they only sense, would now be among the wealthy of the land. I will not upbraid such victims for the past, I would rather cheer and console; I would rather tell them that it is not yet too late, that no one should despair, that there is still balm in Gilead, still a physician there. I would assure them that the oldest and most inveterate habit can be overcome by a simple effort of moral courage, by one virtuous resolution. Habit and custom tyrannise over men, because they want courage to face and oppose their tyrants; but the strongest chain of passsion that ever fettered the soul, and led man's senses captive, can be broken by a bold, a virtuous effort. The pledge which I ask you and others to take, does not enslave, it makes free—free from vice, free from passion, free from an enslaving habit. The fewer passions that rule us, the freer we are; and no man is so free as the man who places himself beyond and out of the reach of temptation; for, as the Scripture says, those who court danger shall perish therein. The freedom which I advocate is one you can obtain without any sacrifice of health, of pleasure, of money, or of comfort. On the contrary, it will add to your health, your wealth, your pleasure, and your comfort. Temperance brings blessings in both hands; blessings for time, and blessings for eternity, Let the drinker of strong drink examine his past life, and he cannot fail to see that the darkest moments of his life have borrowed their murky hue from intemperance. I never knew a young man or young woman to go astray, and walk in the way of lewdness, whose departure from the path of virtue was not chiefly from the influence of strong drink.

. . . .

There is no difficulty in taking the pledge. No man performs his duty better than a teetotaller; no man is better able to brave the vicissitudes of the season. I am now in the habit of travelling constantly during the last nine years, in heat and cold, in rain and snow, by day and night; and I have never suffered any serious inconvenience from it, because I was a teetotaller; and now, thank God, I am as active and as full of energy as ever, and as determined now as I was nine years ago, to devote myself to the great cause of reformation, and moral as well as social advancement. I never knew what true happiness was until I became a teetotaller; for until I became so, I could never feel that I was free or out of danger, or could say to myself, with confidence, that I would not at one time or another be that most degraded thing, *a drunkard*. Let no man tell me that he is safe enough, that he has no occasion to take the pledge, that he is above temptation. There is no one strong enough or firm enough to resist temptation; no one so strong or firm that he may not fall. I have seen the stars of the heavens fall, and the cedars of Lebanon laid low. I have seen the proudest boasters humbled to the dust, steeped to the very lips in poverty, and sunk in dishonoured graves.

. . . .

I am here in the name of the Lord. I am here for your good. This is a time to try men's souls; and that man or that woman must be a monster who would drink while a fellow-creature was dying for want of food. I don't blame the brewers or the distillers—I blame those who make them so. If they could make more money in any other way, they would; but so long as the people are mad enough to buy and drink their odious manufacture, they will continue in the trade. Is it not a terrible thing to think that so much wholesome grain, that God intended for the support of human life, should be converted into a maddening poison, for the destruction of man's body and soul? By a calculation recently made, it is clearly proved that if all the grain now converted into poison, were devoted to its natural and legitimate use, it would afford a meal a day to every man, woman, and child in the land! *The man or woman who drinks, drinks the food of the starving;* and is not that man or woman *a monster* who drinks the food of the starving?

It would be difficult to say in what country or among what people the most active sympathy was displayed towards the suffering people of Ireland. The generosity of the people of England of all classes was most munificent; but the practical benevolence of America was in a special degree cheering and timely. In the great cities of the United States, meetings were held in the early part of 1847, to raise money for the relief of Ireland, and these meetings were attended by the most influential men of the country. Thus, in Philadelphia, the Chief Justice of the Supreme Court presided over a meeting held in that city on the 28th of January 1847; and the noble charity displayed on that occasion wiped out the last trace of the blood shed in the riots of 1844. The Vice-President of the United States presided over a meeting held in Washington. In New York and Boston the same sympathy was felt, and the most active exertions were made to afford the description of relief then most required by Ireland. Providence had vouchsafed that to America which it had, for wise reasons, denied to Ireland—an abundant supply of food for man; and America, in giving from her abundance to her distressed sister, proved how beautiful and holy is that bond of humanity which links nations, the most remote, in one great family, sympathising with each other's joy and sorrow.

On Monday the 13th of April, a noble sight might be witnessed in Cork Harbour; the sun shining its welcome on the entrance of the *unarmed* war-ship 'Jamestown,' sailing in under a cloud of snowy canvass, her great hold laden with bread-stuffs for the starving people of Ireland. It was a sight that brought tears to many an eye, and prayers of gratitude to many a heart. It was one of those things which a nation remembers of another long after the day of sorrow has passed. Upon the warm and generous people, to whom America literally broke bread, and sent life, this act of fraternal charity, so gracefully and impressively offered, naturally produced a profound and lasting impression, the influence of which is felt to this moment.

The captain of that unarmed war-ship was thus favourably introduced to Father Mathew:—

Boston, U. S. A.: March 27, 1847.

DEAR SIR,—This will introduce to you the commander of the United States *unarmed* ship, the 'Jamestown,' Robert B. Forbes, Esq., who has nobly volunteered his services to convey to your shores a cargo of provisions for the relief of the destitute.

It affords me great pleasure to make this philanthropic countryman of ours known to one who is personally known to me, and to millions in both hemispheres, as one of the greatest benefactors of his race. In Mr. Forbes you will find one of nature's nobles, who, leaving the endearments of home at this boisterous season, crosses the ocean to imitate HIS and our SAVIOUR, to feed the hungry and raise the desponding. To you, my excellent friend, I cordially commend him, hoping at no distant day to grasp your hand, and welcome you on our shores, and then assure you that our sympathies and hearts are one, though separated by the ocean and a different faith.

With high esteem, your friend,

JOHN TAPPAN.

The Very Rev. Theobold Mathew.

Father Mathew lost no time in paying his respects to Captain Forbes, who expressed in the strongest terms the pleasure he felt in meeting and knowing the man with whose name he had been so long familiar, and spoke of the impatience of the American people to receive him among them. Captain Forbes concluded by offering Father Mathew a passage in the 'Jamestown;' which offer was gratefully declined, on the ground that the state of the country required the best exertions of everyone who could in any way assist her, and that it would be an unpardonable crime to desert her in the hour of her direst necessity.

The commander of the United States frigate 'Macedonian,' another bread-laden ship of war, also desired to have the honour of taking Father Mathew to the States in his ship:—

United States Frigate 'Macedonian.'
New York: May 15, 1847.

Reverend and respected Father,—This frigate will leave for Ireland and Scotland some time during the present month; and having understood that it was the intention of your reverence to visit this country during the summer, I take the liberty of respectfully offering to your consideration the propriety of returning with me.

It would give me great pleasure to have the honour of your company on my homeward voyage; and I can only assure you, that should you determine to accompany me, no pains shall be spared to make your voyage as pleasant to yourself as it is hoped it will be profitable to my fellow-citizens of the United States.

Accept the assurance of high regard, consideration, and respect from

George C. De Kay,
Commander of U. S. F. 'Macedonian.'

To the Very Rev. Father Mathew, Cork.

It is not within the scope of this biography to enter into a detail of the measures adopted by Parliament and the Government for the relief of Irish distress, or within the province of the writer to attempt a criticism, much less to pass judgement, upon the merits or the shortcomings of those measures, or the manner of their administration. This properly belongs to the historian who writes the history of the Irish Famine. But it is much to be deplored that the works undertaken at that time, with a view to provide employment, were not in most instances of a remunerative character, and that some such scheme as that proposed by Lord George Bentinck—to lend fifteen millions of money for the construction of the earthworks of railways—was not even partially adopted. For, while it would be untrue to state that considerable good was not accomplished by the works then executed, especially in opening up, and rendering accessible to traffic, remote or hilly districts of the country; it would be equally untrue to state that many most useless and unprofitable works were not undertaken. Allowance must, however, be made for a time of panic, which is always fruitful of measures of precipitation, as of blunders and disasters.* The delay in granting work to a parish or district was fatal to life, and the work itself was, in fearfully numerous instances, almost equally fatal. When the work was obtained, the physical energy of the workman was gone; and the very effort to use the spade, the wheel-barrow, or even the hammer, accomplished the destruction of a life which hunger and dysentery had undermined.

In the month of March 1847, there were employed on the public works the enormous number of 734,000 persons, representing, says Mr. Trevelyan, 'at a moderate estimate of the average of each family, upwards of three millions of persons.' It being apprehended that the drawing away of such an enormous amount of labour from the ordinary agricultural operations of the country would dangerously interfere with the harvest of 1847, and thus bring about a renewal of the famine which then afflicted Ireland, it was determined to substitute for those works gratuitous distributions of food; and on the 20th of March a reduction of 20 per cent. of the numbers employed on the works was carried out, and the same plan of reduction was persevered in until the new system of gratuitous relief was brought into full operation. Even the partial diminution of the numbers so employed was attended with the most serious consequences, as it tended to aggravate the distress, which was at its height in the months of April, May, and June. The Temporary Relief Act was brought into effective operation in July, during which month over

* In a note to his article in the *Edinburgh Review*, Mr. Trevelyan has the following—

'A Member of the Board of Works, writing to a friend, observed as follows:—

"'I hope never to see such a winter and spring again. I can truly say, in looking back upon it, even now, that it appears to me, not a succession of weeks and days, but one long continuous day, with occasional intervals of nightmare sleep. Rest one could never have, when one felt that *in every minute lost a score of men might die.*'"

3,000,000 of persons received daily rations. The machinery by which this gigantic system of relief was administered, consisted of Relief Committees in each electoral division, with a Finance Committee and a Government Inspector in each union, the entire being under the control or direction of a Board of Commissioners in Dublin.

This system of relief, which Sir John Burgoyne exultingly described as 'the grandest attempt ever made to grapple with famine over a whole country,' was administered through more than 2,000 local committees, to whose honour and trustworthiness Mr. Trevelyan thus bore testimony:—'It is a fact very honourable to Ireland, that among upwards of 2,000 local bodies to whom advances were made under this Act (the Temporary Relief Act), there is not one to which, so far as the Government is informed, any suspicion of embezzlement attaches.'*

The estimated cost of this relief in food was 3,000,000*l.*; but the amount actually expended was 1,557,212*l.*, being nearly 500,000*l.* less than what had been allowed by Parliament to be raised under the Act.

* Article on the 'Irish Crisis' in the *Edinburgh Review*, Jan. 1848.

CHAPTER XXX.

The Bishopric of Cork—Father Mathew is nominated by the Clergy—Letter from Father Prout—The Capuchin's Beard—Decision of the Holy See adverse to Father Mathew—Addresses from the Clergy and Laity—He bears the Disappointment bravely—His Friends the Rathbones.

THE Right Reverend Dr. Murphy, Catholic Bishop of Cork, one of the most learned prelates of his Church, died on the 7th of April 1847; and at the customary time—a month after—the parochial clergy of the diocese met for the purpose of nominating his successor. The clergy nominate by election; and, as a general rule, the candidate who stands '*dignissimus*' is appointed Bishop by the Holy See. It is usual that the clergyman who stands first of the three who are nominated by the Parish Priests of the diocese, is raised to the dignity of the Episcopate; but it occasionally happens that the Holy See, for reasons which it deems sufficient, selects the second, or even the third on the list, or goes out of the list and beyond the diocese, and appoints a priest who has no connection with the diocese, and who probably never dreamed of the mitre. The election is presided over by the Archbishop of the Province and his Suffragans; and the report forwarded by those prelates to Rome materially influences its decision. The result of the election—which was held in Cork in the month of May—was, that Father Mathew was placed highest on the list; and as there were but rare instances of the election of the clergy being overruled, and the first on the list not being appointed by the Holy See, it was taken for granted, by the public generally, that Theobald Mathew was in reality the future Bishop of Cork.

The election by his brother priests was the crowning honour of his life. It was the most emphatic testimony that could be borne to his public and private virtues. The delight of his fellow-citizens was unbounded ; and whenever he appeared in the streets, he was met with congratulations as sincere as they were enthusiastic.

Father Mathew himself looked with much confidence to his receiving the briefs from Rome in due course, and accepted the congratulations of his friends as upon a matter of which there was no doubt whatever. He believed that the cause which he had so deeply at heart would be served by his elevation to the mitre ; and if he had any apprehension as to the result, it was lest the cause might suffer through his failure. In the General of his order, in Rome, he knew he had an influential supporter ; and an extract from a letter he received from a distinguished townsman and attached friend, the Rev. Francis Mahony, better known to the world of literature as the witty and erudite 'Father Prout,' will show how strong was the interest which the venerable Cardinal Micara, felt in his career. The letter was written from London, on the 20th of May 1847 :—

I left Rome as above stated, but had previously ordered a bust of the *Irish Capuchin, robed in the cowl and habit of his order*, to be executed by Hogan ; and although Cardinal Micara was laid up in bed with the gout when the present arrived in the Barberini Convent, I had the satisfaction, in calling next day, to find it placed conspicuously in his reception room, with the inscription as follows :

FRATER THEOBALDUS MATHEW,
ORDINIS CAPUCCINORUM ; TEMPERANTIÆ
IN HIBERNIA ET UBIQUE TERRARUM
PROPUGNATOR.

The Cardinal several times mentioned to me his displeasure 'that you had never visited Rome,' which I fully explained by the nature of your labours, and the impossibility of interrupting them, save at the sacrifice of so many lives that depended upon your incessant toils. I mentioned that I hoped to induce you to visit him next October, after the harvest.

When the donor of the bust next visited the Cardinal, the latter asked—'Where is the beard of the Capuchin?' 'Beards are not worn in Ireland, your eminence,' replied Mr. Mahony. 'Then is Father Mathew, the Capuchin, ashamed of his order?' demanded the Cardinal, whose silver beard fell low on his breast. The bust was taken back to the Irish sculptor; and when it reappeared in the state room of the Cardinal, it was enriched with a beard, at once orthodox and picturesque.

There were many, however, who, while joining in the universal satisfaction at this signal mark of respect and confidence which had been paid to him by his brother priests, dreaded that his elevation to the responsible position of the spiritual head of an extensive diocese would have the effect of taking him from his great work of moral reformation. Though the Church would gain a popular bishop, the cause might loose its powerful, because trusted leader.

Immediately upon the result of the election being made known, an address was presented to Father Mathew by the Catholic clergy (secular and regular) of the city of Cork. It bore the signatures of twenty-three clergymen, none of whom—inasmuch as they were not parish priests—could have taken part in the election. They not unnaturally desired to show how thoroughly they agreed in the decision arrived at by their reverend brethren, who, possessing the right to vote, had so fully represented the feelings of the general body of the clergy. The address and answer form a fitting portion of this biography.

ADDRESS

FROM THE CATHOLIC CLERGY OF THE CITY OF CORK TO THE VERY REV. T. MATHEW, MINISTER PROVINCIAL OF THE CAPUCHIN ORDER IN IRELAND.

VERY REV. DEAR SIR,—We, the Undersigned Clergymen of the City of Cork, hasten to convey to you our warmest congratulation upon the high position in which you have been placed by the choice of the

Parish Priests of this Diocese. In so placing you, we had not, and, from circumstances, could not have, any part. The decision, however, arrived at by the majority of those with whom the choice rested, merits and obtains our entire approval. This we deem it right to convey to you in the present form.

You, Very Reverend dear Sir, have been associated in the Ministry with some amongst us for many years; to others you are endeared by ties of affection formed in childhood, and strengthened by the experience of a riper age; and you are known and esteemed by all as a most laborious Priest, a consistent and ever-active friend of the Poor, and a truly zealous promoter of every measure which has for its object the interests and honour of God's church and the welfare of God's people.

Should the decision of The Supreme Pontiff confide to your care the charge of this diocese, the attainment of the high objects of the Episcopal office will, in your person, be greatly facilitated by the extensive and well-deserved influence over all classes which your many and exalted virtues, during a long career of unexampled usefulness, have already secured to you.

Accept, Very Reverend and dear Sir, the assurance of warm regard and sincere respect with which we remain your Faithful Friends and Brethren.

Cork, May 8, 1847.

To which address, so honouring alike to its authors and its object, Father Mathew returned the following grateful reply:—

VERY REV. AND REV. BRETHREN, MY VERY DEAR FRIENDS,—I receive with the deepest respect and gratitude the expression of your regard for myself, and of your concurrence in the vote by which the Venerable Parish Priests of this Diocese have conferred on my humble self the highest honour in their power to bestow.

I cannot deem myself worthy of so high and responsible a position, neither am I influenced by any feelings of personal ambition—but I feel deeply at receiving such a testimony from a body of Clergymen in talent and virtues distinguished in the Irish Church, and endeared to me by the closest ties of the friendship of many years.

Whatever may be the decision of the Holy See, I shall during my life treasure up the remembrance of this day; and in any sphere in which it may please God to place me, I trust I shall never forget how much I owe to the kindness and affection of my Brethren in the Ministry.

THEOBALD MATHEW.

The decision of Rome was adverse to Father Mathew, and was also undoubtedly opposed to the wishes of the Catholic community, not only of the city of Cork, but of the country generally. However, after the first burst of disappointment passed away, it became apparent that Rome had decided for the best, and that the wise and learned prelate who had been placed over the affairs of one of the most important dioceses of Ireland was in reality the one who was best suited for the discharge of its duties. It did not require the lapse of many years to deepen this belief into a conviction; and it is due to the Right Rev. Dr. Delany to say, that no bishop of the Catholic Church of Ireland more thoroughly deserves the confidence and affection of his own flock, or the respect of those who differ from him in faith.

In the month of June, the decision of the Holy See in favour of Dr. Delany was announced; and on the 2nd of July there appeared, in the public press of the city, an address from the inhabitants of the City and County of Cork, with one thousand names attached thereto.

From feelings of delicacy, and out of deference to the Holy See, this address was not made public until after it was known that Father Mathew was not to be the Bishop of Cork. It originated with laymen, and every signature of the thousand which it bore was that of a layman; and had an address of the kind been published while the matter was yet undecided, it might have been taken as an attempt to bring pressure to bear upon Rome by a demonstration of lay opinion—a course which would not have been altogether respectful. But the decision being adverse to those who signed the address, it would have appeared cowardly and unworthy, on their part, if they *then* shrank from the public expression of the feelings which they entertained for their illustrious fellow-citizen. Therefore the address was published. It was in the following terms:—

TO THE

VERY REV. THEOBALD MATHEW.

THE ADDRESS OF THE UNDERSIGNED ROMAN CATHOLIC INHABITANTS OF THE COUNTY AND CITY OF CORK.

VERY REV. DEAR SIR,—We, the undersigned Roman Catholic inhabitants of the County and City of Cork, encouraged by the example of our beloved Clergy, venture thus publicly to embody in an address of congratulation the sentiments of heartfelt delight which, in common with the whole nation, animate every class—nay, almost every individual of this great community—at the high tribute paid by the venerated Parish Priests of this Diocese, at the late election for bishop, to your eminent virtues as a Catholic Pastor, and to your enduring services in behalf of a grateful country.

These venerable and venerated men deserve well of Ireland. Forgetting self, and the natural partiality which would suggest no appointment but one from amongst the pious and exemplary members of their own order, they, in the first election for Diocesan ever held here, placed prominently in their list one of the regular clergy—because of his high merits, his great charities, his unaffected piety, his unceasing labours as a minister of God; and because, too, of the unbounded respect and veneration entertained for him by all classes and creeds in the British Empire; thus exhibiting to the world the cordial union existing within the bosom of the Church, and the high religious sentiment which influenced the election.

As humble members of that Church, we may be permitted to rejoice at the prospect of having as our future bishop the man who so triumphantly achieved the moral regeneration of his country, who taught Irishmen the value of self-respect, and—an evident instrument in the hands of Providence—rooted out those degrading habits that weakened the influence of religion, and, while rendering our countrymen the victims of bad passions, brutalised their intellects, and made the name of Irishman a byeword and a shame.

We can well imagine the gratification with which the Supreme Pontiff will receive the selection which has been made. In his Holiness the Christian world recognises one distinguished for those high intellectual qualities that are so eminently adapted for his exalted station—an enlarged mind, a discerning judgement, great firmness of purpose, and an untiring determination to advance the interests of religion. Having constantly in view this, his one great object, we may well conjecture how gratified his Holiness will feel at the opportunity afforded him to obtain for the Church, in a higher sphere of action, the energy, the wisdom and the influence of our venerated 'Apostle;' for amongst the many acts which will illustrate the Pontificate of Pius IX. none, we feel confident, will shed more real lustre on his reign than the appointment of you, Very Rev. dear Sir, to the Irish Episcopacy.

That such may be your destiny is our earnest prayer, not for our own sake, for no rank can give elevation to you—not for your own sake, for we well know how, even now, you would shrink from the eminence into which you have been forced, and how you would delight to pursue your Herculean labours with an humbleness and modesty as characteristic as your zeal—but for the sake of the religion we profess, of the hierarchy we respect, of the country we love, we pray it may be your destiny to be associated in the Episcopacy with the venerated prelates who now shed so bright and enduring a lustre on the Irish Church.

[Here follow the signatures.]

It has been intimated, in an early portion of this work, that Father Mathew was not a theologian—that he lacked that professional knowledge so essentially necessary to the head and ruler of a diocese; besides, it was too notorious that he was reckless in his charities, and crippled in his resources. Had he been elevated to the mitre *before* he had become embarrassed in his pecuniary affairs, or before his habit of scattering money profusely had been confirmed, he would, no doubt, have managed to confine his charities, within something like moderate bounds; and though he would have stripped himself of the last shilling which he could call his own, and denied himself every personal comfort, to relieve the distress of his fellow-creatures, still the responsibility of his position, and the obligation of affording an example to his clergy, would have saved him from the pain and humiliation of pecuniary embarrassment. But he had gone too far to retrace his steps; and the horrors of the famine, which he hourly endeavoured to mitigate by his exhaustless generosity, was plunging him into new difficulties, and into deeper entanglements, from which he was never afterwards emancipated.* Therefore, on this ground alone, and putting strictly professional considerations aside, the decision of the Holy See, though adverse to the wish and feeling of the moment, was soon acquiesced in, as being not only wise and just, but most for the advantage and interest of the Church.

However Father Mathew may have felt the blow—and he *did* feel it acutely—he never in the slightest degree manifested either soreness or disappointment. If the wound bled, it was internally. Indeed, it must be added, there was no cause whatever for bitterness of feeling, for no human being triumphed over him, or sought to mortify him on account of his disappointment; on the contrary, the reverence of the public assumed a character at once deeper and more affectionate, and in every countenance he could read the expression of that respect which was universally entertained towards him. To the work of charity, then, he devoted himself with renewed energy; and in the knowledge that he was assisting to do good, to save life, and mitigate the sufferings of the destitute who besieged his door, he experienced a satisfaction and consolation which no dignity, however exalted, could ever bestow.

In this season of national calamity he made many friendships, which lasted during the remaining years of his life;

* Among his other causes of pecuniary embarrassment was his Church of the Holy Trinity. That a church, to replace the wretched crib in Blackamoor Lane, had been felt to be necessary, not only by its congregation, who constantly overflowed into the lane in front of its entrance, but by the citizens generally, was proved by the eagerness with which it was undertaken. It was unfortunate for Father Mathew's future peace of mind that he did not consent to accept one of the finest sites in the city—on Sullivan's Quay, opposite the Grand Parade—for his new church. At times, he was impetuous, and not a little self-willed; and in hastily obtaining another site (in an impulse of irritation at what he conceived to be an unfair demand), he made a fatal mistake, and acted in opposition to the wishes of his committee. A fatal mistake, indeed; for not only was the site which he adopted a bad one, but a foundation had to be constructed at immense cost. Then, the design was too elaborate in external ornament, and had to be, to a considerable extent, abandoned, as may be seen to this day. Out of a gross sum of 14,000*l.* expended on this building, Father Mathew supplied about half that amount out of his own resources. The state of the country from 1846 seriously interfered with his collections, thereby throwing upon him additional personal responsibility.

and no friends whom he had known at any period of his career were truer, more generous, or more unwearying and unselfish in their kindness towards him, than the Rathbone family. Their friendship never wavered or failed during his life, and it still blooms, fresh and bright, upon his tomb. William Rathbone, the eminent Liverpool merchant, had large quantities of breadstuffs consigned to him from America, for distribution in Ireland; and believing that he could most fully carry out the intentions of the benevolent donors of this welcome relief by a personal visit to Ireland, he went there with his wife and son. On his arrival in Cork, he consulted with his friend Miss Jennings—a lady well known as the most devoted enthusiast in the cause of negro emancipation—as to the best person to whom he could entrust a considerable portion of his consignment. 'I will introduce you to the right man,' said Miss Jennings, who, having effected the promised introduction, was thus the means of originating a friendship to which every successive year but added new strength. 'Father Mathew,' said Mr. Rathbone, 'would you have any objection to let us see, with our own eyes, what your plans are, and how you work out your relief systematically—in fact, what practical steps you have taken to relieve the distress of which you complain?' Father Mathew assured him that, not only had he no objection to show him everything, but that nothing could be more to his wish than that Mr. Rathbone should see everything for himself. Accordingly, next morning, Father Mathew conducted the party—consisting of Mr. and Mrs. Rathbone, Mr. Robert Rathbone, and the captain of the American vessel which had brought the cargo of corn, meal, and flour—to poor schools, in which several hundred children were at breakfast; to work-rooms, in which young girls were provided with a substantial meal; and to food depôts and soup kitchens. The party were greatly impressed with the misery which they witnessed, and the practical relief so wisely administered. 'Al' well,' said Mr. Rathbone; 'no doubt you relieve the poor, and that the distress is very great; but we should like to see some particulars, some individual instances, of this distress.' 'Then,' replied Father Mathew, 'we have only to enter the first house in the first lane we come to.' Arriving at the first house of the first lane to be met with, Father Mathew entered it, leaving the party before the door. He returned in a moment, saying—'This house contains ten occupants, six of whom are in typhus fever at this moment. Come and see them, if you have no objection.' Mr. and Mrs. Rathbone naturally hesitated at accepting so startling an offer; but their son at once volunteered to enter. 'No,' said the captain, 'you must not go in there, in the midst of contagion. I have neither wife nor child belonging to me, and I need not care.' The captain then went in, entered the different rooms, looked about him, and made various enquiries; and when he returned into the street he declared that the misery he had witnessed was beyond description, and that he could not have imagined anything more appalling. The party did not require further proof of the reality of the misery which they desired to relieve.

From that moment Theobald Mathew obtained the confidence of William Rathbone, who soon thoroughly appreciated the nature of the man—its weakness as well as its strength. Merchant and man of business as he was, he could well understand how Father Mathew, who could as soon fly in the air as keep accounts on commercial principles, must of necessity plunge himself in embarrassment, in his eagerness to relieve the distress that surrounded him on every side. He well knew how the first tale of misery whispered in his ear, in the little parlour in Cove Street, would have proved fatal to a balance on the credit side. Writing to the author, in January 1863, of his recollection of Father Mathew in 1847, Mr. Rathbone says:—

Of our first meeting I remember little ; but the pleasing impression of his frank, genial bearing, his clear open countenance—the general impression of goodness and power which his whole appearance and manner conveyed—was very strong. As we saw more of him, we were much struck with his *practical efficiency*, which was not remarkable in some of the committees. One day the soup of one of the relief committees was bad. The committee were at a loss for the cause. Father Mathew was empowered to examine. He saw the oatmeal, tested it, and found it unsound. He himself examined the boilers, at six o clock in the morning, and found a crust an inch thick left from former boilings. This was the right way to come at the cause, and Father Mathew adopted it. . . . . His house had, at that time, little furniture ; no carpets, but remains of straw, for at night it was filled with poor creatures who had no other home.

When he afterwards visited Liverpool, after his first attack, the impression of *goodness* was the same, but the *power* was gone.

CHAPTER XXXI.

O'Connell's Death—Sorrow of the Nation—Alleged Causes of his Death—Father Mathew's respect for O'Connell—Roughly Treated—Successful Remonstrance—His Famine Sermon.

A MEMORABLE year for Ireland was the year 1847. The death of O'Connell added no little to the gloom in which the famine had enveloped every home in the land. Whatever the opinions which were held of the great tribune by persons of opposing politics and adverse parties, it was conceded on all hands that no one loved his country more earnestly and passionately than he did. They may have reprobated his policy, and denounced his agitation, but they could not deny him the merit of patriotic attachment to his country. Perhaps those who most vehemently opposed O'Connell were some of the more extreme of the national party, whose warlike doctrines he had strenuously resisted; but, as time rolled on, the feeling of opposition died out, and gave place to a juster appreciation of the man who had achieved the greatest triumph by the most blameless means, and with whom love of Ireland was ever the uppermost thought of his mind and feeling of his heart. But to the great mass of his countrymen—the Catholic population of Ireland—his death was a heavy blow. They mourned in unaffected sorrow the loss, not only of the Emancipator of his fellow Catholics throughout the British Empire, but the leader to whom for many years they had been accustomed to look for advice and guidance on all public questions. The deep feeling of sorrow with which the sad intelligence from Genoa—in which city he died, on the 15th of May, in the 72nd year of his age, on his way to the Holy City, where he hoped to have breathed his last—was received in Ireland, was as creditable to his fellow-countrymen as it was honouring to the fame and memory of O'Connell.

The death of that great man was attributed to various causes; among others, to the effect which his imprisonment in 1844 had upon him, mentally and physically; and also to the influence which the disasters of his country produced upon a man of a highly impressionable nature, and one who so thoroughly identified himself with its fortunes. Then there was the sudden break up which usually takes place in men of gigantic frame and prodigious strength of intellect and body, the moment the first symptoms of decay are manifested. The consciousness of his having been worsted—even though temporarily—in his struggle with the Government of the day, must have had a depressing effect upon the successful leader, who had so long and so justly boasted that he could 'drive a coach and six through any Act of Parliament;' but the deprivation of his healthful mountain exercise, enjoyed amidst the wild and romantic scenery of his native Iveragh, must also have told terribly on his health. O'Connell delighted in the music of his dogs, as it echoed amid the hills, and he loved the grand roar of the Atlantic, as its waves broke in thunder upon the rocky headlands that girt his home of Derrynane; and not all the flattering addresses which he received from every parish in Ireland, not all the sympathy which was felt from one end of the country to the other for the imprisoned chief, could compensate him for those fresh breezes of the hill and the sea-shore, which made his blood dance in his veins, and his heart feel young again. Then came the failure of 1845, and the crushing disaster of 1846, to say nothing of the struggles and contentions in which the Apostle of Moral Force was continuously engaged with the advocates of the Sword. With the sorrows and the misfortunes of his country, a man like O'Connell could not but sympathise heart and soul; and the contemplation of the ruin which no effort of his could either arrest or prevent, must have tended to bow his spirit and depress his vital energy. The grand old tree was struck by the lightning, and it fell with a crush to the earth, causing a shudder through the land.

From the sorrowing son of the illustrious dead, Father Mathew received the following:—

Gowan Hill, Dalkey: May 31, 1847.

VERY REV. DEAR SIR,—Of your charity, I pray humbly for your prayers for the eternal repose of my dear, dear father.

His beloved remains may be in Ireland in about three weeks, to rest in Glasnevin Cemetery, as there most accessible to the people he laboured for.

Most respectfully,
Your faithful humble servant,
JOHN O'CONNELL.

The Very Rev. Theobald Mathew.

Father Mathew at once responded to the filial appeal of O'Connell's best beloved son, by a letter full of the tenderest sympathy. Dreading the influence of the Repeal agitation on the temperance movement, he was ever on the watch to save his cause from the risk of being compromised by the taint of politics; but he never ceased to admire and feel grateful to the man who was the champion of his Church, and the liberator of its people, its priests, and its altars. An extract from his letter to John O'Connell will sufficiently exhibit this feeling, which was shared in by the priests of the Catholic Church throughout the world:—

. . . . Few have known longer or more intimately, or have more honoured and loved your great and good father. In the Holy Sacrifice I daily present him before the throne of the Most High; and on thousands of altars, from the rising to the setting sun, the tremendous mysteries are celebrated by priests of our holy Church, for the eternal repose of the soul of him who is wept by the whole world. In common with all the inhabitants of the south of Ireland, I regret being deprived of the melancholy consolation of paying my tribute of respectful sorrow to the remains of the illustrious dead. Yet I must acquiesce in the propriety of selecting for the honoured resting-place of O'Connell the metropolis of Ireland. I fervently pray that the Lord may grant to you and your beloved family every spiritual and temporal blessing.

Your faithful and devoted friend,
THEOBALD MATHEW.

John O'Connell, Esq., M. P.

The following from John O'Connell is an evidence of the gratitude with which the kind and consolatory letter of Father Mathew was received in the house of mourning :—

Gowan Hill : June 6, 1847

VERY REV. DEAR SIR,—(Thank God! it will soon be 'My Lord.') God bless you for your kind, consoling, affectionate letter. It *is a consolation*, and a great one to us, in the house of our heavy affliction.

I do assure you, Very Rev. dear sir, *he reciprocated* your kind sentiments, while he deeply, truly, and so deservedly reverenced you.

Ever your most respectfully attached and deeply grateful (DEEPLY AND DOUBLY),

JOHN O'CONNELL.

Very Rev. Theobald Mathew.

The mortality in the city of Cork had now reached to such an extent, that Father Mathew was compelled to close his cemetery against any further interments, or at least until such sanitary precautions had been taken as would prevent injury to the public health. From the 1st of September 1846, to the 1st of June 1847—a period of nine months—10,000 bodies had been buried in this cemetery! This number did not include the burials from the workhouse, for which a separate graveyard had been provided. If it be considered that there were other burial places in the city, and in the neighbourhood of the city, in all of which interments were frequent, some idea may be formed of the mortality of the Famine Years.

Towards the end of May, the Cork District Relief Committee suspended its operations. The food depôts of the city were supported by and under the management of this body, and, as a necessary consequence, were closed when its functions terminated. Father Mathew, apprehending the vast misery which would ensue from their being closed at such a period of distress, took upon himself the entire responsibility of maintaining the Southern depôt—that nearest to his own house; and this he kept open for a considerable time, partly at his personal cost, and partly by the charitable contributions of the benevolent. In addition to the three large boilers belonging to this depôt, Father Mathew erected three new boilers; by which he was enabled, at an expense of 130*l.* per week, to feed between 5,000 and 6,000 famishing human beings. The daily average consumption of Indian meal amounted to one ton and a quarter; and this was made into a wholesome and nutritious stirabout, for which ravening hunger supplied an unfailing appetite. The doors were thrown open at an early hour in the morning, and kept open till one o'clock in the day, and everyone that entered was supplied with a sufficiency of this food.

An undertaking of this nature involved great risk. At the rate specified, the expenditure amounted to nearly 600*l.* a month; and where there were so many other claims upon the public, the difficulty of meeting this large outlay was necessarily increased. Impressed with the serious nature of the responsibility which he had assumed, his brother Charles ventured to remonstrate with him, saying—'It is all very well so long as you have funds to provide for the daily wants of those people. So long as you feed them, they will bless you, and regard you as their benefactor. But suppose your means fail, and you can no longer supply the multitude with their expected food, what will happen then? Why they will turn upon you and revile you, as the author of their misery. For God's sake! think of what you are doing.' 'My dear Charles, I do think of what I am doing, and I trust in the goodness of God. In Him I put my trust, and He will not desert me.' Nor did He; for at the very moment these words were being uttered, a letter was handed to Father Mathew by the servant—and this letter brought intelligence of the arrival in the harbour of a vessel with a cargo of breadstuffs from America, part of which was consigned to him. 'Now, Charles, was I not right in saying that I had no fear, because I trusted in the goodness of God? Glory and honour be to His blessed name!'

The door of the yard of the depôt was shut at one o'clock; but if any poor person had not received the customary dole of food, it was the practice, as a matter of course, for them to turn to the house in Cove Street, from which food was distributed at all hours of the day. On one occasion, some dozen poor people were lingering in the yard of the depôt, having arrived too late, the daily supply having been exhausted at an earlier hour than usual. The appearance of these poor creatures was deplorable; and Donnelly, a member of Father Mathew's staff, now performing the functions of a Relieving officer of the Mathew Commission, desired them to follow him to 'the house.' As Donnelly left the depôt, the number of his followers did not exceed twenty, but they soon swelled to hundreds, and by the time he reached the door of the house in Cove Street, there were not less than a thousand persons massed in front of the well-known dwelling. The bread was at hand, and Donnelly did his best to distribute it impartially. Father Mathew stood meanwhile in the window of his room—for the term dining-room, or drawing-room, would be out of place in this instance—watching the proceedings. Suddenly he rushed down stairs, and, to Donnelly's great amazement, charged him with being a wicked and unfeeling man, and, in fact, a disgrace to humanity. 'Good law! your reverence, what did I do?' 'What did you do? You passed over a poor cripple—a poor helpless creature—who is over there, leaning against the wall. I am ashamed of you, sir.' 'I declare, your reverence, I did my best; but the crowd shoved me about so, that I did n't know what I was doing,' said poor Donnelly. 'Well, sir, I will show you how you ought to manage, so that there will be no confusion in future, and that everyone will have a fair share. Go and divide the people into two rows, one on each side of the street, and I will bring out a basket of bread, you will bring another, and then you will see how easily I can distribute it.' Donnelly did as he was desired, and arranged the crowd into two lines, with a wide space in the centre. Out Father Mathew came, with a large basket of bread in one hand; and Donnelly and another member of the staff followed with similar supplies. 'Now,' said Father Mathew, 'observe what I am doing.' Things went on well for a minute or so, while the priest was imparting his valuable lesson to his follower; but soon the two sides of the living wall closed upon the instructor, and, blocking up the passage, held him a prisoner. He remonstrated and implored, but in vain; their eagerness to clutch at the bread rendered them insensible to all considerations of delicacy; and when he did at length free himself from the tremendous crush, it was at the sacrifice of his best coat, which was slit up from the waist to the collar! For a moment, the good man was in a towering rage, and he vowed 'never to have anything more to do with such nasty and ill-behaved people,' and that they should never receive any further relief at his hands. 'But, sir, said Donnelly to the author, 'there he was at it again next morning, as fresh as ever, and as if nothing had happened, and he kissing the poor little dirty children, and calling them all the tender names in the world. Oh, sir, he *was* a good man.'

Feeling apprehensive of the future safety of the potato crop, in which the people so blindly trusted, Father Mathew used every possible effort to dispel the prejudice which existed amongst the poor against that wholesome and substantial food, Indian meal, or the '*yallow male*,' as it was termed He might frequently be seen standing at his hall-door, with a bright fragment of a well-made cake in his hand, and affecting to eat pieces from it with intense relish. By word, by example, as well as by presents of nice-looking and palatable loaves of this valuable food, he did more than any other man in Ireland to render it not only acceptable to, but comparatively popular with the people, who at first regarded it with aversion.

Father Mathew's influence upon the wealthier classes was most valuable at this trying moment, and he did not fail to exercise it freely in the cause of his clients, the poor. An instance will happily exemplify the value of this influence, and the manner in which it was exercised.

Among the industrial schools and work-rooms to which the famine gave birth, was one to which a number of charitable ladies attached themselves. Besides providing employment for the destitute girls who worked in its classes, the patronesses of the school supplied their pupils with breakfast, thus ensuring to them the certainty of one meal in the day—no light boon at such a time. This breakfast was continued to be given for several months, and with the best results; but the funds falling somewhat low, the ladies became alarmed, and, seeing no immediate prospect of their being replenished, they determined at least to take into consideration the expediency of not giving it beyond a certain period. A day was appointed for the consideration of the proposal; and the subject being one of very grave importance, a large attendance was the consequence. The lady who first expressed her opinion as to the necessity of discontinuing the breakfast now brought the matter forward, and the other ladies felt that its continuance beyond the time specified would involve the institution in debt, and perhaps destroy its usefulness; and the question was about to be decided according to that view, when Father Mathew entered. On being told what had occurred, he seemed greatly moved; and turning to the assembled ladies, many of whom were his most intimate friends, he said that 'the proposal of discontinuing the breakfast surprised and indeed shocked him beyond measure. When he was entering the building, he saw a number of handsome equipages drawn up outside the door, and when he entered he saw the room crowded with ladies elegantly and even sumptuously dressed. Seeing this, he naturally wondered how any such proposal could find support among persons surrounded by such appearances of wealth; and he especially wondered how ladies of their position and circumstances could think of refusing a solitary meal to their poor starving sisters, the virtuous daughters of decent parents, whom God, for His own wise ends, had afflicted with an unexpected calamity.' 'Why,' said he, 'the very ornaments that adorn your persons would provide an abundant breakfast for these innocent young girls for a considerable time.' 'Oh, Father Mathew,' said the lady by whom the proposal had been brought forward, 'forgive me! It was I who made the proposal, and I am sorry for it. I know I did wrong. But there is a friend who will give me 40*l.* to-morrow, and I shall send it to the treasurer. We must not give up the breakfast.' The effect was irresistible, and such arrangements were at once entered into as ensured the continuance of the much-required meal so long as relief of the kind was necessary. The 40*l.* from the 'friend' was from the pocket of the lady herself, who was as generous as she was impulsive. Father Mathew was not without having a personal interview on his own account with the treasurer of the charity.

At no period of his ministry was his preaching more effective than in the very midst of the terrible famine, with misery and sorrow and death on every side. Little time had he to compose an artificial discourse at that moment, when every energy was strained in devising and administering relief. I remember a charity sermon at which I was present, and how the congregation testified, by their emotion as well as by their liberal response to his appeal, their belief in the truth of his descriptions of the horrors which then abounded. The passages quoted are not certainly models of style ; but such was the earnestness and pathos of the preacher, and the belief in the truth of the pictures which he drew from his daily and hourly experiences, that the eloquence of Massillon or Bourdaloue could not have produced a more thrilling or touching effect. They are given here, not only as being characteristic of the man, and descriptive of the time, but also as they represent the sublime charity which was exhibited by the poor to those more wretched than themselves—the latter being a theme on which, because of his admiration of that marvellous charity, and because of the salutary influence which it produced upon the rich, he loved to dwell. The plaintive tones, the wailing voice, the impassioned earnestness of the orator—rather, indeed, of this apostle of charity—more than atoned for any defects of style in passages such as these :—

Were I permitted to rouse the men of wealth from their dream of avarice, the ladies of fashion from their silken lethargy, would they permit me to conduct them for one day, where they ought to go every day, and where they should esteem it a high privilege to be allowed to go—to the abodes of pain and sorrow, to the squalid receptacles of the agonised and the dying—I would answer for their hearts. They are surely of flesh and blood ; but were they hard as adamant, they would not resist the cries of the famishing little creatures tortured by extreme want, and wrung with tormenting pain. There, amidst the chilling damp of a dismal hovel, see yon famine-stricken fellow-creature ; see him extended on his scanty bed of rotten straw ; see his once manly frame, that labour had strengthened with vigour, shrunk to a skeleton ; see his once ruddy complexion, the gift of temperance, changed by hunger and concomitant disease to a sallow ghastly hue. See him extend his yellow withering arm for assistance! hear how he cries out in agony for food, for since yesterday he has not even moistened his lips! See his affectionate wife, though involved in the same distress, tenderly endeavouring to lighten his sufferings, and during the long and sorrowful night supporting his drooping head. See his little children pressing round him with their wants. He fixes upon them his piercing dying looks. Oh! who can conceive the anguish, the exquisite anguish, that now rends the father's heaving breast! Turning his gaze from the killing scene, he lifts his hollow eyes to heaven, and lays before his God his intense grief. O Christians, Christians! is not this wretched man your brother? Is not the Great God of all that wretched being's Father? Can you, men of wealth—can you, my female auditors—contemplate such a dismal spectacle, without feeling the warm tide of sensibility rushing to your bosoms? That abject, that degraded being is not amongst you, who is not now resolved to subtract from costly ornaments, jewellery, and dress, to sacrifice some favourite folly, to retrench even the ordinary expenses of your families, and be content with the simple necessaries of life, and give this day into benevolent hands the honourable savings, that they may buy bread that the poor may eat. The triumph, the pure feast of soul, which this action would afford, would leave at an infinite distance behind, the selfish indulgence of vanity, or the sordid gratification of sense.

. . . .

She is scarcely sixteen. She was once the only darling child of fond indulgent parents. Her father, in early manhood, was cut off by fever, and the mother was left alone to provide for her orphan daughter. Disappointed in every struggle for bread, pressed down by the iron hand of adversity, worn out in the remembrance of the friends of former days, she is obliged to hide herself from the light of day in the gloom and damp of a dark cellar. She soon dies of a broken heart, and leaves her child to the cold charity of a pitiless world. This poor forlorn child being left to herself, she soon fell the prey of the foul seducer. Her black career of sin is soon ended. See her now extended on that scanty bed of straw, pale, emaciated, abandoned by all; no friendly hand to wash away her bloody tears, no pious lips to pour into her broken heart the balm of religious consolation. Shall she be left a prey to despair, to perish for ever? O no, O no! your charity this day, like a summer's sun, will penetrate and cheer her dreary habitation. Your plenteous charity this day, like dew from heaven, will desceud upon her, and this faded flower will bloom again. This poor prodigal will again return, and find here, through Christ, the way to repentance and to heaven.

. . . .

The rich, comparatively speaking, give nothing. That is, there is no proportion between their wealth and their charity. But the poor support the poor; and if there were not an universal destitution amongst the operatives of our city, we would not be branded with the burning shame of being obliged to avow, that in the midst of the blaze of affluence which our city presents, hundreds of our fellow-creatures have perished for want at the very rich man's gates. I could recount instances of heroic charity, amongst the poorest of the poor, at this very period, that would do honour—that are worthy—of the apostolic era. A desolate widow in my immediate neighbourhood, whose sole support is a bed for lodgers, has under her roof, for the last six weeks, an aged stranger, whom nobody knows. She tends him, and feeds him, as tenderly as if he were her brother. There is a lonely plain-work woman advanced in years, who resides in Chamberlain's Alley, in the parish of St. Nicholas, who has for many months supported, out of her scanty earnings, a helpless female; and if she were her mother, she could not love her more. And on last Monday, an interesting child was abandoned in the streets by its unnatural parent; and when it was about to be sent to the workhouse, a poor man, a scavenger, with his broom in his hand, who, with tearful eye, was looking on, came and solicited the child; and when it was given to him, his countenance beamed with joy, he clasped the helpless innocent in his arms, and brought it rejoicing to his humble dwelling. There are, to my own certain knowledge, at this moment, cherished by the very poor in the poorest portion of this city, the parishes of SS. Nicholas and Fin Barr, more than thirty children, whose unhappy parents perished during the famine. On beholding such charity as this, well may I apply to these blessed poor the words of the Saviour to the widow and her mite—'Amen, I say unto you, she has given more than all.' O ye rich! how your merit fades before charity like this. Oh, that I could anticipate the glorious welcome that awaits these merciful beings on the great accounting day. Oh, may my death be the death of the righteous, and may my end be like to theirs! . . .

CHAPTER XXXII.

He receives a Royal Pension—Important Explanation—Invading John's Pantry—John's Refuge—Father Mathew's Pets—Letters to Mrs. Rathbone—His deserved Popularity.

IT had been for some time the intention of the more influential friends of Father Mathew to raise such a sum of money as would provide him with an annuity sufficient to maintain him independently, and thus enable him to prosecute his mission free from the embarrassment of pecuniary cares. His devoted friend Mr. S. C. Hall was one of the most active and untiring on this occasion. The principal result, however, of this organisation was, that the claims of the Moral Reformer of the age were brought directly under the attention of the Government, many members of which were friendly to him, and favourable to the object sought to be attained; and that the services rendered by Father Mathew to the interests of the public peace and the cause of humanity were formally recognised. The fact that Her Majesty had granted him a pension of 300*l.* a year, was thus conveyed to Father Mathew by Lord John Russell, who had acted towards him in a kindly and generous manner on former occasions:—

Chesham Place: June 22, 1847.

REVEREND SIR,—It is with much pleasure I inform you that the Queen has been pleased to direct me that an annual pension of 300*l.* should be settled upon you out of Her Majesty's Civil List, as a mark of her approbation of your meritorious exertions in combating the intemperance which in so many instances obscured and rendered fruitless the virtues of your countrymen.

It gives me great satisfaction to be charged with the duty of making this announcement.

I am, reverend sir, your obedient servant,

J. Russell.

Rev. Theobald Mathew.

The bestowal of this pension was creditable to the Government on whose responsibility it was proposed to Her Majesty, and met with the universal approval of the country. Moderate as it was in amount, it established a sound principle—that the State should thenceforth recognise other victories than those won in the field of battle or on the quarter-deck, and should honour other conquerors than those whose hands were crimsoned with human blood. The approbation of his services by the Sovereign set the royal seal upon that moral reformation which had already earned the applause, not alone of the British Empire, but of the world. Father Mathew was really grateful for this act of kindness, though an occurrence, which took place two years after in America, and in which his feelings were not fairly represented, led many people to hold a different opinion at the time. As there will be no further necessity to refer again to the pension, it may be as well to set at rest this misrepresentation, intentional or unintentional, of his feelings with respect to it, though in doing so we must anticipate the course of events by at least two years. In a letter to his good friend Mrs. Rathbone, he thus explains the occurrence :—

Boston : August 28. 1849.

My dear Mrs. Rathbone,—My object in now writing, after first expressing an earnest hope that every member of your beloved family continues well, is to satisfy your mind on the subject of the reply made by me to the Temperance Society in New York. The fact is, I never give written answers to addresses. My time is so much occupied, now more than ever, I must content myself with a verbal expression of my feelings. Party feeling runs high amongst the Irish in America; and the person who took on himself the publication of the address and my reply, *used expressions which I never uttored.* It would be ungrateful of me, were I to attack the British Government; for though moderate the amount of the pension is, yet it answers the purpose for which it has been appropriated, and I am not unmindful of the exertions made by the Ministry during the recent scenes of destitution and famine. . . . .

With most respectful remembrance to Mr. Rathbone, and to all the family, I am,

Dearest Madam,

Your ever grateful and devoted friend,

THEOBALD MATHEW.

To his friend Miss Jennings, of Cork, he wrote at the same time on the same subject. He says:—

Allow me again to address you on the subject of my reply to the Temperance Society in New York. I find that it has been the subject of remarks from some of the newspapers in England and Ireland.

Not having time to give written answers to addresses, I content myself with verbal ones; and the individual who, on behalf of the Society, took on himself to publish both, made me use expressions which I did not utter.

After the publication of the reply, I was unwilling to correct it, for various reasons, especially as party feeling runs high amongst the Irish in America.

Aware of your desire to serve me, of which I have had so many proofs, I leave it to your prudence to defend me, if necessary.

Father Mathew, as he says, had 'various reasons' for not publicly repudiating the words attributed to him; but the principal reason was, that the person who so compromised him was one whom he had known in Ireland, and for whom he entertained a personal friendship; and he, besides, made allowance for the strong anti-English feelings under which his young friend wrote the reply, in which the writer's own prepossessions against England were, perhaps unconsciously, attributed to one who entertained quite different feelings with respect both to that country and its Government. This is the explanation of a matter which caused considerable discussion at the time, and which, with many, was the occasion of a prejudice against Father Mathew, whom they accused —we now see how unjustly—of ingratitude,—a vice odious in anyone, but the one most opposed to the character and disposition of Theobald Mathew.

Of the pension it is only necessary to say that it was appropriated to the payment of the interest of the insurance on his life, by which he guaranteed his creditors against loss, and secured them the amount of their debts.

For a few days in the summer, he paid his accustomed visit to the old house at Rathcloheen; but the great table was not now so full as in other days, for death had cut down the stoutest members of the family. Tom Mathew had followed Frank Mathew to the grave; and it was by the widowed mothers of their orphan children that the 'Reverend Uncle,' as he was styled, was now welcomed to his beloved Tipperary. He soon surrounded himself with the poor of the neighbourhood, to whom he distributed food with profuse liberality; and he took special pains to associate the young people with himself in the good work, in which he taught them to feel an interest and a pleasure. Here he adopted an ingenious mode of assisting the cottiers and small farmers, without at the same time hurting their pride or lowering their self-respect. He had it circulated abroad that he was in want of all kinds of poultry, which would be very useful at the house. The poor people, who would have made any sacrifice in order to afford him pleasure, or to pay him a compliment, brought to Rathcloheen chickens, ducks, geese, turkeys, and eggs, which they freely offered as presents, but which he insisted on purchasing at his own price, and on his own terms, and much to their advantage.

The reverence of the children for their uncle was proof against the familiarity which he encouraged, the innocent games which he promoted, and the romps in which he did not hesitate to take part. *Butler's Lives of the Saints* is a standard book in the libraries of Catholic families; and when, a few years before the time now referred to, chapters were read for the young people, in which the life of some illustrious servant of God was depicted, it was a common remark for the children to make—'Oh, how like our reverend uncle!' The criticism was just and discriminating.

Short was the rest which Father Mathew allowed himself, and brief was his sojourn at Rathcloheen. In a few days after his arrival in Tipperary, he was addressing a temperance meeting in Dublin; after which he returned to Cork, to superintend the distribution of bread to the poor.

His man John felt personally wronged by the famine, which drove so many people to the house in Cove Street. The poor were at all times obnoxious to John; and when they came, in their rags and their misery, pestering and importuning that aristocratic worthy, whose temper and humanity were about equal, he positively detested them. It was a pleasant sight to see Father Mathew invading John's pantry, and rummaging in his hiding-places, in search of a piece of cold beef or mutton, or a bone of ham, with which to thicken and flavour the soup that simmered on the range, and which soup was one of John's special aversions. There was Father Mathew, eager in his search after John's concealed treasures, and John following him, in despair, but at a respectful distance; and as his master made a grand discovery—perhaps of a leg of mutton, of which but a single cut had been taken—and with his own hands popped his prize into the huge cauldron, John would groan as if he were the victim of some atrocious burglar, who had broken into the house and robbed the larder before his eyes. Occasionally, John would stretch forth his hands, to save the morrow's dinner from confiscation; but the priest would turn on him, and crush him with the tremendous threat, before which he ever recoiled in mortal terror—'John! if you go on in this way, I must certainly leave the house.' John would thereupon abandon the morrow's dinner to its fate, and either conceal himself in his pantry, or seek refuge in bed.

It was no uncommon thing for John to betake himself to his couch at unnatural hours, and even at times when his presence in any other part of the house save his sleeping apartment was much required. John generally contrived to keep a little whisky in the house—for the 'tins' stood frequently in want of brightening, and he had always found that whisky was a grand specific for producing a lustre that made those useful articles shine like silver. It did happen, in some moment of abstraction, that John mistook the right application of the polishing fluid, and used a little of it internally, and that his bed became the most convenient and indeed necessary asylum after such unconscious mistakes. Over John's weakness, the Apostle of Temperance flung his large cloak of charity and affection. 'Poor John is not well to-day, my dear,' would Father Mathew say to his nephew, after a visit to John's attic; but although not a word ever dropped from the master which could indicate the failing of the servant, the sharp eyes and keen observation of inquisitive youth were not to be baffled—and John, on his reappearance in public, sourer and more morose than ever, would have to endure sly hints at the real cause of his retirement. John would also occasionally rebel against an order to prepare dinner for a company more than usually numerous, and rushing to his attic, would plunge into his bed, and there entrench himself. Many a pilgrimage to that attic would the master make, in the hope of softening the obduracy of his domestic tyrant, and bringing him to terms. Even when defeated and driven back by the inexorable despot of the pantry, the priest would still say—'Poor John! really he is not at all well.' He loved the little cross-grained fellow, and petted and spoiled him, and would not hear a word said to his disparagement; and so the little imp played upon his master's affection for his worthless self, and bullied and worried him to his heart's content.

The priest had his pets as well as his torment; and in

the caresses of his dog 'Sober,' or the milder demonstrations of Madam Pinky, his cat, he sought consolation when John was unusually obdurate. He would often tell of the untimelv fate of a dearly cherished pet, a sparrow, that answered to the name of Peter. The sparrow, generally an early bird, was caught napping on one fatal occasion; for while in that unguarded state, he was sat upon by a huge friar, a man of exemplary piety but colossal dimensions. 'My dear, when the friar rose from the chair, there was my poor Peter, quite flat!' said his master, who, after the lapse of more than twenty years, remembered with regret the sad story of his pet sparrow. Sober's fate was more ignominious. Sober, though a model teetotaller, was a dog of morose disposition, and appeared to take a fiendish pleasure in grabbing unwary sinners by the legs. Father Mathew made ineffectual attempts to represent Sober as an animal of a naturally amiable character, whose occasional misconduct arose from innate playfulness of disposition and exhilaration of spirits. But this explanation not having proved satisfactory to a poor woman, in the calf of whose leg Sober had made a severe incision, that much misunderstood animal was consigned to a premature death. Father Mathew did all he could to save the brute; but the injured woman was not to be appeased, and justice was done on Sober, to the sorrow and indignation of his afflicted master.

The following letters to Mrs. Rathbone exhibit his ceaseless exertions in behalf of his clients, the destitute. They also depict the terrible condition to which the unhappy beings that flocked in from the country were reduced. The utmost alarm was felt by the hard-pressed citizens at the daily increasing influx of country paupers, who not only interfered with the stronger claims of their own poor, and drained the resources of the local community, but brought infection and death to many a home. This explanation is necessary to qualify the statement in this letter of the 23rd of July:—

Cork: July 23, 1847.

My dear Mrs. Rathbone,—Your esteemed letter reached me this morning, and it is now late in the evening, and I have not yet recovered from the agitation of mind caused by Mr. Rathbone's letter. The Government Relief Committees, at best, are giving only partial relief, and many of them have not yet commenced, though the period for their operations will expire the 15th of next month. Thousands and thousands would have perished, were it not for the supply of food furnished by the various benevolent associations. Should the charity of our great benefactors in the United States fail, it is horrible to anticipate the consequences of the stoppage of Government relief. The remonstrances of the Board of Health have had no effect on the Relief Commissioners. Even milk, though to be had in abundance at less than one penny per quart, is considered too expensive a luxury for the destitute on the relief lists, and in the Union Workhouses. We are still in fear and trembling for the harvest; but let it be most prosperous, money cannot be procured by the poor to purchase the necessaries of life, unless remunerative employment can be given by the landed proprietors. The New Poor Law Bill, with the cooperation of the party I have named, will effect much good. Self-interest has a powerful influence on the human heart, and, blinded by it, too many of the wealthy allow their wretched dependents to starve, lest the rates should become too heavy. If there was a fund to defray the expense of sending destitute strangers from Cork to their native parishes, it would prevent unutterable calamities. Many hundreds of these wretched creatures are to be seen in the dismal lanes and poor suburbs of our city, craving a morsel of food from beings almost as miserable as they are; and during the night, they lay themselves down to sleep upon the earth, exposed to wet and cold. These doomed beings are called vagrants, and sturdy beggars, and under that appellation are seized upon, should they appear in the public streets, confined like malefactors, without food until next morning, and then placed in carts, and, with two pennyworth of bread each, are driven four or five miles from the city, and left there to perish. Many of them die in the fields, and many find their way back again to Cork. No compassion, no helping hand for these miscalled vagrants—every heart steeled against them. The Relief Commissioners are too ready to listen to reports of frauds upon the committees; but they have no ears for the complaints of the poor against their cruel oppressors. I feel so strongly on this painful subject, I am unwilling to write more, lest I should harrow your feelings.

With kindest compliments to every member of your family, I am,

With profound respect,

Dear Mrs. Rathbone,

Yours affectionately,

THEOBALD MATHEW.

Cork: July 30. 1847.

MY DEAR MRS. RATHBONE,—I regret having caused you and Mr. Rathbone so much pain and trouble. If the 'Macedonian' had put into any other harbour in Ireland, I should not have suffered so much from disappointment. As the 'Reliance' is now in our port, I hope some arrangement, satisfactory to all, will be made. I feel as intensely for the destitute in Galway, Kerry, Mayo, Sligo, Clare, and Donegal, as I do for the perishing poor of Cork. It was the expectations raised, and about to be blighted, that made me so unhappy.

Believe me,

With highest esteem,

Dear Madam,

Your devoted and affectionate

THEOBALD MATHEW.

Cork: August 26, 1847.

MY DEAR MRS. RATHBONE,—Ten thousand thanks for your welcome intelligence, and the charitable interference by which you accomplished so desirable an object. To Mr. Rathbone I am also deeply grateful.

The 300 barrels I shall carefully husband, dispensing their valuable contents like a precious treasure. The lamented death of the benevolent Mr. Beale has prevented me from applying for the flour. I cannot express the delight I felt at meeting my dear friend Samuel at Buncrana. It was so unexpected, and yet so timely, to see him amidst the wilds of Innishowen. I am about to start for Dublin, and have only time to assure you and Mr. Rathbone of the enduring gratitude of,

With profound respect,

Dearest Mrs. Rathbone,

Your devoted and affectionate

THEOBALD MATHEW.

On meeting a friend in the street about this time, Father Mathew, with whom the removal or expulsion of the country paupers, referred to in his letter to Mrs. Rathbone, was uppermost in his mind, at once enquired if his friend had anything to do with those proceedings.

'No, indeed, Father Mathew, I have not; I do n't approve of them.'

'I am delighted, my dear sir, to hear that you have not joined in such a movement. You know, as a Christian man, you are bound to relieve, as far as your means will admit, the distress of every human creature, no matter if he comes from the centre of Africa.'

He did good himself, and encouraged others to do good. A young gentleman of the city, over whose youth he had watched like a father, came to him one day during the very height of the famine, to ask his advice as to what he was to do with a miserable half-starved female infant, that he had discovered, while passing through a field, lying asleep in the arms of its dead mother. 'I came to you, sir, to know what I am to do with the child.' 'God sent you that child, my dear; you can't do better than rear it,' was Father Mathew's reply. No proposal could have been more startling to the young man, who was not yet of age; but the influence of Father Mathew was so great over his friends, that the advice—embarrassing as it must have been—was adopted, and the poor child of the famine was carefully reared by her young preserver.

The ranks of the clergy were decimated in many districts of the country, and the death of an active member of a relief committee was a matter of the most ordinary occurrence. Neither wealth nor luxury could keep the Famine Fever at bay. Born in the hovel, of want and squalor, it was carried about in rags from house to house; and often when the members of a family had to leave or return to their home, they had to struggle through a clamorous group clustered round their door, and to pass through an atmosphere heavy with evil odours. But Father Mathew seemed insensible to everything save the misery he sought to relieve. The famine odour was in his parlour in Cove Street, and at his door, and in the dwellings of the poor whom he daily visited. Nothing, however, could intimidate him. Neither was he disgusted by the most abject or even loathsome squalor. Beneath fetid rags, and accumulated filth, and swarming vermin, he recognised his fellow-creature, made in the image and likeness of his Divine Master. With the courage of the hero, he united the spirit of the Samaritan.

Indeed at no period of his career had Father Mathew a stronger claim upon the admiration of mankind, or the love and veneration of his country. In his own city the feeling in his favour was intense. He was the guardian angel of the poor, their surest and best resource. This feeling found public expression in the month of July 1847, at an entertainment to Captain De Kay (Commander of the 'Macedonian'), and other American gentlemen. The writer had the honour to preside on that occasion; and a short passage from the address of the Chairman, and another from that of the accomplished and brilliant advocate, the late Francis Walsh, familiarly known as Frank Walsh, will afford a just idea, not only of the estimation in which Father Mathew was then held by his fellow-citizens, but of the solid services to humanity on which the public sentiment based. The Chairman said:—

The awful visitation of the last nine months has exhibited Father Mathew in a higher and holier light, in a position and character more sacred than we had hitherto beheld him—as the champion of the poor. Before, he was a leader, at the head of a great popular movement, and sustained by the enthusiasm of the whole country; but he has magnanimously given up that great mission for a time, to remain in Cork, as a protector and friend to the poor; to shield them from the indifference of those who are too often wrongly entrusted with authority, and who, in their devotion to an inhuman policy and a hateful doctrine, are too often indifferent to the misery and sufferings of the wretched recipients of a relief grudgingly given, and pinchingly doled out. I say, then, that the last nine months have endeared

Father Mathew more to us, and have united him closer to our affections, than have all his previous labours and splendid triumphs.

The pleasing theme was thus enlarged upon by Frank Walsh, or, as he was popularly designated, 'the Counsellor':—

What your Chairman has told our American friends of the last nine months' labours of Father Mathew, would be imperfect if we did not also add this to it,—that, while attending with an extraordinary vigilance, with indefatigable watchfulness, with intense care and eager anxiety to the distribution of the food in every petty detail, watching that no official should counteract, no mean minister should frustrate, no petty motives should restrict the value of the bounty, or diminish it to those on whom it was intended to confer relief, he has been in the midst of pestilence, in the most frightful dens, where fever exhibited its most awful and pestilential effects, hanging over the bed where not one but three were stretched, in a room where not one but sixteen were in disease together, perishing of fever. He has risked his life hourly and daily. But in the midst of all his cares, and labours, and toils, it is right to let the world know, as we in Cork do, that besides being one of the most distinguished men of our time, he is one of the most hard working, patient, zealous Catholic priests with whom God has blessed mankind. He had been in Cork, his selected and adopted city, before his name became so justly celebrated, so beloved and honoured for his devotion and anxiety to the poor, that he was one of those most revered as a Christian clergyman; and now, independently of the glorious movement which he represents, by his personal virtues, his charity, his amiability and goodness, he is at present a link of union between Christians of all denominations.

CHAPTER XXXIII.

His Influence with the People of Ulster—A strange Question and a laconic Reply—The incurable Cancer—A poor Breakfast—The disgusted Devotee—Christmas-boxes—The Great Duke.

SO long as there was a necessity for his presence, Father Mathew remained in Cork, whose people had, as he thought, the first claim upon his exertions; but the moment he could safely quit his post, without desertion of duty, he was again off to some distant part of the country, on his temperance mission. In the month of August he was entertained at a soirée in Londonderry, in which city he was hailed with enthusiasm by men who hated his church and not occasionally misrepresented its principles and its teaching; and in the following October we find him in Coleraine, in which thoroughly Ulster town the priest from Munster was received with a respect which was as sincere as it was, in many instances, involuntary. 'Why did you kneel to him?' asked one of the 'True Blues' to another. The answer was a testimony to the influence of the man—'Who the d—l could resist him?—who could help it?—no one could refuse him anything he asked.' Some came to their doors in a spirit half bitter half jeering; but, strong Protestants and Presbyterians as they were, they yielded to an unaccountable impulse, and, falling on their knees, humbly received the blessing of a man of God.

It was in Dublin, some years before, that he said rather an amusing thing in reply to a person to whom he was in the act of administering the pledge. He was hard at work, going rapidly through a large batch, making the sign of the Cross on the foreheads of his postulants, when the man whose brow he then touched said, 'Father Mathew, here am I, an Orangeman, kneeling to you, and you blessing me.' 'God bless you, my dear, I did n't care if you were a *Lemon-man*,' was his reply, as he rapidly passed on, amidst an audible titter from the batch.

Father Mathew had been severely censured by the leading London journal for having dared to stop Her Majesty's mail in the High Street of Athy. On that occasion there were some thousands of solid reasons against the possibility of stirring the coach, in the shape and substance of a dense crowd of people eager to take the pledge. On another occasion, however, the mail was arrested, though for a short time, and from a different motive. The guard had given the signal, the coachman had flourished his whip, and the horses were in motion, when a cry was raised of 'Stop the coach!' A respectable-looking lady, well known as a leading Methodist, was seen running after the vehicle, her bonnet held on only by its strings, and her hair streaming wildly about her face. At so strange a spectacle, the guard was much surprised, and ordered the coachman to pull up. 'I have special business with Father Mathew,' said the lady, as soon as she had sufficiently recovered her breath to make herself intelligible. Father Mathew put his head out of the window, and enquired what the special business was. 'Father Mathew,' said the excellent woman, 'I pray daily that the Lord may preserve you in humility; has He done so?' 'Yes, ma'am,' was Father Mathew's laconic reply, as the coachman, who had overheard the brief dialogue, laid his whip rather smartly on his impatient team.

The three following paragraphs will show that in the months of November and December 1847, he was as active and energetic as at any previous period of his career. The first appeared on the 3rd of November:—

FATHER MATHEW

Leaves town this evening on a Temperance Tour. He is to preach and administer the pledge in Derry, on Sunday the 7th; in Sligo, on Wednesday the 10th; and in Strabane, on Sunday the 14th. He will return to Cork on Thursday the 18th inst.

The second appeared on the 25th of November :—

FATHER MATHEW

Left town last night to preach and administer the pledge at Omagh, county of Tyrone, and also to attend a grand Temperance Soirée at Strabane. He will return to Cork on Saturday, the 4th of December

And the third on the 31st of December :—

FATHER MATHEW

Left town this morning for Limerick, where he is to hold Temperance meetings, and to administer the pledge on New Year's Day, and Sunday. He will return on Tuesday next.

There was one visit he never failed to pay every day during which he remained in Cork : it was the last which he made ere he set out on his journeys, and it was the first which he made on his return. It was to the bedside of a once beautiful girl, who was slowly dying of an incurable cancer. Some years before, she had been confided to his care by her friends in a neighbouring county. When she arrived first in Cork, and gave herself up to his spiritual charge, she was joyous and light-hearted, and her artless gaiety of character lent an additional charm to her uncommon beauty. She was placed in a respectable establishment as an assistant, and was happy and contented with her situation. One day—a sad day for her—a fellow-assistant, who happened to be near her, was tearing a piece of some strong material which a customer had purchased, and in the effort to tear this article, he struck the poor girl violently in the bosom. It was a fatal but an innocent blow. Soon cancer began to spread its deadly fibres through her system, and then commenced the long martyrdom which prepared her for the crown that was to reward her sufferings and her fortitude. Father Mathew, who had watched over her with a father's solicitude, at once came to her assistance, and saved her from the hospital or the workhouse. He supplied her with every necessary, and surrounded her with such comforts as her miserable case was susceptible of; but the sweetest consolation which he afforded her, was when he sat by her bed of pain, and read for her, and prayed for her, and wiped away the drops of agony that stood upon her transparent brow. Sickness imparted an ethereal character to her beauty; and the sweet smile of patience that triumphed over the weakness of poor human nature, had in it something wondrously touching. The light of heaven seemed to chase away the shadow of the grave from that gentle face, whose look of resignation haunted her faithful friend in his journeys, and inspired him with fortitude to bear up against many a trial and many a care. How earnestly she longed for his return! how her large eyes brightened, and her wasted features flushed, as she caught the first sound of his eager step upon the stairs!—for, no matter what the distance he had to come, or the toil he had undergone, he neither changed his dress, nor allowed himself a moment's rest, until he had seen 'his poor Ellen.' The end that was inevitable came at last, and he had the consolation of closing those loving eyes in the holy rest of a happy death, and of laying her in a grave shadowed and perfumed by fragrant shrubs.

A little incident, which occurred in one of his journeys after the fury of the famine had passed, touched him greatly, insomuch as it evinced the poverty and privation still endured by the working classes. While proceeding on his way, he observed a pretty little girl, not more than ten years of age, trotting lightly along the road, carrying on her arm a small basket carefully covered up. With her light quick trot she was keeping pace for some time with the horses. His attention being attracted to the child, he ordered the driver to stop, and called her towards him. 'Where are you going, my dear, in such a hurry?' enquired Father Mathew. Dropping a courtesy, the little girl said, 'Down beyant, sir, with my father's breakfast.' 'And what have you got for your father's breakfast, my dear?' 'Pittaties, sir.' 'Have you nothing with the potatoes—not a drop of milk?' 'No, 'ndeed, sir, an' he's glad to get that same,' replied the child. 'Have you not even a pinch of salt with them, my dear?' said Father Mathew. 'Salt, sir!' exclaimed the little girl, opening wide a great pair of hazel eyes, in amazement at the suggestion of such a luxury—'why then cock him up with salt!' 'Then, my dear, here is something to buy salt with, and here is something for yourself too,' said Father Mathew, who left the child radiant with delight at her good fortune in meeting so liberal a benefactor.

The pious women who were accustomed to attend the Friary on Christmas morning, were usually edified by a sermon from Father Mathew, appropriate to the festival of the day. His discourses on those occasions breathed the spirit of peace and holiness with which his own soul was filled. The disappointment at his omission of the customary sermon was a source of much discomfort to his devoted followers, the regular attenders. One morning he was expected to preach at the early Mass, and the little church was filled with worshippers, a considerable number of whom held lighted candles, to enable them to read their prayer books on that dark winter morning. There was one old lady, who, with spectacles on her nose, was devoutly reading her book, and awaiting in calm contentment the appearance of her favourite preacher. At length there was the flutter of a white surplice seen at the door of the sacristy, and the clergyman made his appearance; but, instead of the noble countenance of Father Mathew, to whom the robes of his ministry added new beauty, the congregation beheld the commonplace features of a fat little gentleman, whose ability as a pulpit orator was of the humblest kind. The moment the full consciousness of her disappointment broke upon the old lady, the candle fell from her relaxed grasp on the floor, and, with a voice in which disgust and bitterness were blended, she audibly exclaimed, 'Why, then, 't is *you* that are welcome to us this blessed morning!'

Christmas-boxes were in Father Mathew's esteem a time-honoured institution, as all his young relatives and many of his young friends could testify. It, however, occasionally happened that some pressing claim of poverty, some more than usually pathetic tale of widow or of orphan, even of repentant profligate, either altogether blighted the full-blown hopes of his nephews and nieces, or reduced the expected present, from being something highly acceptable, to being something, in their eyes at least, very contemptible. Thus, on one occasion, the promised pony was represented by a book; for the money intended for the purchase of the pony had gone to release from the army the only son of a miserable widow, who had been forsaken by her boy for dreams of glory, and visions of fame and fortune, to be won at the bayonet's point. The nephews were indignant with the widow, for having a son who could think of 'listing,' or who, having embraced the profession of a soldier, could sneakingly permit himself to be ignominiously bought out. Now though many a recruit 'took the shilling,' under the influence of drink, it was to the Apostle of Temperance the disconsolate parent of the would-be hero appealed in her distress. On one of these occasions the recruit was the only support of an aged mother, and the father of six helpless children. Father Mathew's exchequer was at its lowest ebb at this time—it was in 1847; so that between the mother's lamentations for 'her darlin' boy, who was the comfort of her ould heart, and the light of her two eyes,' and his own empty pockets, the priest knew not what to do. At last, the idea of appealing to the 'Great Duke,' flashed on his bewildered mind. He did so, on the impulse of the moment, and met with a prompt result; for the noble Duke thus replied by return of post:—

Field Marshal the Duke of Wellington presents his compliments to the Very Rev. Mr. Mathew: he could not refuse his application, and has directed the discharge of the soldier he desired.

CHAPTER XXXIV.

He is attacked with Paralysis—His Fortitude and **Resignation—** His Recovery hailed with Enthusiasm.

IN the year 1848, which, as we have seen by the paragraphs recently quoted, he began so auspiciously, he suffered the heavy penalty of his ten years of unparalleled exertions. His rigorous fasting had also much to do with the catastrophe which occurred. When remonstrated with respecting this severity of life, and implored to relax his austerity in some degree, his answer was—'I am the strongest man in Ireland.' The time was now at hand when that boast could never be repeated.

During the Lent of 1848, which he observed with his customary strictness, and during which he devoted himself with even more than usual fervour to the various duties of the ministry, he was suddenly struck with paralysis. This was the commencement of a sad tribulation, which lasted, with more or less intermission, to the hour of his death, which took place in eight years after. When about rising, as was his invariable rule, at an early hour in the morning, he fell on the ground at his bedside. The noise of his fall at once roused his Secretary, who rushed to the room, and found him stretched on the floor. He was assisted back into bed, and Dr. O'Connor—who, besides being his physician, was also his attached personal friend—was sent for. Alarmed at the intelligence, the doctor hastened to attend him. 'I was sorry, sir, to have heard that you were ill—what has happened?' said Dr. O'Connor. 'My dear doctor,' replied Father Mathew, in the calmest voice, and with the sweetest smile, 'I am paralysed.' 'Paralysed, sir!' 'Yes, my dear friend, I am paralysed in one side; and when I tried to stand this morning, I fell on the floor.' The doctor had never met with such a patient; for here was a man who spoke of a grave calamity as if it were a matter of the very smallest importance. The calmness, which was genuine, was the result of high moral courage and Christian resignation. The blow was great, but the fortitude was still greater.

Dr. O'Connor's description of that morning's professional visit is interesting:—

On further enquiry (says the doctor) I found that the leg and arm of one side were paralysed, but not entirely powerless, and that he also had suffered pain in the head for from some days previously. I remained with him whilst leeches were being applied to his temples by his friend and faithful disciple, A. F. Roche. He entertained us during the time with anecdotes of his temperance travels, and never appeared more cheerful, though conscious that he was labouring under a visitation which more than any other brings terror to the mind of a patient. He remarked 'it was not much matter to him how it terminated. If a priest had done his duty, and was prepared, the time of his death was of little consequence.' Of all the community, among whom the news of his illness soon spread, he was the only one that appeared unconcerned.

With consternation was the sad intelligence received by the local community; and wherever it was heard, it evoked the deepest feeling of sympathy and regret. Crowds surrounded his door, and exhibited, by their awe-struck and mournful aspect, the dismay and sorrow which pervaded every breast. In a few days, however, the anxiety of the public mind was relieved by the glad tidings of his gradual recovery. Day by day he mended, and about the second week in May he seemed to have got over the effects of this his first attack. His recovery was hailed with universal delight, and numerous addresses of congratulation proved to him how strong was the hold which he had upon the affections of his countrymen.

'His mind,' says Dr. O'Connor, 'was not apparently affected by this attack, and the weakness in the limbs soon diminished so much, that the entreaties of friends or physicians could no longer prevent him from resuming his labour in the temperance cause.'

On the 19th of July he left Cork for Dublin, and did not return until the 1st of August. And during the period which intervened between that date and the time of his leaving Ireland for America, he divided his time between his temperance mission, his priestly duties, and his efforts to relieve distress, promote industry, and assist every good work.

Previous to his attack, he had visited the Irish metropolis for the purpose of giving his testimony in favour of Charles Gavan Duffy, who was then about to be placed on his third trial for alleged political offences. Father Mathew entertained a sincere respect for the truth and earnestness of the Young Ireland party, and he naturally admired the ability and eloquence of their writings and speeches. Besides, he was grateful to Mr. Duffy, who had afforded valuable aid to the temperance cause, and had written and spoken of the Apostle of Temperance in the most enthusiastic terms of praise. 'I consider Mr. Duffy a man of the highest integrity and principle. I would not think him a man likely by any means to entertain or favour any project of anarchy or spoliation of property,' said Father Mathew, when giving evidence for his friend. Had he lived to witness the honourable and distinguished position taken by Mr. Duffy, as one of the ablest and most influential public men and ministers in the colony of Victoria, Father Mathew would have greatly rejoiced.

As will be seen by his letter to Judge Lumpkin, he was not insensible to the sufferings of his country; but though he ardently longed for her happiness and prosperity, he sedulously abstained from taking any part whatever in politics. In his earlier life, when questions affecting the liberty of his Church were at stake, he sympathised with the efforts by which Catholic Emancipation was eventually won, and did not fail to exercise his undoubted right as an elector to secure the return of a candidate favourable to a liberal policy; but having on one occasion induced a number of poor voters to risk the consequences of supporting the popular candidate, and having been disappointed in promises made to him in their behalf, he abstained from that hour from taking any part in elections, or mixing himself up in any way with politics or with party. This was a fortunate circumstance, as it removed one formidable barrier to the success of his temperance mission.

It would be a dreary task to follow him through the misery which met him at every step, and surrounded him on every side, during the period that preceded his departure. This misery depressed his spirit, and sickened his very soul, though he courageously fought against its influence, and spared no effort to mitigate it, by relieving it. What man could do, he did—more, indeed, than any ten other men could have done; but his heart died within him as he found how little was the result of all his zeal, his energy, and his self-sacrifice. The movement, too, had lost its former spirit. Many of the rooms had been closed in the terrible famine year; and the bands had, in several instances, been broken up, in consequence of the death, the poverty, or the emigration of their principal members. The pledge was, on the whole, fairly kept; but not a few had yielded to the deplorable influence of evil times, and had sought in the maddening draught temporary oblivion of their sorrows. The banner which once proudly floated in the air, now drooped on its staff. The famine had struck the cause as well as decimated the ranks of its followers.

The following letters, addressed to his devoted friends the Rathbones, afford a last glimpse of the state of the country in

1848, and the profound interest which he took in the hopes and disappointments of its unhappy people :—

Cork : February 7, 1848.

My dearest Madam,—In compliance with your expressed wish, I would have immediately stated to you my impressions as to the prospects of unhappy Ireland, and what appeared to me most advisable in the present destitute condition of our wretched people: but as nothing can be accomplished without pecuniary assistance, I could not reconcile it to my feelings to address you on such a subject. As you have again condescended to apply to me for information, and have stated the benevolent source whence relief can be obtained, without adding to the already too numerous appeals to your private funds, I shall not longer hesitate to lay my sentiments before you.—

The British Association has devoted its supplies of food and money to the relief of destitution in twenty-two poor-law unions, which were pointed out to them by the poor-law commissioners as unable to pay rates sufficient to feed the starving multitude. The children are the peculiar objects of this supplemental charity. There are in the unions not favoured with a portion of this British charity, many thousands who crave a share of this blessing. The unhappy Gregory Clause in the new poor law operates cruelly on the cottier tenants. All tenants of this class who hold more than a quarter of an acre of land are excluded from poor law relief, unless they give up their little farms. Horrified at the prospect of being paupers for ever, they cling to their cottages and farms, and perish by slow starvation rather than abandon their homes; for the moment the tenant leaves his house to enter the workhouse, it is levelled to the ground. Many parents would be able to keep themselves from the workhouse, if a little assistance were given in the way of food to their helpless children. Widows and unmarried females could support themselves, if knitting, plain work, &c. &c. were supplied them. To meet these pressing wants, and to train up the rising generation in habits of industry, has long been my anxious desire. To its accomplishment I have devoted my strenuous efforts. Supplying small farmers with cheap seeds, such as turnip, flax, and potatoes; and assisting industrial schools, in which the children, male and female, are instructed and supplied with the material for remunerative labour, such as weaving, spinning, gardening, &c. &c. In all these efforts for the improvement of the habits of our people, I have succeeded beyond my most sanguine expectations. As the destitute of the city of Cork have multitudinous resources, I have extended my exertions to various parts of Ireland, especially Tipperary, Limerick, Galway, the King's and Queen's Counties. The progress of improvement is slow, and much misery must be endured. But we are, I confidently believe, in a transition to a better social condition. We will soon see a new Ireland.

The recent special commission in Limerick, Clare, and Tipperary, bloody as the issue has been, has proved that, guilty as our wretched people have been, they were not as desperately wicked as represented. That there was not a conspiracy amongst them to murder the landed gentry. That their own class were generally the victims, and that the struggle for the possession of land was the dire cause of the shedding of human blood. The commission has also shed additional lustre on the great temperance movement. *Not a single teetotaller, out of the millions, was implicated in the guilt of blood-shedding. The convicts were all whisky drinkers.* It is to be believed that Ireland would be the most moral country on the face of the earth, if all its inhabitants were total abstainers.

With highest respect,

Dearest Mrs. Rathbone,

Your most devoted and affectionate friend,

THEOBALD MATHEW.

Mrs. Rathbone.

Cork: May 5, 1848.

MY DEAREST MADAM,—Though not an advocate for the extensive cultivation of potatoes, I am of opinion that, to enable our destitute people to recover from the effects of the late calamity, no other food could be so easily had to supply their many wants this season. I know of no object more worthy of your and dear Mr. Rathbone's benevolent sympathy, than the assisting our industrious cottier tenantry to cultivate their little farms, by giving them seed. The generous gift of fifty pounds,* which you have so considerately confided to me for distribution, has been very timely. Now that the season is fast advancing, it will be the means of employing the hitherto desponding farmer and his family in the cultivation of ground that would otherwise remain as waste, and of restoring them to comparative comfort and happiness.

I trust, however, that Government will do something for us, either to assimilate our condition with England, or grant other salutary concessions.

I am, with profound esteem,

Dearest Madam,

Your devoted and affectionate

THEOBALD MATHEW.

Mrs. Rathbone.

* American funds.

Cork: July 21, 1848.

My dear Mr. Rathbone,— . . . You will learn with much gratification, that I have been enabled by your last remittance from the funds of the good people of Boston to wind up in a satisfactory way the affairs of the different charities with which I was connected. They are now able to support themselves by the fruits of their industry.

I saw last week, as I passed through the country, many luxuriant fields of potatoes and turnips, from seed I was enabled to distribute. But, what I deem of more importance, I have witnessed habits of cleanliness, economy, and industry, which promise to be permanent, and to diffuse themselves gradually through the most neglected and the rudest portions of the peasantry. We are, I trust, on the eve of better times for poor Ireland. May God requite all who have contributed to do her good. Presenting affectionate remembrance to the family at Green Bank, believe me,

My dear Mr. Rathbone,

Your most grateful

Theobald Mathew.

W. Rathbone, Esq

Cork: August 13, 1848.

My dear Mr. Rathbone,—I regret that the melancholy task of announcing the *total destruction* of the potato crop has devolved upon me. The blight appeared three weeks back; but it seemed confined to particular places, and affected only the stalks; since then wet weather has been so constant, the blight has become general, and the tubers are rotting with frightful rapidity.

The labouring poor, thank God, are not involved in this calamity, for they have abandoned the *con-acre* system, and depend upon money wages, or the poor law; but the small farmers made a last effort to retrieve their almost desperate affairs, and risked their all upon this season's potato crop. Thousands, who have endured every privation rather than surrender their little farms, and consign their wives and children to the hopeless support of a workhouse, are now in despair. I am grievously disappointed myself. In every way I encouraged the propagation of potatoes. The large sum I received from you, and all that I could beg or borrow myself, I expended in the purchase of the, I now believe, doomed potato. In travelling through the country, that but a few days ago bloomed with a luxuriant harvest, I found the atmosphere everywhere tainted with noxious vapours from the putrefying vegetable, and the wretched people bathed in tears. I could only mingle my tears with theirs.

May the God of all consolation console them in this their great tribulation. Well may they exclaim, with the Prophet Jeremiah, 'All you that pass by this way, attend and see if there be any sorrow like my sorrow.'

With regard to myself, I have only to say, that my health is improving, and if I were free, I would gladly abandon this land of horrors and misery.

Presenting affectionate remembrance to Mrs. Rathbone and your beloved family, I am,

My dear Mr. Rathbone,

Your most grateful and devoted friend,

THEOBALD MATHEW.

W. Rathbone, Esq.

The consequences of the famine are matters of history, and are to be found principally in the sale and transfer of a vast amount of property, and that wondrous emigration which has flowed from the shores of Ireland in a continued stream to this hour, though with more or less diminished volume.

From October 1849 to August 1859, the gross amount realised by the property sold in the Court of Encumbered Estates reached to the prodigious sum of 25,190,839*l*. The sacrifice of property during the first years of the operation of this Court was sad to contemplate. It ruined many and enriched others. It annihilated the owner, robbed the later encumbrancers, and conferred estates for half their real value on purchasers lucky or daring enough to speculate in land at such a period of general depression and alarm.

The famine imparted an extraordinary impulse to Irish migration and emigration. It is ascertained that for the ten years previous to 1841, about 630,000 persons had left Ireland permanently, either to go abroad, or to settle in some other portion of the United Kingdom. From 1841, to 1851, including the Famine years so called, the number of persons leaving permanently, was 1,640,000. From 1851 to 1861, the number was 1,250,000. And if we add 200,000 between 1861 and 1863, who quitted their country ostensibly for ever, we shall have a total of 3,720,000. The great bulk of this enormous subtraction from the population of a single country, emigrated to the United States, Canada, and Australia. A considerable number established themselves in the manufacturing districts and great towns of England and Scotland. It is now computed that the contribution of population from Ireland to the United States, has given to that vast continent the largest portion of its present inhabitants—that is, that the Irish, and the descendants of the Irish, constitute, if it may be so expressed, the largest of the various nationalities which go to make up the whole of its existing population. In England and Scotland, according to the Census Commissioners, there were in 1861, no less than 805,703 of Irish, born in Ireland—to say nothing of their children who were born in those countries.

The rush from Ireland to England during the year 1847 assumed the character of a panic—an unarmed people flying before the face of a pursuing enemy. From the 1st of January to the 1st of November of that year, 278,000 persons landed in Liverpool alone; and of these, 123,000 sailed from that port to foreign countries—the remainder scattering themselves over various parts of England. The total emigration abroad for that year was 215,444. It increased to 249,721 in 1851.

To two very opposite influences were principally owing this extraordinary Exodus—namely, compulsion and persuasion. Hunger and evictions on the one hand—inducements and assistance on the other.

From 1846 to 1848, both years included, the number of ejectments brought in the various courts was 32,193, and the number of persons evicted was 140,835. From 1849 to 1853, both years included, the number of evictions was 47,115, and the number of persons evicted was 239,000. Which would give a total of evictions, during the periods specified, of 79,308, and of persons evicted, 379,845. In 1850, the number of persons evicted was 74,000.

Among the inducements to emigrate, including labour and employment of different kinds, were the invitations from relative to relative—from the son or daughter, to the father and mother, or to the brothers and sisters; and these invitations were accompanied by large remittances, money saved from hard honest toil in a strange country. In 1847, these remittances amounted to 200,000*l.* In 1848, they rose to 460,000*l.*; in 1850 and 1851, they were about 1,000,000*l.* each of those years; and in 1853, they amounted to the enormous sum of 1,490,000*l.*! It is officially ascertained that the total remittances from the Irish emigrants to the States, to Canada, and to Australia, to their relatives in Ireland, amounted up to 1863 to 12,642,000*l.* But this does not represent the entire The Emigration Commissioners, in their report for 1863, thus refer to these remittances:—

It is necessary to repeat that these returns are very imperfect, as they contain none of the remittances through the post or through private hands, or through any of the banks or mercantile houses, which decline to furnish us with information. It would scarcely be unreasonable to estimate *the amount of which there are no returns at half as much again as that of which there are returns.*

According to this statement, the gross amount received by the Irish at home from their kindred abroad, cannot have been less than 19,000,000*l.*—a sum almost fabulous in its magnitude.

In the history of the world there is nothing to surpass this, for generosity, self-sacrifice, and attachment to family and race. If the Irish have their faults—as what people have not?—they nobly atone for them by the most exalted virtues.

Among the results brought about by the great national calamity, was the creation of a better feeling between persons of different religious belief, who became oblivious of doctrinal distinctions in a moment of common peril, and who caught from the very nature of their sacred work the sublime spirit of Christian charity. There were some miserable exceptions, it is true, in which the mortal agony of the destitute was sought to be availed of for the promotion of unholy triumphs over conscience; but such disgraceful attempts were reprobated by every man of sense and feeling in the land, and only assisted, by the contrast, to render more pure and exalted the devoted and disinterested zeal exhibited by those who ministered to their afflicted neighbours as men to men, as brethren to brethren. Mr. Trevelyan, in the article in the 'Edinburgh Review,' to which I have before referred, bears testimony to the harmonious cooperation of the clergy of different Churches:—

> Those (he says) who had never before exchanged words or looks of kindness, met to cooperate in this great work of charity, and good men recognised each other's merit under the distinctions by which they had been previously separated. The Protestant and Roman Catholic clergy vied with each other in their exertions for the famishing and fever-stricken people, and in numerous instances their lives became a sacrifice to the discharge of exhausting, harassing and dangerous duties. To the priests, all were indebted for the readiness with which they made their influence over their flocks subservient to the cause of order; and the minister of religion was frequently summoned to the aid of the public officer, when all other means of restraining the excited multitude had failed.

Appalling as had been the suffering of the Irish people, and terrible as had been the destruction of human life, that suffering would have been far more appalling, and that destruction of life would have been far more terrible, but for the noble charity which had been displayed by the people of Great Britain, and the people of America, France, and many other countries of the world. From every quarter of the globe contributions poured in upon afflicted Ireland; and had it not been for that generous cooperation, which linked nation with nation in one common bond of fraternal sympathy for a suffering member of the family of nations, there would have been more than a million red graves within the circle of the Irish shores. It is difficult to conjecture what was the actual amount of money transmitted to Ireland through various sources and channels; but independently of moneys advanced and granted by Government, or raised by taxation, which amounted in all to about 10,000,000*l.*, there was considerably more than 2,000,000*l.* received and administered through societies or individuals. Mr. Jonathan Pim, who drew up the reliable report of 'The Transactions of the Central Relief Committee of the Society of Friends during the Famine in Ireland,' states that local and central relief associations distributed sums that could not have fallen far short of a million and a half. In these sums are not included the funds received and administered through individuals; nor the money sent by the Irish in America, either to assist their friends at home, or to enable them to emigrate. The Friends had entrusted to their care money and breadstuffs amounting on the whole to about 200,000*l.*; and to their honour be it said, they administered tneir trust wisely and well. The Society of Friends of England contributed over 42,000*l.* of that amount; the rest principally consisted of contributions from America. The British Relief Association, established in London, sent 391,700*l.* to Ireland. Another 100,000*l.* was sent from England through various religious bodies. These large sums are entirely independent of the vast number of contributions sent by persons of every class to private individuals in Ireland. Nor did the poor country itself display less generosity; for, notwithstanding the untold amount of private relief given—given daily and hourly—of which no one but the donor and recipient was ever aware, the local contributions officially announced for 1846 and 1847 exceeded 300,000*l.*

The Catholic Bishops and Clergy in England and Scotland stimulated to the utmost the willing charity of their flocks in aid of their suffering brethren in the old country; but to no one was Ireland more indebted for solace and succour in her hour of misery, than to the saintly and venerable Dr. Briggs, the late Catholic Bishop of Beverley, who has since gone to receive the reward of his long life of usefulness and virtue.

It is only necessary to add that the cry of an afflicted people, suffering from a calamity permitted by Providence, for wise purposes no doubt, elicited a response honouring to our common humanity.

There was something still nobler than the charity of those who came to the relief of the starving Irish—that was the sublime Christian resignation with which the stricken people bowed to the dispensation of Divine Providence. 'It is the will of the Lord,' was ever on the lips of the sufferers. 'They died as martyrs died, and God gave them a reward great beyond this world's conception,' was Father Mathew's frequent assertion, when referring to that disastrous period.

From an able and appreciative article on the career and services of Father Mathew, which appeared in the 'Dublin University' of June 1849, and which derived its materials principally from a sketch from the pen of the late Denis Owen Madden, who had been known from his boyhood to the illustrious subject of his brief but brilliant memoir, I take the concluding passage. The testimony is that of a Protestant contributor to the accredited organ of the Protestant Church of Ireland; and on that account it is the more valuable for my purpose:—

But though the teetotal movement has received a heavy check by the social consequences of the famine, a vast deal of good has been effected. A popular opinion has been raised against drunkenness; and the fact that tens of thousands of Irishmen were induced to abandon spirituous liquors, is in itself a great moral fact in the history of our country. No one can despair of extraordinary moral alterations in this country, who calmly reflects on the apparent hopelessness, some years since, of expecting a change in the national love of strong drinks.

We honour Father Mathew as a man who has given us good grounds for not despairing of the social regeneration of our people. We respect him for his moral elevation of character, his freedom from selfishness, and his contempt for all vulgar ambition. We see in him a man who has done great public benefits to his own detriment. His private resources he cheerfully expended in the cause of temperance, and has given up his time and care to the service of his countrymen. Such a man, who never abused his great influence for political purposes, deserves to be honoured and regarded with affection as one of the worthies of our island. Praise he has had in abundance. Statesmen in both Houses of Parliament have acknowledged his public services. Journals of opposite parties have testified to his disinterestedness. He has won at the same time the respect of the rich and the affection of the poor. May his health be still spared by Providence to enable him to pursue his virtuous career; and when, at some distant day, he will be called to receive the reward due to those who toil in their Maker's service, may his example allure many to follow in the footsteps of Mathew the philanthropist!

CHAPTER XXXV.

Resolves to visit America—Leaves in the 'Ashburton'—The Voyage out—Arrives in America—His Reception in New York—His Levees—The Daughters of Erin—New York his Head-quarters.

THE Apostle of Temperance now, in 1849, thought it time to fulfil his long-standing engagement to visit America, to which country his thoughts had of late constantly been directed. The enterprise, so full of risk to one who had been seriously affected by his attack in the Lent of 1848, was undertaken quite in opposition to the wish and remonstrance of his physician and friends. In his interesting communication to the author, Dr. O'Connor refers to Father Mathew's condition at this time :—

Though a cloud had passed over his mind, and he was no longer the animated brilliant advocate of temperance—though his gate was every day more enfeebled, and intellectual labour became a struggle—still he worked with more ardour than at any time previously, as if he were the more anxious to utilise a life which he felt was now drawing to a close. He was always most punctual in obeying the instructions of his physicians, as far as referred to taking medicines, or submitting to very painful operations, such as cupping, blisters, and setons, which he had to endure. But if the physician attempted to control him in the performance of what he considered to be the duty of his life, he became powerless. A proof of this was soon exhibited, when Father Mathew resolved to go to America to propagate the principle of temperance. His physicians, and those of his friends and relatives who were thought to have most influence with him, waited on him, and urged on him the madness of encountering such labour in the then state of his health. But it was all in vain; he persevered and accomplished his object.

Having taken an affectionate leave of his family and friends, whom he felt he might never meet again in this life, he left for America in the summer of 1849. After a brief stay in Liverpool, as the guest of his devoted friends the Rathbones, he embarked in the ship 'Ashburton,' accompanied by his secretaries Mr. O'Meara and Mr. Mahony, and sailed on his memorable voyage to the shores of the New World.

The voyage was long and tedious, but otherwise favourable. For the first few days, Father Mathew suffered from that malady which is no respecter of persons, and which makes victims alike of the occupant of the state cabin and the steerage. As soon as he gained his sea legs, he was to be found in every part of the ship, but chiefly among the poor emigrants from Ireland, of whom there were some hundreds on board.

There was not one of the entire number with whom he was not at once at home; for there was scarcely a parish in Ireland with which he was not thoroughly familiar, and with respect to which he had not something to say. It was a comfort to those poor people, whom poverty and misery had driven from their native land, to be spoken to of their home, from which every hour was separating them by additional miles of ocean.

The fore part of the vessel was made the scene of his mission while in the 'Ashburton'—hearing confessions, administering the pledge, lecturing and giving good advice, and occasionally replenishing a too scanty purse out of his own not over-abundant means. The monotony of a voyage without any incident, not even a storm, was very trying to a man who longed for action, and who preferred bustle and excitement to repose. To a family from Tipperary he was indebted for a welcome present of 'milky' eggs, which were most acceptable, as the fresh provisions were every day falling rather short. A fog of three days' duration did not tend to render the voyage more agreeable. At length, after a trip fully three times as long as is now made by a 'Cunard, the ship reached Staten Island; and before Father Mathew well knew where he was, he found himself swinging over the side in a chair, and placed in a boat belonging to Mr. J. P. Nesmith, who laid hands on the Apostle of Temperance, and bore him off to his mansion, in which everything had been prepared for the reception of the illustrious visitor. It was a kindly act; for it afforded him an opportunity of recruiting after the fatigues of the voyage, and gathering a little strength for the labours consequent upon his public reception, which was to take place the next day.

On Monday, the 2nd of July, 1849, the City of New York bade Father Mathew welcome in the name of America. The Municipal Council, accompanied by deputations from various public bodies and societies, proceeded in the Sylph steamer to Staten Island, to conduct him to the Castle Gardens, where his arrival was awaited by one of the largest assemblages ever seen in that famous city. The Bay of New York presented a noble picture to the eye of the stranger; its bright waters, which were stirred by a smart breeze, being crowded with the ships of almost every nation of the world, whose flags streamed to the wind in honour of the illustrious man who had come to the New World covered with the renown which he had so well earned in the Old. All was bustle and animation, activity and life, betokening the power and progress of a great country in the first flush of its youthful energy. Strains of music floated in the air, and cheers were heard from many a vessel, as the Sylph steamed on her way to Staten Island. On arriving at the island, the municipal authorities were introduced to Father Mathew, who was thus welcomed by Alderman Hawes in the name and on the part of the Common Council of New York:—

REVEREND FATHER,—As the chairman of the committee charged with the arrangements for your reception, the pleasing duty devolves upon me of bidding you welcome, and in the name of the Common

Council of the city of New York, to tender to you its hospitalities. Though now for the first time you tread our shores, be assured, sir, you are no stranger to us. Your well-earned fame—destined, we trust, to be as enduring as that of the noblest and best of heroes and statesmen—has long since preceded you; while your efforts for the amelioration of the condition of your fellow-man, and the results which have hitherto crowned those efforts with such signal success, claim both the admiration and gratitude of our whole people. Not only in the cottage of the peasant, but as well in the mansions of the wealthy and refined, have your labours and influence been exerted, and successfully blessed; and you now stand forth, modestly and unpretendingly, we know, but not the less preeminently, among the chief of the public benefactors and philanthropists of the age. There lies before you in this, our highly favoured country, a wide and extended field of usefulness in the great cause of temperance, in which you have been so long distinguished at home; and while we doubt not the prayer of every sincere patriot and Christian will invoke the blessings of Providence upon your labours—as Americans, holding dear to us the welfare and happiness of our fellow-countrymen, we rejoice in the prospect that here, as abroad, your labours may be alike successful. Congratulating you, sir, on your safe arrival, I again bid you welcome—a cordial, heartfelt welcome to America.

Father Mathew replied in a subdued tone; everything which he saw and heard, the joyous sights and the glad sounds that hailed his arrival, contrasted so strikingly with the gloom and misery which he had left behind him in his own country. The man was not what he had been three years before, just before the famine burst upon the affrighted land. Then he was full of energy and hope; now he was broken down, his heart filled with sorrow and care. There was no time, however, on a day like this, to devote to melancholy retrospect, for there was much work to be gone through before New York was done that day with Father Mathew; besides, a mournful countenance would have been treason to such eager welcome. There were addresses to be received and replies to be delivered without number; for no sooner had one body presented its address, than its place was occupied by a successor, and so on till the honoured object of all this enthusiasm must have been bewildered in his efforts to say something different in reply to each new form of welcome.

The Sylph steamed along the shores of the Bay, which were crowded with dense masses of the population, nearly the whole of whom had turned out, in holiday attire, to receive the Apostle of Temperance. The wild ringing cheer of the Irish might be heard above all, as they occupied every vantage ground that enabled them to catch a glimpse of their beloved countryman, from whose hands many thousands among them had received the pledge in the old country, and from whose hands likewise hundreds of them had received the bread of life in the famine time.

It was considered, by those who were present when Father Mathew entered the Castle Gardens, that never, on any occasion, was the multitude of people greater, or the enthusiasm more intense. New York is, *par excellence*, the city of ovations; but it seemed as if it were resolved to outdo itself in honour of the moral conqueror. The formal welcome was offered to him by his Honour Mayor Woodhull, who invited him to accept the hospitalities of the city. The Mayor happily referred to the special claim which Father Mathew's services to humanity gave him to a public reception on that historic spot :—

On this spot we have been accustomed to receive the most distinguished men of our own and other lands. The statesman, bearing the highest honours of his much loved country, and the victor, fresh from the field of his proud triumphs, have here been greeted with the salutations of the most elevated in authority, and with the general welcome of the citizens of this metropolis. But you, sir, come among us with a highly different and peculiar distinction. The honours which you wear have been accorded to you by those who revere you for your deeds of love and benevolence. Your titles are written on the hearts of the uncounted masses whom your heroic perseverance in the humble acts of mercy and good will have saved from a fate even more dreadful than the grave. Your victories are not made up of the dead and dying left behind in your path, but of living thousands, whom you have rescued from a fate more remorseless than the conqueror's march. Your trophies are seen in the smiling faces and happy homes of the countless multitudes whom you have won from the deepest abyss of wretchedness and despair. The enemy with whom you have grappled is one of the direst to the human race. Frightful are the ravages of plague, and vast the preparations to stay its desolating curse; but the destroying angel of Intemperance has entombed more victims than any pestilence which has ever afflicted the human family. All seasons are its own, and no physician can baffle its downward progress. Quarantines and sanitary precautions cannot check its career. Yet there is one human power that can subdue the enemy of man. It is the moral power of a persuasive, earnest, and benevolent heart, that summons all its affections, and with heroic sublimity concentrates all its energies to the single work to be accomplished. It is this power which you have so successfully exercised, and by which you have attained such astonishing results.

We shall not ask the reader to follow Father Mathew through the pleasing toils of the remainder of that day, and shall leave to the imagination of each to picture to the mind the brilliancy and splendour of the procession which wound its glittering way through the crowded thoroughfares of New York. Bringing him to the Irving House, we shall allow the reporter of the 'Herald' to describe the manner in which the city had provided for the reception of its guest:—

As you enter the hall, a life-like painting of Father Mathew meets your eye at the farther end, right over the bar; and in the lobby window, immediately behind and a little above these, is a beautiful white satin blind, with the inscription, 'Glory be to God on high, and on earth peace to men of good will;' then immediately underneath, the word 'Temperance.' At the foot of this is an exquisitely painted wreath of flowers, with Father Mathew's autograph, in large hand, in the centre. The suit of rooms are on the second floor, and consist of four—a reception parlour, a drawing-room, and a bed-room all on the same range, and communicating with each other, and a dining-room at the other side of the hall.

These rooms are all furnished with the newest and richest furniture, and in the most modern style of fashion. The tables, chairs, and sofas, of the finest massive rosewood; the carpets, tapestry, velvets, and everything else in keeping. The bedstead is also of rosewood, and has a magnificent lace canopy.

At eight o'clock in the evening, the Common Council entertained Father Mathew at a public dinner, at which healths were drunk in glasses of pure 'Croton.' 'There is as much sincerity,' said the temperance leader, 'in water as in wine; and I beg to give, in a full bumper of this pure liquid, the health and prosperity of the Mayor and citizens of New York.'

Gladly did the wearied object of all this enthusiasm avail himself of the first moment to retire to his apartments, and seek in rest new strength for the toils and labours of the morrow—though not in the grand bedstead of rosewood, and beneath the 'magnificent lace canopy,' but in the bed appropriated to Mr. O'Meara, which was in a back room, and away from the noise of the street.

For the next fortnight, Father Mathew held levees in the City Hall, which was daily thronged with visitors of every class and condition, and representing every sect and party in the States. So great was the inconvenience from the crowding on the two first days, that it became necessary to have one day set apart for the reception of ladies, and the next for the reception of gentlemen. And side by side with the belles of New York, or the darker beauties of the Southern States, were the daughters of Erin, from the highest to the humblest—the wives and daughters of the distinguished soldier, the successful physician, the leading lawyer, or the prosperous merchant—or the young girls who had won by honest toil the grand clothes with which they proudly ruffled it amongst the best of them. Father Mathew was delighted and amused with the appearance and manners of these young girls. The dress was grand in the extreme, the accent a beautiful blending of Irish and American, and the language replete with the salient peculiarities of both countries. Their greeting of the priest of their Church, while it was affectionate and reverential, had strong dash of independence in its tone; and they who, in their old home, might have been but too humble, and even servile, now evinced in many ways —in word, in air, in manner, and in carriage—the consciousness of being citizens of a country in which all stood on an equality—at least, in the abstract. 'From what part of the old country are you, my dear?' would Father Mathew enquire, as some unmistakably Irish face presented itself; and when he was told the county and the parish whence his visitor had come, he had something to tell her in return, which brought the colour to her cheek, and the tear to her eye, and perhaps a sob to her throat. What visions of bye-gone happiness or sorrow—alas! generally the latter—which his gentle and familiar words conjured up to the memory of those exiles, who looked back with tender regret, even from their hardly-won prosperity and independence, to the humble home and the lowly lot in the land of their youth!

Father Mathew had to make visits and return visits, as well as to receive them; and then, after sufficient time had been devoted to sight-seeing, or sacrificed to courtesy, there was his mission to prosecute. The month of July was one of incessant labour and excitement; but the excitement, though drawing largely upon the resources of a constitution grievously impaired, rendered him insensible to fatigue, and enabled him to go through his work without faltering for a moment. Rising at an early hour in the morning, he said mass in one church or other, and lectured and administered the pledge; and after breakfast, there were visits or visitors, meetings and pledge-giving—and so on till a late hour in the evening.

Thus, before he quitted New York for Boston, he had administered the pledge to a vast number, principally Irish, and had done much, both by exertion and by influence, to add strength and vigour to the temperance organisation of the great city by which he had been so nobly received.

After having remained the guest of the city for some ten days or fortnight, he then retired to the hospitable residence of Archbishop Hughes, whose letter of invitation had been one of the chief inducements to his coming to America. New York he frequently visited during the next two years, and generally made it his head-quarters, from which he travelled in various directions, according either to the state of his health or the engagements he had to fulfil.

CHAPTER XXXVI.

The Slavery Question—The Abolition Party—Necessity for Prudence—Scylla and Charybdis—Correspondence with Judge Lumpkin—Coming Events casting their Shadows before them.

IN Boston, which city received him with every honour and distinction, he was subjected to much annoyance, from the unthinking zeal of a partisanship which would make no allowance for the peculiarity of his position and the exclusive character of his mission. It is necessary that his conduct with respect to the question of slavery should be placed in its true light, as being highly creditable to his judgement and good sense. Had he acted in any other manner than as he did, he would have been open to the gravest censure, and justly amenable to the charge of having sacrificed a great cause to a wanton intermeddling in a question full of complicated difficulties, and exciting passions which, though then slumbering in the hearts of the American people, have since, as the world but too well knows, burst forth in fierce and desolating flame. Father Mathew did not visit America to accomplish the emancipation of the negro, but to advocate and promote the cause of temperance; and any attempt to play the part of the abolitionist would have been in bad taste and in worse judgement.

Scarcely had Father Mathew arrived in Boston, when he received a letter of invitation to be present at a meeting to celebrate 'the anniversary of the most thrilling event of the nineteenth century, the abolition of slavery in the West Indies.' In this letter of invitation he is reminded of the fact that, in 1842, he had signed an address from the people of Ireland to their countrymen in America, in which the latter were called upon to treat the coloured people as their equals, to hate slavery, and to cling to the abolitionists. He is also asked 'to improve every suitable opportunity, while he remained in the country, to bear a clear and unequivocal testimony, both in public and private, against the enslavement of any portion of the human family,' and more to the same effect. This letter was handed to him on the 26th of July; and on the next day Mr. William Lloyd Garrison, accompanied by Dr. Bowditch and another gentleman, waited on him, in order, says Mr. Garrison, in his account of the interview, 'to obtain an introduction to Father Mathew, and to be sure that the letter of the Committee, inviting him to participate in the celebration of that great and glorious event, the entire abolition of British West India slavery, failed not to be put into his hands.' These gentlemen were determined, if possible, to make their own of so famous a 'lion' for their approaching celebration. It was nothing to them, or to those whom they represented, if Father Mathew, by complying with their request, annihilated his influence on their platform, and thus rendered necessary his speedy and ignominious retreat from the shores of America. In 1849 the Northern States were divided on the question of slavery, and the abolitionists were neither popular nor influential in any one of those States; and the very name of an abolitionist was odious in the South. Yet into a subject of the kind, which evoked such bitter hostility and such fierce passions, the Apostle of Temperance was invited to plunge headlong! Partisanship is indeed as exacting as it is inconsiderate.

The letter of invitation is again thrust into his hand, and he is told to read it at his leisure, and answer 'as he may think duty requires.' Taking the letter 'with some agitation and embarrassment of manner,' he answered in language which ought to have satisfied any fair man, but which disgusted the disappointed abolitionists.

'I have as much as I can do,' said he, 'to save men from the slavery of intemperance, without attempting to overthrow any other kind of slavery. Besides, it would not be proper for me to commit myself on a question like this, under present circumstances. I am a Catholic priest; but, being here to promote the cause of Temperance, I should not be justified in turning aside from my mission, for the purpose of subserving the cause of Catholicism.'

What other answer could Father Mathew have given? Or, what other answer would have been worthy of the man who, of all others in the world, was the one most responsible for the success of a cause which recognised no difference, whether social, political, or religious? Of course, in that interview, Mr. Garrison delivered a very eloquent discourse, and taunted Father Mathew in a manner quite satisfactory to the feelings of the speaker; but what gave him, as he said, 'special surprise, and inflicted the deepest wound upon his spirit,' was Father Mathew's apparent lack of all sympathy for the slave, of all interest in the Anti-Slavery movement.

Father Mathew had been invited to the South—was, in fact, to visit it in the course of a couple of months, with one object, and one object alone; and yet he was expected to commit himself to the expression of sympathies, opinions, and a policy which would have either rendered his visit wholly impossible, or, should he have the hardihood to persevere in his intention, would have closed every door in the South against him, and irretrievably damaged the cause which it was his first duty to promote and protect from injury.

In bitterness of heart, Mr. Garrison concludes his account of the memorable interview—'Not a syllable fell from his lips, expressive of pleasure that the American slave has his faithful and devoted advocates—or of joy at the emancipation of eight hundred thousand bondsmen in the British Isles. I is with great sorrow of heart that I lay these facts before America, Ireland, and the world.'

Father Mathew had, like every Christian man, rejoiced in the emancipation of the bondsmen to whose freedom Mr. Garrison accused him of being insensible; but he thought of the thousands of his own race and country, who, in the cities of the South, were the victims of a still more deadly slavery; and, with a prudence and reticence that did him honour, he resolved that no word should drop from his mouth which could prevent him from coming to their rescue, and effecting their freedom.

From among several letters which Father Mathew received from home, expressing a just approval of the course which he had taken, in not allowing himself to be ensnared into the meshes of the abolitionists, one may be quoted, inasmuch as it was written by an enthusiastic friend of the slave, and one of the most zealous supporters of the abolition cause. Miss Jennings of Cork, whose name, because of whose services to the Anti-Slavery Society, was well known in Boston, thus wrote to Father Mathew:—

My dear Mr. Mathew,—Although I feel that I would gladly lay down my life, were it needed, in the Anti-Slavery cause, yet I also feel that you would injure the temperance cause were you to devote any of your time to the Anti-Slavery question. One great philanthropic object you have devoted your mind to try and accomplish; and, if you succeed in destroying intemperance in the Slave States, you lay the axe at the root of slavery. . . . By devoting your whole mind to temperance, you will do far more good than if you allowed yourself to be distracted by any other great philanthropic movement. Slavery, it has been truly said, demoralises the slave, and demoralises the master. *I know you abhor slavery in your heart*, and I trust that its hideousness will not purposely be concealed from you, as it is too often done.*

* Even in the year 1862, an enlightened and kind-hearted gentleman, Mr. James Haughton of Dublin, spoke of Father Mathew in the following words, which he afterwards published in the form of a tract, for general circulation. In a paper

Mr. Garrison published his account of this famous interview on the 10th of August, and with it the letter presented to Father Mathew, as well as the address of 1842, from the Irish people to their countrymen in America. This publication was the source of new troubles to the man who honestly endeavoured to maintain a position of complete neutrality.

The Massachusetts Anti-Slavery Society, in their Annual Report of 1850, are obliged to admit that the American press almost universally justified Father Mathew, and condemned the conduct of the abolitionists, 'as uncalled for and impertinent.' The abolitionists, however, consoled themselves with the assertion, that in the British Islands there was but one opinion entertained of Father Mathew's conduct—that of 'unqualified condemnation.' An assertion, we verily believe, which owes much to the imagination of the compilers of the Report in which it is made.

This was the Scylla. There was also a Charybdis.

Father Mathew had received an invitation to visit Georgia through Governor, or Judge, Lumpkin, President of the Temperance Society of that State; which invitation he had gratefully accepted. But no sooner had the account of the interview in Boston and the Irish address been published,

entitled 'Ireland and Father Mathew,' read for the International Temperance and Prohibition Convention, held in Hanover Square Rooms in September 1862, Mr. Haughton thus refers to one of the 'few dark passages in Father Mathew's life, which,' as the writer remarks, 'serve to show us that even the best men have serious imperfections of character:'—

'When he proposed accepting the invitation to America, I entreated him not to go, for I knew the danger; and he fell beneath the wiles of the slaveholder. He failed to maintain in the South the noble principles of freedom for the coloured race which he had always advocated at home. Like the great Kossuth, he, too, was unable to withstand the blandishments of American men stealers, and both sunk, not a little, in the estimation of the world for this false step. Such is the righteous judgement which follows glaring deviations from the path of rectitude—Father Mathew never recovered his health and spirits after his return from America.'

Father Mathew's health was broken *before* he left Ireland—sacrificed to his superhuman exertions in the famine years. His health was further injured by the excitement which he underwent in New York; and the reader will see how his marvellous labours during his stay in America utterly ruined an already shattered constitution.

than indignation was excited in the minds of the pro-Slavery party, who, overlooking the admirable prudence displayed by Father Mathew on the 27th of July, 1849, condemned him for having signed the address of 1842. Writing from Athens, on the 4th of September, Governor Lumpkin says :—

REV. AND DEAR SIR,—Your favourable response to the invitation of the Temperance Convention of Georgia to visit our State, caused a throb of joy to fill every heart. All looked forward with delightful anticipation to the time when we should take you by the hand, and welcome in our midst the friend of humanity and deliverer of his countrymen from the most galling servitude that ever cursed our race. In the full fruition of these happy hopes, the following document has found its way into our newspapers, purporting to be a circular addressed by the late Mr. O'Connell and yourself, together with 70,000 other inhabitants of Ireland, calling upon 'Irishmen and Irishwomen' in this country, by all the memories of their native land, to cling to the abolitionists in America, and to unite with them to put an end to slavery here, by all peaceable means in their power. Duty to you, sir, duty to ourselves, and to the common enterprise in which we are embarked, constrains me to bring this publication to your notice, and to enquire respectfully whether or not it be genuine; and if so, to ask whether you still cherish the same sentiments which are there embodied? And to say to you, in all candour, that on your answer to these interrogatories will depend your capacity for usefulness in the South. Justice to our families, our firesides, everything dear to us, forbid that we should call any man 'brother' who unites with our enemies in waging an unprovoked and most relentless warfare upon our hearths and homes, our peace and prosperity.

I will only add, in conclusion, that the pain which I feel in making this communication is greatly aggravated by the consciousness that it is calculated to inflict a wound on a generous heart, which I would most gladly shield at any sacrifice, save that of the interests involved in this matter.

Believe me to be, most respectfully yours,

THOS. HENRY LUMPKIN.

Never was man placed in a more awkward position than was Father Mathew between these two angry parties. If he proclaimed, what in his heart he felt, hatred of Slavery, not only was the South barred against him, but his influence in the North was gone; for the abolitionists did not then—whatever they may have since claimed to do—represent the public sentiment of that portion of the great confederacy. If he retracted the opinion pronounced in the document of 1842, and to which he had committed himself by his signature, he would have damaged his reputation for consistency and sacrificed his self-respect, and also have raised a storm about his ears which would have compelled his retirement from the new and important field of his mission. By a letter marked 'private,' he endeavoured to appease Governor Lumpkin without compromising his honour; but the Governor was not to be appeased. In a letter of his, dated the 12th of October, there is this passage:—

> Under these circumstances, with a clear comprehension, I trust, of the responsibility thus incurred, and with the most profound regret as to the miscarriage of our hopes, *I herewith*, so long as I have the power, at least, *and with the hearty concurrence and approval of the Executive Committee of the Convention, withdraw the invitation so cordially and sincerely offered.* Viewing our cause as we do, as the chief hope of man, we must not permit it to be wounded in the house of its friends. We will welcome no one, knowingly, among us, who fraternises himself, or encourages others to do so, with a faction which would recklessly shiver the Union into fragments; which would reek its unhallowed hands red as crimson in human blood; which, in a word, seems to combine in one mass all the worst elements of thought, action, and feeling, peculiar to our troublous times.

The very language adopted by Governor Lumpkin, and which no doubt met with the sympathy and approval of the powerful party and vast interest which he represented, only the more clearly demonstrated the danger of the slightest intermeddling in a question so charged with explosive materials.

Father Mathew, in a letter dated Richmond, the 22nd of December 1849, assures Governor Lumpkin, that had he known the high position of that gentleman better, he would not have marked his former letter 'private,' but would have left it to his own prudence to have acted as seemed best to the cause which was equally dear to both. He then continues:—

The second letter which you kindly forwarded I have never seen, as on its reaching Boston I was confined, at New York, by a severe illness, and my physician, Dr. Frazer, and my secretary, deemed it advisable not to speak to me on such an exciting subject.

I find, with regret, that my single-mindedness in the advocacy of the, to me, all-absorbing cause of temperance is not, in this great country, well understood. In my own beloved country, though groaning under the weight of the heaviest burden of misery that ever a nation bore, I endured every species of calumny, rather than risk the infliction of the slightest injury to the temperance cause, by advocating the Repeal of the Union between England and Ireland. In referring your Honour to the conversation I held with Mr. Garrison, in the Adam's House, Boston, I vainly thought my solemn declaration *of being firmly resolved not to interfere in any, the slightest degree, with the institutions of this mighty republic*, would have been amply sufficient to calm the anxieties of even the most sensitive American. I now, dear and honoured judge, renew this declaration; and I most respectfully urge that no man who himself enjoys freedom in this emphatically free country, can require more from one who has merely come amongst you to advocate the high and holy cause of temperance, bearing in his hand the pure and spotless white banner, with the divine motto inscribed, 'Glory to God on high, peace on earth to men of good will.'

And this letter, which an unbiassed person would pronounce to be creditable to the wisdom and good feeling of the writer, was characterised in the Report of the Massachusetts Anti-Slavery Society, as a humiliating production, than which 'the force of servility could no further go.' Such is the blinding influence of fanaticism in any cause, however good it may be.

We shall see, a little farther on, in what manner the Senate received the proposal to grant him free admission to the floor of the House, and how there were then—at the close of 1849—felt the premonitory tremblings of those passions which exploded in the early part of 1861, and are now convulsing the States in the throes of the deadliest struggle recorded in history. The graver the question at issue, the more commendable was Father Mathew's prudence in holding himself entirely aloof from both parties.

CHAPTER XXXVII.

His Secretary's Diary—Ill in New York—His indefatigable Labours —Arrives in Washington—Debate in the Senate—Entertained by the President.

I HAVE in my possession a diary which was kept by Father Mathew's secretary, Mr. O'Meara, during their stay in America. It was written simply for his own satisfaction and guidance, partly as a chronicle of his daily impressions, and partly as a reference for facts—what had been done in such a place, or on such a day. But though, when writing this diary, Mr. O'Meara did not imagine that any eye but his own would have ever scanned its pages, it was freely placed at my disposal as soon as I had resolved on undertaking the biography of the great man whom he so truly loved, and so faithfully served.

I have read this diary through with the greatest care and attention; and the more I read, the more profound was my admiration of the man whose daily doings it recorded. There is scarcely a page which does not reflect his true character—his charity, his goodness, his humility, his compassionate nature, his love of the human family, his holiness of life and purity of thought. But these are not what excite astonishment, for they are belonging to his whole life; what most surprise us are his amazing energy, his endurance of fatigue, and his unconquerable courage and perseverance. Seriously afflicted with paralysis in Ireland, we see him confined to bed in New York, in the month of November, with a painful illness; and yet, in a few days after, we behold him again at work. A few extracts from the diary will exhibit this more clearly than any mere statement of the fact can do:—

Sunday, November 18th.—Father Mathew improved in health to-day, though still confined to bed. This evening he bled rather profusely.

Monday, 19th.—Improving, but not able to be up. Though in bed, received several visitors.

Tuesday, 20th.—Father Mathew better. After breakfast, sat up, but felt weak. The motion in his limbs still perceptible. At 12 o'clock he had an interesting interview with the Hon. Henry Clay.

Wednesday, 21st.—After breakfast, he dressed and remained up the entire day. Received several visitors, but did not go down stairs.

Thursday, 22nd.—Considerably better. Breakfast down stairs. Several came to take the pledge. The doctor, at one o'clock, took Father Mathew out driving. . . . . . He gave the Rev. Mr. ——— ten dollars, and promised to write to his Bishop to take him back.

Friday, 23rd.—Still improving. Got up before breakfast. . . . Paid visits. Several took the pledge to-day.

Saturday, 24th.—Father Mathew had rather a troublesome night, the side painful. Gave young ——— 1*l.*

Sunday, 25th.—Father Mathew said mass at the S.S. of Mercy, Houston Street. Returned to the Irving at 11 o'clock, but still not free from pain. Dined in the Hall—his first appearance in public. . .

Monday, 26th.—Father Mathew had a troublesome night with his side. Better this morning. Hon. Mr. Fillmore, Vice-President of the United States, called to pay his respects. Also General Cass. Several to take the pledge. Gave to ——— twenty dollars, and to ——— five dollars. The doctor and ——— took the pledge.

Tuesday, 27th.—Father Mathew much better. . . . . . . In the evening was waited on by the Mayor and Board of Aldermen, who came to bid him adieu.

Wednesday, 28th.—Left per rail and steamer this morning for Philadelphia. Arrived privately, and proceeded to the residence of the Bishop, Dr. Kendrick.

We shall now see how this feeble man, who had just risen from a bed of sickness, was employed on Sunday the 2nd of December:—

Father Mathew said mass at half-past six o'clock this morning, in the Bishop's private chapel, which was crowded. Immediately after, gave the pledge; and when he had breakfasted, proceeded with the

Rev. Mr. Gartland to Gloucester, five miles across the river, to attend the dedication of a new church, to which the Rev. Mr. O'Donoghue, of Waterford, is appointed pastor. Father Mathew preached the dedication sermon, delivered in his usual good style, notwithstanding his illness. After the ceremonies, he administered the pledge. The weather became very severe and extremely cold, and snow fell heavily throughout the entire day. After dinner, returned to the Bishop's, and remained administering the pledge until eight o'clock. Several came.

On Wednesday the 5th, he said early mass, and having lectured on temperance, administered the pledge. Then after having paid and received visits, he commenced again to administer the pledge, and 'did not close until nine o'clock P. M. Six hundred disciples were the result of his day's work.

On Thursday the 13th, he is still suffering from his side; nevertheless, he is up at six o'clock on the following Sunday, on which day he lectures twice, preaches to a large congregation, and administers the pledge to about 800 persons, including many distinguished people of different religious persuasions. He is thus engaged 'the entire day.' The same description might be given of each day during his visit to Philadelphia. And such, indeed, was the manner in which he prosecuted his mission in every city in which he stopped during his prolonged tour in America.

On the 18th, he left for Washington, but not before he had received, during that morning, a considerable number of converts to temperance.

As soon as his arrival was made known in the Capital, a resolution was unanimously carried in Congress, admitting him to a seat on the floor of the House—the very highest distinction which could be conferred upon the subject of another country, by the representatives of that great Republic. When Father Mathew availed himself of this flattering permission, the members rose to receive him. Had he been a crowned monarch, the respect thus paid to him by that free assembly could not have been more impressively exhibited.

The same proposition was made in the Senate, and gave rise to a most animated discussion, which conclusively proved how wise was the reserve which he maintained in his interview with Mr. Garrison. The opposition to which the proposal gave rise was of great value, as it enabled Father Mathew's friends to place his mission, his objects, and his motives, in their true light before the American people, thereby rescuing him from the misrepresentations of those who desired to damage by traducing him.

The resolution, which was proposed by Mr. Walker, Senator for Wisconsin, was as follows:—'*Resolved*—that the Rev. Theobald Mathew be allowed a seat within the bar of the United States Senate during the period of his sojourn in Washington.'

Mr. Clements, who moved a negative to the resolution, thus justified his opposition:—

> The reason which prompted me to make the objection was, that I had been informed that the individual named in the resolution had been charged with denouncing a portion of this confederacy with the maintenance of an institution which he was pleased to characterise as a sin and a crime; and when respectfully invited by the Governor of Georgia to express his views in relation to the institution of slavery, he refused to answer. Under these circumstances I do not think I could conscientiously suffer such a resolution to pass. I do not myself regard slavery as a sin, and I do not believe that I could be induced so to regard it by any representation on the part of any person; but if it be so, at all events it is an institution not to be interfered in by foreigners. I shall object now to the adoption of the resolution as I did yesterday, because there is in reality no necessity for its adoption, and, as it appears to me, there would be no propriety in adopting it.

Mr. Clay expressed his regret that any opposition should have been offered to such a proposal, which was simply intended as a compliment and mark of respect to a distinguished individual; and thus continued:—

I think it ought to be received as a just homage to a distinguished foreigner, for his humanity, his benevolence, his philanthrophy, and his virtue, and as properly due to one who has devoted himself to the good of his whole species. It is but a merited tribute of respect to a man who has achieved a great social revolution—a revolution in which no blood has been shed; a revolution which has involved no desolation, which has caused no bitter tears of widows and orphans to flow; a revolution which has been achieved without violence, and a greater one, perhaps, than has ever been accomplished by any benefactor of mankind. Sir, it is a compliment that is due from the Senate, small as it may be, to the gentleman indicated in the resolution, as an illustrious Irish patriot; and I put it in all seriousness, and in a spirit of perfect kindness, to the honourable Senator from Alabama, whether placing this subject of slavery in connection with the proposition that has been offered is not imprudent and unwise, in respect to the very subject which he has so much at heart?

Mr. Seward concluded an eloquent eulogium upon the object of the intended compliment in these words :—

I must be allowed to say, with all respect, that I hope the American Senate will give evidence, by the unanimity with which we pass this resolution, of the sentiment which is almost unanimous amongst us, that if slavery be an error, or if it be a crime, or if it be a sin, we deplore its existence amongst us, and deny the responsibility of its introduction here; and that, therefore, we should not withhold this token of respect from virtue, merely because it happens to be found residing in the mind of a person who has expressed an opinion unfavourable to the existence of slavery, but who is celebrated for his devotion to virtue and the rights of man.

'The question,' said Mr. Davis of Mississippi, 'resolves itself into this :—

Whether the Senate, having upon its floor those who represent a slaveholding constituency, shall vote an extraordinary compliment to one known as the ally of O'Connell, and in whose expressed opinions he openly coincided? Why, if he came here as a guest to share our hospitality, and not to disturb the peace of our country, did he not say that our domestic affairs are our own, and that he did not come here to disapprove of any portion of them; that he came here to express no opinions in relation to slavery? He comes covertly, a wolf in sheep's clothing; and I hold the Senator from New York to be the very best authority upon that subject.'

Mr. Walker, the mover of the resolution, vindicates its proposal:—

So far as we have had intimation of the character of the mission of Father Mathew, it is one of peace and good will to all mankind, and not of aggression upon any class of the community. Regarding him in this light, as a man who has not only accomplished a great amount of good, but who is now engaged in the good work of endeavouring to reform and improve the social condition of society, I have thought it appropriate that this mark of respect should be tendered to him, without regard to what his individual opinions may be upon other subjects.

Mr. Hale voted for the resolution, 'as a tribute to the virtues, the philanthropy, and the meritorious exertions of Father Mathew,' although he disapproved of the course which he had taken on the slavery question.

Mr. Badger objects to the proposal, as not only being without precedent, but establishing a dangerous and embarrassing precedent for the future:—

In the first place, it is without precedent, so far as I know, and so far as I have been able to ascertain from gentlemen around me, who have had opportunities of being better informed than I am. I say it is without precedent, because it is impossible to conceive that the case of Gen. Lafayette can be supposed to furnish a precedent for this resolution. He stood upon such grounds of preeminence as to render it a case altogether distinct from any that can now occur, where an individnal, who is not a citizen of the United States, is to reeeive a particular mark of respect.

Mr. Cass deprecated the introduction of the slavery question, respecting which the public mind was already 'in a high state of excitement,' and thus placed the proposition on its right ground:—

This is but a complimentary notice to a distinguished stranger just arrived among us. And well does he merit it. He is a stranger to us personally, but he has won a world-wide renown. He comes among us upon a mission of benevolence, not unlike Howard, whose name and deeds rank high in the annals of philanthropy, and who sought to carry hope and comfort into the darkest cells, and to alleviate the moral and physical condition of their unhappy tenants. He comes to break the bonds of the captive, and to set the prisoner free—to redeem the lost, to confirm the wavering, and to aid in saving all from the temptation and danger of intemperance. It is a noble mission, and well is he fulfilling it. I need not stop to recount the evils which the great enemy he is contending with has inflicted upon the world—evils which are the source of a large portion of the vice and misery that human nature has to encounter. But the inundation is stayed. Higher motives, nobler aspirations, the influence of religion, and the hopes of life are coming to the rescue, and are doing their part in this great work of reformation. You grant a seat here to the successful warrior returning from the conquests of war. Let us not refuse it to a better warrior—to one who comes from the conquests of peace, from victories achieved without the loss of blood or life, and whose trophies are equally dear to the patriot and the Christian.

Mr. Foote spoke in favour of the resolution; and the passage which is quoted is not only an evidence of the bitter feeling existing between the two parties, but is a further proof of the wisdom of Father Mathew's conduct in maintaining the strictest neutrality in a cause of so much anger and animosity. Mr. Foote said:—

I regret to learn that, when addressed by citizens of Alabama and Georgia as to his views upon the question of slavery, he either declined responding, or responded by letters withheld from publication at his own request. I think that in this transaction he committed a great mistake, and one which will greatly impair his efficiency as a champion of temperance. But, until I receive conclusive evidence to the contrary, I must believe that he still adheres to the resolution which he assumed and made public shortly after his arrival in this country, not to connect himself at all with any of the domestic controversies in progress on this side of the Atlantic. I well recollect the scene which occurred somewhere in the State of Massachusetts between certain fierce abolition agitators and Father Mathew, in which these wicked incendiaries made a most indecent and ungentlemanly attempt to inveigle this venerable personage in their nefarious schemes, and to wield the influence of his name and character against the institutions of the South; and I have not forgotten the dignified and severe rebuke which he administered to these infatuated factionists, nor the scurrilous denunciations which they showered down upon him so plenteously afterwards. These facts are too recent not to be recollected by all of us. Did I regard Father Mathew as deserving any part of the commendation bestowed upon him, in connection with the cause of abolition, by the honourable Senator from New York, instead of recognising him as a noble philanthropist, I should feel compelled to class him with thieves, and robbers, and murderers, and midnight incendiaries. Did I suppose that the honourable Senator from New York had been duly authorised to give expression to the sentiments of Father Mathew upon the question of slavery, I should regard it as insulting to this body to have his name even uttered in our hearing. I might suppose, until proof to the contrary shall be adduced, that the honourable Senator from New York, whether designedly or not I will not undertake to decide, has done serious injustice to a worthy and unoffending personage, and that in his fiery eagerness to advance a favourite but infamous cause, he has attempted to drag to his aid the influence and popularity of a great and potential name, in a manner that cannot fail to prove displeasing to all the disinterested friends of the temperance reform, to be found upon the habitable globe.

Mr. Downs, while vindicating the principles which he held, and which he represented, did ample justice to the wisdom and good taste manifested in Father Mathew's conduct. The following extract is the last which it is necessary to give of a debate which had a material influence in rendering successful in all portions of the States which he visited, the mission of the Apostle of Temperance. Thus spoke Mr. Downs :—

It is said that long ago, before he came to America, he expressed opinions opposed to slavery. Well, suppose he did, is it reasonable or proper in us of the South to require of him to retract these opinions? He comes among us, not as a propagandist either of religious or political doctrines, but on a benevolent mission of humanity, to make mankind better and happier, like the Saviour of the world who preceded him—on a mission scarcely less divine. He has, when approached, refused to commit himself, or in any manner to interfere in public affairs or opinions on that subject in our country. Is not this a course which all must approve of? Could he, with propriety, or without defeating the success of his mission, have pursued a different course? For myself, I confess, coming to the United States for the benevolent purpose he did—an object to be accomplished in no particular section, or by no particular party or sect, but throughout our broad land, from north to south and from east to west, and by the cooperation of the well-disposed of all—if he had taken any part in political discussions, or obtruded his opinions on all occasions, I should not have approved of his course, even if it had been in favour of our side of the question, but should have considered him wanting in that wisdom and discretion necessary for the success of his mission. Besides, sir, we of the South believe ourselves to be right in our opinions on the subject of slavery; that our course will bear the test of scrutiny and examination; that people abroad entertain erroneous opinions of our institutions, which would be removed by visiting our country and ascertaining the true state of the case. Would it not then be inexpedient and unwise to ask Father Mathew, before he has visited our section of the country, and had an opportunity of judging for himself, to change opinions previously formed? Would the world say this was the conduct of a people confident of the justice of their cause? or would it not rather say there is something to conceal, or there would not be such precaution? For myself, I do not believe that he has evinced any disposition to interfere in our institutions; on the contrary, it seems to be admitted on all sides, that when approached by the abolitionists on the subject, he refused to concur with them in their views, or give them any encouragement. But, even if he was so disposed, I have too much confidence in the justice of our cause and the strength of our institutions, to suppose he could do us any harm. Mr. President, I shall vote for this resolution upon another ground. This distinguished gentleman is upon a mission which I consider of vast importance to the people of the United States and to all the world. I believe his efforts are to be of immense advantage, and I concur in the object of them, and I wish them success, and am disposed to advance them in every possibly way.

The original resolution was carried by a majority of 33 to 18; and an honour which had been only previously conferred by the representatives of the American people on Lafayette, who had brought his name and his sword to the cause of their freedom, was now accorded to the humble Irish friar, who had won a name even more glorious by his services in the cause of suffering humanity.

On Thursday, the 20th of December—the day after the discussion in the Senate—Father Mathew was entertained by the President of the United States at a grand dinner, to which fifty guests, including the foremost men in the country, had been specially invited. The President presented each member of the distinguished company to Father Mathew, who dated the commencement of many valuable friendships from that occasion. The dinner was served in sumptuous style ; but though the choicest wines of Europe sparkled on the board, scarcely any wine was used by the company, and none by the host, out of respect to the guest of the evening.

CHAPTER XXXVIII.

How he employed his Sunday in Richmond—A Sunday in Savannah—As Generous as ever—His Success at New Orleans—He believes the Irish Exodus Providential—His Appeals to the Irish —Arrives at Little Rock—A Mission in the Woods.

AN extract from the diary will exhibit the manner in which he was employed in Richmond on Sunday the 23rd of December, while he was yet suffering from the effects of his recent attack :—

Said mass at seven, and gave an exhortation particularly addressed to the Irish. Administered the pledge. At eleven o'clock the church crowded—the majority Dissenters. Father Mathew preached again in his best style, after reading from the Gospel, 'Prepare ye the way of the Lord, make straight His paths.' The congregation delighted. Immediately after mass, again spoke with very great ability on temperance. *He astonished myself.* Administered the pledge to about two hundred. Had some friends to dine with us. Again at vespers attended, and spoke briefly to a crowded audience. It is astonishing how he is able to labour so much. The Dissenters delighted with his discourses, which were very good. The evening becoming cold, and snow falling, retired to the house at five o'clock.

On Sunday the 30th, he is at Wilmington. Says the diary :—

This will be a memorable day in Wilmington. Father Mathew, as usual, celebrated the holy sacrifice at half-past seven o'clock, lectured and administered the pledge; and at eleven o'clock preached—his text, 'The Lord in His holy temple.' The sermon universally applauded by all present. The little church was never filled so much before. Three-fourths were Dissenters, and many known to possess strong prejudices. All most orderly and respectful. Immediately after the sermon, spoke on temperance with much ability and force. His arguments, as usual, most conclusive, replete with scriptural quotations. The majority of the Catholic community, and several others, most respectable people, took the pledge. The Rev. Thomas Murphy and the boys on the altar were the first. The impression made by Father Mathew's sermon and discourses has had a most beneficial effect, especially with those of different opinions and strong prejudices.

During the day, we are told, 'he had some Americans, whose accession was much applauded, and who acknowledged they would not take a pledge from any other individual.' 'It is extraordinary,' continues the diary, 'the effect produced by Father Mathew's influence.'

On the 5th of January, while in Charleston, he is complaining of his leg; and yet on the next day, Sunday, he undergoes an amount of fatigue which would try a robust constitution. Two sermons and two discourses on temperance were rather many for a man in his condition.

Farther on, we have blisters, and plaisters, and other applications; and the next day we find him commencing his work in the morning, and 'continually occupied until eight o'clock P. M.'

Here is the account of a Sunday in Savannah :—

Sunday, 27th Jan., 1850.—Father Mathew had a large congregation at eight o'clock. Exhorted in the usual style; text from the Book of Exodus. Congregation chiefly Irish. Some took the pledge. At half-past ten o'clock, again preached at High Mass; text, 'I was dumb.' After High Mass again exhorted, and administered the pledge to a large number, some hundreds, including the principal Catholics, and many Americans. The church was not capable of containing a single individual more than were in it. Numbers remained outside. Father Mathew's voice was strong, notwithstanding the day was extremely hot. Dr. Prendergast had us all to dine with him, and some strangers. At half-past three o'clock Father Mathew resumed. After vespers introduced various temperance arguments, not exactly in the same words, but to the same purpose. The anxiety to take the pledge increased. Father Mathew announced 700 before vespers, and 300 more joined during the evening, making 1,000 for the day. Remained engaged until eight o'clock, when we returned to supper, all friends waiting for us. Spent a pleasant evening.

Considering that the same kind of work was continuously carried on, without the cessation of a single day, unless when travelling by rail or steamer, it is not surprising to hear that 'Father Mathew was very tired,' or that 'he had not recovered from his fatigue,' or that 'his leg was again troubling him,' or that 'his side was giving him annoyance,' or that he had 'passed a troublesome night.' But nothing short of a complete break-down could stop him, so long as there was work for him to do; and so long as there was a drunkard to be reclaimed, a profligate to be received back into the fold, or an emigrant from Ireland to be preserved from danger, there was work for Father Mathew. Thus, for instance, after having attended a levee of the citizens in the Concert Hall in the City of Columbus, he 'went to the prison to give the pledge to its inmates.'

His hand, too, was for ever in his pocket. 'Give, give, give!' was his motto in America as in the old country; and though he met little squalor or mendicancy during his sojourn in the States, scarcely a day passed that some one did not appeal to his compassion or excite his sympathy. To children and coloured people he gave medals without charge, and silver medals were presented in great number to those who served or who patronised the cause. Thus, what with money left in the hands of the clergyman for some useful charity, or sums given to applicants, or voluntarily offered, and the cost of travelling and lodging, and other causes of expense which it would be impossible to particularise, Father Mathew often found it hard to pay his way, although he was frequently made free of boat and rail, and often accepted hospitality eagerly pressed upon his acceptance. An extract or two will illustrate the liberality which was his daily habit, and at the same time exhibit with what zeal he prosecuted his mission, in spite of his infirmity of body:—

Wednesday, 27th February, 1850.—Distributed upwards of 100 cards and medals gratis.

Thursday, 28th.—Distributed nearly 300 cards and medals gratis, the majority to children and coloured people.

Monday, 11*th March.*—He gave to the S. S. for the female orphans twenty dollars, and twenty dollars to the Brothers for the male orphans. . . . Preaches well, but not so energetically as formerly; was complaining of his limbs being infirm, and felt nervous. He feels the effects of his exertions always more the day after. Went to Dr. M'Nally, who applied an issue in his neck, which he says will be of great service. The operation was very painful to him.

Wednesday, 13*th March.*—Yesterday witnessed the festival at which, by his contribution, Father Mathew entertained the orphans. Poor creatures, they were quite happy, and so was Father Mathew—it was so like former acts of his in the old country. . . Gave a poor woman two dollars.

This was how he spent Patrick's Day in Mobile :—

Father Mathew said mass at half-past seven o'clock. Many of those who took the pledge were communicants. The morning very warm, as hot as our summer days. At half-past ten, went to the High Mass, at which Father Mathew preached in good style; text—'Why have the nations raged,' &c. When the ceremonies were over, several presented themselves for the pledge. Dined in company with the Bishop at Mrs. Brown's, a respectable and good Catholic lady. Returned to vespers, and at the close had about forty more to join. Father Mathew, though he did not pretend it, felt much excited and nervous from his exertions. He is not so strong as he was some time since. At seven o'clock adjourned to St. Vincent's church, with the Rev. Mr. Hackett, who preached the eulogy of St. Patrick. A good many took the pledge.

During his stay in Mobile he addressed the following to his friend Mrs. Rathbone :—

Mobile. Alabama : March 8, 1850.

My dear Mrs. Rathbone,—Since my departure from your hospitable mansion, I have, as you are aware from the papers, endured much toil and anxiety; and though the mild climate in which I now sojourn is very beneficial to me, yet I find myself weak, and my limbs are become infirm.

You will be glad to hear that the storm attempted to be raised against me in the South has subsided. The inhabitants I find, in general, as you represented, courteous and affable. I now perceive the necessity that existed for my having firmly adhered to the resolution I had formed when coming to this country, not to interfere with its institutions. Had I done anything to prevent my journey through the Southern States, I should never have forgiven myself. There are tens of thousands of my beloved countrymen scattered over the South; and all are cheerfully coming forward, at my invitation, to rescue themselves from the wiles of intemperance. The consequences might have been dreadful, as many who had been slaves to this debasing habit were anxiously expecting me. . . .

In my journey through this country, I have hitherto, thank God, been most fortunate in escaping accidents. I cannot feel sufficiently thankful to the Almighty for preserving me from a dreadful calamity that occurred yesterday on the Alabama river, in the steamboat in which I had but come to this city the day previous. She accidentally caught fire, and nearly forty passengers perished.

In the course of another week, I go on to New Orleans, and from thence up the mighty Mississippi.

Present, my dear Mrs. Rathbone, my respects to my esteemed friend Mr. Rathbone, and believe me to be,

Dearest Madam,

Your ever grateful and devoted,

THEOBALD MATHEW.

Mrs. Rathbone, Green Bank, Liverpool.

From Mobile, where he had been the guest of the Catholic Bishop, he proceeded to New Orleans, in which city he was welcomed with equal warmth by its spiritual head.

He received and declined an invitation through the Mayor from the municipal authorities to accept the hospitalities of the city. Notwithstanding his correspondence with Judge Lumpkin, the feeling for Father Mathew in New Orleans was most friendly. 'Although,' says Mr. O'Meara, in his diary, 'the Bar-rooms are extremely numerous,' in about ten or twelve days after his arrival, he had given the pledge to more than 6,000 persons, including many of the wealthier classes. 'The change is already most perceptible,' adds Mr. O'Meara; 'not a single drunkard seen in the streets during Easter Saturday night.'

Sunday, 14th April, 1850.— . . . I never heard him preach better. It was for the establishment of schools. Many of the most respectable and influential citizens, including Protestants and Dissenters, present —an immense congregation. Five hundred took the pledge to-day. Gave twenty dollars for religious purposes. He visited the charity hospital, and gave five dollars.

Thursday, 18*th April*.— . . . At two o'clock dined with Mr. Cohen and his family, all of whom took the pledge. He is a Jew. . . . . The statement of his affairs by his brother Charles most distressing to him, and makes a sad impression on his mind.

Monday, 22*nd April*.—Father Mathew had a feverish cold, and remained in all day.

Writing from New Orleans on the 3rd of May, to Mrs. Rathbone, Father Mathew says :—

As far as my temperance labours in New Orleans are concerned, you have been made acquainted, through the press, with my progress and unqualified success. Already upwards of 12,000 have taken the pledge in this city, and I expect an increased accession of three or four thousand more. This I consider an adequate compensation for any sacrifice I made of my feelings on the slavery question. New Orleans is a great and populous city, and apparently as healthy as any other portion of this great Republic ; though the yellow fever occasionally carries off many, the city is wholly free from consumption and other maladies which make such ravages in the old country. My general health is improved ; but the incessant speaking and attendant excitement have occasioned an increase of the paralytic lameness in my left leg, which I find very inconvenient, as I am obliged to be constantly in motion. . . . I have cautiously avoided any act that would afford grounds for the suspicion of my being influenced by mercenary motives ; but I find it difficult to make out sufficient funds to defray my own and secretary's expenses.

We continue to make further extracts from the diary :—

Monday, 13*th May*.—Gave an Arminian priest four dollars—four dollars for postage for the two last days—five dollars for servants and cabs. Many coming to take the pledge in a shocking plight—cut faces and black eyes, and not a cent in their pockets.

Friday, 16*th May*.—Father Mathew met with an accident, which frightened us a little. On getting into a cab, the horse started, and he was dragged along in the gutter. He sent for me and for clothes, and he continued his farewell visits. More than 13,000 have already taken the pledge in New Orleans.

Tuesday, 21*st May*.—Though few joined to-day, yet amply compensated by the consolation afforded to him as well as to families of respectability, who have reason to be rejoiced at his arrival. One in particular, Mr. ———, at whose house we dined, declared that Father Mathew was the saviour of his son, and that he had now no fear of him—that he was one of the best men in the country. Many other respectable families similarly circumstanced.

Wednesday, 22nd May.—In the Princess steamer, on our way to Natchez. Father Mathew enjoyed this day. Was full of anecdote He is strongly opposed to capital punishment. He was much struck by the appearance of two criminals in chains, bound for Baton Rouge. Among other things he mentioned, he told of his having once attended a penitent who was dying; and after having prepared him and administered the viaticum, &c., the poor innocent man turned to him and asked with great coolness, 'What 's the news?' Father Mathew told him he should be thinking of something else, and that he should prepare to meet his God. 'I know that, your reverence,' was the reply; 'but I should like to take to my friends in the other world the latest news.'

Saturday, 25th May.—Gave thirty dollars for religious purposes—ten dollars to the Sisters for a feast for the children.

Tuesday, 28th May.—Visited the hospital and the prison, and had postulants in both.

As Father Mathew reached Vicksburg, a city which has since then acquired a terrible celebrity, the weather, which had become overpoweringly warm, greatly oppressed him, although he continued to exert himself as long as he could resist the weakness which was daily increasing. In Vicksburg, as in every village and town and city which he passed through, he met with old friends—either those whom he had personally known in Ireland, or their children; and while some were in rather indifferent circumstances, many were prosperous and respected, occupying good positions, and possessing considerable influence. The Catholic clergy were almost invariably Irish, the exception being French. He also met several Irishmen in command of the finest boats on the Mississippi and its tributaries. The following extract from the diary was written on board the 'Cotton Plant,' which was then bound for Little Rock :—

Saturday, 15th June, 1850.—Had a very troublesome night with the mosquitos, which were most annoying during the time the boat lay up at night. The day became very agreeable. Reading nearly all day. Father Mathew saw several inhabitants as we passed on the river—some of them Irish. Strange that the Irish are to be found everywhere. It is so different from the Germans, French, &c., who emigrate in colonies, and always settle down in one place. Father Mathew, in defending his countrymen from the fault thus attributed to them, gave it as his opinion, that it was much better the Irish should be scattered amongst the people of this great country. He instanced St. Giles's, London, where they congregated, and were found so troublesome and dissatisfied. 'Independent of this, he felt that the children of such a nation, whom the Almighty permitted to endure so much suffering and misrule, were destined by that all-wise Providence to propagate the Faith amongst the nations of the earth where infidelity reigned. No other people were more respected by the Americans than the Irish who respected themselves. That one blot on their escutcheon was their only crime, and, with the Divine blessing, he would remove that stain from their character. Though French, Spanish, and German are good Catholics, he said, yet no people have done more to promote the Faith, and to support their pastors, than the Irish. That generous noble disposition is not to be found amongst other nations. Wherever a few Irish Catholics settle down, their first effort is to raise a temple to the God of their fathers. The zeal that glowed in the breasts of their ancestors still glows in theirs. It is to be deplored, said Father Mathew, that many who came from Ireland to settle in distant portions of this country have lost the Faith, in consequence of their not having pastors or Catholic temples. This occurred chiefly when the first settlers arrived.'

Father Mathew was painfully struck at reading on the tombstones of the grave-yards which he visited on his route, many familiar names, and finding that his countrymen of the working class died off at an early age. He attributed this premature decay to several causes, including the inordinate use of tobacco (which weakened the powers of digestion), to strong drink, to the too frequent use of fresh meat, which was also eaten too rapidly, and to over work, to which they were urged by contractors, who thought more of the accomplishment of their undertakings than of the lives of their workmen.

He availed himself of every opportunity to appeal to the pride and patriotism of his countrymen, and employed every topic which he thought most calculated to impress them with the necessity of sustaining the character of their race and the honour of their country in their adopted home. The glory of their ancestors, the piety and heroism of their fathers, the sorrows and sufferings of their country, the great work—the spreading of the Faith, which, by God's providence, they were destined to accomplish—these and like topics produced a powerful effect upon his Irish hearers, whose cheeks flushed, or whose eyes filled with unbidden tears, as the words of the speaker awakened their pride or stirred the depths of their hearts. Father Mathew knew the Irish nature as thoroughly as any man ever did, and he used that knowledge for the best and noblest purpose—the moral purification and social advancement of an exiled race.

Little Rock was reached on the 16th of June. The Bishop was an Irishman. His priests—O'Reily, Corcoran, and O'Donoghue—were also Irish. Their names smacked racily of the old country. The welcome was—*Irish.* It may be mentioned, as one item of the expense to which Father Mathew was put by his constant travelling through the States, that he had to pay 24 dollars, or about 5*l.*, passage money for three persons, from Napoleon to Little Rock. Here, according to the following from the diary, Father Mathew was comparatively happy, though still anxious :—

> The exertions of Dr. Byrne were very great when first he came as Bishop. He had to stop at the hotel, there being scarcely any Catholics in Little Rock. Now, through his untiring zeal, he has laid the foundation of a prosperous diocese. . . . Weather very fine, but extremely warm; agreeing with Father Mathew very well. He feels comparatively happy. One matter makes him somewhat uneasy, as we have been for nearly two months exceeding the limits prescribed by the Insurance Company, which arranged that he could stay in the South, to the extent of 33° north latitude, up to the 1st of May. . . . . In the evening visited the young ladies' academy, where an address of welcome was spoken by one of the pupils, to which Father Mathew replied. . . . . Much anxiety expressed by the citizens to hear him speak.

Greater numbers flocked to his standard in many other American cities, but in none was he received with a warmer affection, or did he feel more thoroughly at home. Those who differed from him in religion treated him with respect and confidence, crowded the little cathedral to hear him preach the Gospel, and received the pledge at his hands. The good bishop and his priests surrounded him with every attention, and sought to induce him to remain with them during the summer, until his health, which was painfully infirm, should be somewhat restored. The bishop asked him to remain with him entirely, and become his coadjutor; but Father Mathew's mind was fixed upon returning as soon as he could to the country for which his heart yearned with passionate longing. Such, however, was the debility which was but too apparent, that Dr. Byrne secretly expressed his wish to Mr. O'Meara, that should it please Providence to close that saintly life in America, his honoured remains might find a resting place at Little Rock. Hope was entertained that his visit to the Springs of Arkansas would have a beneficial effect on his constitution, and he was now on his way to visit those famous waters, and test their efficacy by a trial of some duration.

Father Mathew was much amused with the missionary adventures of his friend Father O'Donoghue, one of the three priests of Little Rock. This excellent man, whose death occurred during the course of the summer, was the true type of the spiritual pioneer. Possessing considerable ability and ready powers of argument, full of wit and humour, and enjoying the gift of an imperturbable temper, he was more than a match for those who occasionally challenged him to controversy, in sustainment of the truth of his religion. He was by no means aggressive, but he was at all times ready to put the lance in rest in defence of his faith. The extended nature of his spiritual fold, and the wide tract of country over which his flock were scattered, called for the constant display of courage and endurance as well as zeal. He had to ride for days through tangled forests, the home of wild animals, against whose attack he had to be ever on the watch. Frequently he lost his way, and had to sleep under some shelter which he ingeniously improvised. One day he was very near being strangled by a wild vine, and on another his hat was sacrificed to the same kind of obstruction, and he had to ride bare-headed for several miles, until he reached the first log cabin to be met with in the depths of the verdant wilderness. When he was lucky enough to enjoy the shelter of a roof, he either slept on the floor, his head pillowed on his saddle bags, or, if he stretched his weary limbs on the bed, he found himself the companion of a slain bear, which the hunter had flung in that receptacle for game. But, whether on the floor, or by the side of a shaggy monster, the slumber of the brave missionary priest was profound and unbroken. However, this constant strain upon every faculty of mind and body was soon to bring him to an early grave.

To show how missions prosper where they are energetically worked, it may be mentioned that when Father Mathew was in Little Rock, there still existed the log hut in which Bishop Byrne had taken up his episcopal residence seven years before; and that although he was then too poor to employ a regular servant, he had within that time built a cathedral—not very large, and with only three regular pew-renters—a dwelling house and a seminary, and had also established a college at Fort Smith, opened a mission at Pine Bluff, and accomplished a number of things which, considering the smallness of his means and the poverty of his congregation, were literally marvellous.

CHAPTER XXXIX.

He sets out for the Springs of Arkansas—Delightful Journey—Spends his Time pleasantly—Letter to Mrs. Rathbone—Bigotry rebuked —Scene in the Navy Yard of Pensacola—He objects to 'Lecture' —His wonderful Memory—Causes of his pecuniary Embarrassment.

ON Tuesday the 25th of June, Father Mathew set out for the Sulphur Springs, having previously distributed 100 dollars for various charitable purposes, besides having given a number of cards and medals gratis. The barouche and wagon cost him twenty-one dollars more. The journey was delightful, through a beautiful country, full of variety—hill, plain, rock, mountain, gushing streams and winding rivers, majestic trees as well as fragrant shrubs—and the most perfect stillness reigning over all. No song birds filled the air with their music, and not a sound was heard in this beautiful solitude, save the murmur of the babbling brook, a rustle amid the branches, or the clatter of the horses' feet over the track which was called a road, and which was occasionally but a passage, cleft, as it were, through a dense mass of living verdure. It seemed as if these lovely wilds of Arkansas had never been trodden by the foot of man, who had not yet come to claim as his own an earthly Paradise which had been rendered so well suited for his enjoyment. The settlers were few, and the attempts at clearing were rare.

Father Mathew for a time flung aside his cares, his load of anxiety and trouble, and resolutely left behind him the haunting shadow of debt—more terrible to him than the spectre of Death on the Pale Horse—and became himself once more. He revelled in story and anecdote and humorous incident, recounted events of his early life, and gave his impressions of public men in the New world and the Old; and when he had contributed far more than his share to the enjoyment of the day, he called forth the recollections of his young companions, who were delighted to see the cloud of care banished from his brow, and the anxious look no longer in his eyes. The travellers reached their resting place late in the evening, and were regaled with a supper of milk and honey, and pure bread, and butter fragrant from sweet pasture. The next morning at five o'clock, the carriage was in motion, and the journey was resumed. The same variety of scenery, the same beauty, the same loneliness—the same cheerful gaiety in the carriage, as Father Mathew referred lovingly to incidents of his boyhood and to the memory of his mother, and to scenes and circumstances in the early years of his mission. And when he sought to impress any great truth on his young friends, he illustrated its wisdom by a parable, or its value by some striking fact, borrowed from history or the biography of a great or good man. Having rested for the night at the Hot Springs, where they found friends from New Orleans and Natchez, they arrived next day at the Sulphur Springs, eight miles from the Hot Springs. Here, then, in a lonely log cottage, in the very heart of the solitudes of Arkansas, tenanted by a widow and her son, and not another human being nearer than two miles, or more than two or three nearer than the Hot Springs, the wearied Apostle of Temperance sought a short repose from labour such as scarcely any other man had ever gone through. If thought and care could have been cut off by a barrier of mountains, or by a giant hedge of forest trees, or by rushing streams and flowing rivers, all would have been well; but from this Paradise the serpent could not be banished—it would intrude unwished for and unbidden.

In the lovely Washitau, which wound its graceful course,

now through woods, now between noble hills, Father Mathew was reminded somewhat of the Suir, which flowed through his native county. In the woods, by the banks of the Washitau, or by the side of a smaller stream, he rambled, when the heat was less intense; and he talked wisely and pleasantly to his companions, whose minds he directed, without apparent aim, but with instinctive purpose, to the contemplation and the love of the good. He picked blackberries, too, as of old in the woods of Thomastown; and the ripe berry of Arkansas tasted the sweeter from the association. Thus they spent the two first days in this retreat, reading, talking, rambling from one charming spot to the other, and making small explorations into the forest. And on the Sunday Father Mathew offered up the holy sacrifice on the piazza of the cottage, under the canopy of heaven. The congregation consisted of Mr. and Mrs. Kelly, who had come over from the Hot Springs, and the two secretaries, Mr. O'Meara and Mr. Mahony. It was the first time, in all probability, that the voice of the Priest had been raised in adoration in that part of the forests of America; and the solemnity and stillness of all around contrasted with the scenes of that day twelvemonth, when he first landed on the shores of the New World.

With intense interest, he watched the arrival of the papers from Ireland, which was then slowly emerging from the effects of the Famine. A passage from the diary will exhibit his opinion on a question of much importance to his country:—

Speaking of the changes about to take place in Ireland by the transition of land, Father Mathew remarked how at first it became encumbered. 'The first proprietors were gentlemen and would-be gentlemen, who let the land to what are termed "middle men." They, to make the most of it, usually let the ground to *conacre tenants*, calculating that—suppose the middle-man's take to be 200 acres, at 4*l*. per acre—by letting half in conacre, at say 10*l*. the acre, the rent was over paid. The next year the other half was let in the same way, while he had the produce of the other portion, which was unlet. Thus the poor labourer, strictly speaking, had to bear the burden of all. The present contemplated changes will not be effectual, unless a clause be inserted in every lease *against subletting.*'

The post brought him some letters that gladdened his heart, but more that filled him with sorrow and anxiety. To one of the former, he thus replied :—

Sulphur Springs of Arkansas :
9th July 1850.

My dear Mrs. Rathbone,—I thank you, I thank you, for your more than sisterly solicitude, and for the unexpected and unexampled generosity of Mr. Rathbone. His generous present arrived most seasonably, at a moment when I was quite bewildered, not knowing what to do. The cause of this distress of mind was an unexpected notice I received from the agent of the Insurance Company, to pay 150*l.*, the amount of the second year's extra premium for the permission to travel into the Southern States. The 700 dollars I received from my countrymen in New Orleans, I sent to pay the interest of the bills in the Banks at Cork. I ignorantly flattered myself that the extra premium I paid before I left home would free me during my sojourn in this country. . . . . I shall continue at the cold Sulphur Springs for another fortnight, and then remove seven miles distant, to the celebrated Hot Springs, and after a sojourn of a few days, proceed to visit the Indian nation—the wretched degraded remnant of the once mighty proprietors of this vast continent. I go in the name of the Lord, to seek and to save the poor victims of oppression and drunkenness.

These unhappy people, round whom Cooper and other writers had flung the charm of romantic interest, excited the liveliest compassion of Father Mathew; but he was never able to realise the hope that he had so long cherished, of visiting them in their villages, and rescuing them from the deadly tyranny of the 'firewater'—a worse enemy than the white man, and more fatal to the Indian than the steel or the bullet of the foe.

The fashionable world of America was at this time absorbed in a case of peculiar interest, upon which much was said on both sides, the question of who was in the wrong being discussed with keen partisanship. A gentleman had won for his bride, from a host of competitors, a reigning belle, the loveliest girl of the circle in which she moved. Fortunate prize-winner, he prepared a gilded cage for his lady-bird; and so sumptuous and costly were the bridal chamber and boudoir, that they were thrown open, first to the scrutiny of the *élite*, and then to the devouring curiosity of the vulgar. In twelve months after, while Father Mathew was plunged in the verdant solitudes of Arkansas, the fashionable world was startled by hearing of the separation of the 'happy pair,' and reading in the public prints advertisements from the husband crying down the credit of his wife! One of the heavy charges urged by the disenchanted husband was that his lovely bride was addicted to the free use—not of cognac—but of rouge and cosmetics. 'There are people in this world,' remarked Father Mathew, 'who, if they have no real troubles to vex them, will create troubles for themselves by their own folly.' And thereupon he told many strange things which he had seen in his experience.

After a month's rest at the Sulphur Springs, where he spent some of the happiest moments of his life, Father Mathew left for the Hot Springs. He had become greatly interested in poor Molly, the negro woman, and her little son Peter, whose woolly pate he was constantly caressing; and he much regretted the poverty which alone compelled him to relinquish the desire of purchasing both mother and son, and setting them at liberty. Molly and Peter might have been bought for 350 dollars; but there was no such sum in Father Mathew's exchequer.

While at the Hot Springs, an old lady sent for him to come to her at once. The distance was eight miles. Fortunately, there was no vehicle to be had, and therefore he could not comply with her request. But as Father Mathew could not come to the old lady, she came to him. Though very old and sickly, she mounted a horse and rode over to see him, and to request that he would cure her! At first it was thought she was a Catholic, but she was a Baptist. Father Mathew denied that he possessed the power which the old lady persisted in attributing to him; but he did what he could to soothe and console her.

Generally, and indeed as a rule, the manner in which Father Mathew was treated by members of the different sects in America was in the highest degree creditable to their good feeling. They paid him every honour and respect; they thronged the Catholic churches in which he preached; and, in the addresses which emanated from their communities and associations, they bore the most generous testimony to the value of his services, and the disinterested purity of his motives. In a little village of Arkansas was displayed one of the very rare exceptions to this almost universal expression of courtesy and good feeling. During his stay at the Hot Springs, he visited a Sunday School, where his presence was expected, for an address had been prepared for his reception. Besides the children and their teachers, there were several grown persons in attendance. He was welcomed for various reasons, but he was expressly assured *not* because of his being a Priest of the Roman Catholic Church—an assurance equally gratuitous and offensive. This was a challenge which Father Mathew could not fail to accept; and, in his reply, he said 'he felt justly proud of being an humble minister in that holy church which had done so much for the glory of God and the civilisation of mankind, which had stood bravely in the van from age to age, unchanged while all else was changed, and which had outlived, and would outlive, both calumny and oppression.' Feeling that he had sufficiently vindicated the dignity of his Church, and his allegiance to her faith and authority, he resumed his accustomed gentleness, and expressed his regret that his young friends should have thought it necessary to make the allusion which they did; for, in advocating temperance, he recognised no religious denomination whatever. A sweet smile and a cordial shake of the hand set matters at rest; and the proceedings were happily concluded by the enrollment of a number of 'postulants,' and the presentation of a card and medal to each.

But the scene which was witnessed on Sunday the 29th of December 1850, in the Naval dockyard of Pensacola, afforded the most remarkable testimony to the reverence in which Father Mathew was held by all classes in America. His reception by the Commodore, by whom he was splendidly entertained on the Saturday, was most flattering. When he arrived, he was met by his host, who wore his full dress uniform, and introduced to the numerous company who had been invited to meet him. As the greater number of the guests were officers of the navy, or officials in the establishment, uniforms were generally worn. Had the guest of the evening been the President of the United States or some potentate from the other side of the Atlantic, instead of a simple Irish Priest, he could not have been entertained more sumptuously, nor could he have been treated with more marked respect. Grace was said by Father Mathew, and thanks were returned by the Rev. Mr. Lewis, the Protestant clergyman.

On the morrow there was assembled in the spacious Hall of the Naval Hospital—which had been placed at the disposal of Father Mathew by the Commodore—a congregation of more than 600 persons. It included the very first people in connection with the great establishment, and represented the leading churches of the United States. The hall had been fitted up with an altar and every requisite for Catholic worship; and good ladies willingly assisted Father Mathew, like as of old in Ireland, to render the appearance of the altar and sanctuary as beautiful and as becoming as possible. Among the first that arrived in this extemporised Catholic church were the Commodore and his family, accompanied by military and naval officers, all in full dress uniform. Among the other members of that remarkable congregation was the Rev. Mr

Lewis, who, in order to afford his flock an opportunity of hearing Father Mathew, had word sent round to them that he would not have service on that morning. The decorum and gravity observed by all present could not have been surpassed by any congregation, or in any church in the world. Nor was the congregation disappointed in the Christian minister who preached the word of God to their willing hearts.

He seemed for the moment to have recovered the fire and animation of his best days; and he preached with so holy a sincerity of manner, with such convincing confidence of belief in the truth of what he uttered, and with such fervour and earnestness, that he carried his hearers with him from the beginning to the end of his discourse. At the conclusion of the ceremonies, he again addressed his audience, but on the subject of his mission; and the effect of that appeal was the addition of one hundred followers, most of them of respectable position, to the ranks of temperance.

It was disheartening to Father Mathew that he received but little benefit from his visit to the Springs of Arkansas. His limbs were tremulous and shaky, and his mind was at times grievously depressed. Neither were the accounts from home of the most enlivening character, whether of a public or a private nature. Great misery still amongst the poor—workhouses crowded—employment scarce—trade bad—and emigration on the increase. Then, temperance reading-rooms were abandoned, and their members scattered; and, lastly, there were pressing pecuniary claims. Thorns were scattered in the path of this tottering and toil-worn man; still he bore up bravely, and rather courted than avoided new scenes of labour and excitement. Rest, if it extended beyond a few days, became irksome to him. He longed to be again in the harness, doing his work, adding to his hundreds of thousands of disciples in America. His anxiety of mind, which fretted at inaction, prevented his obtaining the advantages of repose, and of the regular and easy life which he led while at the Springs.

There was one thing, however, to which he had a decided objection—that was, to 'lecture;' and this was the very thing which he was most frequently requested to do. If he travelled by steamer on one of the great rivers, it was intimated to him that the saloon could be converted into a convenient lecture-hall, and that he was sure of a large and appreciative audience; or if the boat stopped at the smallest place—some city on paper, whose future glory was represented by a few log houses—there came a request from the 'citizens' that he should land and lecture. He almost invariably rejected these polite overtures, preferring to read, or to be read to, or to visit the passengers of the humbler class, amongst whom he was sure to find some of his own country people, whose resources were not the most abundant. Frequently are such passages as these to be met with in the diary of his Secretary:—'Went among our countrymen of the lower deck. Some took the pledge. Father Mathew assisted them in a pecuniary way also.' 'To a respectable young man in distress, Father Mathew handed ten dollars privately.' 'In St. Louis, the day before leaving, Father Mathew handed sums of money to old acquaintances in struggling circumstances.' 'The condition of the poor emigrants from Ireland excites his compassion, and he freely shares with them his scanty resources; so much so, that I am anxious for his departure, before they are entirely exhausted.'

There was not a face he met that did not recall some circumstance to his memory, which was prodigious. The man or woman whom he had spoken to years before, in any part of Ireland, he at once recognised, whether in the streets of New York or New Orleans, or on the lower deck of a steamboat on the Mississippi. Many a poor exile's heart was cheered by the salutation—'How are you, my dear?—when did you leave ——?—when did you hear from your father and mother?' Names as well as faces he retained in that wonderful memory; and often was his Secretary surprised at hearing him address people, whom he could not have seen later than six or eight years before in a northern county in Ireland, familiarly by their name, as if he had only left them the day before. He possessed this faculty of memory in the highest degree. And perhaps no faculty is more useful in a leader; for the followers of a great man are not always willing to make allowance for his oblivion of their identity, and expect that their Christian names, if they had half a dozen of them, should be remembered as well as their surnames.

This volume might be swelled with instances of his goodness to these poor wanderers. Here he bestowed money—there gave protection to helpless girls; here procured situations—there induced some compassionate matron to befriend a young creature who stood trembling in the very jaws of danger.

While on his first visit to New Orleans, a number of the brethren of a religious order in Ireland landed in that city. They were on their way to one of the Western States, there to establish a convent and a colony. The money necessary for their purpose was to have been remitted to them in New Orleans; but days passed, and no remittance arrived. The poor men were in great distress of mind, being naturally alarmed at their helpless condition, when they fortunately thought of applying to Father Mathew for advice and assistance. The assistance was readily granted by one who could feel for their position of embarrassment; and in a day or two after, the brothers were on their journey up the Mississippi, with a sum of more than 200*l.* in their possession, advanced to them by Father Mathew. The money was faithfully returned, but not sooner than a year after.

'What shall we do, sir?—we are at our last dollar!' was more than once the anxious demand of his Secretary

'Trust in God, my dear; He will give us enough,' was the invariable reply. It was the same reply which he had often given in the Famine time; and when more money came then into his possession, it was bestowed on new objects. And so it also was in America.

While at Pensacola, a strange circumstance occurred. A young foreigner, named Demetrius Reoboe, died, and Father Mathew officiated at his funeral. The body, which was borne by the friends of the deceased, was first carried to the church, where the service for the dead was chanted, and then to the burial ground, where Father Mathew read the usual prayers. This funeral took place on Monday, December 16, 1850; and on Wednesday, the 18th, there was another funeral, at which he also attended. This was the funeral of a cousin of Demetrius. A compact had been made between them, that the first who died should prepare a place in heaven for the other, who was to follow immediately. Demetrius was buried on the Monday, and in twenty hours afterwards the cousin was a corpse; and in twenty-four hours more, both cousins were tenants of the same tomb. What was the cause? Possibly, it was the effect of imagination upon a system depressed by sorrow at the loss of a beloved friend. Whatever the explanation, the facts were as they have been stated.

Writing to Mrs. Rathbone from St. Louis, on the 20th of October, 1850, Father Mathew says:—

The success that has attended my exertions in the city of St. Louis has exceeded my most sanguine expectations. Nine thousand persons have taken the total abstinence pledge; and when you are informed that I have not been able to lecture in the temperance halls, from infirmity, you must deem it a very considerable number.

You do not appear to approve of my protracted stay in America. Neither do I myself; as I could advance the cause as much, and even more, in England, Ireland, and Scotland. To be candid—for I disguise nothing from one whom I love as a sister—I yearn after the old country, and I envy this letter which is so soon to reach its shores; but I fear to return home, so much is expected by my creditors. If I had foreseen my illness, I would not have incurred debt, which makes me miserable, and detains me in exile. But apprehending no impediment to my career, and having well-grounded pecuniary expectations, I imprudently yielded to my feelings, and. to uphold the teetotallers, and to feed the hungry during the famine, I unhappily incurred liabilities which can only be liquidated by my death—an event which in any case cannot be far distant.

CHAPTER XL.

Politeness to a Female Slave—Her Reply—An **impressive Lesson** —Jenny Lind—Barnum—New World Notions—Another **Attack** —Embarks for Europe—His Farewell **Address—Advice** to his Countrymen—His Mission in America.

FOR nearly three months of the year 1581, Father Mathew made New Orleans his head quarters. He frequently stopped with attached friends, whose acquaintance he had made or renewed on his first visit—for he had known not a few of them in Ireland. Among the most devoted of these was Colonel Mansel White, who had emigrated years before from Tipperary, and who then held a high position in his adopted country. While enjoying the hospitality of this devoted friend, Father Mathew, who, as a true gentleman should be, was always kind and considerate to servants, apologised to a coloured woman for the trouble which his visit had caused her. Her answer much amused him ;—'I do n't consider it any trouble at all ; besides, we can't get along any how in this world without it.'

Though Father Mathew was received with the greatest kindness by slave owners, and though slavery did not present itself to his view in abhorrent colours, he still maintained the same aversion to it as an institution which he had ever expressed. Yet he fully appreciated the difficulty of dealing with a question so vast, and with interests so complicated ; and he could not but think that wisdom, not passion, was essential to its solution. Nor, it must be said, was he much impressed with the feeling evinced to the Negro in the Free States. A single circumstance will often produce a stronger effect upon the mind, than the grandest professions of liberality. He was one day in an omnibus in New York ; and as the vehicle was dashing along through a crowded thoroughfare, it knocked down and rolled over a coloured man. To Father Mathew the African was really a man and a brother, and he got out of the vehicle and assisted to raise the poor fellow from the ground. 'Lift him in,' said the Samaritan, 'and we can take him to the nearest doctor.' 'No, no,' said the passengers—among whom perchance there might have been an abolitionist—'we can't travel with coloured people.' The rejection of the insensible and wounded fellow-creature from that carriage was a lesson which Father Mathew learned in the Broadway of New York, and which he held in his recollection so long as he remained in the United States.

During his stay in New Orleans, Father Mathew made the acquaintance and admired the extraordinary powers of the Swedish Nightingale, the celebrated Jenny Lind, who was at that time creating a sensation in that fair city of the South. Father Mathew found her simple, unaffected, and unspoiled, natural in manner and interesting in conversation ; for even then she spoke English fluently, though with a foreign pronunciation. On two occasions he heard her sing. Declining to attend her concerts, which were held in the evening, he was invited to her rehearsals ; and from a private box in the St. Charles theatre, Father Mathew and his enraptured Secretary heard the nightingale to the best advantage. His Secretary was in an ecstacy ; but we doubt much if the Apostle of Temperance, who in other days nodded so approvingly to the wildest efforts of the village band, and so cordially thanked the artists of a month's teaching for their 'beautiful music,' did not think much more of her kindness than he did of her execution. Mr. O'Meara began to speculate as to what must be the nature of heavenly melody, when, as he remarked in his diary, 'we are so fascinated with the charms of the voice of one of our fellow-creatures.'

Barnum—*Mr.* Barnum is altogether out of place—who was the manager of Jenny Lind's musical engagements in America—was polite and kindly to Father Mathew; but, curiously enough, he delivered a lecture on temperance, of an hour's duration, and never once made mention of the name of the leader of the movement, although he was then in the same city! Surely this was an illustration of the play of *Hamlet* without the character of *Hamlet*

Frequently, in his rambles through New Orleans, as well as in other cities which he visited, Father Mathew recognised, in rather menial capacities, and engaged in the very rudest labour, young men who at home in the old country would have disdained the idea of work. But there they should work, or go to the wall; and many, who had been reared tenderly, and whose education had cost what would then be a grand capital to commence the world with, resolutely fought their way, by sturdy industry, to the social position which they had lost in the miseries of their native land. The doctor, the lawyer, the son of the country gentleman or of the respectable shopkeeper, might be seen serving as a waiter at the bar, toiling as a workman on the quays, or acting as a porter in a grocery store; but those who held on, and exchanged the Irish 'spirit' for the American notion, were sure to change places ere long—that is, to employ instead of being employed. One accustomed to the old world notions would have been amazed, as Father Mathew was, to know that the young fellow who waited on him while at the Hot Springs, had been elected Justice of the Peace the day before; and that the unassuming looking person who drove two of the boarders in a wagon to Little Rock, was the Sheriff of the County! When the Irish caught the American spirit and set to work, and when they combined steadiness with energy, they were sure to go ahead; and Father

Mathew was delighted to find his countrymen filling positions of honour and credit in every part of the States which he visited. How many he redeemed from a degrading and enthralling vice—how many he assisted to rise in the world—how many owed their future independence to his visit—it would be hard to say; but when it is computed that he administered the pledge to more than 600,000 persons in the United States, it must be admitted that his footsteps were followed with blessings, for the good which he did to the children of his race in a strange land.

On his way from New Orleans to Nashville, and while steaming up the Mississippi, he experienced another attack of his old malady. This occurred one day preceding the thirteenth anniversary of the commencement of his mission,—his twelve years of incessant labour—of heart, brain, and body—such labour as not one man in a million could endure, or would think of undertaking. Shattered, broken down, worn out, he was; but he had done a great work, and won a great fame; and let us hope that the consciousness of the good which he had wrought for his fellow-man soothed his pillow of pain.

We must not follow him further in his American tour; nor is it necessary that we should. We should have to recount much of the same which has been already presented to the reader,—the same wonderful triumph of the moral over the physical man—the same holy zeal in the cause of humanity impelling him to efforts beyond his strength—the same unconquerable resolution—the same boundless charity—the same tenderness and compassion for the erring and the sorrowing. We shall not speak of the honours that were offered him wherever he went, the reverence which the highest and the proudest in that great confederacy of free States repeatedly testified to him, or of the friendships that followed him through the few remaining years of his life: we shall rather allow the touching words spoken in reply to an address which he delivered in Cincinnati, in a few months after his last attack, to conclude our account of his long, laborious, and memorable mission to America :—

In the protracted warfare which I have waged against the wide-spread evil of intemperance, and which, I trust, has ever been conducted in a spirit of Christian charity, I have had many serious difficulties to encounter, and much interested hostility to overcome. The growing infirmities of age, aggravated by repeated attacks of a dangerous and insidious malady, now demand retirement and repose. At the close of a long, and thank Heaven, a successful campaign, I find myself, it is true, enfeebled in health, shattered in constitution, and destitute of this world's wealth; yet, with the Apostle, 'I glory in my infirmity,' contracted, as it has been, in the noblest of causes, and I still feel, that no sacrifice, whether of health, of property, or of life itself, is too great to save from ruin and perdition the humblest of those for whom our divine Saviour has willingly shed His most precious blood.

On the 8th of November, he embarked on board the 'Pacific,' one of the Collins' line of steamers, on his return to Europe. Previous to his embarkation, he published his 'Farewell Address to the Citizens of the United States,' from which a passage or two may be appropriately quoted. It thus begins :—

My mission amongst you closes to-day. I cannot take my final departure from the shores of your great and generous country, without publicly recording my deep and grateful appreciation of the generous sympathy, the delicate attention, and the unremitting kindness, which I have experienced in every section of this vast Union. The noble reception which you have spontaneously tendered to a stranger, known merely as an humble missionary in the cause of moral reform, proves the devotion of your people to the interests of humanity, however feebly championed, and has endeared America and her people to me by a thousand ties too sacred for utterance. Though the renewed attacks of a painful and insidious malady have rendered it impossible that I could (without imminent danger to my life) make those public exertions which were never spared by me in the days of my health and of my vigour, I yet thank Heaven I have been instrumental in adding to the ranks of temperance over 600,000 disciples in America. I have been much cheered during the past week, by the receipt of letters from all parts of the States, bearing unimpeachable testimony to the strict fidelity with which this voluntary obligation is observed. I need scarcely add, that virtue, and the duties which religion inculcates, together with peace, plenty, domestic comfort, health, and happiness, everywhere followed in its train.

Having borne grateful testimony to the aid which he had received from the public press of America, and the kindness and friendship which had been shown to him by many distinguished individuals, he then addresses his own countrymen :—

To my own beloved countrymen I most affectionately tender a few words of parting advice. You have, my dearly beloved friends, relinquished the land of your birth, endeared to you by a thousand fond reminiscences, to seek on these distant shores that remuneration for industry and toil too often denied you at home. You are presented here with a boundless field of profitable employment, and every inducement is held out to persevering industry. You are received and welcomed into the great American family with feelings of sympathy, kindness, and friendship. After a few years you become citizens of this great republic, whose vast territorial extent abounds in all the materials of mineral, agricultural, and commercial wealth; the avenues to honour and fame are liberally thrown open to you and to your children, and no impediment (save of your own creation) exists to prevent you attaining the highest social and civic distinction; and will you any longer permit those glorious opportunities to pass unimproved, or, rather, will you not, by studying self-respect, and acquiring habits suited to your new position, aspire to reflect honour alike on the land of your birth and of your adoption? I implore you, as I would with my dying breath, to discard for ever those foolish divisions —those insensate quarrels—those factious broils (too often, alas, the fruits of intemperance) in which your country is disgraced, the peace and order of society violated, and the laws of Heaven trampled on and outraged.

He thus eloquently concludes :—

Friends and fellow-countrymen,—I now bid you a reluctant, a final farewell. A few hours more will separate me from the hospitable shores of America for ever. I carry with me, to the 'poor old country,' feelings of respect and attachment for its people, that neither time nor distance can obliterate.

Citizens of the United States,—I fervently pray that the Almighty Disposer of human events, in whose hands are the destinies of nations, may continue those blessings and favours which you have so long enjoyed—that your progress in every private and public virtue may keep pace with your unexampled prosperity—that you and your children's children may be ever true to the great destiny that awaits you, and to the spirit of those institutions under the fostering care of which you have so rapidly progressed. May your country still extend the hand of succour to the helpless exile, afford an asylum to the persecuted, and a home to the oppressed—and thus inseparably connect her future destiny with the interests of universal humanity.

The 'New York Herald,' of the same date, bears the following most interesting testimony to his mission in America :—

On reviewing his exertions for the past two years and a half, we are forcibly struck with the vast amount of physical fatigue which he must have undergone in the discharge of his onerous duties. Over sixty years of age, enfeebled in health, and shattered in constitution, he has yet, with all the ardour of his former zeal, vigorously prosecuted his 'labour of love.' He has visited, since his arrival in America, twenty-five States of the Union, has administered the temperance pledge in over three hundred of our principal towns and cities, has added more than half a million of our population to the long muster-roll of his disciples; and, in accomplishing this praiseworthy object, has travelled thirty-seven thousand miles, which, added to two voyages across the Atlantic, would make a total distance nearly equal to twice the circumnavigation of the globe. Though labouring under a disease which the slightest undue excitement may render fatal, never has he shrunk from his work of benevolence and love. North and south, east and west, was he to be seen, unostentatiously pursuing the heavenly task of reclaiming his fallen brother, welcoming the prodigal son back into the bosom of society, uttering the joyful tidings that no man is past the hour of amendment; dealing in no denunciation, indulging in no hypocritical cant or pretensions to pharisaical sanctity, by quietly and unobtrusively pursuing his peaceful course, and, like his illustrious sainted prototype, reasoning of 'temperance, justice, and judgement to come.' When his physicians recently recommended absolute repose, in the midst of his labours in a crowded city, as indispensable to his recovery from the last attack of paralysis, 'Never,' replied the venerable man, 'will

I willingly sink into a state of inglorious inactivity; never will I desert my post in the midst of the battle.' 'But your life,' replied his physicians, 'is at stake.' 'If so,' said he, 'it cannot be sacrificed in a better cause. If I am to die, I will die in harness.'

He returned to Ireland in the month of December 1851.

CHAPTER XLI.

Returns to Ireland—The confirmed Drunkard—Glad to see Beggars again—The last of John—His Visitors at Lehenagh--Insanity of Drink—The hundred Invitations to Dinner.

WHILE in Dublin, he spent some days in visiting friends whom he desired to see once more. Going out one morning with this intention, he suddenly said to his nephew, by whom he was accompanied—'Tell the driver to stop, my dear. There is poor ——,' mentioning the name of an unhappy artist whom he had often befriended, and whom he had ineffectually endeavoured to redeem from confirmed drunkenness. The driver pulled up; and there, on the side-path, stood a shabby-looking battered man, blear-eyed, red-nosed, dirty and uncombed, his coat buttoned up to conceal the want of a shirt. The recognition had been mutual. Though Father Mathew's hair was now grey, and gradually approaching to white, there was no mistaking that well-known countenance, which preserved its nobleness of outline and unchanging sweetness of expression. As the miserable creature approached the carriage he burst into a kind of drunken cry, and, seizing the hand of his old benefactor, he kissed it passionately, his emotion depriving him of the power of articulation. Tears streamed down the face of Father Mathew, who could only murmur, 'Poor child, poor child!' as he slipped a bank note into the hand of the prodigal. So long as he could keep him in sight, Father Mathew's glance was fixed on the unhappy being, who remained motionless in the same spot, a miserable object to contemplate. The carriage turned the corner of the street, and the two men never again saw each other in this world. The drunkard died as he had lived—in misery and shame.

About the same time, a beggar, who had accosted him in the usual way, imploring his charity—'for the love of the Lord and for all the sowls that ever left him'—was surprised and overjoyed at finding his appeal responded to by the bestowal of half-a-crown. 'That 's an immense sum, sir, to give to a mere beggar, who would be well content with a penny,' said the nephew. 'Oh, my dear,' replied Father Mathew, 'I delight in relieving the poor. It is my great happiness. I scarcely ever met a beggar in America—for months together I could not see one; and it was a privation to me to have no one to relieve and make happy for a moment.' The good man did not do himself justice when he thus spoke; for though he rarely met a professional mendicant in the United States, he was in the daily habit of relieving distress, and making many happy by his bounty.

His altered appearance, as he returned to Lehenagh, inspired his family with sorrow and apprehension. But however striking the change in his health, his nature and disposition were still the same,—the same benevolence and kindness—the same thoughtfulness and consideration for the wishes and feelings of others.

One cannot be absent for two or three years from his home without finding, on his return, that changes have taken place, or that Death has been at work, even in his own family circle. Father Mathew had not to deplore the loss of any member of his family; but there was one long-familiar face which he was never to see more. That was the sour visage of his man John. It was against John's most solemn warning and appalling prophecy that the priest resolved on going to America. To John's accurate conception of that country, it was the abode of blacks and 'wild Ingins,' and tomahawks and scalps were constantly associated with his ideas of its civilisation.

'Do n't leave your own fine country, sir,' pleaded John, 'and I will never desert you. The boards will carry me out of this house.' 'What does John mean by "the boards" carrying him out, sir?' asked his nephew. 'He means his coffin, my dear,' said Father Mathew, who was intimately acquainted with the figurative style which in moments of strong emotion his venerable domestic indulged in. 'Do n't, sir, do n't go to them bloody-minded savages,' were John's parting words. But his master went, and John remained behind, well provided for. But having been abandoned by its leader, what had John to do with temperance? Nothing. With bitter disdain, John flung off the mask he had but partially worn, and celebrated his liberty in a series of wild and prolonged potations. When the tidings of his master's illness reached home, John's grief was to a great extent softened by the triumph of his predictions. He always knew how it would be, and he told *him* what would happen; for sure a country of blacks and 'Ingins' was no place for a Christian. Sourer and more saturnine became John's temper—deeper and deeper his potations; until one day death surprised him in a sickness which John solely attributed to his intense grief at the continued absence of his master, but which others, including the doctor who attended him, accounted for on very different grounds. However, the little man was carried in 'the boards' to his last resting-place, a considerable time before the return of the priest from the land of 'blacks and Ingins.' Father Mathew thought of John as Prince Hal spoke of Falstaff—he could have 'better spared a better man.' The very weaknesses of the cross-grained little sinner only the more endeared him to his tolerant and indulgent master.

No sooner was it generally known that Father Mathew had taken up his residence at Lehenagh, than the quiet of that secluded home was at an end. His old friends the beggars flocked to visit the benefactor who had never troubled them with searching examinations to test the truth of their story, but who relieved them at every risk—even of his donation being converted into the fiery devil against which he waged incessant war. Under the shade of a spreading tree in summer, or on the door-steps, the beggars mustered; and the same impostors frequently received the dole three or four times in the same day. Nor was Father Mathew obliged to anyone who exposed the imposition. It afforded him happiness to bestow charity, and he did not care to enquire too minutely into the merits of each case. The proof of their imposture would only have caused him pain.

Soon the clatter of the drum and the braying of the trumpet scared the rooks in the old avenue, as some temperance band, which had survived the famine, roused him with its familiar strains; and soon, too, the spacious hall became redolent of strange odours, of which that of bad whisky was the most marked and the most easily discerned. So long as he remained at Lehenagh, he had constant visits from repentant drunkards, whom he received with unfailing benignity. He appeared to think everything else secondary to the reclamation of an erring mortal, and the sooner he could devote himself to this duty, the greater his satisfaction. To the last, he rose at an early hour, and, until his strength utterly gave way, he said mass frequently on weekdays, and always on Sundays and holidays —the household forming his congregation. No excuse would be taken by him for the absence of one of the young people, who were obliged to be most punctual in their attendance.

Though he rose at five o'clock, he did not usually leave his room until it was time for breakfast. The intermediate hours were occupied in prayer and meditation, and in religious exercises which he never omitted to perform. But he would at any time leave his breakfast or dinner if he happened to catch a glimpse of a 'case' which he thought demanded his immediate attention; and the family were compelled to adopt various precautions against intrusion during those hours. Once, however, that the breakfast—with him a scanty meal—was despatched, he was from that moment on the look-out for his unfailing beggars and his repentant profligates.

Many an absurd and many a painful scene was witnessed before that hall-door, as some tattered creature broke away from his wretched wife, and was captured and brought to Father Mathew, who had witnessed the flight and capture with intense interest, and tottered down the stone steps and along the avenue, to meet the prize half way. Once within his influence, opposition was out of the question.

Even the great dog, to which a beggar was an object of profound mistrust, seemed to take kindly to the pledge-seekers and the pledge-breakers; for he would thrust his nose amicably into the hand of some poor fellow who had not spent the Saturday night and the Sunday in the most creditable manner.

'Dan, that's a fine dog,' remarked a teetotaller to an erring friend whom he had in charge. 'He is, Maurice, a fine baste, and a mighty friendly one, too.' 'Dan,' resumed his sober friend, 'I'm thinking that dog has more sense than you.' 'Wisha, that would be aisy for him, the Lord knows,' was the humble reply. 'See, Dan!—there's that dog, and the devil himself would n't make him take a taste of sperits; but the devil can't keep you from it—and that dog, we're tould, has no raison, and you have.' 'I ought to have it, Maurice, sure enough; but when I take a drop at all, I'm bothered complately.' 'Right, my dear,' said Father Mathew, who had heard the dialogue with delight, 'we lower ourselves far below the brute, when we indulge in a degrading passion, that robs us of our most glorious birthright—our reason. The Great Being who made us, did not render us dependent upon a vicious stimulant for our health and happiness. We do n't require it, and we are better without it. Do not mind anyone who says to the contrary.'

The men were not always the most difficult to deal with. Women were brought to him by their husbands, whose means they had destroyed, and whose happiness they had wrecked. Some were dogged and stubborn, others insensible to every feeling of shame or compunction, and more were labouring under the influence of that terrible malady, *delirium tremens.* 'There is a devil in me—there is a devil in me!' shrieked out a young woman, whose flushed face, wild stare, and frantic gestures proved that she was suffering from the insanity of drink. 'Yes, indeed, the devil of drink possesses you, my poor woman,' said Father Mathew. 'There! he says I 'm a devil—that the devil is in me! I knew it—I knew it—I 'm damned!—I know I 'm damned—the devil is dragging me down to hell! There! there! there!' Wilder and wilder grew her shrieks, as the paroxysm of the madness increased in intensity. The poor husband's dejected appearance, as he gazed upon the fury with a look in which shame and affection were blended, spoke a volume of domestic misery and disappointed hope. When the paroxysm subsided, Father Mathew brought his influence to bear on her; and ere many weeks had passed, a modest, blushing wife fell on her knees before him, kissed his hand with passionate fervour, and thanked him, amidst sobs and tears, for the peace of heart and home which she then enjoyed. The husband's fervid, 'God bless your reverence!' was fully as expressive in its gratitude.

As long as he could, he kept up his visits to old friends; and, with that purpose, he frequently drove into the city, which was about two miles distant from Lehenagh. One day he returned unusually animated. 'Something must have pleased you very much, sir?' remarked Mrs. Mathew. The priest then told how he had been invited to dinner by the little son of a respectable mechanic whom he met in the street. 'Father Mathew,' said the little fellow, 'do come and dine with us—we have such a nice dinner.' 'What have you, my dear?' enquired Father Mathew. 'We have a fine leg of mutton, and we have turnips, and we have potatoes,' replied the child. 'Have you no cakes, my dear?' said Father Mathew. 'No, sir,' answered the little fellow, with an abashed air, as if he had no right to have given an invitation under such circumstances. 'Then, my dear, you must have them,' said Father Mathew, putting a half-crown into the hand which he held in his own.

The next day he returned from the city with a more than usually depressed air. 'What is the matter, sir?—has anything annoyed you?' enquired his sister-in-law. 'My dear, I received a hundred invitations to dinner from a hundred little boys, to-day!' was his reply, in a mournful tone of voice. He could not for a time enjoy the amusement which the story evidently caused to his listeners.

There were other visitors to Lehenagh beside beggars, impostors, and people to take the pledge. These were persons who had come in the hope of being cured of their bodily ailments.

CHAPTER XLII.

Father Mathew's alleged Power of effecting Cures—General Belief in this Power—The chronic Headache—Dr. Barter's Testimony —Instances of his strange Influence—Pilgrimages to his Grave.

WHATEVER may be the opinions entertained as to Father Mathew's reputed power of effecting cures in certain cases of disease, the subject, however delicate, is one to which I cannot avoid alluding. Were I to refrain from noticing it, I should appear as if shrinking from the risk of hostile criticism; and I would moreover fail in adequately representing the veneration in which he was held by the Irish people. The subject is one which occasioned much interest during his lifetime, and since his decease.

That Father Mathew was the *cause* of cures being effected, I cannot deny myself the belief. That he *effected* cures, is what many persons, in every way trustworthy as to character and intelligence, have repeatedly asserted. The belief in this alleged power appears to have been entertained even before his connection with the temperance cause; but from that time to the hour of his death, it certainly existed very generally throughout Ireland. Even on his first visit to Dublin, in 1840, he was besieged by crowds of afflicted people, suffering from different ailments, who imagined that his touch and his blessing would prove more efficacious to them than all the ministrations of science. Farther on I shall prove, from evidence which, to me at least, seems conclusive as to the fact, that Father Mathew conferred instantaneous relief, and in some instances permanent benefit, on persons labouring under various bodily affections; and I shall now endeavour to represent the manner in which those who had no doubt as to the *fact*, accounted, or sought to account, for what was to them, as to others, a subject of wonder and speculation.

Those who suffer from any physical malady are naturally impatient of their affliction, and are generally willing to adopt any means of relief which they are assured, or which they imagine, will serve them, whether those means commend themselves to their reason, or are reconcilable to their good sense and judgement. Indeed, it would seem as if the sick or afflicted person becomes more or less of the nature of a child, and unreservedly surrenders reason and judgement to the physician, whether that physician be a mere pretender, or a man of approved ability and experience in the treatment of disease. We know what an effect is produced through the mind upon the body, and how the most harmless and simple medicine—the coloured water, or the bread pill—can be made to play an important part in the cure of disease, and the restoration of health.

It is not difficult to conceive how a naturally religious people should believe in the efficacy of a good man's prayer, and how, enfeebled and suffering from one malady or another, they should implore his interposition in their behalf. There are very many who, believing in the power and mercy of God, equally believe that, even in these times, as in days of old, that power and that mercy are wonderfully manifested; and that good and holy mortals are now, as then, selected as the fitting instruments through which blessings are dispensed to individuals and communities. Those who sought Father Mathew's aid were profoundly impressed with the conviction of his goodness and holiness. They looked upon him as a man of God, one chosen by Providence for the accomplishment of a great work. This they were told by bishops and by priests, who constantly spoke of the Apostle of Temperance in this spirit. Even those of another faith did not hesitate to speak of him and to address him in language of the same nature. Thus the conviction of his goodness and holiness was general—indeed, universal; and this conviction was most favourable to the idea of his being able to work some benefit for those in whose behalf he petitioned Him whom he so faithfully served, and whose honour and glory he so zealously laboured to promote. With this conviction and this belief firmly rooted in the minds of persons suffering from a malady in which the mind could in any way become a useful agent in assisting or effecting a cure, it is not surprising that many returned from Father Mathew considerably improved, if not wholly cured. That they *did* so return, I can state on authority which I cannot question; but what was the exact cause, or mode, or means of cure, is what I shall not venture to explain, save in so far as I have already indicated.

Father Mathew persistently represented to those who came to him in the expectation of relief, that he had no power whatever to effect cures, or to work miracles. It was to no purpose that he shewed them his paralysed limbs, saying, 'Surely, I would cure these if I could; but I have no power to cure anyone.' His patients were ready with an answer, saying—'It is because you took the sickness of others on yourself that you are so afflicted.' That he could not cure himself was no proof to them that he could not cure others; and, frequently, he was accused of insensibility to sufferings, which those afflicted with them believed he could relieve, if he only earnestly set about doing so. Having declared that he had no such power as that attributed to him by his petitioners, he never refused to bless them, or pray for their recovery, if such recovery were pleasing to God. He naturally thought that his blessing could do them no harm, and besides he would not refuse to grant that which was so earnestly implored.

The total abstinence which the pledge imposed, really did effect what seemed to be miraculous cures; and the sound advice which he frequently imparted to those who applied to him for relief, greatly assisted the operation of nature. Then, in not a few instances, it was at the very turning point of the disease that his aid was implored; and pious gratitude readily attributed to the effect of his touch, his blessing, or his prayers, what was about to happen as the natural result of a favourable change. Mothers, in the frenzy of a mother's alarm, brought him their children, upon whose marble features the seal of death seemed to be impressed; and there are letters to which I could refer, in which, in spite of his earnest disclaimer, the writers persisted in attributing the recovery of the beloved ones to his holy intercession.

The reader may account for the following, which I give because it is within my own personal knowledge, in any way he thinks best; all I desire to do, is to state that which I know to be a fact. A young lady, of position and intelligence, was for years the victim of the most violent headache, which assumed a chronic character. Eminent advice was had, but in vain: the malady became more intense, the agony more excruciating. Starting up one day from the sofa on which she lay in a delirium of pain, she exclaimed—'I cannot endure this torture any longer; I will go and see what Father Mathew can do for me.' She immediately proceeded to Lehenagh, where Father Mathew was then sick and feeble. Flinging herself on her knees before him, she besought his prayers and blessing. In fact, stung by intolerable suffering, she asked him to cure her. 'My dear child, you ask me what no mortal has power to do. The power to cure rests alone with God. I have no such power.' 'Then bless me, and pray for me—place your hand on my head,' implored the afflicted lady. 'I cannot refuse to pray for you, or to bless you, my dear child,' said Father Mathew, who did pray for and bless her, and place his hand on her poor throbbing brow. Was it faith?—was it magnetism?—was it the force of imagination exerted wonderfully? I shall not venture to pronounce which it was; but that lady returned to her home perfectly cured of her distressing malady. More than that—cured completely, from that moment forward.

I might quote letters from persons who thoroughly believed that Father Mathew had cured them of various affections—that he had instantaneously restored sight to eyes almost blind, and power to limbs altogether helpless; but I prefer, in a matter so full of delicacy, and respecting which opinion is so certain to differ, to rely on the written testimony of a gentleman above all suspicion, and to whom it is impossible to attribute what may probably be designated 'the credulity of superstition.' Besides, as will be seen, he attributes what he saw to a very different cause from that which is so readily accepted by those who believe in the efficacy of prayer, and the miraculous power of faith.

The writer of the following statement is a Protestant gentleman—Dr. Barter of Blarney—whose hydropathic establishment of St. Anne's, is one of the best known in the United Kingdom. This statement is the result of a conversation which I recently had with Dr. Barter, as to the alleged power of working cures attributed to Father Mathew, and in which the doctor mentioned such facts—which came under his notice in the summer of 1853—as induced me to request that he would be good enough to reduce them to writing. This he willingly did, at the same time giving me permission to make the fullest use of his name. The following is the document written by Dr. Barter, and bearing his signature:—

As a resident for months in my establishment, to which Father Mathew had come for the restoration of his health, I had ample opportunity of studying his character and habits; and well do I remember his unceasing labour in the cause of suffering humanity.

The crowds that came daily from distant parts of the country to seek his aid were legion; yet to every one, from the highest to the lowest, he was ever accessible, and never seemed tired of doing good. I often remonstrated with him on the injury which must follow from such severe physical and mental labour, but to no purpose; his love for his fellow-man, and his goodness of heart, banished from his noble breast every selfish feeling, and he disregarded my repeated warnings.

Several came to be cured of painful disease; *and I often witnessed great relief afforded by him to people suffering from various affections, and in some cases I was satisfied that permanent good was effected by his administration.* Such satisfactory results, on so large a scale too, made him the more earnest in his purpose, and gave the recipient unbounded faith in his power; and the result, from such a favourable combination of circumstances, could not be otherwise than beneficial to the patient. *Father Mathew possessed in a large degree the power of animal magnetism*, and I believe that the paralytic affection from which he suffered, and which brought his valuable life to an untimely end, was produced by an undue expenditure of this power. His nervous power was lowered by imparting his health and vigour to thousands. I have often seen injurious results from such a cause, and have experienced them in my own person. Ought not this to endear his memory to us, and more particularly to those who have received benefit from the exercise of his power?

The doctor's theory is, that the magnetic power controls and directs the nervous power, thereby substituting a healthy for a morbid action of the system. Upon this theory or principle—whether it be sound or erroneous, I offer no opinion—Dr. Barter accounts for what he himself witnessed during a period of some months at his establishment in Blarney, and of which many others were equally cognisant. I value his testimony on this account—that it furnishes the evidence of an intelligent and unprejudiced witness as to the *fact* that, from whatever cause, or through whatever means or agency, Father Mathew did afford relief to persons suffering from disease.

From a long letter, overflowing with gratitude to the memory of Father Mathew, written by a man of good character and credibility, who states that he had received his education in the school which his benefactor had established shortly after he commenced his mission in Cork, I extract the following passage, merely adding that *I know* the writer to be that which I have represented him:—

I could tell you of people that he cured, only it would occupy too long, but I can tell you what happened to myself. My eyes got very bad, and I was afraid I was going to lose my sight entirely, which would have brought me to ruin. I was obliged to stay away from my business in the market, I became so blind, so I said I would go over to Cove Street and see his reverence, which I did. I was so bad that I got a boy to lead me in the streets. Father Mathew was there before me, and was glad to see me and shook hands with me, as he always did; he was kind to simple and gentle, and there was no sort of pride in him at all. So I told him how bad I was, and sure he saw that, for he asked me how did I get so bad. I knelt down, and he prayed for me and put his hand on my head, and made the sign of the cross on my eyes, and he said it would n't signify, and that I would be well shortly; and sure I was, for I walked home without the boy helping me, and I was as well as ever that day. I brought my wife to him another day, and he cured her of a sore bosom, as all the neighbours know.

Not only were those afflicted with bodily ailments brought to him, but those likewise who suffered from mental infirmity. A young man was being taken by his friends to the Lunatic Asylum of Cork, and the treatment which he received at their hands was not such as to improve his condition. Bound on a car, his limbs tied with cords, and his head exposed to the rays of a fierce sun, he was thus being conveyed to the Asylum, when the conductors conceived the idea of first taking him to Father Mathew. The idea was fortunately acted upon, and they turned the horse's head towards Lehenagh. Father Mathew's heart was filled with compassion at the spectacle of a human being bound like a wild beast, uttering strange cries, and foaming at the mouth. He spoke to him kindly and gently, and thus soothed his chafed spirit; and he then desired his friends to loose the cords that bound him, and to protect his head from the sun. The effect of the kind voice, the gentle words, and the soothing touch, was marvellous upon the patient, who had suffered violent paroxysms shortly before. The poor fellow recognised Father Mathew, in whose power to serve him he seemed to have confidence, and he promised that if he were brought back home, he would do everything that he was asked to do; and upon Father Mathew's intercession, he was brought back, instead of being placed in the Asylum. In a month afterwards, a fine handsome young man, well dressed and well-mannered, came to Lehenagh, to return him thanks for 'what he had done for him.'

Another case, which I shall mention, was that of a young girl from Macroom, who was brought to him by her parents, who were afraid that she would die of starvation, as she had obstinately refused to eat anything for a number of days, or to utter a single word. Her head was seriously affected, and she could not sleep. She was taken three times to Father Mathew. Through the first visit some good was effected, and after the third visit she was perfectly restored to her natural appetite and sleep. Before she left Lehenagh, she ate and drank what was offered to her, and spoke rationally, and without reluctance.

Another girl, whose hands were tightly clenched, and the nails of whose fingers were buried in the flesh of her palms, was also brought to him by her parents. For weeks she had been in that condition; and though the physicians who had been consulted endeavoured to open her hands, they tried in vain. 'Allow me, my dear,' said Father Mathew, in his winning voice; and taking her hand in his, and gently unlocking and extending her fingers, he brought it into its natural form. This was a case of pure hysteria affecting the limbs, such as is frequently seen in the hospitals.

Cases such as these—which will be accounted for in various ways—confirmed the people in the belief of his power to cure. When he was asked by members of his family, or by his more intimate friends, how he could himself account for some cures which were too patent to be denied or doubted, his invariable reply was—'It is faith—the great faith of the people.'

That this faith took rather a wide range of latitude at times, a trifling incident, which occurred during the early days of the temperance movement, will show. A poor woman having a little boy in her arms, came towards him, saying—'Oh wisha, yer reverence, put yer hand on this little gossoon; he 's the divil intirely! 'Surely, my good woman,' said Father Mathew, 'that poor child is not a drunkard?' 'No, yer reverence,' replied the anxious parent, 'but he 's the divil at the pipe; and I want you to take the "shaugh" out of him.'

To Father Mathew's own words, spoken in Dublin, in the year 1840, and quoted at page 140 of this volume, I would refer the reader—those words being an authentic exposition of his ideas and feelings on this delicate subject.

I shall conclude my allusion to it with the mention of an appropriate fact,—that, in accordance with the time-honoured custom of praying at the graves of holy men who had been remarkable for the sanctity of their lives, numbers of people—most of them afflicted with ailments of various kinds—constantly come to pray at the tomb of Theobald Mathew. The sexton of the cemetery relates many instances of relief being obtained, or cures being effected, through visits to his grave. One thing is certain—that people who entered as cripples, supported by crutches, have left their crutches inside the railings of the tomb, and returned without aid or assistance to their homes. Votive offerings of this description have been frequently found in the same place, but have been invariably removed, by order of the clergymen to whom the charge of the cemetery belongs. I mention the fact of such visits being made, and of such testimonies being offered, by pilgrims to the tomb of Father Mathew, as an evidence of that belief in his holiness and sanctity which exists—and which no doubt will long continue to exist—in the minds of a grateful and religious people.

CHAPTER XLIII.

Another Attack of Apoplexy—His Visit to Madeira—**Getting** worse—Goes to Queenstown.

WHILE at Lehenagh, after his return from America, he was seized with a fit of apoplexy, which demanded the most active treatment. On the 1st of February 1852, at five in the evening, he fell in a fit while alone in his bedroom. The noise of the fall was heard by the family, who were apprehensive, from their knowledge of his condition; and on entering the room, they found him lying senseless on the floor. It was for a time feared that he would never recover from the insensibility in which he was plunged; but his friend and physician, Dr. O'Connor, was soon at his bedside; and by that bedside his attached and faithful secretary, Mr. O'Meara, watched during the entire night. The patient passed from insensibility into a profound sleep; and so entirely unaware was he of having been ill, that, on awaking at early dawn, his first words were, 'This is the Feast of the Purification. David, I must prepare to say Mass.' He recovered very rapidly from this attack, and could not be restrained from immediately resuming his wonted duties.

In a letter addressed to the 'United Kingdom Alliance,' dated Cork, February 21, 1853, Father Mathew gave his warmest adhesion to that association. He says:—

My labours, with the Divine aid, were attended with partial success. The efforts of individuals, however zealous, are not equal to the mighty task. The United Kingdom Alliance strikes at the very root of the evil. I trust in God the associated efforts of the many good and benevolent men will effectually crush a monster gorged with human gore.

It would be a painful task to trace the sure and steady progress of the malady which had marked as its victim this best friend of his country. Alike sanguine as desponding, he looked upon freedom from pain, or a faint improvement in his limbs, as the forerunner of certain recovery. As soon as he felt strong enough to resume his functions as a clergyman, he took up his abode on Charlotte Quay, near his church of the Holy Trinity, which had been consecrated during his absence in America. But the labour which, in spite of every remonstrance, he would impose upon himself, soon developed worse symptoms; and he was recommended to go to Madeira, as much for the climate as to rid him, even for a time, of the toil which he daily underwent, and which no entreaty could induce him to relinquish.

He left for Madeira in October 1854, and did not return until August in the following year. From a letter which he addressed to Dr. Hayden of Dublin, dated from Funchal, January 22, 1855, the following extract is taken:—

As I flatter myself it will afford you pleasure, I inform you that, under the influence of this genial climate, my paralysed limbs are much improved. I still suffer from lameness, which prevents me from exercising on foot, the streets being so steep. I lament this, as we have no vehicles except cars drawn by oxen on the hills by which the little city of Funchal is encompassed. I am almost prevented from taking the air, as the charge for the ox-cars is too expensive—two shillings and three pence the hour. There are vehicles called palanquins, and others named hammocks, carried by two men, which are more expensive than the ox-cars. I have never suffered myself to be carried in those lazy palanquins and effeminate hammocks. I do not deem myself feeble enough (thank God) to be carried by my fellow-creatures. These vehicles are generally used by delicate ladies, or gentlemen in deep consumption. It is frightful to meet in the narrow streets these awful vehicles, in which the miserable sick are extended at full length.

We enjoy in Madeira a perpetual spring, in which the thermometer never falls in the shade lower than sixty-four, but often rises to seventy-four. It is to be feared that on my return to Ireland, I shall suffer severely from the cold.

As for myself, the only wish I have for improved health, is that it may enable me to resume my labours for the few remaining years of my life, in the sacred cause of temperance. Should it be the merciful will of the great God not to restore my health, I fervently pray that the Almighty may, in His goodness, call me to Himself, that I may not be a burthen to my friends.

If he could have freed himself from the care and anxiety that perpetually haunted his mind, and that, like a shadow, dimmed the beauty of that lovely island, he might have had a chance, not of recovery, but of prolonging his life for some years. But he chafed at his forced inaction, and was impatient to be again at work. To die in harness seemed to be his destiny, and it certainly was his desire. There was no necessity for him to preach temperance to the abstemious people by whom he was surrounded, but he contrived to find amongst the poorest of the islanders constant objects for his bounty. By the residents, as well as the visitors to the island, he was treated with the greatest consideration, and the regret was general when his intended departure was announced.

While in Liverpool, on his way to and his return from Madeira, the invalid received many evidences of respect and veneration; but the kindness of his steadfast friends, the Rathbones, whom he then saw for the last time, was as affectionate and generous as ever.

Believing that he had derived much benefit from his visit to Madeira, he again undertook duties for which his shattered health rendered him wholly unequal, and he was once more compelled to return to his brother's house at Lehenagh, where he resumed the old routine. Day by day he became more feeble and helpless; still he would totter down the steps, and limp along the avenue to meet a poor drunkard half way, or to anticipate the arrival of a friend whom he had recognised from the window or the door. Many were the sweet words of counsel that fell from his lips during the last year of his life. Sweetness, humility, and holiness, marked every hour of his declining days. Even while surrounded by his brother's family, he was constantly engaged in silent prayer ; and when he spoke, his words breathed the very spirit of devotion. When reference was made in his presence to his services to his fellow creatures, or to his acts of goodness, he would say with the greatest earnestness—'Oh ! do not, do not, my dear, give me any merit for what I have done. How I wish my motives had been always pure in the sight of God !'

Throughout his life as a priest it afforded him the greatest consolation and happiness to offer up the Holy Sacrifice. It was to him the most solemn moment for communing with his God ; and though at all times his manner at the altar was in the highest degree edifying, towards the close he appeared wholly absorbed in his devotions. On each of the two Christmas days preceding his death, he celebrated three masses, the greatest number a priest is allowed to celebrate, and only on that solemn festival. About ten months before his death, he was observed to stagger at the altar, just after the consecration. The clerk at once came to his support ; but the priest made a strong mental effort, and so far rallied as to go through the ceremony to the end. He made no remark afterwards as to what had happened, but he accepted the warning, for he never ventured to say mass again. To one of his fervent piety, this was a sad privation ; he however accepted it with his usual resignation.

Frequently the cloud, which had been so long gathering, would settle on his brain, and shroud him in a kind of mournful apathy. Every artifice which affection could suggest would then be resorted to, to cheer him, but in vain ; and the sadness that seemed to hang like a pall upon his brow, would communicate its gloomy influence to the group around him. Few could recognise, in that drooping figure, and mournful and dejected countenance, the Father Mathew of other days. Where was now the elastic step, the vigorous frame, the clear bright eye, the smile so full of charm? Disease and affliction had effected the painful transformation. Loving hearts ached at that sad spectacle of human decay.

The knowledge that his death could not be far removed was constantly present to his mind. So long as he remained at Lehenagh, he would before retiring at night shake hands with his brother and sister-in-law, and kiss the younger members of the family; and did he happen to leave the sitting-room without having done so, he invariably came back, even from the bottom of the stairs leading to his bed-room, to give them this salutation. The earnestness of the manner in which this nightly leave-taking was gone through, excited the surprise of his brother and Mrs. Mathew, who made no remark at the time; but afterwards, while at Queenstown—where he died—the priest explained what had appeared so strange from its impressiveness. 'I feared,' said he, 'that I might die before the morning, and it was as if I were every night taking my last farewell of those I loved.'

His prediction that he would suffer from the cold on his return from Madeira, was painfully realised. Fires had to be kept up at Lehenagh even during the early summer; but the rooms were large, and the poor invalid sighed for the warmth of Funchal, or thought with regret of those genial cities of the Southern States, in which for a time he had forgotten his bodily infirmity. Another voyage to Madeira was then out of the question, and he resolved to try the milder atmosphere of Queenstown.

Thither he would go, in spite of the earnest entreaty of his relatives, who desired to have him near them, and to watch over him to the last; but he was not to be moved from his purpose once that he had resolved upon it It was shrewdly suspected that one of his reasons (his chief reason) for quitting Lehenagh for Queenstown was to avoid giving further trouble to his family, to whom he felt he had been so long a cause of anxiety and solicitude.

Tender and sad was his leave-taking of his affectionate relatives, with whom he had spent most of the happiest days of his life, and who rejoiced when he was glad, and suffered when he was oppressed with sorrow or with care. Beneath those spreading trees what happy groups had assembled at his bidding! Upon that lawn how many a time were witnessed the innocent sports, and were heard the joyous shouts, of the young people whom he had invited to holiday and to feast! Before that door how often had he beheld the beloved banner flutter at the head of some faithful society, and listened with delight to strains which were ever harmonious to his ear! Tenderly and sorrowfully he bade a long adieu to a spot consecrated by countless memories of happiness and affection, of pleasure and of pride; for he knew in his heart that he would never see it more—he was going to Queenstown to die.

CHAPTER XLIV.

Has Father Mathew's Work survived him?—The Spirit lives.

AND now, before the curtain falls, and we catch the last glimpse of him whose character and career I have endeavoured, however feebly and imperfectly, to depict, I would say a word upon a question which has been put to me repeatedly, and which will naturally suggest itself to the mind of the reader—namely, has Father Mathew's work survived him? Conscientiously speaking, I feel convinced *it has.* Nay more, I believe it is impossible to destroy and undo that work. Father Mathew taught his generation this great lesson,—that, as a rule, alcoholic stimulants are not only unnecessary but injurious to the human being—that drunkenness is an odious and disgusting vice—that poverty and misery and disease and crime are born of this vice—that the man who altogether abstains is safer than the man who is moderate in his enjoyment of that which is so full of risk and danger; and that not only is there no possible safety for those liable to excess, and unable to resist temptation, save in total abstinence, but that there is redemption—social, moral, and physical—to be found in the pledge for the most confirmed and abandoned drunkard. This is a grand lesson to have taught; and this lesson, which has become part of the world's wisdom and experience, cannot be obliterated—certainly not from the memory of the Irish people. In so far, then, he has left his work as a great lesson and legacy to posterity; and whenever again the vice against which he waged so vigorous and successful a strife for many of the best years of his life assumes a formidable aspect—dangerous to society and perilous to morality, industry, peace, and order—there is no fear that the lesson will not be applied, or that Providence will not inspire, or even raise up, those who will put it into practice as Father Mathew did, for the sake of religion, humanity, and country. If they will not preach total abstinence, they will at least counsel and promote temperance for the mass, and rigid sobriety for those who know not how to limit themselves within the bounds of moderation.*

* As an instance directly in point, I would refer to the extraordinary work accomplished in his arch-diocese, by the Most Rev. Dr. Leahy, Catholic Archbishop of Cashel and Emly. He has succeeded in inducing the publicans within the limits of his episcopal jurisdiction to close their houses, and not to sell anything spirituous, on Sundays; and this he has effected with the most beneficial results to the morality and good order of the arch-diocese. Dr. Leahy is favourably known to the English public for his successful suppression of stupid feuds and wicked faction fights, and for the public and solemn reconciliation of two of the most powerful factions that existed in Tipperary. In a public letter addressed 'To the Very Rev. John Spratt, D.D., and James Haughton, Esq., of Dublin,' Dr. Leahy describes the means by which he enforces his Sunday-closing law, and which, no doubt, requires similar circumstances for its enforcement and success in other places. The principal of these must be that the people, as throughout the district in question, should be of one religious faith. The letter from which this extract is quoted, is dated 'Thurles, 23rd of April, 1863,' and was repeatedly referred to in the House of Commons, in the debate on Mr. Soames' Bill, on Wednesday the 2nd of May. The extract is as follows:—

'Now, what are the means by which we have been enabled to enforce this law? The authority of the Bishop, the cooperation of the Clergy, who from the first threw themselves into the cause with commendable zeal, the influence of religion coupled with the frequentation of the Church's sacraments, the people's strong religious sentiments, their respect for the ordinances of their Church, their deep reverence for their clergy, especially for the word of their Bishop—with them sacred;—these, and these only, are the means by which we have enforced this law, and enforced it so effectually, that in a few years it has acquired all the stability of a time-honoured ordinance, and is observed by the people as exactly as any law of Church or State in this realm;—observed, too, let me add, not as an unpleasant restraint, but most willingly by those on whom it imposes the sacrifice of appetite, nor less willingly by those of whom it requires the sacrifice of a gainful trade—observed by the poor and by the rich alike, by the small hard-struggling publican all the same as by the wealthy merchant, in the village and at the cross-road just as in the populous town. It is to myself a marvel how the people observe this law.'

That the mass of the Irish people have not adhered to the pledge, is true; but, assuming the possibility that they would have done so, had Father Mathew retained for some years longer the same vigour of constitution and physical activity which he enjoyed in the height of the temperance agitation, and had he been able to devote his undivided attention to the completion of his work—is it within the bounds of human possibility that any moral movement could have withstood the combined influence of such discouraging causes as those which the temperance movement had to encounter? Let us be just to Father Mathew, and to his followers; and let us remember the succession of events which pressed with disheartening effect upon the temperance cause and the Irish people,—the terrible and protracted famine—the political disturbance of 1848, and the reaction which necessarily followed the impaired health of Father Mathew—his long absence from Ireland, extending over a period of two years and a half, from June 1849 to December 1851—his gradual decay, which admitted but of feeble and intermittent efforts on his part—and the depression and want of public spirit, which the poverty and misery of the country induced. What human cause—what cause which relied for its sustainment upon a high moral tone and pride of spirit, individual as well as national—could have resisted influences such as these? The wonder is, not that they acted so injuriously as they did,

It is but fair to the Archbishop to quote a preceding passage, where he describes the manner in which he dealt with his flock previous to his attempting the reform that secured their sobriety on the Lord's Day.

'As I went the round of the diocese from parish to parish in performing the duty of visitation, seldom or never did I omit to make temperance a subject of exhortation to the people, following up exhortation with the practical work of administering a pledge, sometimes to individuals, generally to large groups of persons gathered around the sanctuary rail. The pledge was—not to get drunk at any time, nor to frequent public-houses on Sundays or holidays—and bound for no longer a time than three years, or say, till the Bishop's next coming to the parish. A pledge for life, except in rare instances, or of total abstinence, except in the case of confirmed drunkards, I have seldom, if ever, administered, preferring easy temporary pledges as more likely to do good to the mass of the people.

but that they did not act more fatally than they did ; for, in spite of all that has happened to discourage and depress, the organisation is not destroyed. In every city, in every town, in every parish, there are still numbers who have remained faithful to the practice of total abstinence, and there are everywhere to be found the ready elements of future revival. Living examples of the value of sobriety—its value to character, to position, to worldly prosperity, to domestic happiness and public esteem—are to be found in every part of the country ; and these examples preach a lesson more eloquent than words can frame or tongue can utter. I personally know, not a few, but many men of worth and respectability, who owe all they possess and enjoy to temperance, and who glory in proclaiming their undying gratitude to the author of their happiness and independence. They are to be found in every rank of life ; and their fidelity to the cause is the more resolute and enthusiastic from the memory of the misery and degradation from which they were rescued and redeemed.

There is then the improved moral tone of society, and the change in the public sentiment. Formerly, drunkenness was regarded rather as a fault for which there were numberless excuses and palliations ; now, drunkenness is looked upon as a degrading vice, and the drunkard finds no universal absolution from the judgement of society. Whatever opinion may be held as to the necessity of total abstinence, or the wisdom of moderation, there is but one opinion as to excess—that is, one of just and general condemnation. Formerly, there was not a circumstance in one's life, or an event in one's family, or in the family of one's friend or acquaintance, that was not a legitimate excuse for a poor fellow 'having forgotten himself,' or 'being overtaken by liquor ;' but a sterner verdict is now pronounced upon the delinquent—and that sterner verdict, which evidences a higher tone of public wisdom and morality, is another of the results of Father Mathew's teaching. And in this way, too, his work has survived the mortal life of its author.*

* James Haughton, of Dublin, writing from that city on the 1st of May, 1863, says :—

'I am happy to say that Father Mathew's influence for good is still extensive in this city, where many who took the pledge from him have since lived happy and blameless lives. I cannot give you the least idea of the number of teetotallers in Dublin. Father Spratt is constantly enrolling members, but he does not keep any record of them. Every Sunday evening we hold a meeting in Cuffe Street, where from one to three hundred persons constantly take the pledge.'

In Cork a healthful spirit of revival is manifesting itself—the result principally of the efforts of a few earnest men, more distinguished by their zeal than by their social position or personal influence.

The temperance cause is deeply rooted in other portions of the United Kingdom ; and wherever Father Mathew preached, in the Old World or in the New, there are to be found propagandists of his doctrine, and living examples of its practical utility and advantage to the human race.

CHAPTER XLV.

In Queenstown—His Christian Humility—The ruling Passion strong in Death—His last Moments.

DURING the autumn of 1856, a white-haired venerable man, of a countenance noble in outline and sweet in expression, might be seen slowly creeping along the sunny places of Queenstown, his tottering steps assisted by a young lad, on whose shoulder one hand of the invalid rested for support. This was Theobald Mathew, the Apostle of Temperance, whose voice, a few years before, rang in the crowded hall, and was heard far above the heads of listening multitudes, and whose physical energy then seemed almost indestructible. There was not one who did not bow to him with respect, as he passed slowly by ; and no eye glanced at that halting gait and that shattered frame, without a look of the deepest sympathy. Hour by hour, step by step, that martyr to the public good was on his way to his last resting-place. Hour by hour, too, the cloud darkened around him, rendering him more sad and silent than at any former period of his malady. Occasionally he rallied out of this gloom and depression, when visited by one of his old friends in the ministry, or by his faithful followers in the temperance cause.

One day an attached friend called to pay him a visit. The visitor ascended the stairs, and, finding everything quiet, pushed in the door of the sitting room, which was partly open, and entered. There he found Father Mathew on his knees, buried in prayer, wholly abstracted from things of the earth. Not wishing to disturb him at such a moment, the friend was about retiring, when the servant said—'Mr. —— is here, sir.' Father Mathew rose from his knees, and, tottering towards his visitor, warmly embraced him. 'Pardon me, sir,' said the gentleman, 'for disturbing your devotions.' 'My dear friend,' said Father Mathew, beseechingly, 'you must join with me in my prayer to God. Pray for me, dear ——' 'For you, sir!' 'Yes, my dear—I was praying that God would prepare me for leaving this world, and would forgive me for the sins I have commited.' Taking his visitor by the hand, he again asked him to kneel with him. 'What necessity is there for my praying for you, Father Mathew?' 'Oh! my dear, who can be pure in the sight of God!' was the reply. 'But you have done so much good for mankind.' 'No, no,' said the humble man, in still more earnest tones; 'I have done nothing—and no one can be pure in the eyes of God. Kneel with me, my dear, and pray with me to the Father of Mercy.' His earnestness could not be resisted; and by the side of that true Christian, the strong man knelt, overwhelmed with emotion. When both rose from that solemn prayer, the face of the priest was radiant with a holy light; that of the strong man was bathed in tears. 'Promise me, promise me that you will remember me in your prayers during the Holy Sacrifice,' were the last words which Father Mathew uttered, as the two men parted for ever in this world; and when next that face was beheld by the friend who loved him in life, it was when it reposed in the sleep of death.

For more than two hours every day, he was to be found in the church, absorbed in prayer and meditation; and whatever time he could spare from visitors, and the exercise which he endeavoured to sustain, were devoted to the great purpose of the brief remainder of his life—preparation for a holy death.

But even in these his last moments, the ruling passion was strong as ever. About six weeks before his death, his brother Charles came to see him; and on entering the sitting-room, he was surprised to perceive a rather large table elaborately laid out for several guests. Charles expressed his surprise, and remonstrated with his brother, saying—'Surely you ought not to take such trouble on yourself, now that you are so delicate. Who are to dine with you?' Father Mathew was not at all pleased at being thus caught in his old habit of feast-giving, and he never ceased hinting to Charles that 'he would most certainly lose the train if he remained much longer;' and though Charles had really come to spend the evening with him, he could not find it in his heart to interfere with an enjoyment in which the invalid took such intense delight, and he left the poor feeble host to dispense his last hospitality. The explanation of the dinner party was this—his young attendant pursued his studies during several hours of the day at a school in the town; and Father Mathew, to afford him pleasure, gave him permission to invite a number of his companions to dinner. This little feast recalled, no doubt, the happy joyous days of old, when he entertained the Josephians in his house in Cove Street; and his anticipation of the gratification of the young people, at the good things prepared for them, dispelled the heavy cloud for a time. His brother was surprised at what he considered to be an improvement in his health; but it was only the result of momentary excitement.

That one so good and gentle, and so considerate to others, should inspire the warmest interest in every member of the household amid which he spent the concluding days of his life, is what might naturally be expected; and nothing was wanting on the part of the excellent man in whose house he lodged* to render him as comfortable as possible. The very desire which he always expressed, to avoid giving trouble, only made those around him more anxious to anticipate his wants; and the care and solicitude of this kindly man and his family were unceasing to the last.

* Mr John Sullivan, of Queenstown.

There is little more to be told. The curtain was soon to fall. Some days before his death, he received the final shock. When dressing in the morning, he fell heavily to the ground, without however losing his senses, except for a short time. He was placed in his bed, speechless and powerless, save for some slight motion of his fingers, and with partial loss of hearing. He rallied somewhat during the day; but it was apparent, even to an unprofessional eye, that his days were numbered. His faculties were not nowever more dim than they had been hitherto, or at least for a year previously. He made signs that he desired to have a clergyman sent for, and his wish was at once complied with; and the clergyman who had acted as his spiritual director during his residence in Queenstown, was quickly at his bedside, and afforded him the consolations of religion. Thus fortified, he lay tranquilly and in peace, without pain, but with an expression of great sadness upon his countenance. As the members of his family came about him, he could only smile and press the hand of each with feeble grasp. He at first made efforts to speak to them; but the voice which had moved the hearts and awakened the consciences of so many, which had comforted so many a bruised and broken spirit, which had soothed so many death-beds, was never more to be heard by mortal ear. He intimated, with sufficient significance, his wish that any one who desired to see him should be admitted to his room; and even those who had come to take the pledge, before the news of his severe attack had spread abroad, were brought to his bedside. By that dying couch they knelt; and they themselves repeated the well-known formula, after which he contrived to make the sign of the cross on their foreheads with his palsied hand. And this was the last act in the life of Theobald Mathew, who, if he were the Apostle, was also the Martyr of Temperance.

For several days he continued free from physical suffering, as far as could be judged. He observed everything that occurred in the room, and looked his thanks for any little friendly office, in a way that was deeply affecting. The Sisters of the Queenstown Convent watched and prayed constantly by his beside. 'Theobald, would you wish to be buried with Frank and Tom?' his brother Charles enquired of him, as the last hours were approaching. The dying man signified a negative. 'Is it in the cemetery?' 'Yes,' was plainly indicated. 'Is it under the Cross?' A sweet but faint smile, and fainter pressure of the almost lifeless hand, was the only reply. This was the spot which he had many years before marked out as his resting place. There was no violent convulsion, no mortal agony, no awful struggle of nature, in his last moments. Death stole upon him as gently as sleep upon a wearied man. He died in peace, without the slightest movement. But it would seem as if, in some inexplicable way, an expression of pain moulded itself upon his features. It was like the lingering shadow of the sorrow which had long brooded over his spirit, and which, for some years past, had been so rarely and so briefly dispelled. 'Ah, surely, somebody is vexing him,' said an old and loving follower, when admitted to the bedroom. And yet if one may predicate such of mortal, he must have been then, after a life of fever, toil, and pain, experiencing that happiness which is promised to those who on this earth walk in the light, and imitate the life of the Lord. Thus passed away, in the 66th year of his age, and in the 42nd of his ministry, Theobald Mathew, the Apostle of Temperance. The 8th of December 1856, belongs to history as the date of that event.

CHAPTER XLVI.

Feeling caused by his Death—Expressions of Opinion respecting his Character—Protestant Testimony—His Funeral—His Statue.

THE knowledge that Father Mathew had been for some years declining in health, and that the event of his death could not possibly be far off, did much to prepare the public for its announcement. Had he been struck down in the vigour and activity of his life, the effect upon the mind of the country would have been for a time overpowering, so much was he loved by all classes of the people of Ireland; but even as it was, and prepared as the public were to receive at any moment the sad tidings of his death, the announcement that he was no more, was received with a feeling of genuine and universal sorrow. That sorrow was however mitigated by the consciousness that he had been released from a state of pain and misery, and that his weary spirit was at rest. Though the people of his own city mourned for him as for a father whom they had lost, they derived a holy consolation from the conviction that he was then 'a saint in heaven.'

The tidings of Father Mathew's death elicited a strong and general expression of public opinion in his favour. From every quarter came earnest and eloquent testimonies to his character, his services, his motives; and the public press of the British Empire faithfully reflected the feeling entertained towards the illustrious dead by every class of his fellow subjects.* No harsh word was uttered against

* Testimonies from the public press might be given in great number, but the space remaining is too scant for their quotation. I shall therefore content myself

one whose happy fortune it had been to disarm hostile criticism, and convert enemies into friends. The few shades in his character were absorbed in its brightness; and none thought, but with tenderness, of the self-will which had evinced itself at times, or of the jealousy which had been rarely displayed: these two were easily accounted for by the earnestness and ardour of his nature, and his long habit of authority and leadership. It was of his large heart, his great soul, his tender and compassionate nature, his intense love of his fellow creatures, his generosity, his self-sacrifice, his nobleness of spirit, his devotion to the poor, his long life of toil and labour spent in the service of God—it was of these men thought, and not of the specks upon the sun.

'I never saw a man,' said the venerable Thomas George French, of Merino—a Protestant gentleman of high rank,—'so untainted by the world as Father Mathew. He was the model of what a Christian clergyman ought to be. I never

with a single testimony from the *Cork Constitution*, the well known Protestant organ of the South of Ireland. It is the more valuable because of the source from which it emanates, as well as from the daily opportunity which the writer had of thoroughly understanding the character and career which he depicted:—

'Yesterday passed from among us a man who filled a large space in the eye, not of Cork only, but of the world. His reputation was not Irish or English, but European and American. By multitudes in every land his name was syllabled and his memory revered, and by tens of thousands will be hallowed both for resolutions inspired and for benefits enjoyed. We speak not of Mr. Mathew as a friar or as a priest. Whatever our objections to his creed, his motives, we believe, were single, his humanity was genuine, and his benevolence was great. Great, too, beyond precedent was the revolution he wrought in the habits of a people given beyond precedent to the excesses of "strong drink." He laboured honestly and energetically, sparing neither health nor time, deterred by no difficulty, confronting with cheerfulness opposition where he ought to have had cooperation, and persevering humbly but earnestly until obstinacy was overcome and incredulity convinced, and until not a parish in the country could refuse to receive as a benefactor one whom it at first regarded as a cheat . . . Dislike as we may the accessories, it is a great thing to see drunkenness giving place to sobriety, slovenliness to cleanliness, sloth to industry, discord to content; and to see parent and child, wife and husband, going forth in the hours of relaxation to enjoy together the comforts acquired by release from the brawls, and bondage, and beggary of the public-house. It is for his agency in this desirable consummation that we bestow this brief notice on a man whose health was broken, if not his life shortened, by his efforts to achieve it. For some years he has been in a state of debility which everyone witnessed with regret; for, apart from his amiability of disposition, his unassumingness of deportment, and his abstinence from participation in political or polemical contention, there is something melancholy in the visible day-by-day decay of powers and faculties which but lately were instinct with life and energy; and that possibly from a consciousness of our own liability to a similar visitation, disposes us to look with a sympathising eye on any on whom the afflicting hand has thus heavily been laid. Such, at all events, was the feeling with which professors of all creeds regarded Mr. Mathew.'

heard a word from him that ought not to emanate from a man of good heart and pure mind. If one were likely to be influenced by a clergyman of another persuasion to change his creed, it would be by such a man as Father Mathew—not because of any peculiar talent he possessed, but from his manner and the example of his own life.'

'Father Mathew was always engaged in good and charitable works, and in trying to serve and benefit his fellow creatures. I never knew a more benevolent man or a more perfect gentleman' said John Cotter of Cork, a man of patriarchal age, and whose own benevolence had become a proverb—'as charitable as John Cotter.'

This is the manner in which he was spoken of by Protestants who had known him intimately, long before he became connected with the temperance movement.

For myself (wrote Smith O'Brien,) whether he be or be not canonised as a saint by the Church of Rome, I am disposed to regard him as an Apostle who was specially deputed on a divine mission by the Almighty, and invested with power almost miraculous. To none of the ordinary operations of human agency can I ascribe the success which attended his efforts to repress one of the besetting sins of the Irish nation. If I had read in history that such success had attended the labours of an unpretending priest, whose chief characteristic was modest simplicity of demeanour, I own that I should have distrusted the narrative as an exaggeration; but we have been all of us witnesses to the fact that myriads simultaneously obeyed his advice, and, at his bidding, abandoned a favourite indulgence.

Long before the time of his death, even the most sceptical had admitted that the Apostle of Temperance had no selfish object in the promotion of a movement to which his own family were among the first victims; and the fact that he died in poverty—that, save his watch and altar plate and sacred vestments, which belonged to him as a priest, he had nothing to give or bequeath—dispelled the last lingering suspicion which had its origin, years before, in ignorance and misconception. His death paid the debts for which he had heavily insured his life ; and, with the exception of members of his own family, who had more than once generously made large sacrifices to assist him in his pressing difficulties, there were none whom the insurance did not satisfy.

The Corporation of his adopted city only expressed the public feeling when they resolved on honouring the memory of their illustrious fellow citizen by a public funeral. The body was brought up on Thursday from Queenstown by a number of his oldest and most attached followers, and placed in the Church of the Holy Trinity, which was another monument of his priestly zeal for the glory of God's House. Thousands crowded the sacred building so long as an opportunity was afforded to the public of taking a last look at those beloved features, which were exposed to view for some time before the funeral. With timid step and bowed head the poor entered the Church, which was shrouded in sombre drapery, and approached the coffin in which lay all that was mortal of their friend and benefactor. As they gazed with tearful eyes on that face, so calm, and pale, and rigid, as if chiselled out of marble, sobs broke from their labouring breasts, and they gave way to passionate bursts of sorrow. Noble and beautiful was that countenance in the stillness of death ; and though the traces of suffering and care were discernible in its worn and wasted lineaments, there was still, as strikingly visible as in life, the same expression of benevolence, which was the most marked and unchanging characteristic of his nature.

On Friday the 12th of December, 1856, Cork poured out its population in the streets to pay the last tribute of respect to the memory of its greatest citizen ; and through a living mass the funeral cortège—extending nearly two miles in length—wound its slow and solemn way. Every class, every rank, every party, every creed, had its full representation in that sad procession, which was closed by the truest mourners of all—the poor. Never before were there so many persons assembled in the cemetery to which its founder was now borne. It was computed that more than 50,000 mourners—for all that day were mourners—crowded the adjoining roads, and filled every avenue and walk, and covered every available part of that beautiful burial place, as the Catholic bishop and the attendant clergy—more than 70 in number—received the body at the entrance. The impressive solemnity of the sublime service for the dead hushed for a time the convulsive sobs that broke from that vast assemblage; but as the precious remains were deposited in the tomb prepared for their reception, the great sorrow burst forth again, telling how deep and strong was the feeling which the people bore to one whom they had so much reason to honour and to love. Amidst the tears and prayers of his fellow citizens, who that day represented a mourning nation, the body of Theobald Mathew was consigned to the grave for which his spirit had long yearned; and there, in that chosen spot, beneath the cross which his own hands had reared many years before, his ashes now repose.

In a few weeks after the grave closed over the mortal remains of the Apostle of Temperance, the citizens of Cork assembled in the public Court-house, to consider the most appropriate means of paying a tribute of respect to his memory. That meeting was of itself a tribute to his memory, no less than an evidence of his teaching,—it was a happy fusion of class, of party, and of creed; and in a spirit of harmonious concord, inspired as it were by the lessons of the sainted dead, all united for the performance of a duty which was at once an honour and an obligation. The Protestant and the Dissenter vied with the Catholic in the eloquent expression of affection for the man, and veneration for his character; of sorrow for his loss, and of pride in his citizenship. Never was feeling more harmonious, never was testimony more unanimous. In obedience to the almost universal wish, it was resolved that a statue of Father Mathew in some way typical of his temperance mission, should be erected in one of the public thoroughfares of the city—thereby affording the most gratifying consolation to the people whom he loved as a father, and amongst whom he had lived for more than forty years. An unavoidable delay, occasioned by the death of Mr. Hogan, the eminent sculptor to whom the task of executing the statue was originally confided, prevented the committee from carrying out their delegated trust as soon as could have been desired; but ere the close of this year (1863) a statue by Foley—replete with the charm of life and grace which genius can alone impart to marble or to bronze—is to be erected in the most public and conspicuous position. And while this statue will faithfully represent those beautiful and long-familiar features, and recall that mission to which he devoted many of the best years of his life, and to which he sacrificed his happiness and his health, it will visibly associate the memory of its most famous and illustrious citizen with the city of his adoption,—that city which was the scene of his holy labours as a minister of religion, and the birth-place of that great moral reformation which has conferred, and which will long continue to confer, countless blessings on mankind.